Toronto Magnetical and Meteorological Observatory

Abstracts of meteorological Observations made at the Magnetical Observatory, Toronto, Canada West

During the Years 1854 to 1859, inclusive

Toronto Magnetical and Meteorological Observatory

Abstracts of meteorological Observations made at the Magnetical Observatory, Toronto, Canada West
During the Years 1854 to 1859, inclusive

ISBN/EAN: 9783337186944

Printed in Europe, USA, Canada, Australia, Japan

Cover: Foto ©ninafisch / pixelio.de

More available books at **www.hansebooks.com**

ABSTRACTS

OF

METEOROLOGICAL OBSERVATIONS

MADE AT THE

MAGNETICAL OBSERVATORY, TORONTO,

CANADA WEST,

DURING THE YEARS 1854 TO 1859, INCLUSIVE.

TORONTO:
PRINTED BY LOVELL AND GIBSON, YONGE STREET,
1864.

CONTENTS.

	PAGE
INTRODUCTION	vii

General monthly meteorological abstracts, 1854 to 1859 inclusive, giving the daily mean values of the meteorological elements, the daily resultant directions, resultant velocities and mean velocities of the wind, the daily extremes of temperature, with the amount and approximate duration of rain and snow for each day on which rain or snow fell 2

TABLES

I.—Monthly means of the temperature of the air at each of the six observation hours, from 1854 to 1859 inclusive 74

II.—Monthly and annual means of the temperature of the air, furnished by six daily observations from 1854 to 1859 inclusive 78

III.—Differences of the monthly and annual means of the temperature of the air from 1854 to 1859 inclusive, in excess or defect from the normal monthly and annual means, both being derived from six daily observations .. 78

IV.—Monthly means of the temperature of the air at each of the six observation hours, for the period 1854 to 1859 inclusive 79

V.—Differences of the mean monthly temperature at each observation hour, in excess or defect from the normal mean monthly temperature of the same hour, together with the means of the six hourly differences ... 79

VI.—Monthly mean differences, without regard to sign, between the normal temperatures of the day and hour and the observed temperatures at the same day and hour, for each month of the years 1854 to 1859 inclusive 80

VII.—Monthly mean differences, without regard to sign, between the normal temperatures of the day and hour and the observed temperatures, for each of the six observation hours, for the period 1854 to 1859 inclusive .. 80

VIII.—Mean differences, without regard to sign, between the temperatures observed at 2 P.M. on consecutive days, for each month in the years 1854 to 1859 inclusive, the effect of the annual variation being eliminated.. 81

IX.—Shewing for each month (for the period 1854 to 1859 inclusive) the number of cases in a hundred when the change of temperature observed at 2 P.M. on consecutive days was increasing, with the average values of the increasing and of the decreasing changes 81

X.—Mean difference of the temperature of the air, from the normal at the hour of observation, for each of the sixteen points of the wind's direction, with the number of observations from which the means are derived, for the years 1853 to 1859 inclusive 82

XI.—Monthly means of the diurnal change of temperature, exclusive of that due to annual variation, from 6 A.M. to 6 A.M., for the period 1854 to 1859 inclusive, arranged according to the daily resultant direction of the wind 83

XII.—Frequency of increasing changes of temperature, the total number in each month and direction being 100.. 83

XIII.—Aggregate of increasing changes for each direction, the joint aggregate of increasing and decreasing changes for any one month and direction being expressed by 100 83

CONTENTS.

TABLES PAGE

XIV.—Monthly and yearly means of the diurnal change of temperature, without regard to sign, and excluding that due to annual variation, from 6 A.M. to 6 A.M., for the period 1854 to 1859, arranged according to the daily resultant direction of the wind 84

XV.—Comparative diurnal changes of temperature in the same month that are due to different winds, being the numbers in Table XIV. expressed in terms of the arithmetic mean change in that month for all winds .. 84

XVI.—Comparative diurnal changes of temperature that are due in different months to the same wind, being the numbers in Table XIV. expressed in terms of the annual arithmetic mean for that wind 84

XVII.—Monthly means of the daily maxima, minima, and ranges of temperature, for the years 1854 to 1859 inclusive 85

XVIII.—Highest and lowest temperatures in each month, and monthly ranges of temperature, for the years 1854 to 1859 inclusive 86

XIX.—Monthly means of the barometer at each of the six observation hours, from 1854 to 1859 inclusive 87

XX.—Monthly and annual means of the barometer, furnished by six daily observations, 1854 to 1859 inclusive.. 91

XXI.—Differences of the monthly and annual means of the barometer, for 1854 to 1859 inclusive, in excess or defect from the assumed normal monthly and annual means, both being derived from six daily observations 91

XXII.—Monthly means of the barometer at each of the six observation hours, for the period 1854 to 1859 inclusive 92

XXIII.—Differences of the mean monthly readings of the barometer at each observation hour, in excess or defect from the assumed normal for the hour, together with the means of the six hourly differences 92

XXIV.—Monthly mean differences, without regard to sign, between the observed readings of the barometer and the assumed normals proper to the day and hour, for each month of the years 1854 to 1859 inclusive 93

XXV.—Monthly mean differences, without regard to sign, between the observed readings of the barometer and the assumed normals for the day and hour at each of the six observation hours, for the period 1854 to 1859 inclusive 93

XXVI.—Mean differences, without regard to sign, between the heights of the barometer observed at 2 P.M. on consecutive days for each month, in the years 1854 to 1859 inclusive 94

XXVII.—Shewing for each month (for the period 1854 to 1859 inclusive) the number of cases in a hundred when the height of the barometer observed at 2 P.M. on consecutive days was increasing, with the average values of the increasing and of the decreasing changes 94

XXVIII.—Mean difference of the reading of the barometer from the normal at the hour of observation, for each of the sixteen points of the wind's direction, with the number of observations from which the means are derived, for the years 1853 to 1859 inclusive 95

XXIX.—Monthly and yearly means of the diurnal change in the readings of the barometer (corrected to temperature 32°) from 6 A.M. to 6 A.M., for the period 1854 to 1859 inclusive, arranged according to the daily resultant direction of the wind 96

XXX.—Frequency of increasing changes in each month, the total number in each direction being 100 96

XXXI.—Aggregate of increasing changes for each direction, the joint aggregate of increasing and decreasing changes in the month for any one direction, being expressed by 100 96

XXXII.—Monthly and diurnal means of the diurnal change, without regard to sign, in the readings of the barometer (corrected to temperature 32°) from 6 A.M. to 6 A.M., for the period 1854 to 1859, arranged according to the daily resultant direction of the wind 97

XXXIII.—Comparative diurnal changes in the height of the barometer in the same month that are due to different winds, being the numbers in Table XXXII. expressed in terms of the mean change in that month for all winds 97

CONTENTS.

TABLES		PAGE
XXXIV.	Comparative diurnal changes in the height of the barometer that are due in different months to the same wind, being the numbers in Table XXXII. expressed in terms of the annual arithmetic mean for that wind	97
XXXV.	Highest and lowest readings, and monthly ranges of the barometer in each month, from 1854 to 1859 inclusive	98
XXXVI.	Monthly means of the pressure of dry air at each of the six observation hours, for the years 1854 to 1859 inclusive	99
XXXVII.	Monthly and annual means of the pressure of dry air furnished by six daily observations, for 1854 to 1859 inclusive	103
XXXVIII.	Monthly means of the pressure of dry air at each of the six observation hours, for the period 1854 to 1859 inclusive	103
XXXIX.	Monthly means of the pressure of vapour at each of the six observation hours, for the years 1854 to 1859 inclusive	104
XL.	Monthly means of the relative humidity at each of the six observation hours, for the years 1854 to 1859 inclusive	106
XLI. & XLII.	Monthly and annual means of the pressure of vapour and relative humidity, furnished by six daily observations, for 1854 to 1859 inclusive	112
XLIII. & XLIV.	Monthly means of the pressure of vapour and relative humidity at each of the six observation hours, for the period 1854 to 1859 inclusive	113
XLV.	Monthly means of the extent of sky clouded at each of the six observation hours (the hemisphere being unity) for the years 1854 to 1859 inclusive	114
XLVI.	Monthly and annual means of the extent of sky clouded, from six daily observations, for 1854 to 1859 inclusive	116
XLVII.	Monthly means of the extent of sky clouded at each observation hour, for the period 1854 to 1859 inclusive	116
XLVIII.	Mean clouded sky for each of the sixteen points of the wind's direction, with the number of observations from which the means are derived, for the years 1853 to 1859 inclusive	117
XLIX.	Comparative view of the annual variations of certain meteorological elements derived from the series 1842 to 1848, and from the series 1854—59	118
L.	Comparative view of the diurnal variations at the six observation hours, for the same two series	118
LI.	Resultant direction, resultant velocity, and mean velocity of the wind for each month	119
LII.	Monthly and annual resultant directions of the wind for each hour of Toronto astronomical time, for the period 1854 to 1859 inclusive	120
LIII.	Monthly and yearly resultant velocities of the wind, for each hour of Toronto astronomical time, for the period 1854 to 1859 inclusive, the velocities being in miles per hour	121
LIV.	Monthly and yearly mean velocities of the wind for each hour of Toronto astronomical time, for the period 1854 to 1859 inclusive, the velocities being in miles per hour	122
LV.	Mean velocity of the wind for each of the sixteen points of the wind's direction, with the number of observations from which the means are derived, for the years 1853 to 1859 inclusive	123

Tables

LVI.—Ratios shewing the comparative duration of different winds in each separate month, being the absolute durations of the different winds in the month, expressed in terms of the monthly mean duration for all winds 124

LVII.—Ratios shewing the comparative duration of each separate wind in the different months, being the numbers in Table LVI. expressed in terms of the annual means given at the foot of each column 124

LVIII.—Ratios shewing the comparative duration of different winds for each separate hour, being the absolute durations for the hour, expressed in terms of the duration of all winds for the same hour.................. 126

LIX.—Ratios shewing the comparative duration of each separate wind in different hours, being the absolute durations for the hour, expressed in terms of the mean duration of that wind for all hours 128

LX.—The number of days in which rain fell, its approximate duration in hours, and depth in inches, for each month of the years 1854 to 1859 inclusive... 130

LXI.—The number of days in which snow fell, its approximate duration in hours, and depth in inches, for each month of the years 1854 to 1859 inclusive 131

LXII.—The number of days in which either rain or snow fell, their approximate duration in hours, and depth in inches, for each month of the years 1854 to 1859 inclusive; one inch of snow being reckoned as equivalent to one-tenth of an inch of rain.. 132

LXIII.—Comparative duration of the several winds during the days in any part of which rain or snow fell, from observations in the years 1853 to 1859 inclusive 133

LXIV.—Comparative duration of the several winds during the hours in any part of which rain or snow fell, from observations in the years 1857 to 1859 inclusive 134

LXV.—Comparative duration of the several winds during the days in any part of which snow fell, from observations in the years 1853 to 1859 inclusive, the snow storms being arranged in four classes, according to the amount of snow, and each class being taken to include all the higher classes 135

LXVI.—Comparative duration of the several winds during the hours in any part of which snow fell, from observations in the years 1857 to 1859 inclusive, the snow storms being arranged in four classes, according to the amount of snow, and each class being taken to include all the higher classes 136

INTRODUCTION.

The Toronto Magnetic and Meteorological Observatory is situated in the grounds of the University of Toronto, in Latitude 43° 39'.4 N, Longitude* 5h. 17m. 33s. W., 108 feet above Lake Ontario, and approximately 342 feet above the level of the sea.

The early history of the Observatory, including the circumstances which led to its establishment by the British Government in 1839–40, are given in detail in the introduction to the 1st Volume of the Observations, published under the superintendence of General Sabine, R. A., which, together with the 2nd and 3rd volumes, contain the magnetical and meteorological observations, from 1840 to 1848 inclusive.

The operations of the Observatory as an imperial establishment were brought to a close in the early part of the year 1853. The magnetical observations, which had ceased preparatory to the removal of the instruments, were resumed under the authority of the Provincial Government in July of the same year, while the meteorological observations were continued without intermission. The non-commissioned officers of the Royal Artillery, Messrs. Walker, Menzies and Stewart, who had acted as observers under Captain Lefroy, R. A., and other officers of the Royal Artillery, were permitted by the indulgence of the Military authorities to continue in the same capacity till they became permanently attached to the Observatory on their retirement from the army in 1855.† The general supervision was committed to the Professor of Natural Philosophy‡ in University College, Toronto, till the appointment of the present director, G. T. Kingston, M.A. in August, 1855.

In the Autumn of 1853 a new building was commenced, to take the place of the old Observatory. The principal part of the present structure is in form rectangular, about 54 feet from North to South, in the direction of the magnetic meridian, 44 feet from East to West, and 16 feet in height, exclusive of the roof. Its western portion is occupied by the entrance, the two offices, and the dark room, which communicate towards the east with the principal room containing the magnetical differential instruments, mounted on their original stone pedestals, which latter, during the progress of the work, were boxed over for protection.

In the north-west corner, and included in the same horizontal dimensions, is a square tower, side 16 feet and height 43 feet, including a balustrade 2½ feet high.

---

* Determined by electric telegraph with Boston in January, 1857. It accords with the result of chronometric comparison with Boston in 1840, see Toronto Observations, p. 17, Vol. I. The heights 108 feet and 342 feet refer to the level of the mercury in the cistern of the barometer.

† The staff of observers was increased in January, 1857, by the appointment of Mr. W. F. Davidson.

‡ J. B. Cherriman, M.A., late Fellow of St. John's College, Cambridge.

INTRODUCTION.

The whole of the main building, together with the tower, are of stone, whose freedom from magnetism had been carefully ascertained, prior to its employment in the construction. The nails and other fastenings are either copper or zinc.

From the southern face of the chief room extends a passage 4½ feet wide, which communicates at its southern extremity with a room 20 feet by 13, appropriated to the observations of absolute magnetic intensity. On the east and west of the passage, and communicating with it by a second transverse passage, are two small rooms, the former for observing transits, and the latter for the observations of absolute declination. The three rooms with their connecting passages form a cross 72 feet from north to south, 73 feet from east to west, and 8½ feet in height. The extreme length of the whole building is thus 126 feet, and its greatest width 73 feet.

The three small rooms are built of stone, the passages being of lath and plaster on stone foundations. These buildings, which were the first erected, were used as offices during the demolition of the old observatory and the erection of the large room and tower, which latter work was commenced in June, 1854 and completed in June 1855.

The meorological observations for the years 1854 to 1859, the results of which are given in this volume, were made with the following instruments :—

The Standard Barometer, by Newman, is described on page lxxiii. of the 1st volume of the Toronto osbervations. The interior diameter of the tube is 0.6 inches. In conformity with the practice in the preceding observations, the corrections for capillarity amounting only to .002 inches, have not been applied.

The Standard Thermometer is the instrument described on pp. xcvii. and xcviii. of the 2nd volume of the Toronto observations. It is by Fastré of Paris, and is graduated à l'échelle arbitraire.

All the observations on the temperature of the air were made by this thermometer, excepting when the temperature fell lower than the limits of the scale, (about —8°) when the thermometer employed was one supplied from the Kew Observatory.

The wet bulb thermometer is also by Fastré, and is graduated according to an arbitrary scale.

The position occupied by the thermometers till June 24, 1854, was on the outside and near the middle of the north wall of the principal room in the old building. They were protected above by a double projecting roof, and on the east and west and north by double venetian shutters descending to about 4 feet from the ground. The thermometers were attached to horizontal strips of wood extending east and west, and were read from an aperture in the wall made for that purpose, and fitted with a shutter and sliding window. The bulbs, which were perfectly free, were about 4½ feet from the ground.

On June 24, 1854, the thermometer shed was removed from the wall, and placed against the south fence of the Observatory enclosure. The thermometers remained under the shed in this position till the completion of the new Observatory. On June 15, 1855, at 3 P.M, they were moved to the new thermometer shed on the outside of the north wall of the tower. The projecting roof above, and Venetian or rather Louvre shutters of the new shed are single and painted white, instead of being double and green as in the old shed.

The interior length of the new shed, from east to west, is 13¼ feet, the distance of the northern shutter from the northern wall of the Observatory 5 feet, and the height, exclusive of the slope of the roof, 9½ feet. The shutters extend down to a distance of 2 feet from the ground. The thermometers are attached to horizontal strips of wood extending east and west, their bulbs, which are perfectly free, being 4½ feet from the ground, and 14 inches from the inside of the shutters. The shed is entered by a door communicating with the interior of the building, but the thermometers can also be read through a window by the aid of a telescope.

The self-registering thermometers, for recording the extremes of temperature in the shade, are attached to the same horizontal strip of wood with the standard and wet bulb thermometers.

The anemometer (Robinson's) prior to June 1854, was mounted over a temporary shed attached to the N. W. corner of the old Observatory. The floor of this shed, its roof and the horizontal plane in which the cups revolved were respectively 6 feet, 12 feet and 20 feet above the floor of the Observatory.

On June 26th, 1854, the anemometer was moved to the top of a conical wooden tower standing at a distance of about 20 feet N.W. from the N.W. corner of the main building. This tower, originally built for Osler's anemometer, was about 30 feet in height. The anemometer continued in operation in this latter position from June 28th, 1854, till June 11th, 1855, when it was mounted on the tower of the new Observatory. The centres of the cups in the present position of the anemometer revolve in a horizontal plane 4¼ feet above the balustrade. The clockwork and papers for recording the direction and velocity of the wind are supported by a platform immediately under the deck roof of the tower.

The Rain Gauge in use is simply a rectangular vessel with an aperture of 10 inches by 20 inches, placed 7 feet above the ground, and communicating by a pipe with a receiver beneath. The volume of water received is measured by a glass graduated to cubic inches and parts of an inch.

The frame supporting the rain gauge stands in the enclosure surrounding the Observatory, and at a distance from other objects sufficient to secure it from the effect of eddy winds.

The barometer, standard thermometer and wet-bulb thermometer were read six times each day, namely, at 6 A.M., 8 A.M., 2 P.M., 4 P.M., 10 P.M., and midnight, excepting on Sundays, Christmas Day, and Good Friday, when these instruments were read at 6 A.M. and 2 P.M. only. These latter readings, though recorded in the daily registers, are not included in the hourly means for those hours. From the temperature of the air and of evaporation, the pressure of vapour and the relative humidity were deduced by hygrometric tables. Prior to the 1st January, 1858, Kupffer's hygrometric tables were in use, but after that date the tables employed were those calculated by Professor Coffin, of Lafayette College, Pennsylvania, from the more recent experiments of Regnault.

The differences between the barometric pressure and the pressure of vapour were recorded at each observation, in conformity with ordinary usage, as the *Pressure of Dry Air*.

At the same six observation hours, a record was also made of the direction and velocity of the wind, with the general appearance of the sky, including the class, distribution, and motions of the clouds.

The meteorological day having been regarded since the establishment of the Observatory as beginning at 6 A.M., local civil time of the day of date, the custom was introduced in January, 1856, of reading and setting both the maximum and minimum self-registering thermometers at 6 A.M., terminating the day of date, with the view of ascertaining the highest and lowest temperatures that occurred within each successive space of twenty-four hours.

B

INTRODUCTION.

As the reading the minimum thermometer at 6 A.M., from the proximity of that hour to the time of minimum temperature, necessarily led to the loss of many of the true minima, and to the record as such of other lower temperatures which were in fact not true minima; and since the aggregate of the temperatures recorded as minima was consequently lower than the aggregate of the true minima, the hour of reading the minimum thermometer was changed, January 1, 1858, from 6 A.M. to 2 P.M., the temperature being recorded as the minimum of the day that included the hour of reading. By thus reading the minimum thermometer at an hour near to the ordinary time of maximum, no minimum could be lost, excepting when the temperature at 2 P.M. was lower than any that had occurred during the previous twenty-four hours. The maximum thermometer continued to be read as before, at 6 A.M., the temperature that it indicated being recorded as the maximum of the twenty-four hours just terminated.

From Robinson's Anemometer a record was made of the general direction of the wind during each hour of every day (Sundays and other holidays *included*), and the mean velocity or number of miles travelled by the wind during the same hour, the space of each hour being designated by the hour with which it commenced. For each of the six observation hours, the instantaneous direction and approximate velocity at the hour was also recorded, such velocity being the number of miles travelled by the wind during the half hour preceding and the half hour following the hour of observation.

The resultant direction and resultant velocity for any day or other group of consecutive hours, or for a group consisting of like hours on different days, were calculated from the directions and velocities in the several hours composing the group by the formulæ

$$\tan \bar{\theta} = \frac{\Sigma (V \sin \theta)}{\Sigma (V \cos \theta)}; \quad \overline{V} = \frac{\Sigma (V \cos \theta)}{n \cos \bar{\theta}}$$

Where θ represents the angular distance to the right of north of the point from which the wind blew during the hour, V the corresponding velocity, $\bar{\theta}$ and $\overline{V}$ the values of θ and V corresponding to the resultant, and n the number of hours in the group under consideration.

The depth of the rain or snow recorded as having fallen during any day was measured at 9 A.M. of the following day, prior to January 1, 1856; but after that date the time was changed to 6 A.M., the termination of the meteorological day as regards the other elements.

In the general monthly abstracts in pp. 2 to 73, the numbers given in the six columns headed "*daily means*" are the daily averages of the observations made at the six observation hours, and are uncorrected for diurnal variation. The resultant directions and velocities and the mean velocities of the wind are derived from the twenty-four hourly directions and velocities.

The numbers at the bases of the columns of daily means, as well as those of the mean velocity of the wind, and of the extremes of temperature, are the averages of the numbers under which they stand, Sundays being excluded only in the first six columns. Under the columns containing the daily resultant directions and resultant velocities of the wind are entered the monthly resultant directions and velocities; and under the columns for the rain and snow are entered the sums of the numbers which those columns respectively contain. In the rain or snow columns, the occurrence of a star (*) indicates that the amount was inappreciable, or the duration less than half an hour. Where rain and melted snow are combined, ten inches of snow are reckoned as equivalent to one inch of rain.

INTRODUCTION.

REMARKS ON THE TABLES.

The normals to which reference is made in the temperature tables (Tables I. to XVIII.) are the normal temperatures proper to Toronto in its actual circumstances, and not those proper to the parallel of latitude on which Toronto stands. They have been deduced from the table of twenty-four-hour daily means (*a*) given by General Sabine in his paper on "the periodic and non-periodic variations of temperature at Toronto," by applying the diurnal variations (*b*) contained (though with contrary signs) in a table given in the same paper.

The normals thus computed have been tabulated, and are kept as standards to which the actual temperatures are referred; the abnormal variations, with their proper signs, being entered in the daily register side by side with each observed temperature.

Table I. gives the monthly means of the temperature of the air at each of the six observation hours in the years 1854 to 1859 inclusive. The numbers in the last column on the right are the means of the numbers in the six preceding columns, and are uncorrected for diurnal variation.

The final columns for the several months in Table I. are exhibited at one view in Table II., which contains the monthly and annual means of temperature, furnished by six daily observations, in each of the years 1854 to 1859 inclusive, as well as for the period consisting of the same six years.

In Table III. the monthly means of temperature given by Table II. are compared with the corresponding normal means, namely, those derived from the normals proper to the six observation hours. It will be seen that on the average of the six years the temperatures have been in excess of the normals in the summer and autumn months, and in defect throughout the winter and spring, the mean of the whole year being 0°.36 in defect.

The numbers at the foot of each of the several monthly parts of Table I. are collected in Table IV. which shews, on the average of the six years, 1854 to 1859, the monthly means of temperature for each month, at each of the six observation hours.

In Table V. the hourly means in Table IV. are compared with the corresponding normals.

The *extent* of the oscillations of temperature above and below the normals proper to the day and hour are shewn by Table VI. which contains the average abnormal variations or digressions of temperature, without regard to sign, for every month and for the mean of the twelve months in each of the six years of observation. From the final column we learn, that taking one month with another, the temperature on the average of the whole series made oscillations to the extent of 6°.7 above or below the normal proper to the time of observation, and that their mean amplitudes in different years never differed by more than 0°.5 from the average (6°.7). The progression from month to month in the monthly mean digressions is not perfectly continuous, but the general character of the annual period is shewn by the quarterly averages of the six-year means at the foot of the table, which are 6°.2 in spring, 5°.2 in summer, 5°.9 in autumn, and 9°.4 in winter.

In Table VII. a comparison is made for each month between the abnormal digressions of temperature, without regard to sign, at each of the six observation hours.

(*a*) Philosophical Transactions for 1853, pp. 154-159.
(*b*)   "   "   "   pp. 145, 146.

INTRODUCTION.

If the annual means alone be regarded, there is nothing to warrant the belief that one hour is, to any great extent, more subject than another to thermic disturbances; but if the numbers in the columns for 10h., 12h., 18h. and 20h. be compared with those for 2h. and 4h., it will be seen that in the six winter months (October to March) the former group are in nearly every case, number for number, greater than the latter group, and that exactly the reverse takes place in the other six months. The winter half-yearly means are in every case greater, and the summer half-yearly means less at each of the hours, 10h., 12h., 18h. and 20h. than at 2h. and 4h.. The half-yearly means for the two groups, each taken collectively, are as follows:

At 10h., 12h., 18h. and 20h., winter half-year, 8°.25 : summer, 5°.13;
" 2h. and 4h., " " 7°.48; " 5°.90;

From this it appears that in the winter half-year there is on the average a greater steadiness of temperature at 2h. and at 4h. than at the other observation hours, and also that this is reversed in the summer half-year, the greater steadiness of the temperature being then at the hours of the night and morning.

The mean abnormal digressions, while they shew the *extent* of the temperature oscillations, do not afford any measure of their *duration*, nor do they indicate whether the temperature passes gradually or suddenly from one abnormal condition to another.

The rate per day at which the temperature changes, irrespective of diurnal and annual variation, will be found by taking the algebraical differences between the abnormal digressions at the same hour of consecutive days. These differences being taken for 2 P.M., their monthly averages without regard to sign have been collected in Table VIII. From inspecting the table it will be seen that one day with another through the year, the average difference in the temperature at 2 P.M. on consecutive days was 5°.83; the maximum 7°.58 occurring in January, and the minimum 4°.73 in August; while the quarterly means were 7°.17 for winter, 5°.70 for spring, 5°.24 for summer, and 5°.21 for autumn.*

The ratios at the foot of the table, which express the means of each month in terms of the mean for the year, exhibit the comparative changeableness of temperature in the different months.

In Table VIII. no distinction is made between the increasing and the decreasing changes of temperature, and it does not appear whether the changes of one sign are numerous and of small magnitude and those of the opposite sign few and abrupt, or whether the changes in either direction are on the average equal in number and magnitude. These points are considered in Table IX. The numbers in the first line are each obtained by dividing 100 times the number of all the *increasing* changes that occured in the group of months of the same name by the *total* number of changes in the same group of months. The numbers in the third line are the quotients arising from the division of the *sum* of all the increasing changes in the group of months of the same name by the *number* of increasing changes. The numbers in the fifth line are derived in an analogous manner. It appears from the table that in eight months in the year there is a preponderance in the number of increasing changes of temperature, the mean percentage in the year being 54, that the average value of an increasing change is 5°.44, and

---

* The differences were subsequently taken between the temperatures at 6 A.M. on consecutive days, for the purpose of forming Tables XIV. to XVI, in which the differences are connected with the daily resultant winds. The quarterly and annual means thence derived are 9°.41 for the winter, 5°.31 for the spring, 3°.90 for the summer, 6°.75 for the autumn, and 6°.35 for the year.

The fact stated with reference to Table VII., namely, that the temperature at 2 P.M. is systematically more irregular in summer and less irregular in winter than at 6 A.M., will explain why the summer mean is less and the winter mean greater when the differences are taken between 6 A.M. That the annual mean is also greater in the latter case is owing to the circumstance that the temperature at 6 A.M. is more irregular on the average of the year than at 2 P.M.

of a decreasing change 6°.34. For the different seasons the average percentage of the numbers of increasing changes of temperature, and the average values* of the changes are as follows:

	Percentage.	Average Increase.	Average Decrease.
Winter	51	6.95	7.49
Spring	55	5.16	6.38
Summer	55	4.73	5.87
Autumn	54	4.92	5.61

Hence it appears that the descending changes of temperature are systematically more sudden at all seasons than the ascending changes.

In Table X. the abnormal variations of the temperature with their proper signs are arranged according to the different directions of the wind at the six ordinary hours of observation. Regarding each point in the table as including an angular space of 11° 15' on each side of it, it appears that the temperature was above or below the normal at the time of observation, according as the wind blew from a point lying to the south or to the north of a line drawn from N.E. b E. to S.W. b W. The greatest depression of temperature 3°.58, accompanied a wind from N.N.W., and the greatest elevation 3°.61 occurred with a S.S.W. wind, giving a range of 7°.19.

In Table X. the dependence of the actual temperature on the actual direction of the wind is considered, but no regard has been had to the duration of the wind in its actual direction, cases being embraced in which the wind had just begun to blow from a given direction, as well as those in which it was about to shift. If it be admitted that in the long run the epoch of observation may be considered as occurring at the middle of the space of time in which the proposed wind was blowing, the mean observed effect on the temperature, corresponding to a given direction, will be a combination of the effect due to the actual wind during half the time of its action, and that due to the preceding winds. To escape from the difficulty which these considerations involve, instead of employing as a standard of reference the normal temperature of the day and hour, which includes the joint effect of all the winds, it would seem better to refer the actual temperature to that which existed when the actual wind began to blow. Where hourly observations both of temperature and of wind are recorded, the question might be investigated, though with some labour, as to the rate of change per hour in the temperature effected by a given wind; but in the absence of hourly observations of temperature, the effect of a certain wind may be approximately known by arranging the changes of temperature after consecutive intervals of twenty-four hours, according to the resultant direction of the wind during the interval. The resultant direction of the wind having been computed at Toronto for every day, commencing and ending at 6 A.M., at which hour the temperature is recorded every day, Sunday included, the differences between the temperatures at 6 A.M. on consecutive days throughout the series 1854 to 1859 have been arranged in separate months, and in eight groups corresponding to the eight principal points of the compass, each difference or change of temperature being placed in the group most nearly corresponding to the resultant direction of the wind during the day in which the change occurred. The algebraical sum of the changes of temperature that accompanied a given resultant wind during a group of months of the same name, being divided by the number of times that this resultant wind occurred in the same month, the quotient will be the number in Table XI. corresponding to that month and wind.

* The quarterly averages are found independently of the separate months, by dividing the quarterly sums of the increasing or decreasing changes by the corresponding numbers.

INTRODUCTION.

In tracing the connection between a change in the value of any meteorological element and the direction of the wind during the interval of time in which the change occurred, the practice of referring the change to the *resultant* wind is admissible, provided that the direction undergoes no great change during the interval; but if the change of the wind's direction be great, the resultant computed in the ordinary way, although geometrically equivalent to the several component winds, in the direction with which they reach the anemometer, may possibly be far from equivalent in physical effect, and should it be from a direction for which the resultants are comparatively few, errors may thus be introduced sufficient possibly to disguise the true character of the relation sought, unless the errors be subdivided and thus rendered inappreciable by the combination of a series of sufficient length. From these considerations, the results arrived at, where the series, as in the present instance, comprises only six years, will possibly demand modification when combined with the observations of future years, and particularly with regard to the conclusions relative to single months.

It will be seen on examining Table XI. that in every month with a resultant wind from N., N.W. and W. the temperature was lowered; in every month with a resultant wind from S.W., S., S.E. and E. the temperature was raised; and that with a resultant wind from N.E. the temperature was raised in some months and depressed in others, the collective effect in the whole year being a rise of temperature with a resultant wind from the N.E. Taking the average of the year, with the wind from any point between N.E. through East and South to S.W. inclusive the temperature was raised, and with the wind from any point between West and North both inclusive the temperature was lowered. The S.E. wind accompanied the greatest rise, and the N.W. wind the greatest depression, the opposite effects being nearly equal, and the range $9°.1$.

The greatest ascent of temperature occurred with the S.E. wind in seven months; but in January, March, July, November and December, a south wind corresponded to the greatest rise. The greatest depression of temperature occurred with a N.W. wind in all months but March, when the most cold producing wind was from the west, and August and October, when the North wind accompanied the greatest depression.

Table XII. gives for each resultant direction—for each month and for each year, the number of days that an increase of temperature occured out of a hundred days, in which the resultant wind was from the same direction in the same month.

Cases of a rise of temperature exceed the number of falls with the resultant wind from N.E., E., SE., S., and S.W., in all months, with three exceptions for N.E. and one exception for each of the points East, South and S.W.

The temperature fell more frequently than it rose in all months with the resultant wind from W. N.W. and N. Taking the year round, the number of cases in which the temperature rose exceeeded those in which it fell, with the wind from N.E., E., S.E., S.,and S.W., the mean percentage being 69, while with the wind from W., N.W. and N.,the number of increasing changes fell short of the depressions, the mean percentage being 34.

In Table XIII. we have for each month and for the year the relative *amount* of the ascending change of temperature with each wind, as compared with the whole amount of ascending and descending changes with the same wind.

In Table XIV. are given, for each month and for the year, the means (without regard to sign) of the changes of temperature in twenty-four hours that accompany different resultant winds. The

INTRODUCTION.   xv

numbers in the final column are not the arithmetic means of those in the preceding columns, as they would be if the wind blew an equal number of times in all months, but are obtained by dividing the aggregate amount of all the changes, without regard to sign, for the corresponding wind, by the number of times that that wind occurred. The numbers at the foot of the table are the *arithmetic* means* of the numbers in the columns under which they stand.

In Table XV. the effects of different winds in the same month are compared by aid of the ratios of the numbers in table XIV. to the arithmetic means over which they severally stand. For the most part the South wind would seem to be most productive of change in the colder months, and the N.W. wind in the summer months, while for the whole year the effects of the cold winds seem to be greater, and those of the warm winds less than the average effect of all winds.

In Table XVI. the effects of the same wind in different months are compared. It has been already seen from Table VIII. that the average change of temperature in twenty-four hours, irrespective of the direction of the wind, is least in the warmer months and greatest in the colder months. Table XVI. shews that this holds also for each wind taken separately, the greatest contrasts between the effects in cold and hot months being those presented by the north and south winds, the effect produced by the north winds in January being more than four times its effect in July, and the effect of the south wind in January and December being at least five times that produced in June.†

Table XVII. gives the monthly means of the daily maxima, minima, and ranges of temperature, and Table XVIII. the absolute maxima, minima, and ranges for each month and for the year, in each of the years 1854 to 1859, and on the average of the six years.

BAROMETRIC TABLES.

The means or approximate normals employed as standards of comparison in the barometric tables (Tables XIX. to XXXV. inclusive), are the hourly means in each month, derived from the observations of seven years for the first nine months, and from the observations of six years for the rest of the year.

Table XIX. gives the monthly means of the height of the barometer, corrected to temp. 32° Fahrenheit, at each of the six observation hours in the years 1854 to 1859. The numbers in the last column are simply the monthly six-hour means, or the means of the numbers in the six preceding columns.

The final columns for the several months in Table XIX. are exhibited in one view in Table XX, which contains the monthly and annual means of barometric pressure furnished by six daily observations in each of the years 1854 to 1859, as well as for the period consisting of the same six years.

In Table XXI. the monthly means of the barometer given by Table XX. are compared with the corresponding approximate normal means.

The numbers at the foot of each of the several monthly parts of Table XIX. are collected in Table XXII. which shews, on the average of the six years, the monthly means of barometric pressure, for each month, at each of the six observation hours.

---

* These means are of course not the same as those from which the quarterly averages are derived, that are given in the foot note to the remarks on Table VIII.

† Tables XIV. to XVI. were formed for the purpose of tracing the connection (should such connection exist) between the resultant directions of the wind and thermometric movements generally, without reference to the directions or signs of those movements. As the computations were made, the tables have been given, though the results do not indicate anything very definite. A combination with a few additional years, might possibly lead to more satisfactory conclusions.

In Table XXIII. the hourly means in Table XXII. are compared with the corresponding assumed normals.

Table XXIV. is designed to shew the monthly averages of the extent of the barometric abnormal oscillations. The numbers whose averages are tabulated are the differences between the actual heights of the barometer and the assumed normal heights proper to the month and hour.

The annual distribution of these mean abnormal variations of the barometer resembles in its general character the corresponding distribution in the abnormal variations of temperature. The maximum is 0.249 in January, the minimum 0.119 in August, and the mean 0.183. The quarterly means of the abnormal digressions are 0.230 for the winter, 0.190 for the spring, 0.122 for the summer, and 0.191 for the autumn.

Table XXV. shews the distribution of the abnormal variations of the barometer at the different hours. The diurnal progression, unlike that shewn in the corresponding table for temperature, is well marked on the average of the twelve months. The greatest digression, which took place at 8 A.M. on the average of the year, maintained the same hour in every month but February and December. The minimum digression occurred on the average of the year at 10 P.M., and at either 10 P.M. or midnight in every month but November, when it took place at 4 P.M.

The numbers in Table XXVI. are obtained by dividing the monthly sums of the differences between the corrected readings of the barometer at 2 P.M. on consecutive days by the number of the days in the month. The average change in the whole year was 0·195, the maximum, 0·232, being in December, and the minimum, 0·123, in July; while the quarterly means were 0·267 for winter, 0·210 for spring, 0·125 for summer, and 0·182 for autumn.* The ratios at the foot of the table exhibit the relative rate of the diurnal change in the barometer in the different months.

From Table XXVII. it is seen that on the whole the barometric pressure passed from one condition to another by gradations, of which those in which the pressure increased are nearly equal in number and magnitude to those in which the pressure diminished, the average magnitudes of the ascending and descending changes being respectively 0·194 and 0·107.

Table XXVIII. gives the mean abnormal variations of the barometer, with their proper signs, arranged according to the actual direction of the wind at the six ordinary observation hours. According to the table the barometer was above the normal when the wind was blowing from any point between east and south, both inclusive, and below the normal with the wind from any point between S.S.W. through west to N.W.

The change in the state of the barometer dependent on the direction of the wind has been sought by a method similar to that employed in the temperature tables, namely, by collecting in Table XIX. the monthly and yearly means of the differences between the corrected readings of the barometer at 6 A.M. of consecutive days, arranged according to the resultant direction of the wind.

From this table we learn that the barometer rose during the twenty-four hours when the resultant wind was from West, N.W. and North, in all months; that it fell with a wind from N.E., E., S.E. and S. in all months, and that with a wind from S.W. it rose in some months and fell in others. Taking

---

* The quarterly means given in the text are nearly identical with those obtained from the differences taken between 6 A.M. and 6 A.M. on consecutive days, namely, 0·269 for winter, 0·211 for spring, 0·121 for summer, 0·189 for autumn, and 0·198 for the whole year. In connection with this subject, it may be noticed that the annual mean abnormal variations given in Table XXV. for 6 A.M. and 2 P.M. are nearly identical.

the year collectively, the barometer rose with a wind from W., N.W., and N., and fell with a wind from N.E., E., S.E., S., and S.W.

From Table XXX. it appears that a rise of the barometer was more frequent than a fall in all months with a resultant wind from W., N.W., and N., that a fall was more frequent than a rise in all months with a wind from E., S.E., and S., and that with a wind from N.E. and S.W. the number of ascents of the barometer exceeded the number of descents in some months and fell short of it in others, the number of months in which the number of descents preponderated being greater in both cases than the number of months in which the number of ascents preponderated. Taking the year collectively the barometer rose more frequently than it fell with a resultant wind from W., N.W., and N., and it fell more frequently than it rose with a resultant wind from N.E., E., S.E., S., and S.W., the mean percentage in the number of ascents being 78 for the first group of winds and 27 for the latter group.

In Table XXXI. a comparison is made between the *amounts* of the ascending and of the descending changes of the barometric pressure corresponding to the different resultant winds. The joint amount of the change of both signs for each wind and month being represented by 100, the number in this table will of course exceed or fall short of 50, according as the signs in Table XXIX. are positive or negative.*

Table XXXII. gives for each month and for the year the mean changes in the height of the barometer, irrespective of sign, between 6 A.M. and 6 A.M. on consecutive days, arranged according to the resultant direction of the wind.

In Table XXXIII. the relative influence of each of the several winds is compared for each month separately, as well as for the year, by expressing the numbers in Table XXXII. in terms of the monthly and annual arithmetic means for all winds. Taking the year collectively, it will be found that the N.W., S.E. and E. winds were most productive of barometric change, and that the least change accompanied the South wind. The greatest change corresponded to the N.W. wind in May, June, July, and October, and to either the E. or S.E. winds in the other months. The least change corresponded to either the South or S.W. winds in seven months, and to other winds in the remaining five months.

In Table XXXIV. a comparison is made of the relative influence of the same wind in different months, by expressing the twelve monthly numbers for each wind in Table XXXII. in terms of the arithmetic means of the same monthly numbers. The table shews that for each wind separately, as well as for all winds collectively, (as shewn by Table XXVI.) the minimum change of barometric pressure in twenty-four hours took place in one of the cold months, occurring in January for four directions in December for two directions, in February for one, and in March for one. For each wind also, the minimum change of barometer occurred in June or July, excepting that the minimum for the N.E. wind was approximately the same in October as it was in July. †

Table XXXV. gives the highest and lowest readings of the barometer recorded each month in the several years 1854 to 1859, and their differences or the monthly ranges. The final column in the table of ranges gives the difference between the highest and lowest readings in each year. On the average of the six years, the greatest monthly range occurred in December and the least in July. The mean monthly range for all months was 1.035, being 0.793 for the six months, April to September, and 1.277 for the remaining six months.

---

* In January and August, although the number of ascending changes that accompanied a S.E. wind were respectively .20 and .08 of the number of all the changes in these months for the S.E. wind, the amounts of increasing changes were in each case less than .005 of the whole change, and are therefore represented as (0) in Table XXXI.

† See note to remarks on Tables XIV. to XVI.

xviii   INTRODUCTION

The monthly and annual means at each observation hour for the separate years, 1854 to 1859, and for the period embracing these years, are given in Tables XXXVI. to XLVII. inclusive, for the following elements, namely, pressure of dry air, pressure of vapour, relative humidity and extent of sky clouded.

From Table XLVI. it appears that 0.59 was the average amount of cloudiness in the year, December and August being, respectively, the most cloudy and the least cloudy months.

Table XLVII. shews that, among the six observation hours, 2 P.M., on the average of the year, was the most cloudy hour, and midnight the hour most free from clouds.

In Table XLVIII. the numbers expressing the extent of sky clouded are classified according to the sixteen principal directions of the wind. If the sixteen points be arranged in four groups, each embracing four contiguous points, and the mean cloudiness for each point be treated as though it were of equal weight, it appears that the means of cloudiness during winds from directions included within the four quadrants, with their respective differences from the general mean, 0.59, were as follows:

Centres of groups, N.E.b.E.	S.E.b S.	S.W.b.W.	N.W.b.N.
0.72	0.54	0.61	0.51
+0.13	−0.05	+0.02	−0.08

From this we gather that the sky was most cloudy on the average during winds from N.E.b.E., and most clear with winds from N.W.b.N., and that there was a second maximum for winds from S.W.b.W. and a second minimum for winds from S.E.b.S.

In forming Tables XLIX. and L, that give a comparative view of the annual and diurnal variations of certain meteorological elements, as derived from the series 1842–48, and from the series 1854–59, the monthly and annual means of temperature as given by six daily observations have been reduced to the twenty-four-hour means by applying corrections derived from the table on pp. cxxvi-vii. of the introduction to the second volume of the Toronto observations. The independence of the annual variations of temperature for 1854-59 will therefore be affected to the extent of the differences between the monthly and annual values of these correction—differences which in no case exceed $0°.11$.

The independence of the diurnal variations of temperature for 1854-59 will be affected by the annual mean value of the correction, a quantity amounting only to $0°.02$.

RESULTANT DIRECTIONS OF THE WIND IN THE DIFFERENT MONTHS.

The comparison of the monthly resultants derived from the period 1854 to 1859, and given in Table LI., shews that the general direction of the atmospheric current is considerably more from the westward in the winter than in the summer months, the monthly resultants oscillating about N. 43° W. from April to September, inclusive, and about N. 72° W. during the remaining six months.

There is a much nearer approach to uniformity of direction in the different years for some months than for others; thus taking the angular difference between a monthly partial resultant on a particular year, and the corresponding monthly resultant for the six years, as a rough measure of the irregularity of the partial resultant, it is found that the averages of these differences are 7° for January, and about 75° for June and July. The quarterly averages of the differences are, for winter (commencing December 1st) 20°, for summer 53°, for spring 29°, and for autumn 27°; their half-yearly averages being 46° from April to September, and 19° during the rest of the year.

INTRODUCTION. xix

RESULTANT VELOCITIES AND MEAN VELOCITIES IN THE DIFFERENT MONTHS.

The resultant velocities and mean velocities have each their maximum in March and their minimum in July. The change from month to month is regular in both, with the exception of a small interruption of continuity in August and another in December.

RESULTANT DIRECTIONS OF THE WIND IN THE DIFFERENT HOURS.

Confining our attention in the first instance to the annual resultants given in Table LII. we find that during the hour commencing noon the resultant wind is from N. 103° W. its extreme distance left of North. From this point at which the wind is nearly steady during the three hours commencing at noon, it draws round towards the north regularly and continuously till it makes its nearest approach to the North (N. 39° W.) at 5 A.M. About this point it remains nearly steady from midnight to 7 A.M. and then rapidly recedes again to the westward.

The extreme recession of the resultant direction from the north takes place during the first three hours after noon in all months excepting November, when it occurs between 11 A.M. and noon, and in December, when it is between 3 P.M. and 5 P.M. It occurs in May between 1 P.M. and 2 P.M., but in a contrary direction to that of all other months, being 108° to the *east* of north.

The hours of nearest approach to the north are not so well marked, and are included within wider limits. In most months they are found between midnight and sunrise, but in May, June, and November, they occur in the early part of the night. The angular diurnal range in the direction of the resultant is 180° in July (its maximum), and 15° in November (its minimum). The quarterly averages of the diurnal ranges are 25° from December to February, 85° from March to May, 152° from June to August, and 65° from September to November. The half yearly averages are 135° from April to September, and 29° from October to March.

MEAN RESULTANT VELOCITIES OF WIND IN THE DIFFERENT HOURS.

By Table LIII. it is seen that the maximum resultant velocity for the whole year occurs during the hour commencing 1 P.M., and the minimum during the two hours between 4 A.M. and 6 A.M.; the progression being continuous from the maximum to the minimum and to the maximum again, if the second place of decimals be disregarded.

The maximum takes place in one of the three hours commencing noon in every month but April and May, when it is found in the hours commencing respectively at 9 P.M. and 7 A.M. The hours of minimum are not well marked; and in July, August, and September there is a double progression.

MEAN VELOCITY OF THE WIND IN THE DIFFERENT HOURS.

On the average of the year as shewn in Table LIV. the maximum velocity is from 1 P.M. to 2 P.M. and the minimum from 1 A.M. to 2 A.M. The maximum occurs in every month during one of the four hours commencing noon, and the minimum in most months within three hours of midnight, a prominent exception being December, when the minimum is at 7 A.M.

MEAN VELOCITIES OF THE WIND IN DIFFERENT DIRECTIONS.

From Table LV., which includes only winds at the six observation hours, we learn that the wind has a maximum velocity of 10·90 miles per hour when it blows from N.W., and a minimum velocity of 5·22 miles per hour when it blows from S.E. There is an interruption to the continuity of the progression amounting to a second minimum at about N.N.E., and a second maximum at about E.N.E.

ANNUAL DISTRIBUTION OF THE DIFFERENT WINDS WITH RESPECT TO DURATION.

The results given in Table LI. to LIV. depend on the *velocities* as well as on the *durations* of the different winds, and as the average velocities in some directions are much greater than in others, these tables convey but indirect information as to the comparative prevalence of the different winds with respect to their duration. Tables LVI. to LIX., which are given to supply this want, were computed in the following manner:—From the monthly abstracts which give the direction of the wind during each hour of each day, tables were formed for each month in the seven years 1853 to 1859, containing the number of times during like hours that the wind blew from the sixteen principal points, as well as the number of absolute calms in each group of like hours. By combining these tables the two following auxiliary tables were then prepared.

Table A giving the absolute duration in hours of the different winds and of the calms for the several months, each month embracing the observations of seven years.

Table B. giving the absolute duration of the different winds and calms for each of the* twenty-four hours, each hour including all the winds recorded for that hour in the seven years.

Table LVI is derived from table (A) by expressing the absolute durations of each wind in each month and in the year, in terms of the monthly and annual mean durations for all winds. It is designed to give, for each month separately, and for the year collectively, a comparative view of the durations of the different winds.

It appears from this table that winds from between S.S.W., through West to North, have a more than average duration as compared with other winds, taking the whole year collectively; but it is only those from N.N.W. that have a duration exceeding the average in each separate month.

Winds from E.N.E. and E. are above the average on the whole year as well as in each separate month, but December, January, February, and August. The North wind is above the average on the whole year and is above the average in some months and below it in others, but without any perceptible annual period.

The South wind is below the average on the whole year collectively, and in each separate month but May, June, July, and August.

The wind of maximum duration for the whole year collectively is N.N.W., and the wind of minimum duration S.E., with a second maximum at East and a second minimum at N.N.E.

The principal maximum is found at some point between W.S.W. and N.N.W. in seven months; but in April, May, and June, East winds are the most frequent, and in July and September the most frequent wind is from S.S.W.

The wind of least duration is from S.E., S.S.E. or South in seven months; but in May, July, August and September† the least frequent wind is from W.S.W., and in June it is from N.N.E.

---

* The space of the hour has been always designated by the point of time with which it commences, thus, the winds for noon are those between noon and 1 P.M.

† In September the duration of the E.S.E. wind is nearly identical with that of the W.S.W. wind.

In Table LVII. the durations of the same wind in different months are compared. As the months are of different lengths, instead of comparing the absolute durations, which for the longer months would be unduly great, this table is obtained by expressing the numbers of table LVI. in terms of the annual arithmetic means for the several winds.

The change in duration from month to month, exhibited by this table, is for most winds very irregular, the only instance of a distinct period being in the case of the South wind, which decreases in duration regularly from its maximum in June to its minimum in December; the maximum being to the minimum nearly in the ratio of 8 to 1.

If N_3 be taken to denote the ratio which the duration of the winds, from the three points N.N.W., North, and N.N.E. in the six winter months (October to March), bears to the duration of the winds from the same points in the summer half year, and N_7 the corresponding ratio when the winds from North are associated with those from the three points on either side of it, from W.N.W. to E.N.E; the ratio for the analogous combinations about the three other cardinal points being represented by S_3, S_7, E_3, E_7, W_3, W_7; it will be found that

$$N_3 = 0.91; \quad S_3 = 0.49; \quad E_3 = 0.65; \quad W_3 = 2.24$$
$$N_7 = 1.01; \quad S_7 = 0.91; \quad E_7 = 0.70; \quad W_7 = 1.39$$

Again if the durations of the winds in the Northern and in the Western groups be compared with those of the groups diametrically opposite, and $\left(\frac{N}{S}\right)_3$ be employed to denote the ratio whose first term is the duration of the winds from the three points about North, the ratios between other groups being expressed in an analogous manner; we have

In Winter $\left(\frac{N}{S}\right)_3 = 1.94; \quad \left(\frac{N}{S}\right)_7 = 1.36; \quad \left(\frac{W}{E}\right)_3 = 2.18; \quad \left(\frac{W}{E}\right)_7 = 2.25.$

In Summer...... = 1.04; ..... = 1.22; ..... = 0.63; ..... = 1.13

Year............ = 1.34 ..... = 1.30 ..... = 1.25 ..... = 1.59

DIURNAL DISTRIBUTION OF THE DIFFERENT WINDS WITH RESPECT TO DURATION.

The comparative duration, for each hour, of the sixteen winds and the calms are obtained by dividing the absolute duration of each wind in the hour by the average duration of all winds, including calms, in the same hour. From Table LVIII., in which the results are given, the following facts may be gathered.

I. The durations of the winds from W.S.W. to N.N.W. inclusive, for each hour separately as well as for all hours collectively, are above the average duration of all winds.

II. The durations of winds from E. and E.N.E., taking the twenty-four hours collectively, are above the average; and one or other or both of these winds are above the average at all hours, excepting from 2 A.M. to 3 A.M.

III. The durations of the North winds are above the average for the whole day collectively and have a marked diurnal period, their duration being above the average duration of all winds from 9 P.M. to 9 A.M., and below the average from 9 A.M. to 9 P.M.

IV. The South winds have a duration less than the average, taking one hour with another, and they also have a diurnal period, their durations being above the average duration of all winds from 10 A.M. to 6 P.M., and below the average during the rest of the twenty-four hours.

The principal maximum occurs with the wind from S.S.W. from 11 A.M. to 4 P.M., that is to say, during a portion of the time when the duration of the South wind is above the average, and it occurs with the N.N.W. and North wind mostly at the hours when the duration of the North wind is above the average; a second maximum vibrating from East to E.N.E. during the whole of the day and night. From 9 A.M. to 11 A.M. and from 4 P.M. to 7 P.M., namely, when the North and South winds respectively are near their average as compared with other winds, and when the winds in the N.W. quadrant are more equally distributed among its several points, the easterly or second maximum surpasses in value the westerly or principal maximum.

The character of the diurnal periodicity of the different winds is better seen by Table LIX., in which the duration of each wind at each hour is expressed in terms of the average duration of that wind in the twenty-four hours.

If the columns corresponding to the four cardinal points be examined, it is found that the West wind during the night is mostly above the twenty-four-hour average, and below the average during several hours of the day; but the range is small, the maximum being to the minimum in the ratio of 1.36 to 1.

The East wind from 8 A.M. to 9 P.M. is above the average of twenty-four hours for that wind, and is below the average from 9 P.M. to 8 A.M.; its diurnal range, or the ratio of the maximum to the minimum being 2.40 to 1.

The North wind is above the average from 10 P.M. to 9 A.M., and below the average from 9 P.M. to to 10 P.M., the range being 3.44 to 1.

The South wind is above the average from 10 A.M. to 7 P.M., and below it from 7 P.M. to 10 A.M., and its range is 4.82 to 1.

Calms occur eight times as often between midnight and 1 A.M. as they do between 1 P.M. and 2 P.M. The hours of maximum and minimum frequency of calms are very nearly the same as the hours of minimum and maximum mean velocity, a correspondence, which, as appears from Table LVII., does not hold in the case of the *annual* distribution of calms.

RAIN AND SNOW.

The approximate durations of rain and snow forming parts of Tables LX., LXI., and LXII. are found by the addition of the durations in hours recorded on each day from *estimation*. The numbers given are probably not far from the truth, but must not be regarded as strictly accurate.

The monthly average number of days in which rain fell, as given by the six years terminating with 1859, are month for month, with one exception, either equal to or greater than the corresponding monthly averages for the series of 15 years terminating also with 1859, the excess on the whole year being 12 days in favour of the shorter series. The same remark applies, and without any exception, to the monthly averages of the number of days of snow as well as to those of rain and snow, where the two are regarded indiscriminately; the number of days of either rain or snow for the whole year, given in the shorter series, being 24 days in excess of the number given by the series of 15 years.

With respect to the *quantity* of rain the case is reversed, the average annual depth in the six-years series being less than that in the fifteen-years series by about 0.6 of an inch; but this deficiency in the amount of rain is in part made up by a greater amount of snow; so that in combining together the rain and snow, the average amount generally of aqueous precipitation in the year differs only by little more than a tenth of an inch in the two series; and this difference would disappear if eight inches of snow instead of ten inches were taken as equivalent to one inch of water.

RELATION BETWEEN RAIN AND SNOW AND THE DIRECTION OF THE WIND.

As no instrument was in use during the years 1853 to 1859 for recording the hours in which rain fell, an attempt has been made to trace the connection between the fall of rain and the direction of the wind by means of the ratios which express the duration of each wind, on the days in any part of which rain fell, in terms of the whole duration of the same wind during the same series of years. The method employed will be understood by referring to Table LXIII.

Column (1) contains the number of hours that each wind blew during the days on which rain fell, in the years 1853 to 1859. Column (2) contains the corresponding numbers for snow, and column (3) the numbers for rain or snow. The latter are not accurately the sums of the numbers in columns (1) and (2) from the fact that when both rain and snow fell on the same day, the duration of each wind on that day is reckoned *twice*, namely, in both of the columns (1) and (2), whereas it is reckoned once only in column (3).

If each wind blew an equal number of hours through the year, the numbers in column (1) or rather the ratios that they severally bear to their mean for all winds, would exhibit the comparative frequency of the different winds during rainy days; but as the numbers of hours during which the different winds blew were not equal, it is necessary that the numbers in column (1) should be divided by the numbers in column (4) that express the *whole* duration of the corresponding wind during the years 1853 to 1859. From the quotients, which are given in column (5), we learn that of 1000 hours in which the wind blew from E.N.E. as many as 545 hours were comprised in days during some part of which rain fell, but that of 1000 hours of North wind, only 248 hours belonged to days of rain.

Similarly from column (6), 330 hours in 1000 hours of West winds, and only 86 hours in 1000 hours of South winds were included in days in which snow fell; also from column (7), 637 hours in 1000 hours of winds from E.N.E., and 412 hours in 1000 hours of South winds were included in days in which a fall occured of either rain or snow.

Column (8) contains the numbers in (5) expressed in terms of their arithmetic mean for all winds, and columns (9) and (10) are derived in a similar manner from columns (6) and (7).

From column (9) it appears that during days of rain, winds from N.E. through South to S.W. are above or not below the average duration of all winds, and that winds from N.N.E. through North to W.S.W. are below the same average; also, that the most rainy wind is from E.N.E. and the winds for which rain is most rare are from North and N.N.W.

In the case of the snow the winds whose durations are above the average of all winds are from N.E. through North and West to W.S.W., and the winds that have a less than average duration are from E.N.E. through South to S.S.W., the greatest number of winds relatively that occurred during days of snow being from the West with a second maximum at N.E., and the least number being from South and S.S.W.

The two sets of ratios in (8) and (9) produce by their superposition a double progression in column

xxiv   INTRODUCTION.

(10), the chief maximum being at E.N.E., with a second maximum at West; the winds that are least frequently accompanied by rain or snow being those from the north and south points.

During the years 1857 to 1859 a record was made each day of the *hours* during any part of which rain or snow was seen to fall, or was believed to have fallen, from the best evidence that could be procured at the time when the entries were made. The want of any suitable instrument during that period precluded any more certain mode of procuring the requisite facts; but although the entries do not claim the same confidence as those made at the observation hours, or by self-registering instruments, it is believed that they furnish very fair data for determining approximately the relative frequency of the winds that blew during the same hours with rain or snow.

The distribution of the winds that blew during the same hours with rain or snow is given in Table LXIV.

Column (1) gives the number of hours during any part of which rain fell during the years 1857 to 1859, arranged according to the direction of the wind during the same hour. Column (2) gives the corresponding numbers for snow; and column (3) those for rain or snow. For a reason already explained, the numbers in (3) are frequently less than the sum of those in (1) and (2).

Column (4) contains the whole number of hours that each wind blew during the years 1857 to 1859. The quotients arising from the division of the the numbers in (1) by those in (4), and which are contained in column (5), are measures of the frequency of rain for each wind. Thus, it rained during some part of each of 219 hours out of 1000 hours in which the wind was from E.N.E., and 39 hours only out of 1000 hours of N.W. wind.

Similarly from column (6), derived in a like manner from (2) and (4), it is seen that snow was falling during part of each of 140 hours in 1000 hours of N.E. wind, and only 18 hours in 1000 hours of South wind.

Column (7) shews that of 1000 hours of E.N.E. winds (and the same is true for N.N.E. winds), it rained or snowed during parts of each of 282 hours, whereas it rained or snowed only 84 hours in 1000 hours of N.W. wind.

Columns (8), (9) and (10) give the ratios of the numbers in (5), (6) and (7) to their respective means for all winds.

From (8) it appears that during rain, winds from N.N.E. through East to S.S.W., with an interruption at South, have a duration above the average for all winds, and that winds from North through West to S.W. have a duration below the same average.

The most rainy wind is from E.N.E.; and the N.W. wind is that which is least frequently accompanied by rain.

During snow, winds from North to E.N.E. are decidedly above the average, the wind of greatest frequency being that from N.E. Winds from the remaining points of the compass do not follow any regular progression. They are for the most part below the average; but there is a trace of a second maximum between W.N.W. and W.S.W.

In column (10) the second maximum is obliterated by the superposition of the two sets of ratios; the progression becomes single and is uninterrupted, excepting that at the South point the winds are slightly less numerous than at either S.S.E. and S.S.W., and that the ratio at N.E. is rather less than at either of the contiguous points. During precipitation generally, making no distinction between rain and snow, the winds whose relative durations are above the average, are limited to N.N.E., N.E., E.N.E., East, and E.S.E.; the relative durations of other winds being all less than the average.

Comparing the ratios in Table LXIV. with those from Table LXIII., which have been placed side by side with them for that purpose, it may be noticed that the range is much greater in the former than in the latter table; and also that during snow, the west wind, instead of being, as in Table LXIII, the wind of greatest frequency, now touches or is slightly below the average, the principal maximum being transferred in Table LXIV to N.E.; at which point the wind is two and a half times as frequent as the west wind during the *actual fall* of snow, although during days of snow, the west wind blows for more hours than the N.E. wind.

RELATION BETWEEN RAIN AND THE DIRECTION OF THE WIND WHEN THE LIGHTER AND THE HEAVIER FALLS ARE EXAMINED SEPARATELY.

As it is probable that in the enquiries that have been made with reference to the distribution of the different winds during rainy days and during hours of rain, the lighter showers may have given by their number a greater prominence to certain winds than is their due, and have diminished also in some degree the preponderance of those which are properly the rainy winds; tables LXIII. (*bis.*) and LXIV. (*bis.*) have been formed, for the purpose of shewing the distribution of the winds among the several points of the compass, under different circumstances as regards the amount of rain in the day.

The ratios in these tables are obtained in a manner precisely similar to that employed in computing the final columns of tables LXIII. and LXIV.

Table LXIII. (*bis.*) contains the ratios which express the relative* durations of each wind during days of rain, in terms of the mean of the relative durations of all winds during days of rain; (1) when the rain that falls in a day is less than half an inch; (2) when the rain is not less than half an inch; and (3) when light and heavy rain are taken together.

When the rain that falls in the day is less than half an inch, it is shewn by column (1) that the points for which the relative duration of the wind is above the average, as well as the points of the greatest and least relative duration, are the same as when the heavy and light rain are taken together; the range also is very nearly the same, being slightly less than 2 to 1.

When the heavy rains only are taken into account, the winds whose relative durations are above the average, are limited to the six points from N.E. to S.S.E.; the wind of maximum relative duration remains as before at E.N.E., but the minimum is transferred to W.S.W., and the range greatly increases; the E.N.E. winds having a relative duration nearly nine times that of the W.S.W. winds. The increase in the relative durations of the winds from the six points N.E. to S.S.E. inclusive, as compared with those of the other ten winds, is shewn by the averages of the corresponding ratios in columns (1), (2), and (3.)

	(1.)	(2.)	(3.)
Averages of ratios for the six points, N.E. to S.S.E.	1.18	1.75	1.25
Averages for remaining ten points	0.89	0.59	0.85

The ratios in table LXIV. (*bis.*) express the relative duration of each wind during the hours, in

---

*The term *relative duration* is here employed to denote the ratio of the absolute duration of a given wind during rainy days, or during hours of rain, to the whole absolute duration of the same wind, with and without rain, during the same period.

any part of which rain fell, in terms of the mean of the relative durations of all winds during hours of rain.

When rain under half an inch is taken alone, the winds of more than an average duration, if we except an interruption that occurs at N.E., are the same as when no account is taken of the amount that fell in the day; the wind of least duration is still from N.W., but that of the greatest duration is no longer so decidedly at E.N.E.

When rains amounting to less than half an inch are omitted, the most rainy and least rainy winds are still from E.N.E. and N.W.; but the relative duration of the E.N.E. wind is eighteen times as great as that of the N.W. wind. The winds also whose relative durations are above the average, are limited to the four points N.N.E., N.E., E.N.E., and East.

TABLE LXIII.—(Bis.)

Ratios comparing the relative durations of the several winds during days in any part of which rain fell, from observations in the years 1853 to 1859 inclusive, the falls under half an inch in the day, those of half an inch and upwards, and rain generally, without reference to its amount, being considered separately.

TABLE LXIV.—(Bis.)

Ratios comparing the relative durations of the several winds during the hours in any part of which rain fell, from observations in the years 1857 to 1859, the falls under half an inch, those of half an inch and upwards, and rain in general, without reference to its amount, being considered separately

Direction of the wind.	Rain under half an inch. (1)	Rain half an inch and upwards. (2)	Rain generally. (3)	Direction of the wind.	Rain under half an inch. (1)	Rain half an inch and upwards. (2)	Rain generally. (3)
N.	0.73	0.64	0.72	N.	0.68	0.67	0.68
N.N.E.	0.76	0.88	0.77	N.N.E.	1.40	2.18	1.68
N.E.	1.01	1.40	1.06	N.E.	0.93	1.55	1.10
E.N.E.	1.41	2.71	1.58	E.N.E.	1.66	4.37	2.41
E.	1.36	2.43	1.50	E.	1.34	1.71	1.44
E.S.E.	1.17	1.61	1.23	E.S.E.	1.68	0.83	1.45
S.E.	1.06	1.12	1.07	S.E.	1.29	0.67	1.12
S.S.E.	1.07	1.20	1.09	S.S.E.	1.17	0.75	1.05
S.	1.04	0.73	1.00	S.	1.00	0.60	0.89
S.S.W.	1.14	0.88	1.11	S.S.W.	1.20	0.67	1.05
S.W.	1.07	0.80	1.03	S.W.	0.79	0.83	0.80
W.S.W.	0.94	0.30	0.85	W.S.W.	0.64	0.43	0.58
W.	0.86	0.34	0.79	W.	0.68	0.36	0.59
W.N.W.	0.80	0.47	0.76	W.N.W.	0.58	0.28	0.49
N.W.	0.81	0.43	0.76	N.W.	0.50	0.24	0.43
N.N.W.	0.77	0.45	0.72	N.N.W.	0.64	0.39	0.57
Calms.	1.00	0.62	0.95	Calms.	0.74	0.48	0.67

RELATION BETWEEN SNOW AND THE DIRECTION OF THE WIND WHEN THE SNOW STORMS ARE DIVIDED INTO CLASSES ACCORDING TO THE QUANTITY THAT FELL DURING THE TWENTY-FOUR HOURS.

In Tables LXIII. and LXIV., which contain the ratios that exhibit the comparative frequency of the different winds during days of snow or during the actual fall of snow, no distinction is made between snow storms of different magnitude; light falls, lasting for a few minutes, and the heaviest storms being ranked together indiscriminately. With a view of examining whether the distribution of the winds found to prevail during snow generally, is maintained in the case of the heavy falls, the methods employed in computing Tables LXIII. and LXIV. have been applied to the following four classes of snow storms:—

Class I. including every instance where snow was recorded.

Class II. limited to those cases in which the snow in twenty-four hours was equal to or exceeded one inch.

Class III. limited to falls of three inches and upwards.

Class IV. limited to falls of six inches and upwards.

In Table LXV. is shewn the distribution of the winds during *days* of snow, arranged in the above-named four classes, and in Table LXVI. the distribution of the winds during the *hours* in any part of which snow fell, the falls of snow by this method also being arranged in the same four classes.

On comparing the four final columns of Table LXV., we find that the second maximum at N.E. in column (10) becomes very decidedly the principal maximum in column (11) wherein snow amounting to less than an inch in the day is excluded, and increases greatly as the storms become more heavy. The West wind also, which was the principal maximum when light snow was included, is now decidedly below the average, and rapidly decreases in frequency in columns (12) and (13). The North wind maintains a more than average frequency till the falls of snow are limited to those of six inches and upwards.

The progressive increase in the predominance of winds from the five points, N.N.E. through East to E.S.E. in passing from Class I. to Class IV., and the diminished frequency of other winds, are made apparent by the averages of the ratios for the former five points, and of the remaining eleven points. The averages are as follows:—

	AVERAGE RATIOS.			
	Class I.	Class II.	Class III.	Class IV.
Five winds from N.N.E. to E.S.E.	1.00	1.70	2.10	2.55
Eleven remaining winds	1.04	0.74	0.57	0.35

On turning to Table LXVI. we find that the principal maximum at N.E., in column (10), increases rapidly in the higher classes, and that the second maximum at or near West in column (10) disappears when the snow amounts to one inch. The North wind continues above the average during falls of snow whereof all less than an inch are excluded, but is below the average when falls of less than three inches are excluded, and is wholly absent when the storms included are only those of six inches and upwards.

It appears further, with reference to the heaviest snow storms, that although during some part of the day in which the storm takes place, the wind may blow more or less from any point of the compass, during the actual fall of snow the directions of the wind are limited to the four points N.N.E., N.E., E.N.E., and East.

The increasing frequency in the easterly group of winds from N.N.E. through East to E.S.E., *during the actual fall of snow*, as more and more of the lighter falls are excluded, and the diminishing frequency of all other winds, are shewn by the averages of the corresponding ratios in the manner already employed with reference to table LXV.

The averages are the following:—

	Class I.	Class II.	Class III.	Class IV.
Five winds from N.N.E. to E.S.E.	1.41	2.16	2.59	3.22
Eleven remaining winds	0.84	0.52	0.33	0.00

The distribution of the winds among the several points of the compass during falls of snow in which the amount in the day falls short of one inch, will be found by subtracting the relative durations in column (7) from those in column (6). The progression in the resulting series, omitting minor irregularities, becomes single; the maximum is decidedly between the three points W.N.W., West, and W.S.W.; and the minimum is in the S.E. quadrant, the winds from N.E. being well below the average.

TORONTO

METEOROLOGICAL OBSERVATIONS.

GENERAL METEOROLOGICAL ABSTRACT,—JANUARY, 1854.

TORONTO METEOROLOGICAL OBSERVATIONS.

Days	DAILY MEANS.						WIND.			EXTREMES OF TEMPERATURE.			RAIN.		SNOW.		RAIN AND MELTED SNOW.	
	Temperature of the Air.	Pressure of Vapour.	Relative Humidity.	Barometric Pressure.	Pressure of Dry Air.	Clouded Sky.	Resultant Direction.	Resultant Velocity.	Mean Velocity.	Maximum.	Minimum.	Difference.	Depth in Inches.	Approximate duration in hours.	Depth in Inches.	Approximate duration in hours.	Depth in Inches.	Approximate duration in hours.
	°							Miles.	Miles.									
1	16.00	0.081	86	29.717	29.635	0.8	S 74 W	5.56	5.71	26.4	13.2	13.2	...	...	...	...	...	...
2	23.89	.120	88	.717	.626	1.0	S 77 W	8.98	9.10	19.8	3.0	13.9	...	...	...	...	...	...
3	30.42	.210	86	.646	.325	0.6	S 12 E	2.36	4.29	40.2	13.0	27.2	...	...	...	...	...	...
4	34.35	.183	61	.635	.393	1.0	S 88 W	3.89	8.38	46.4	28.8	17.6	...	...	...	...	...	3.0
5	20.60	.086	75	.576	.751	1.0	N 96 E	3.60	7.38	41.0	25.2	15.8	0.255	10.5	...	...	0.020	...
6	17.60	.082	81	.837	.703	0.7	N 57 W	6.67	7.96	27.5	13.0	14.5	...	...	...	...	.255	10.5
7				.785		1.0	S 74 W	6.76	6.84	20.5	12.4	8.1	...	...	...	...	...	...
8						1.0	N 7 W	3.37	4.12	20.2	0.2	20.0	...	...	...	...	...	...
9	14.80	.076	83	.659	.683	0.7	N 49 W	3.83	5.73	27.8	4.0	23.8	...	...	0.8	4.0	.080	4.0
10	29.60	.146	88	.525	.378	0.8	N 89 E	1.11	1.81	37.5	21.5	16.0	...	...	...	...	*	...
11	30.75	.156	88	.551	.395	1.0	N 64 E	6.02	7.10	40.6	20.2	20.4	.485	12.0	...	...	.485	12.0
12	39.40	.229	95	29.880	28.600	1.0	S 70 W	4.14	7.73	44.2	30.5	13.7	.190	7.0	...	...	.190	7.0
13	30.32	.151	88	29.100	28.949	1.0	S 74 W	9.70	10.24	35.6	18.4	17.2	...	...	0.2	4.0	.040	4.0
14	25.23	.117	84	.668	29.552	1.0	N 45 W	4.95	5.29	28.2	23.2	5.0	...	...	*	...	.180	9.0
15						0.6	S 69 E	3.67	4.57	35.2	21.0	14.2	...	...	...	...	.090	6.0
16	31.78	.156	66	.509	.353	1.0	N 78 W	3.72	3.76	36.4	19.4	17.0	.080	2.0	1.5	4.0	.150	4.0
17	22.10	.093	76	.838	.740	0.3	N 50 W	3.99	5.24	28.4	15.0	13.4	...	...	...	...	.080	2.0
18	19.85	.095	85	.857	.762	1.0	N 43 E	5.05	6.06	26.0	17.3	8.7	...	...	...	...	.060	...
19	26.90	.133	89	.778	.646	1.0	N 57 E	6.24	7.54	31.0	21.6	9.4	...	...	...	...	.040	4.0
20	30.63	.164	94	.098	28.930	0.8	N 89 E	1.23	8.46	37.6	22.8	14.7	5.0	...	...	...	.090	6.0
21	15.65	.086	83	.444	29.358	0.6	S 87 W	15.77	15.83	15.2	-1.0	16.2	.090	5.0	4.0	4.0	.090	4.0
22						1.0	N 85 W	7.01	7.14	12.0	-2.8	9.2	...	...	...	...	...	...
23	5.37	.043	79	.001	.953	0.3	S 98 W	11.43	11.66	12.2	2.4	9.7	...	...	...	...	...	2.0
24	6.32	.044	71	29.940	29.905	0.2	N 46 W	4.30	5.24	-5.4	-14.2	19.6	...	...	2.0	2.0	.060	2.0
25	11.92	.074	77	.919	.846	0.9	S 75 E	6.39	7.66	14.2	-3.4	39.6	...	...	4.0	4.0	.060	4.0
26	32.70	.169	80	.364	.195	0.8	N 62 W	7.21	7.50	36.2	15.8	24.2	...	...	...	...	.180	...
27	17.47	.082	79	.608	.526	0.5	N 69 W	7.43	8.21	40.0	15.8	25.8	...	...	1.0	1.0	.020	1.0
28	1.58	.039	76	30.131	30.098	0.1	N 21 E	5.45	8.70	22.8	-3.0	8.2	...	...	4.0	4.0	.070	4.0
29						1.0	N 73 E	5.13	5.52	5.6	-2.6	8.2	...	...	0.8	0.2	*	0.2
30	33.18	.164	96	29.588	29.424		N 26 W	5.61	6.98	27.4	9.8	17.6	.060	1.5	0.7	...	.060	1.5
31	35.47	.189	92	.210	.021	1.0	S 63 W	2.35	2.51	36.8	25.0	11.9	.110	0.5	...	...	.110	0.5
	23.57	0.122	84	29.607	29.485	0.8	N 77 W	2.44	6.91	29.31	13.53	15.78	1.270	39.5	7.5	42.2	2.020	81.7

* Inappreciable.

GENERAL METEOROLOGICAL ABSTRACT,—FEBRUARY, 1854.

Days	Temperature of the Air	Pressure of Vapour	Relative Humidity	Barometric Pressure	Pressure of Dry Air	Clouded Sky	Resultant Direction	Resultant Velocity	Mean Velocity	Maximum	Minimum	Difference	RAIN Depth in Inches	RAIN Approximate duration in hours	SNOW Depth in Inches	SNOW Approximate duration in hours	RAIN AND MELTED SNOW Depth in Inches	RAIN AND MELTED SNOW Approximate duration in hours
1	37.12	0.198	90	29.168	28.970	1.0	N 44 W	Miles 3.15	Miles 4.40	42.8	16.2	26.6	*	*	0.8	3.0	0.080	3.0
2	9.48	.063	83	.591	29.529	0.7	N 1 W	9.22	9.48	18.2	−10.8	29.0	...	...	1.5	9.0	.150	9.0
3	4.62	.048	79	.805	.757	0.3	N 55 W	2.79	3.62	14.9	−4.2	19.1	...	...	...	...	...	...
4	8.27	.057	82	.935	.878	0.8	N 19 W	1.04	2.34	18.8	1.8	17.0	...	...	1.0	2.0	.100	2.0
5	...	...	...	...	...	...	N 45 E	5.31	6.68	23.4	−5.2	28.6	...	...	1.0	3.0	.100	3.0
6	10.80	.068	79	30.079	30.011	0.5	S 73 W	1.03	1.08	23.6	−3.4	27.0	...	...	...	...	...	...
7	22.87	.106	83	29.856	29.748	1.0	S 62 E	6.33	6.56	31.0	13.8	17.2	...	...	3.2	10.0	.320	10.0
8	32.87	.171	91	.150	28.979	0.8	S 56 W	2.67	6.44	36.0	22.5	13.5	.465	5.7	0.2	5.7	.465	5.7
9	28.55	.138	87	.199	.060	0.9	S 82 W	7.09	8.39	35.4	15.0	20.4	.020	...	...	2.0	.020	2.0
10	15.07	.076	82	.761	.685	0.5	N 55 W	4.74	4.91	20.2	−3.5	23.7	...	...	*	*	*	*
11	11.07	.067	84	30.118	30.051	0.6	S 82 W	4.31	5.95	22.2	0.4	21.8	.685	10.0	...	...	.685	10.0
12	...	...	...	...	...	1.0	S 97 E	10.83	10.93	36.0	16.4	19.6	.085	3.5	0.2	1.5	.085	5.0
13	36.10	.203	96	29.447	29.245	1.0	N 4 E	4.64	5.52	38.6	27.5	11.1	*	*	0.5	4.5	.050	4.5
14	28.10	.142	91	.484	.342	1.0	N 74 E	8.61	9.46	33.0	23.5	9.5	...	...	...	...	...	...
15	27.98	.141	90	.461	.320	1.0	S 81 W	7.07	7.62	35.2	20.6	14.6	...	...	0.1	2.0	.010	2.0
16	21.22	.101	85	.737	.636	0.7	N 83 W	4.84	4.98	24.8	7.2	17.6	...	...	...	...	...	...
17	17.85	.088	87	.916	.832	1.0	S 74 W	7.59	7.69	26.0	9.4	16.6	...	...	0.2	3.7	.020	3.7
18	31.28	.161	90	.568	.407	1.0	N 81 W	6.25	8.63	41.0	15.6	25.4	...	...	...	...	...	...
19	...	...	...	...	...	0.2	N 19 E	3.86	4.52	24.6	17.2	7.4	...	...	...	...	...	...
20	20.53	.069	78	.621	.533	0.6	N 69 E	9.04	9.78	24.8	15.0	9.8	...	...	0.1	1.0	.010	1.0
21	25.57	.121	85	.605	.484	1.0	S 31 W	2.56	4.17	38.9	17.0	10.9	.105	1.0	2.5	2.5	.250	2.5
22	26.60	.145	92	.412	.267	1.0	N 54 W	8.81	13.19	26.6	−0.5	37.1	.140	5.0	...	...	...	...
23	10.55	.061	79	.941	.880	0.4	N 70 W	5.00	6.66	23.2	0.3	22.9	...	...	0.2	1.6	.020	1.6
24	25.23	.124	87	.860	.736	1.0	N 18 E	4.57	8.39	35.1	8.4	26.7	...	...	1.0	2.0	.205	3.0
25	17.70	.090	87	.997	.907	0.8	S 88 E	10.87	10.99	34.0	13.0	21.0	...	...	6.5	13.0	.690	18.0
26	...	...	...	...	...	0.0	N 60 E	9.87	12.49	31.6	−0.6	32.4	...	...	...	...	...	...
27	15.37	.053	87	.972	.889	0.0	N 6 E	6.93	0.99	31.6	8.2	23.4	...	...	...	...	...	...
28	21.25	.110	85	.991	.881	0.7	S 88 W	0.56	1.63	...	...	...	...	...	...	...	...	...
	21.09°	0.110	86	29.695	29.584	0.7	N 7 E	1.73	6.91	29.63	9.15	20.47	1.460	25.2	18.0	60.8	3.260	86.0

GENERAL METEOROLOGICAL ABSTRACT.—MARCH, 1854.

Days	DAILY MEANS.					WIND.			Extremes of Temperature.			RAIN.		SNOW.		Rain and Melted Snow.	
	Temperature of the Air.	Pressure of Vapour.	Relative Humidity.	Barometric Pressure.	Pressure of Dry Air.	Clouded Sky.	Resultant Direction.	Resultant Velocity.	Mean Velocity.	Maximum.	Minimum.	Difference.	Depth in Inches.	Approximate duration in hours.	Depth in Inches.	Approximate duration in hours.	Depth in Inches.	Approximate duration in hours.
	°							Miles.	Miles.									
1	30.72	0.148	85	29.896	29.738	0.2	N 24 W	2.78	3.59	37.5	20.5	17.0						
2	33.98	.185	94	.681	.396	1.0	N 87 E	10.56	10.66	39.0	32.0	7.0	.875	14.5			.875	14.5
3	39.07	.209	89	.308	.095	0.2	S 63 W	8.59	8.79	42.0	30.2	11.8						
4	35.12	.160	80	.389	.228	0.4	N 81 W	7.45	9.65	42.8	25.5	17.3						
5							N 70 W	6.57	7.04	33.7	22.4	11.3						
6	29.75	.141	85	.871	.730	1.0	N 34 E	1.34	3.01	33.8	25.2	8.6						
7	34.90	.184	91	.524	.340	1.0	S 68 E	3.15	3.38	37.8	31.8	6.0	.240	2.0			.240	2.0
8	35.02	.197	93	.135	28.948	1.0	N 61 E	3.19	5.03	37.4	31.0	6.4	.240	4.0			.240	4.0
9	32.67	.177	96	.436	.259	1.0	N 82 E	4.59	5.12	35.6	30.0	5.6	.685	19.0			.685	19.0
10	34.68	.187	93	.387	.200	0.8	N 34 W	5.20	6.73	36.6	24.2	12.4	.040	12.4			.040	12.4
11	33.70	.165	85	.781	.616	0.2	S 30 W	4.91	7.39	40.2	27.0	13.2						
12							S 39 W	4.96	4.96	43.8	32.8	11.0						
13	44.00	.212	84	.595	.353	0.8	S 82 E	3.12	4.52	55.0	35.0	20.0	.040	2.5			.040	2.5
14	41.50	.245	93	.487	.242	1.0	S 89 W	3.23	4.98	49.8	31.8	18.1	.045	1.0			.045	1.0
15	41.67	.237	85	.219	28.982	0.8	S 27 W	1.75	2.84	48.6	35.5	13.1						
16	49.33	.241	89	.053	28.812	0.7	N 68 W	10.22	10.60	55.1	28.0	27.1						
17	27.15	.139	89	.097	28.961	0.7	N G1 W	10.23	13.03	34.2	10.0	24.2						
18	18.05	.081	79	.624	29.543	0.8	N 57 W	14.43	14.68	21.2	16.0	5.2			2.2	5.0	.220	5.0
19							N 62 W	10.17	11.14	30.2	13.0	17.2						
20	18.58	.080	75	.940	.869	0.4	N 20 W	5.41	6.48	24.5	12.4	12.1	.020	1.0	0.2	1.0	.020	1.0
21	26.43	.120	82	.901	.731	0.3	S 56 E	4.10	5.08	31.4	21.2	10.2						
22	32.80	.168	90	.207	.099	0.8	S 73 E	6.66	7.50	36.8	29.0	7.8					.140	9.7
23	33.37	.153	80	.131	28.984	0.8	N 62 W	12.26	12.94	41.4	15.2	26.2	.100	5.5	0.4	4.2		
24	17.47	.085	84	.316	29.231	0.9	N 41 W	11.03	11.38	22.5	11.8	10.7						
25	20.05	.090	78	.376	.286	0.7	N 49 W	14.02	14.17	30.0	13.5	16.5						
26							N 49 W	10.42	10.00	24.2	7.4	16.8						
27	17.58	.055	82	.737	.652	0.3	N 31 W	8.13	8.37	25.5	8.2	17.3						
28	17.17	.063	61	.949	.896	0.1	S 31 W	1.55	4.94	29.8	13.4	16.4						
29	21.83	.095	70	30.013	.928	0.0	S 88 E	9.04	9.18	29.2	7.2	27.0						
30	29.42	.139	84	29.755	.618	0.4	N 88 E	3.63	6.30	45.0	32.2	12.8	.160	2.0			.160	2.0
31	38.22	.205	89	.394	.190	1.0												
	° 30.68	0.158	85	29.525	29.369	0.6	N 53 W	3.39	8.03	36.32	22.94	13.38	2.425	62.9	2.8	10.2	2.705	73.1

GENERAL METEOROLOGICAL ABSTRACT,—APRIL, 1854.

Days	DAILY MEANS					WIND			Extremes of Temperature			RAIN		SNOW		RAIN AND MELTED SNOW	
	Temperature of the Air.	Pressure of Vapour.	Relative Humidity.	Barometric Pressure.	Pressure of Dry Air.	Clouded Sky.	Resultant Direction.	Resultant Velocity.	Mean Velocity.	Maximum.	Minimum.	Difference.	Depth in Inches.	Approximate duration in hours.	Depth in Inches.	Approximate duration in hours.	Depth in Inches.	Approximate duration in hours.
	°							Miles.	Miles.	°	°	°						
1	32.50	0.155	83	29.418	29.203	0.8	N 62 W	11.95	12.58	38.8	20.2	18.6			0.2	1.0	0.020	1.0
2	35.03	.158	78	30.032	.904	0.5	N 75 W	4.88	6.17	33.2	22.2	11.0						
3	40.27	.204	82	29.877	.673	0.4	S 21 E	6.50	6.75	39.8	27.8	12.0						
4	44.65	.259	88	.704	.445	0.7	S 13 E	2.66	3.10	51.0	29.0	22.0						
5	47.00	.250	77	.458	.158	0.7	S 33 W	3.48	3.65	55.2	35.4	19.8	.040	0.3			.040	0.3
6	48.53	.162	83	.892	.730	0.6	N 63 W	6.95	11.78	60.2	24.4	35.4						
7	41.83	.233	87	.674	.441	0.9	N 57 E	2.51	5.48	40.6	24.4	16.2	.185	1.2			.185	1.2
8							N 81 E	5.88	6.42	47.8	33.2	14.6	.840	10.0			.840	10.0
9							N 72 E	6.53	7.29	43.4	28.4	14.0	.105	2.5			.105	2.5
10	37.32	.199	90	.394	.195	0.7	N 21 E	7.88	8.21	43.0	29.0	14.0						
11	36.20	.170	81	.720	.550	0.0	S 24 W	2.41	4.29	34.0	15.0	19.0						
12	43.72	.206	74	.719	.512	0.3	S 2 W	0.71	4.98	43.5	28.2	15.3						
13	33.37	.160	84	.977	.817	0.4	N 88 E	5.27	5.27	54.0	31.5	22.5						
14							N 83 E	5.16	5.83	41.7	25.0	16.7						
15	35.12	.151	74	.674	.523	0.9	N 74 E	12.12	12.31	33.8	27.2	6.6						
16							N 74 E	9.82	10.21	39.0	30.5	8.5	.060	1.0			.060	1.0
17	37.10	.166	76	.633	.466	0.5	N 70 E	10.05	10.60	39.5	29.0	10.5	.070	1.0			.070	1.0
18	34.07	.159	56	.586	.428	0.9	S 70 E	3.18	5.25	45.4	25.5	19.9						
19	42.60	.223	88	.476	.253	0.9	N 89 W	1.40	4.29	54.8	32.0	22.8						
20	43.60	.223	80	.468	.245	0.4	N 90 E	1.44	2.67	51.5	35.0	16.5	.020	1.0			.020	1.0
21	48.35	.248	76	.554	.306	0.2	S 55 E	2.25	3.65	51.5	30.2	21.3	.185	12.0			.185	12.0
22	46.12	.283	92	.359	.076	1.0	N 86 E	5.05	5.40	61.0	40.4	20.6						
23							N 46 E	6.06	6.67	53.5	31.2	13.5						
24	50.98	.247	67	.640	.393	0.2	N 6 E	7.94	8.00	61.8	31.8	30.0	.630	2.6	2.0	2.6	.630	2.6
25	54.15	.292	73	.426	.134	0.7	S 35 E	1.75	2.69	59.0	41.0	18.0	.575	4.8	0.5	3.0	.575	2.2
26	50.23	.327	91	.173	28.846	1.0	S 83 E	2.92	3.05	64.5	40.0	24.5	.050	3.0			.050	
27	33.63	.165	87	.581	29.415	1.0	N 28 E	5.74	7.30	60.2	30.5	29.7	.375		●		.375	
28	36.48	.144	68	.993	.851	0.4	N 27 E	11.28	11.35	36.0	25.8	10.2	.070	6.0		2.3	.070	8.3
29	37.32	.194	68	.869	.674	1.0	N 20 E	9.88	9.97	43.8	30.5	13.9	.105	2.0			.105	2.0
30							N 35 E	7.67	8.00	40.8	32.2	8.6						
31							S 42 W	3.15	4.30	46.4	36.0	10.4						
	41.04	0.207	80	29.638	29.430	0.6	N 50 E	2.57	6.81	47.82	30.09	17.13	2.685	41.8	2.7	8.9	2.935	50.7

GENERAL METEOROLOGICAL ABSTRACT,—MAY, 1854.

TORONTO METEOROLOGICAL OBSERVATIONS.

Date	DAILY MEANS						WIND			EXTREMES OF TEMPERATURE			RAIN		SNOW		RAIN AND MELTED SNOW	
	Temperature of the Air	Pressure of Vapour	Relative Humidity	Barometric Pressure	Pressure of Dry Air	Clouded Sky	Resultant Direction	Resultant Velocity	Mean Velocity	Maximum	Minimum	Difference	Depth in Inches	Approximate duration in hours	Depth in Inches	Approximate duration in hours	Depth in Inches	Approximate duration in hours
1	46.75	0.246	78	29.487	29.241	0.6	S 17 E	2.94	3.56	59.0	37.5	21.5						
2	47.52	.239	85	.495	.116	0.9	S 31 E	2.09	3.85	54.5	37.2	17.3	0.205	7.5				
3	46.02	.265	85	.506	.240	0.5	N 3 W	1.82	7.15	56.0	33.0	23.6	.025	1.0				
4	51.53	.261	71	.519	.258	0.1	S 16 E	3.08	6.90	62.0	42.0	20.0						
5	40.78	.231	74	.476	.245	0.5	N 45 W	10.60	10.73	53.8	29.2	24.6						
6	33.63	.119	63	.638	.519	0.2	N 20 W	11.37	11.94	39.0	25.2	13.8						
7							N 22 W	9.37	9.46	48.8	27.5	21.3						
8	47.80	.196	69	.601	.406	0.1	S 35 W	2.79	4.29	59.8	31.8	27.0						
9	45.83	.211	69	.393	.182	0.7	S 73 E	3.15	3.33	57.0	36.8	20.2	.235	3.5				
10	50.53	.263	85	.306	.043	0.7	N 45 E	0.38	4.05	62.4	31.8	30.6						
11	50.72	.263	73	.505	.242	0.3	S 48 W	6.74	5.25	62.3	30.8	21.5	.040	0.8				
12	55.07	.254	62	.743	.479	0.0	N 64 E	5.06	8.17	64.8	43.3	16.4	.455	6.0				
13	52.43	.234	69	.696	.312	0.4	S 82 E	7.08	6.02	71.4	55.0	28.0						
14							S 40 E	1.16	7.38	63.2	35.2	30.8						
15	56.70	.347	76	.557	.211	0.5	S 75 W	2.78	4.92	66.0	36.8	14.0	.915	4.0				
16	54.72	.316	76	.596	.290	0.2	S 89 E	7.38	6.25	60.8	39.2	20.6						
17	59.18	.401	82	.183	.281	0.8	S 46 E	3.00	8.38	68.8	37.0	21.6	.505	3.8				
18	55.38	.318	76	.853	.035	0.8	N 35 W	7.07	3.35	63.4	35.7	26.4	.275	5.0				
19	50.12	.298	80	.615	.327	0.3	S 11 E	8.81	5.33	64.5	35.2	19.7	.315	3.0				
20	49.08	.287	83	.567	.280	0.6	S 43 W	4.46	4.82	59.2	35.5	23.0						
21							S 66 W	2.11	3.63	59.5	35.2	20.6						
22	48.28	.257	81	.876	.619	0.3	S 66 W	2.59	3.90	58.0	32.0	26.8						
23	50.88	.260	73	.917	.657	0.1	S 41 E	3.55	3.55	61.4	36.8	24.0	.765	5.0				
24							S 09 E	4.17	4.17	64.0	43.4	20.6	.835	0.6				
25	61.15	.469	87	.141	.022	0.6	N 42 W	2.02	3.50	69.6	49.8	21.2						
26	58.68	.392	90	.066	.273	0.0	N 72 W	1.14	2.30	69.8	39.8	20.8						
27	59.99	.344	69	.697	.342	0.1	S 78 E	2.28	2.63	71.0	41.0	30.0						
28							S 56 E	1.04	1.37	70.0	47.8	22.2						
29	60.98	.331	65	.601	.270	0.6	N 65 E	5.11	5.54	68.2	47.2	21.0						
30	59.55	.254	51	.596	.332	0.2	N 73 E	4.85	5.85	68.8	35.8	32.2						
31	49.03	.184	54	.858	.674	0.0	S 74 E	4.15	4.65	56.8	33.0	23.8						
	52.20	0.288	74	29.566	29.278	0.4	East	0.40	5.38	61.82	37.90	23.92	5.630	39.7				

TORONTO METEOROLOGICAL OBSERVATIONS.

GENERAL METEOROLOGICAL ABSTRACT,—JUNE, 1854.

Date	DAILY MEANS.						WIND.			EXTREMES OF TEMPERATURE.			RAIN.		SNOW.		RAIN AND MELTED SNOW.	
	Temperature of the Air.	Pressure of Vapour.	Relative Humidity.	Barometric Pressure.	Pressure of Dry Air.	Clouded Sky.	Resultant Direction.	Resultant Velocity.	Mean Velocity.	Maximum.	Minimum.	Difference.	Depth in Inches.	Approximate duration in hours.	Depth in Inches.	Approximate duration in hours.	Depth in Inches.	Approximate duration in hours.
	°							Miles.	Miles.	°	°	°						
1	64.25	0.269	66	28.919	29.650	0.2	S 83 E	1.69	2.95	63.8	35.2	28.6	...	...	...	...	...	...
2	58.55	.289	60	.832	.543	0.0	S 42 W	1.64	2.55	69.0	40.8	28.2	...	...	...	...	...	...
3	62.28	.370	69	.709	.339	0.0	S 1 W	1.40	1.70	74.8	44.0	30.6	...	...	...	...	...	...
4	...	...	...	...	...	...	S 28 E	1.53	2.69	78.0	45.8	32.2	...	...	...	...	...	...
5	67.28	.434	68	.511	.077	0.6	N 40 W	1.00	2.15	79.0	49.8	29.2	...	...	...	...	...	...
6	60.67	.378	73	.427	.049	0.6	N 81 E	5.69	5.81	70.0	49.8	20.2	0.085	1.5	...	...	...	...
7	60.05	.402	86	.384	.082	0.9	N 81 E	5.24	5.69	72.4	44.8	27.6	.085	2.0	...	...	...	...
8	53.60	.380	94	.308	.023	1.0	N 81 E	1.69	2.83	56.7	46.4	10.3	.635	12.0	...	...	...	...
9	56.58	.411	92	.436	.098	1.0	S 88 W	2.22	3.87	61.0	41.4	19.6	.055	3.0	...	...	...	...
10	59.85	.430	86	.703	.273	0.7	S 47 W	3.33	4.07	70.0	49.2	20.8	...	...	...	...	...	...
11	...	...	...	...	...	...	N 85 E	2.15	3.88	66.6	49.0	17.6	...	...	...	...	...	...
12	63.92	.453	78	.535	.062	0.4	South	1.36	2.67	76.4	50.0	26.4	...	...	...	...	...	...
13	66.80	.459	73	.430	.030	0.3	N 65 W	1.86	3.55	79.8	52.8	27.0	.105	2.0	...	...	...	...
14	67.92	.439	66	.507	.067	0.4	S 72 W	2.03	3.63	78.0	50.2	27.8	.020	1.0	...	...	...	...
15	70.62	.514	70	.539	.025	0.4	N 15 W	3.59	4.94	82.0	51.4	30.6	...	...	...	...	...	...
16	59.87	.347	69	.750	.408	0.3	S 54 E	2.20	3.62	69.8	39.4	30.4	...	...	...	...	...	...
17	58.50	.301	64	.738	.437	0.7	N 84 E	3.98	4.45	68.8	44.0	24.5	...	...	...	...	...	...
18	...	...	...	...	...	...	S 65 E	0.84	1.65	76.4	54.0	22.4	...	...	...	...	...	...
19	71.46	.546	72	.601	.055	0.2	N 37 W	3.12	3.12	81.6	57.2	24.4	.105	0.5	...	...	...	...
20	67.82	.432	66	.607	.175	0.4	N 86 E	2.14	5.21	73.5	55.0	18.5	...	...	...	...	...	...
21	63.92	.402	80	.434	.973	0.8	N 85 E	4.82	5.44	70.0	53.0	17.0	.090	1.0	...	...	...	...
22	60.37	.471	74	.454	.928	0.8	S 69 E	2.62	6.39	77.8	54.2	23.6	.255	2.2	...	...	...	...
23	61.58	.447	83	.466	.019	0.6	N 46 W	2.86	3.04	73.6	47.2	26.4	...	...	...	...	...	...
24	...	...	...	...	...	...	N 24 W	5.92	4.85	71.8	51.4	20.4	...	...	...	...	...	...
25	...	...	...	...	...	...	S 37 W	1.44	3.82	77.2	53.2	24.0	...	...	...	...	...	...
26	75.67	.673	77	.457	.784	0.4	...	...	...	92.5	66.0	26.5	...	...	...	...	...	...
27	70.38	.544	75	.530	.936	0.1	N 49 W	6.90	9.87	82.4	60.0	22.4	...	...	...	...	...	...
28	73.00	.498	67	.481	.983	0.7	N 88 E	1.51	1.57	89.2	47.4	41.8	.130	1.0	...	...	...	...
29	63.97	.460	79	.467	.007	1.0	N 21 W	10.26	10.43	76.0	58.0	18.0	...	...	...	...	...	...
30	68.67	.444	67	.499	.065	0.2	...	...	...	78.4	54.6	23.8	...	...	...	...	...	...
31	...	...	...	...	...	...	...	...	...	...	...	...	...	...	...	...	...	...
	65.12	0.434	74	29.551	29.117	0.5	N 24 E	0.71	4.15	74.53	49.84	24.60	1.460	26.2	...	...	...	...

NOTE.—On the 24th, 25th, and 27th, the observations were imperfect, in consequence of the removal of the instruments preparatory to the demolition of the old Observatory building.

GENERAL METEOROLOGICAL ABSTRACT,—JULY, 1854.

Days	DAILY MEANS.						WIND.			EXTREMES OF TEMPERATURE.			RAIN.		SNOW.		RAIN AND MELTED SNOW	
	Temperature of the Air.	Pressure of Vapour.	Relative Humidity.	Barometric Pressure.	Pressure of Dry Air.	Clouded Sky.	Resultant Direction.	Resultant Velocity.	Mean Velocity.	Maximum.	Minimum.	Difference.	Depth in Inches.	Approximate duration hours.	Depth in Inches.	Approximate duration in hours.	Depth in Inches.	Approximate duration in hours.
	°							Miles.	Miles.	°	°	°						
1	69.50	0.430	64	29.782	29.342	0.3	S 80 E	1.73	3.10	83.8	54.6	29.2	...	...	...	...	...	...
2	81.32	.650	63	.555	28.905	0.1	S 76 E	2.72	2.82	83.0	55.0	28.0	...	...	...	...	...	...
3	78.60	.635	63	.424	28.789	0.7	S 19 W	2.20	2.25	95.4	64.5	30.9	...	2.5	...	...	...	...
4	69.55	.509	72	.582	29.073	0.1	S 63 W	2.86	4.58	95.8	51.8	44.5	0.895	...	...	...	...	...
5	71.83	.554	73	.699	.146	0.2	N 29 W	0.62	3.77	96.3	50.4	30.0	...	...	...	...	...	...
6	73.00	.531	69	.657	.126	0.9	N 49 E	1.09	1.86	81.0	65.0	19.2	...	...	...	...	...	...
7	79.23	.738	76	.522	28.784	0.6	S 88 E	3.31	3.37	84.2	62.0	21.2	...	4.0	...	...	...	...
8							N 88 E	7.03	6.24	88.2	60.0	20.4	.350					
9							S 70 W	7.20	7.26	92.2	62.0	21.2						
10	67.28	.420	66	.709	29.280	0.0	N 32 W	2.02	2.98	72.6	47.4	25.2		0.5				
11	67.87	.478	72	.653	.175	0.0	S 17 W	0.79	4.03	81.0	50.5	30.5	.075					
12	62.40	.318	59	.808	.485	0.3	S 58 W	7.60	7.72	82.5	43.8	38.7						
13	61.98	.386	71	.818	.432	0.1	N 23 W	3.87	4.55	73.6	43.0	30.6						
14	72.15	.504	67	.690	.186	0.4	N 78 E	0.82	2.68	76.0	45.2	30.8						
15	72.13	.498	66	.726	.227	0.2	N 73 E	1.39	2.42	83.6	53.4	30.2						
16							S 14 E	1.67	3.32	87.0	54.0	33.0						
17	79.42	.515	54	.744	.229	0.3	S 83 E	3.55	4.51	85.4	62.2	23.2		8.5				
18	74.93	.531	70	.688	.102	0.2	S 78 E	2.39	4.55	86.4	64.6	25.8	.1135	0.6				
19	72.83	.671	86	.547	.000	0.5	S 84 W	3.00	2.56	86.4	62.0	24.4	.640					
20	79.95	.738	78	.521	28.783	0.3	S 71 W	1.10	3.12	95.4	66.4	31.6						
21	75.23	.666	78	.636	28.960	0.4	N 72 E	1.26	3.12	96.8	67.0	29.8						
22	75.22	.666	79	.588	28.922	0.6	N 41 E	1.53	3.07	84.4	69.0	15.4		0.0				
23							S 10 E	0.78	2.02	86.2	64.4	21.8	.565					
24	75.45	.606	72	.698	29.022	0.4	N 67 E	2.77	2.77	82.0	66.2	15.8						
25	78.98	.676	71	.887	28.711	0.5	S 5 E	5.06	6.97	86.9	66.8	20.1						
26	73.12	.451	63	.566	29.112	0.3	N 86 W	11.75	12.32	88.6	67.8	20.8						
27	64.52	.397	69	.506	.416	0.0	S 16 E	12.22	3.61	80.4	53.0	27.4	.395	8.0				
28	71.70	.543	74	.913	.197	0.6	S 21 E	3.09	2.88	76.8	52.6	24.2	.675	3.5				
29	73.32	.614	77	.740	.197	0.6	S 87 W	2.46	2.83	81.6	66.2	15.4	.075	0.5				
30							S 57 W	6.99	7.89	85.4	62.0	23.4						
31	65.98	.518	83	.469	28.855	0.7	S 87 W	1.04	2.22	87.9	61.4	26.5						
				.715	29.197	0.4	S 82 E	0.07	0.69	76.5	61.0	15.5						
	82.47	0.550	71	29.640	29.090	0.4	S 46 W	0.37	4.08	84.79	58.46	26.33	4.805	28.7	...	...	...	...

TORONTO METEOROLOGICAL OBSERVATIONS.

GENERAL METEOROLOGICAL ABSTRACT,—AUGUST, 1854.

Date	DAILY MEANS.						Clouded Sky 7.	WIND.			EXTREMES OF TEMPERATURE.			RAIN.		SNOW.		RAIN AND MELTED SNOW.	
	Temperature of the Air.	Pressure of Vapour.	Relative Humidity.	Barometric Pressure.	Pressure of Dry Air.			Resultant Direction.	Resultant Velocity.	Mean Velocity.	Maximum.	Minimum.	Difference.	Depth in Inches.	Approximate duration in hours.	Depth in Inches.	Approximate duration in hours.	Depth in Inches.	Approximate duration in hours.
1	77.12	0.733	81	29.510	28.776	0.5		S 82 W	Miles 2.22	Miles 3.29	89.4	60.5	28.9	.025	1.0	...	...	...	...
2	70.10	.448	65	.606	29.157	0.2		N 45 W	6.35	6.72	84.0	48.6	35.4	...	...	...	...	...	...
3	65.45	.470	77	.559	.089	0.8		Calm	0.00	0.00	77.6	55.8	21.8	...	...	...	...	...	...
4	67.85	.551	83	.475	28.925	0.9		N 67 W	1.30	2.43	78.2	56.0	22.2	.210	2.5	...	...	...	...
5	67.23	.504	78	.557	29.053	0.4		S 22 W	1.85	2.07	80.2	57.4	22.8	...	...	...	...	...	...
6	59.95	.255	54	.720	.466	0.1		N 73 W	10.39	10.73	78.1	48.0	30.1	...	...	...	...	...	...
7	63.48	.412	70	.836	.494	0.0		N 57 W	9.60	9.71	71.8	48.8	23.0	...	...	...	...	...	...
8	64.22	.392	67	.773	.381	0.7		S 69 E	0.44	3.42	74.5	46.4	28.1	*	*	...	...	...	...
9	67.92	.462	71	.645	.188	0.9		N 05 E	3.66	3.92	74.2	52.5	21.7	...	...	...	...	...	...
10	69.07	.550	80	.596	.046	0.7		N 82 E	1.83	2.06	81.4	63.0	18.4	*	*	...	...	...	...
11	71.65	.582	78	.526	28.944	0.7		S 24 E	1.10	1.58	81.4	65.5	16.2	.210	...	...	...	...	...
12								N 72 W	9.28	9.62	88.2	65.5	22.7						
13								S 18 E	0.65	3.17	86.0	49.4	36.6						
14	63.45	.344	63	.739	29.395	0.3		N 81 W	7.81	8.26	74.5	49.5	25.0	...	...	...	...	...	...
15	62.98	.380	70	.406	.116	0.7		N 65 W	9.07	9.36	75.8	47.2	28.6	...	...	...	...	...	...
16	64.45	.354	63	.630	.276	0.4		N 60 E	2.19	4.10	78.2	52.8	25.4	...	...	...	...	...	...
17	58.60	.331	69	.689	.358	0.3		S 86 W	2.53	2.85	78.4	49.8	28.6	...	...	...	...	...	...
18	64.83	.368	64	.779	.410	0.0		S 37 E	2.09	2.29	81.4	50.3	31.6	...	...	...	...	...	...
19	66.28	.423	70	.633	.210	0.0		S 1 E	2.29	3.33	82.2	54.5	27.7	...	...	...	...	...	...
20								N 26 W	6.87	7.33	86.4	52.6	33.8						
21	74.87	.550	66	.634	.094	0.0		S 54 W	3.93	5.02	88.5	55.4	33.1	...	...	...	...	...	...
22	77.07	.561	62	.658	.097	0.4		N 2 W	6.94	6.94	91.0	60.9	30.1	...	1.0	...	...	...	...
23	62.40	.444	81	.748	.304	0.9		N 72 E	2.20	2.29	69.8	57.0	12.8	.105	...	...	...	...	...
24	80.43	.590	64	.572	28.982	0.3		N 80 W	8.58	8.79	99.2	60.8	38.4	...	...	...	...	...	...
25	69.22	.463	68	.646	29.183	0.4		N 71 E	2.08	2.76	76.4	58.4	18.0	.040	0.3	...	...	...	...
26	73.45	.588	73	.547	28.964	0.3		S 64 W	4.06	4.80	89.4	54.4	35.4	...	...	...	...	...	...
27								N 51 E	1.22	1.96	72.2	54.4	17.8						
28	65.65	.413	70	.786	29.373	0.2		S 60 E	1.64	1.80	78.2	54.2	24.0	...	...	...	...	...	...
29	67.42	.530	81	.713	.188	0.2		S 82 E	2.10	2.40	81.4	63.0	18.4	.075	0.5	...	...	...	...
30	74.87	.649	76	.620	28.971	0.6		S 13 W	2.80	4.35	91.8	67.0	24.8	...	...	...	...	...	...
31	67.20	.665	87	.735	29.230	1.0		N 71 E	3.66	3.96	69.8	62.0	7.8	*	*	...	...	...	...
	68.08	0.478	72	29.648	29.170	0.5		N 64 W	1.76	4.60	80.72	55.26	25.46	0.455	5.3	...	...	...	...

GENERAL METEOROLOGICAL ABSTRACT,—SEPTEMBER, 1854.

TORONTO METEOROLOGICAL OBSERVATIONS.

Days	DAILY MEANS.						WIND.			Extremes of Temperature.			RAIN.		SNOW.		Rain and Melted Snow	
	Temperature of the Air.	Pressure of Vapour.	Relative Humidity	Barometric Pressure.	Pressure of Dry Air.	Clouded Sky.	Resultant Direction	Resultant Velocity.	Mean Velocity	Maximum.	Minimum.	Difference.	Depth in Inches.	Approximate duration hours.	Depth in Inches.	Approximate duration in hours.	Depth in Inches.	Approximate duration in hours.
1	68.97	0.526	91	29.732	29.206	1.0	N 71 E	0.40	2.06	67.6	61.2	6.4	.330	4.6				
2	71.40	.641	94	.631	28.990	0.9	N 68 W	0.49	0.88	90.4	64.4	26.0		1.0				
3	71.83	.611	80	.664	29.053	0.0	N 42 W	1.23	2.20	87.0	65.6	21.4	.595					
4	77.95	.676	75	.550	28.874	0.2	S 79 E	1.26	2.33	81.0	64.8	16.8						
5	77.63	.666	73	.524	28.858	0.7	S 18 W	4.31	1.85	80.8	64.5	29.1	.020	0.5				
6	77.08	.487	77	.714	29.277	0.3	S 73 W	5.33	5.22	93.6	50.8	35.0	.250	0.6				
7	60.17	.407	81	.607	.200	0.9	N 60 W	4.38	5.77	92.7	48.2	31.4						
8	57.95	.414	88	.508	.089	1.0	N 14 B	4.00	4.60	79.6	48.2	20.4	.705	15.0				
9							N 22 B	4.38	5.35	70.2	60.0	8.0	.030	6.1				
10	60.42	.415	81	.582	.167	0.6	S 71 E	5.32	5.63	70.2	44.6	25.6						
11	64.68	.441	78	.592	.150	0.4	N 21 W	2.60	3.30	70.8	45.5	25.3						
12	56.57	.336	74	.846	.512	0.6	N 68 E	7.61	8.49	76.6	46.4	30.2	.395	5.0				
13	61.23	.408	98	.623	.190	1.0	S 6 E	4.59	5.01	68.5	47.5	21.0	.140	10.0				
14	54.93	.312	74	.886	.524	0.4	N 11 W	1.98	2.08	65.6	55.5	10.1						
15	53.85	.295	72	.983	.658	0.4	N 11 W	6.36	6.44	72.0	41.0	31.0						
16							N 61 E	2.42	2.90	69.6	43.5	26.1	.165	1.0				
17							N 22 B	1.36	0.99	63.2	44.8	18.4	.245	2.5				
18	63.37	.485	83	.632	.147	0.6	S 41 W	3.22	3.69	74.0	45.2	29.4						
19	66.92	.488	78	.386	28.878	0.4	N 75 W	9.37	10.87	77.5	48.2	29.3	.005	0.2				
20	48.51	.219	66	.751	29.532	0.4	N 15 W	8.02	8.92	89.2	17.6							
21	50.77	.257	72	.998	.631	0.6	N 70 W	2.89	4.93	60.0	35.8	24.2						
22	51.98	.292	76	30.081	.789	0.0	S 7 E	1.87	3.16	64.0	36.0	28.0						
23	56.78	.357	79	29.825	.493	0.0	S 23 W	3.41	3.69	71.2	41.0	30.2	.080	1.5				
24							S 5 E	1.08	1.54	75.0	51.2	23.8	.050	1.0				
25	63.55	.509	89	.464	28.955	0.5	S 46 W	1.36	1.43	73.2	51.5	21.7						
26	62.85	.484	86	.568	29.084	0.4	S	1.10	1.31	73.8	52.0	23.8		0.5				
27	66.08	.534	87	.547	.013	0.2	N 68 W	3.48	1.95	80.2	46.4	33.8	.365					
28	59.03	.346	73	.700	.354	0.1	N 2 E	2.42	4.22	70.4	47.8	22.6						
29	50.70	.272	76	30.048	.776	0.1	N 60 E	2.64	3.84	60.6	37.6	23.0	•					
30	51.47	.269	73	29.993	.654	0.4	S 41 E	2.06	2.45	61.0	46.4	14.6		0.3				
	61.04	0.430	79	29.701	29.271	0.5	N 22 W	1.38	4.04	72.59	49.09	23.50	5.375	49.8				

GENERAL METEOROLOGICAL ABSTRACT,—OCTOBER, 1854.

Days.	DAILY MEANS.					WIND.			EXTREMES OF TEMPERATURE.			RAIN.		SNOW.		RAIN AND MELTED SNOW.	
	Temperature of the Air.	Pressure of Vapour.	Relative Humidity.	Barometric Pressure.	Pressure of Dry Air.	Clouded Sky.	Resultant Direction.	Resultant Velocity.	Mean Velocity.	Maximum.	Minimum.	Difference.	Depth in Inches.	Approximate duration in hours.	Depth in Inches.	Approximate duration in hours.	Depth in Inches.	Approximate duration in hours.
	°							Miles.	Miles.	°	°	°						
1	51.55	.251	69	29.453	29.202	0.2	N 58 W	1.87	3.59	64.2	39.0	25.2	.145	2.5				
2	55.77	.365	83	28.885	28.619	0.9	S 33 W	6.62	2.83	65.2	43.8	21.4						
3	47.35	.224	70	29.313	29.089	0.5	S 34 W	10.40	7.86	63.8	44.0	19.8	.465	2.2				
4	45.33	.229	78	.856	.626	0.0	N 72 W	10.07	10.40	57.0	29.8	27.4						
5	54.05	.285	69	.837	.552	0.0	S 88 W	2.37	2.72	57.0	34.0	23.0						
6	61.48	.404	77	.840	.436	0.3	S 65 W	4.27	4.34	65.0	44.2	20.8	.005	0.1				
7							S 65 W	1.36	1.58	75.4	53.2	22.2						
8	57.18	.370	80	.629	.259	0.9	N 87 E	1.27	1.54	70.0	50.8	19.2	.035	1.0				
9	50.05	.309	87	.748	.468	1.0	N 6 E	1.76	3.21	70.9	48.6	22.3	.275	2.3				
10	56.82	.387	85	.549	.162	0.7	N 71 E	5.26	5.35	52.8	46.6	6.2	.110	3.5				
11	56.10	.337	81	.524	.137	0.8	S 39 W	2.17	2.55	69.0	47.2	21.8	.015	1.2				
12	46.07	.252	77	.715	.465	0.8	N 24 W	3.89	5.03	65.0	41.4	23.6	.205	1.5				
13	45.97	.239		.385	.146	0.5	N 70 E	3.19	3.53	51.5	40.2	11.3						
14							N 42 W	13.10	13.80	54.8	34.8	20.0						
15							N 44 W	10.18	10.62	45.7	29.0	16.7	.010	3.0				
16	43.05	.230	84	.324	.094	0.9	N 45 W	6.72	7.25	52.6	35.5	17.1						
17	40.75	.212	80	.580	.368	0.9	S 78 W	2.46	3.57	52.0	31.8	20.2						
18	36.60	.149	70	.743	.694	0.7	N 33 W	9.40	9.19	43.2	26.4	16.8						
19	35.78	.158	76	30.033	.876	0.4	S 71 W	1.47	2.23	45.5	30.2	15.3						
20	43.85	.211	74	30.019	.808	0.8	N 57 E	0.97	2.08	45.2	35.4	17.6						
21	44.50	.202	71	29.995	.793	0.1	N 45 E	1.61	2.44	56.8	39.8	17.0	.065	5.0				
22							N 69 E	0.78	7.13	54.2	44.3	9.9						
23						1.0	East.	3.54	3.69	53.6	49.0	5.6						
24	51.40	.292	78	.490	.598	0.4	S 52 E	0.11	0.80	53.6	43.8	19.0						
25	52.77	.314	80	.975	.661	0.7	N 75 E	0.39	1.02	63.8	44.8	20.8						
26	53.32	.326	81	30.087	.759	0.0	N 35 E	0.94	1.76	62.0	41.2	20.0	.040	8.0				
27	48.72	.287	84	30.036	.749	0.6	N 85 E	0.25	0.29	61.0	40.2	20.8	.015	7.5				
28	46.22	.289	92	29.942	.653	0.7	N 52 E	1.90	2.34	57.4	37.4	20.0	.050	6.0				
29	50.90	.327	89	.839	.512		N 58 E	2.19	2.30	60.8	45.2	15.6	.035	1.0				
30	58.02	.401	84	.574	.173	0.8	N 75 E	3.83	3.95	57.8	53.6	4.2						
31	53.42	.371	92	.311	28.940	1.0	S 64 E	8.27	10.40	65.4	55.0	10.4		0.5				
	49.52	0.287	80	29.096	29.408	0.6	N 45 W	1.52	4.57	58.97	41.32	17.65	1.405	46.3	*	*	*	*

GENERAL METEOROLOGICAL ABSTRACT.—NOVEMBER, 1854.

Days	DAILY MEANS.						WIND.			EXTREMES OF TEMPERATURE.			RAIN.		SNOW.		RAIN AND MELTED SNOW	
	Temperature of the Air.	Pressure of Vapour.	Relative Humidity.	Barometric Pressure.	Pressure of Dry Air.	Clouded Sky.	Resultant Direction.	Resultant Velocity.	Mean Velocity.	Maximum	Minimum	Difference.	Depth in Inches.	Approximate duration in hours.	Depth in Inches.	Approximate duration in hours.	Depth in Inches.	Approximate duration in hours.
	°						°	Miles	Miles	°	°	°						
1	45.82	0.227	76	29.428	29.201	0.4	S 87 W	9.42	9.70	53.0	34.0	19.0	0.095	0.7			0.095	0.7
2	47.35	.217	69	.535	.318	0.6	S 85 W	10.23	13.77	55.4	34.0	21.4	.005	0.1			.005	0.1
3	37.67	.156	69	.844	.689	0.6	N 32 W	7.82	8.77	42.2	27.8	14.4						
4	24.38	.069	66	30.143	30.064	0.7	N 2 W	8.95	9.01	30.0	15.0	15.0	*	*	*	*	*	*
5							N 2 E	7.13	8.00	44.0	14.9	29.1						
6	44.49	.223	77	29.230	29.007	1.0	S 40 W	8.87	9.54	46.2	28.4	18.4	.140	0.1			.140	0.1
7	37.82	.175	77	.243	.068	0.6	N 45 W	5.73	6.74	47.8	29.0	18.8	.020	3.7			.020	3.7
8	34.10	.145	73	.605	.460	0.6	N 46 W	6.19	6.72	49.4	29.6	19.8		0.6				0.6
9	34.08	.155	80	.825	.670	0.8	N 75 E	5.37	5.70	37.8	30.2	7.6						
10	44.50	.255	86	.501	.246	1.0	S 87 E	3.01	3.75	50.2	35.2	15.0	.150	6.0			.150	6.0
11	42.82	.224	81	.517	.293	0.4	N 72 W	3.59	4.32	49.4	27.6	20.8						
12							S 59 W	10.27	10.41	48.5	34.2	14.3	.315	6.0			.315	6.0
13	37.00	.179	83	.435	.256	0.7	S 54 W	6.90	9.93	44.4	30.8	13.4	*	*	*	*	*	*
14	35.33	.178	86	.396	.218	0.9	N 3 E	8.52	8.94	39.4	33.0	6.4	.040	2.4	0.2	5.0	.045	7.4
15	38.88	.207	89	.186	28.979	1.0	N 51 W	2.30	2.41	42.2	34.0	8.2	.045	3.0			.045	3.0
16	34.38	.160	81	.370	.210	1.0	S 45 W	4.53	8.35	38.8	30.0	8.8	.040	3.0			.040	3.0
17	37.92	.184	82	.917	.733	0.7	N 65 W	5.53	5.71	40.2	27.6	12.6	.035	3.0			.035	3.0
18	34.05	.161	82	29.151	28.990	0.6	N 29 W	3.98	4.23	42.8	30.8	12.0	*	*	*	*	*	*
19							N 34 W	5.25	5.30	36.4	28.0	8.4						
20	31.30	.153	87	29.548	29.391	0.6	N 85 E	1.80	1.92	35.2	18.6	16.6	.010	2.5	0.1	2.5	.010	2.5
21	30.75	.149	85	.616	.467	1.0	S 49 E	3.77	4.48	36.2	22.2	14.0	.020	3.0	0.2	3.0	.020	3.0
22	34.10	.172	88	.504	.332	0.8	N 14 W	0.07	0.07	38.2	31.0	7.2	.080	6.0	0.8	6.0	.080	6.0
23	42.72	.233	86	.330	.097	1.0	S 61 E	1.27	1.56	48.6	37.4	11.2						
24	48.05	.297	90	28.800	28.503	0.9	S 68 W	4.35	6.10	51.5	39.2	12.3						
25	38.98	.188	50	28.825	28.637	0.7	S 47 W	9.95	10.22	42.2	33.0	9.2	*	*	*	*	*	*
26							S 68 W	12.77	13.87	36.6	26.3	10.3						
27	33.37	.154	80	29.562	29.408	0.8	S 82 W	9.30	10.40	39.8	27.2	12.6	.030	1.5			.030	1.5
28	32.37	.147	80	.637	.510	0.7	N 49 W	10.57	10.90	36.6	27.0	9.0	.135	3.5			.135	3.5
29	34.93	.162	78	.523	.361	0.7	N G8 W	9.18	12.78	36.0	27.0	9.0	.005	0.5			.005	0.5
30	20.77	.085	73	.733	.648	0.4	N 49 W	11.67	12.05	25.5	13.8	11.7	*	*	*	*	*	*
	36.84	0.180	80	29.439	29.259	0.8	West.	3.44	7.54	42.08	28.13	13.94	1.115	34.1	1.3	16.5	1.245	50.6

TORONTO METEOROLOGICAL OBSERVATIONS.

GENERAL METEOROLOGICAL ABSTRACT,—DECEMBER, 1854.

Days	DAILY MEANS.							WIND.			EXTREMES OF TEMPERATURE.			RAIN.		SNOW.		RAIN AND MELTED SNOW	
	Temperature of the Air	Pressure of Vapour	Relative Humidity	Barometric Pressure	Pressure of Dry Air	Clouded Sky	Resultant Direction	Resultant Velocity	Mean Velocity	Maximum	Minimum	Difference	Depth in Inches	Approximate duration in hours	Depth in Inches	Approximate duration in hours	Depth in Inches	Approximate duration in hours
	°							Miles	Miles	°	°	°						
1	28.70	0.129	79	29.498	29.369	0.8	N 70 W	9.48	11.50	34.0	10.0	*			0.2	3.0	0.020	3.0
2	20.88	.079	66	.656	.578	0.9	N 70 E	4.17	7.11	27.6	13.8	24.0			3.0	12.0	.300	12.0
3	15.28	.064	70	.241	.177	1.0	N 16 E	13.76	17.67	28.2	14.6	13.8			3.0	8.0	.300	8.0
4	17.85	.090	77	.226	.146	1.0	N 32 W	22.10	22.87	19.2	4.8	18.6			3.5	8.0	.300	8.0
5	24.78	.120	87	28.954	28.834	1.0	N 87 W	14.24	15.73	18.8	14.4	14.4					.350	
6	11.22	.052	66	29.377	29.326	0.7	S 76 W	11.22	13.24	22.8	12.8	10.0			2.0	4.5	.200	4.5
7	8.63	.059	81	.919	.860	0.4	N 23 W	14.96	15.49	28.6	13.8	14.8			0.2	1.0	.020	1.0
8	26.60	.133	89	.887	.754	1.0	N 53 W	8.28	8.35	44.8	-2.8	17.6						
9							S 12 W	3.71	4.04	21.0	0.9	20.1						
10	24.75	.111	79	.760	.649	0.9	S 79 W	6.78	7.32	33.8	19.5	14.3						
11	23.23	.098	76	.708	.610	0.8	S 81 W	9.02	9.57	39.0	28.8	10.2	*	*	0.1	1.0	.010	1.0
12	37.53	.181	81	.402	.221	1.0	S 74 W	7.40	10.60	32.0	15.1	16.9			0.1	0.5	.010	0.5
13	35.33	.163	80	.484	.321	1.0	S 46 W	6.71	7.14	34.8	18.8	16.0						
14	38.28	.206	91	.323	.114	1.0	N 64 W	4.73	4.97	41.0	27.0	14.0						
15	24.87	.101	74	.529	.428	0.5	N 4 E	3.15	5.66	40.9	29.0	11.9	.030	1.5	0.4	5.0	.030	5.0
16							N 31 E	9.78	10.88	44.8	27.5	17.3			2.5	10.0	.040	10.0
17	6.47	.050	79	.644	.694	0.0	N 27 W	7.30	7.07	29.2	10.0	19.2					.250	
18	2.02	.046	88	.782	.779	0.2	N 27 W	3.99	4.23	12.4	2.4	10.0						
19	20.77	.092	79	.389	.481	1.0	N 32 W	3.19	3.65	13.8	-4.8	18.6						
20	14.58	.073	79	.518	.591	0.6	S 62 W	8.53	8.73	14.2	-7.0	21.2	.060	*	0.6	4.0	.060	4.0
21	3.27	.046	81	.083	30.064	0.8	N 6 W	10.76	11.9	25.4	18.5	11.9						
22	21.83	.102	81	29.952	30.054	1.0	N 27 E	5.59	12.08	28.0	-3.2	31.2					*	*
23							S 86 E	3.75	6.20	18.0	-2.0	20.6			*	6.0	.190	7.5
24							S 47 W		7.10	35.6	18.0	17.6	.080		1.6			
25							S 59 W	3.13	5.44	39.4	34.8	4.6						
26	37.23	.204	92	.594	.990	1.0	N 79 E	5.40	6.69	39.2	34.8	4.4	.185	3.5			.185	3.5
27	36.80	.190	88	.588	.396	0.9	N 7 E	1.69	2.81	36.6	33.5	3.1	.055	3.0			.055	3.0
28	34.48	.179	87	.323	.144	0.9	N 45 W	10.48	14.36	40.0	31.4	8.6	.330	11.0			.330	11.0
29	12.47	.061	74	.780	.719	0.8	N 23 W	11.95	12.40	39.1	15.0	24.1					*	*
30	19.20	.098	82	.752	.654		S 5 E	0.45	0.52	19.4	2.3	17.1			*	*		
31							N 58 E	4.12	4.17	33.0	27.0	6.0						
	21.88	0.109	80	29.587	29.478	0.8	N 44 W	4.30	8.56	29.46	14.38	15.08	0.590	19.0	17.2	63.0	2.310	8.20

GENERAL METEOROLOGICAL ABSTRACT.—JANUARY, 1855.

Date	DAILY MEANS.					WIND.			Extremes of Temperature.			RAIN.		SNOW.		RAIN AND MELTED SNOW	
	Temperature of the Air.	Pressure of Vapour.	Relative Humidity.	Barometric Pressure.	Pressure of Dry Air.	Clouded Sky.	Resultant Direction.	Resultant Velocity.	Mean Velocity.	Maximum.	Minimum.	Difference.	Depth in Inches.	Approximate duration in hours.	Depth in Inches.	Approximate duration in hours.	Depth in Inches.	Approximate duration in hours.
								Miles	Miles	°	°	°						
1	29.40	0.129	82	30.011	29.881	1.0	N 78 E	9.40	9.50	31.0	25.4	5.6	...	...	...	...	...	...
2	38.85	.148	77	30.011	29.862	0.4	N 80 E	4.84	4.95	41.2	29.0	12.2	...	...	...	...	...	...
3	38.08	.184	80	29.963	29.760	0.5	S 78 E	1.17	1.19	45.8	34.0	11.8	.070	2.8	...	...	.070	2.8
4	39.15	.210	88	30.024	29.814	0.0	N 59 W	2.80	3.02	49.2	23.0	25.2	.040	1.5	...	...	.040	1.5
5	39.17	.182	84	30.271	30.138	0.9	N 81 E	10.65	10.65	39.4	22.2	17.2	.015	1.0	...	...	.015	1.0
6	41.87	.235	89	29.881	29.646	1.0	N 29 E	3.91	3.91	49.0	37.0	12.0	...	...	...	...	...	...
7	27.58	.123	50	30.394	30.270	0.4	S 52 W	8.64	8.72	48.2	20.2	28.0	...	...	0.2	3.5	.020	3.5
8	31.73	.131	73	30.067	29.936	0.2	S 68 E	0.16	0.17	34.6	20.5	14.1	...	...	...	...	.040	0.5
9	33.23	.108	54	30.127	30.019	0.6	N 71 W	4.33	5.44	40.8	19.0	21.8	...	...	...	...	.030	1.0
10	30.00	.160	92	29.427	29.277	1.0	S 69 E	1.84	4.41	28.2	18.8	9.4	...	...	0.2	1.0	...	...
11	37.28	.199	90	.231	.032	1.0	S 34 W	1.40	10.3	36.5	26.2	10.3	.040	0.5	...	...	.040	0.5
12	21.85	.096	75	.404	.208	0.6	S 73 W	0.13	0.13	43.8	29.0	18.8	...	...	0.2	4.0	.020	4.0
13							N 45 W	17.56	17.87	29.6	–5.4	35.0	...	...	0.7	2.0	.070	2.0
14	26.42	.115	78	.530	.424	1.0	S 36 W	6.38	6.61	35.2	–1.2	26.4	...	...	0.3	...	.030	...
15	22.85	.106	85	.691	.595	1.0	N 60 W	1.52	3.69	29.4	16.2	13.2	...	...	...	...	...	...
16	33.55	.165	76	.860	.185	0.9	S 68 E	3.55	3.87	32.0	16.0	16.0	...	...	...	...	...	...
17	31.10	.137	82	.469	.332	1.0	S 64 E	0.92	2.95	39.8	20.6	19.2	...	...	0.2	0.5	.020	0.5
18	25.33	.109	90	.304	.205	1.0	N 66 W	7.29	7.69	37.2	24.0	13.2	...	...	0.7	4.0	.070	4.0
19	26.60	.131	99	.359	.258	0.9	N 40 W	4.86	4.96	28.4	20.0	8.4	...	...	0.3	2.0	.030	2.0
20						1.0	N 86 W	0.34	0.85	30.2	21.5	8.7	...	...	*	*	*	*
21	21.02	.107	89	.097	28.990	0.6	N 64 E	6.28	14.76	37.0	25.4	11.6	...	...	3.0	8.0	.660	12.0
22	9.95	.090	81	.628	29.573	0.7	S 63 W	16.14	16.30	25.4	3.9	21.5	...	4.0	...	...	...	...
23	10.37	.051	67	.697	.636	0.2	S 78 W	6.13	6.21	17.2	2.8	14.4	...	...	...	...	...	...
24	16.80	.086	88	.462	.396	2.4	S 69 W	2.63	2.65	21.4	2.4	19.0	...	...	7.0	14.0	.700	14.0
25	16.97	.087	83	.075	28.988	0.7	N 20 E	5.76	7.87	28.3	3.4	19.9	...	...	3.5	9.0	.350	9.0
26	16.10	.074	76	.294	29.160	0.9	N 18 W	14.64	15.96	24.2	9.8	14.4	...	...	0.1	1.0	.010	1.0
27						1.0	N 75 W	12.35	12.76	21.8	10.8	10.8	...	...	6.5	12.0	.550	12.0
28	28.28	.117	91	.080	28.963	1.0	N 61 E	8.55	10.11	28.5	12.8	15.7	...	...	2.0	4.0	.200	4.0
29	19.77	.092	83	.496	29.399	1.0	S 40 W	15.46	16.54	29.0	16.2	12.8	...	...	0.4	5.0	.040	5.0
30	20.88	.096	81	.730	.634	0.9	S 61 W	13.59	13.76	24.0	16.4	7.6	...	...	0.2	6.0	.020	6.0
31							N 43 W	4.26	6.26	28.4	14.6	13.8						
	25.95	0.123	83	29.690	29.514	0.8	N 73 W	1.91	7.26	32.83	17.54	15.29	0.525	9.8	23.3	70.1	2.855	79.9

GENERAL METEOROLOGICAL ABSTRACT,—FEBRUARY, 1855.

Days	DAILY MEANS.							WIND.			EXTREMES OF TEMPERATURE.			RAIN.		SNOW.		RAIN AND MELTED SNOW	
	Temperature of the Air.	Pressure of Vapour.	Relative Humidity.	Barometric Pressure.	Pressure of Dry Air.	Clouded Sky.	Resultant Direction.	Resultant Velocity.	Mean Velocity.	Maximum.	Minimum.	Difference.	Depth in Inches.	Approximate duration in hours.	Depth in Inches.	Approximate duration in hours.	Depth in Inches.	Approximate duration in hours.
								Miles.	Miles.	°	°	°						
1	12.27	0.070	78	29.524	29.454	0.8	N 83 W	6.41	7.47	28.2	-2.4	30.6	....	....	0.5	4.5	0.050	4.5
2	17.08	.080	80	.260	.180	0.9	S 75 W	10.74	11.40	23.4	3.2	20.2	....	....	0.4	4.0	.040	4.0
3	8.12	.052	75	.350	.298	0.5	N 87 W	11.79	13.97	15.6	-14.5	30.1	....	....	0.5	3.0	.050	3.0
4	....	....	....	....	....	....	N 3 E	4.08	4.13	4.2	-13.2	17.4	....	....	0.3	5.0	.030	5.0
5	-7.62	.025	66	.457	.432	0.4	N 3 W	7.93	8.27	8.8	-25.4	31.2	....	....	0.1	0.5	.010	0.5
6	-14.38	.023	68	.753	.730	0.7	N 26 E	0.18	9.19	-6.2	-25.0	18.8	....	....	2.5	10.0	.250	10.0
7	-0.28	.039	85	.546	.508	1.0	N 38 E	13.12	13.21	6.8	-7.2	14.0	....	....	2.5	15.0	.250	15.0
8	11.12	.063	80	.484	.421	1.0	N 4 E	6.77	6.92	16.4	7.0	9.4	....	....	0.1	1.0	.010	1.0
9	9.29	.064	84	.591	.527	0.6	N 59 E	3.29	3.52	19.4	-2.5	21.9	....	....	*	*	*	*
10	17.67	.082	69	.691	.609	1.0	N 40 W	5.71	6.06	27.2	10.8	16.4	....	....	4.0	3.0	.400	3.0
11	....	....	....	....	....	....	N 48 W	1.64	2.07	30.6	4.0	26.6	....	....	....	9.0	....	9.0
12	24.18	.118	87	.759	.641	0.9	S 78 E	10.84	11.14	33.0	15.0	18.0	....	....	5.0	9.0	.500	9.0
13	33.50	.175	92	.571	.396	1.0	N 83 E	12.04	12.36	37.4	31.5	5.9	1.705	17.5	....	....	1.705	17.5
14	34.83	.193	95	.480	.287	1.0	N 71 E	2.19	2.44	38.4	30.5	7.9	.065	3.0	....	....	.065	3.0
15	33.07	.171	91	.473	.302	0.9	N 43 W	6.40	6.65	39.0	27.0	12.0	....	....	4.0	17.0	.400	17.0
16	28.60	.148	90	.428	.280	1.0	S 85 W	4.57	4.80	36.4	22.0	14.6	....	....	1.5	12.0	.150	12.0
17	26.80	.130	87	.567	.437	0.6	N 84 W	5.25	5.51	33.6	24.2	9.4	....	....	0.2	1.0	.020	1.0
18	....	....	....	....	....	....	N 40 W	11.25	11.50	34.1	21.7	12.4	....	....	*	*	*	*
19	23.90	.114	86	.719	.603	1.0	N 29 W	13.74	13.95	28.8	19.2	9.6	....	....	0.2	3.0	.020	3.0
20	23.15	.100	78	.910	.810	0.5	N 29 W	8.70	8.83	32.8	9.0	23.8	....	....	....	....	....	....
21	20.75	.090	75	.936	.846	0.1	N 43 W	1.81	1.95	34.2	11.0	23.2	....	....	....	....	....	....
22	26.47	.126	86	.712	.586	0.9	N 39 W	0.82	1.76	27.2	4.2	23.0	....	....	....	....	....	....
23	4.63	.041	69	.842	.801	0.2	N 18 W	7.57	7.77	12.2	-8.0	20.2	....	....	....	....	....	....
24	2.25	.042	75	.797	.756	0.4	N 69 W	6.77	6.90	14.4	-12.4	29.0	....	....	....	....	....	....
25	....	....	....	....	....	....	S 89 W	12.47	12.66	16.4	4.2	12.2	....	....	*	*	*	*
26	11.70	.058	73	.433	.377	1.0	N 66 W	12.58	12.75	16.4	5.8	10.6	....	....	....	....	....	....
27	11.30	.059	75	.705	.646	0.4	N 34 W	8.79	8.87	19.0	0.9	18.1	....	....	....	....	....	....
28	11.40	.051	67	30.011	.960	0.1	N 30 W	2.01	2.65	21.4	-3.6	25.0	....	....	....	....	....	....
	15.41	0.088	80	29.625	29.537	0.7	N 40 W	4.34	8.17	23.19	4.81	18.38	1.770	20.5	21.8	98.0	3.950	118.5

GENERAL METEOROLOGICAL ABSTRACT.—MARCH, 1855.

Days.	DAILY MEANS.					WIND.				EXTREMES OF TEMPERATURE.			RAIN.		SNOW.		RAIN AND MELTED SNOW	
	Temperature of the Air.	Vapour. Pressure of	Relative Humidity.	Barometric Pressure.	Pressure of Dry Air.	Clouded Sky.	Resultant Direction.	Resultant Velocity.	Mean Velocity.	Maximum.	Minimum.	Difference.	Depth in Inches.	Approximate duration in hours.	Depth in Inches.	Approximate duration in hours.	Depth in Inches.	Approximate duration in hours.
1	19.22	0.097	82	30.001	29.904	0.5	S 53 W	7.40	7.74	34.4	2.9	37.3						
2	29.65	.151	90	29.798	.647	0.9	S 42 W	5.27	5.46	35.2	25.1	10.1			1.0	4.0	0.010	4.0
3	33.32	.170	90	.625	.455	1.0	S 75 W	4.77	4.98	38.6	26.2	12.4						
4							S 57 W	5.56	7.00	42.4	33.8	8.6						
5	37.65	.192	85	.182	28.990	0.9	S 82 W	13.57	15.41	43.7	25.4	18.3	.170	8.0			.170	3.0
6	26.50	.126	85	.482	29.356	0.6	N 39 W	7.57	8.97	25.8	16.8	18.6	.005	1.0	3.0	3.0	.005	1.0
7	23.35	.111	85	.584	.473	1.0	N 20 E	1.65	2.10	20.5	9.0	20.5			4.5	4.5		
8	24.43	.117	86	.691	.474	1.0	S 64 E	2.14	2.42	33.6	16.4	17.2			1.2	0.5	.200	3.0
9	24.42	.116	94	.501	.385	0.7	N 42 W	19.70	20.72	33.8	6.2	27.6			0.1		.120	4.5
10	19.38	.092	80	.880	.788	0.6	N 15 E	1.31	3.75	29.4	8.0	20.4					.010	0.5
11							N 54 E	6.05	7.27	32.4	22.0	10.4						
12	27.95	.120	79	.605	.605	0.2	N 65 E	6.33	7.58	36.2	21.8	14.4						
13	29.17	.139	88	.352	.213	1.0	S 80 E	2.09	3.47	43.8	24.2	19.9	.680	9.0	6.0	9.0	.600	9.0
14	36.57	.179	83	.344	.163	0.9	S 16 E	20.02	20.74	43.8	36.0	7.8	.415	4.0			.680	9.0
15	36.10	.181	86	.310	.129	0.7	S 64 W	6.12	10.92	42.2	22.3	19.9				1.5	.415	4.0
16	31.13	.135	78	.730	.595	0.4	N 64 E	1.22	2.18	39.2	27.0	12.2			0.1		.010	1.5
17	35.83	.159	79	.323	.164	1.0	S 41 W	4.79	17.70	41.9	29.2	12.9	.215	3.0			.215	3.0
18							S 85 W	6.70	6.83	39.8	21.2	18.6						
19	28.80	.129	77	.506	.377	0.3	S 32 W	6.86	9.72	40.2	19.4	20.8			0.5	0.2	.050	0.2
20	28.73	.098	76	.613	.515	1.0	S 89 E	17.90	18.35	29.8	15.2	14.6				2.0		2.0
21	24.03	.114	66	.934	.820	0.9	N 70 W	4.92	5.25	30.8	15.2	15.8						
22	25.43	.097	69	.652	.555	0.0	S 81 W	10.44	10.99	34.6	20.0	14.6			0.1	2.5	.010	2.5
23	29.57	.133	79	.780	.849	0.9	N 81 W	12.25	16.31	35.0	6.8	28.4			0.3	4.0	.080	4.0
24	17.15	.076	74	.266	.189	0.4	N 62 W	16.47	18.46	25.4	6.4	19.0						
25							S 85 W	12.46	12.72	35.6	23.0	12.6						
26	27.82	.134	87	.118	.979	0.9	S 1 W	0.60	10.88	33.2	19.	14.2			0.3	3.0	.010	3.0
27	28.12	.109	85	.439	.320	0.7	N 44 W	11.63	12.52	31.3	11.2	20.3			6.5	10.0	.080	10.0
28	24.77	.102	75	.559	.457	0.9	N 85 W	14.41	14.82	31.7	20.6	11.1						
29	33.47	.131	69	.521	.390	0.0	S 73 W	10.34	10.55	44.2	27.0	17.2						
30	37.55	.160	72	.540	.380	0.5	S 55 W	5.90	6.74	47.4	32.4	15.0					.030	3.0
31	39.82	.194	81	.308	.114	0.4	S 65 W	4.20	0.74	49.4	21.8	27.0					.650	10.0
	28.46	0.132	81	29.518	29.381	0.7	N 88 W	4.70	9.95	30.52	19.63	16.89	1.485	20.0	18.1	44.2	3.295	64.2

TORONTO METEOROLOGICAL OBSERVATIONS.

GENERAL METEOROLOGICAL ABSTRACT,—APRIL, 1865.

Days	DAILY MEANS.						WIND.			EXTREMES OF TEMPERATURE.			RAIN.		SNOW.		RAIN AND MELTED SNOW	
	Temperature of the Air.	Pressure of Vapour.	Relative Humidity.	Barometric Pressure.	Pressure of Dry Air.	Clouded Sky.	Resultant Direction	Resultant Velocity.	Mean Velocity	Maximum.	Minimum.	Difference.	Depth in Inches.	Approximate duration in hours	Depth in Inches.	Approximate duration in hours	Depth in Inches	Approximate duration in hours
1	23.10	0.076	68		29.529	0.2	N 53 W	26.29	26.40	26.6	10.7	15.9			0.1	2.0	0.010	2.0
2	27.62	.112	72		.875	0.3	N 49 W	21.77	22.10	32.4	16.2	16.2						
3	33.37	.132	71		.872	0.4	N 29 W	1.40	3.09	38.4	20.5	17.9						
4	38.10	.182	81		.483	0.9	S 27 E	1.38	1.48	46.4	27.0	19.4						
5							S 28 E	1.59	3.08	48.8	30.6	18.2						
6	32.10	.131	73		.508	0.1	N 37 W	10.88	12.25	45.4	20.0	25.4						
7							S 5 W	4.69	5.16	41.6	27.4	14.2	.035	1.0			.035	1.0
8							S 64 W	4.95	5.88	55.8	32.2	23.6	.015	0.5			.015	0.5
9	42.63	.197	77		.516	0.3	S 70 W	6.50	6.95	54.5	32.8	21.7			1.4	5.0	.140	5.0
10	36.17	.163	79		.506	0.9	N 64 W	11.52	14.53	49.2	27.0	22.2						
11	37.47	.160	74		.808	0.2	N 26 W	21.04	21.09	45.4	28.5	16.9						
12	40.37	.146	63		.914	0.4	N 17 W	7.61	7.98	52.2	32.4	19.8						
13	36.70	.181	84		.687	0.9	N 77 W	3.97	4.88	41.8	34.5	7.3	.655	4.5			.655	4.5
14	47.30	.242	78		.442	0.7	N 46 W	6.57	7.01	69.4	32.2	37.2	.010	1.0			.010	1.0
15							S 8 W	0.98	1.99	52.2	30.0	22.2	.055	4.5			.055	4.5
16	43.62	.221	72		.750	0.0	S 83 E	1.69	2.17	65.3	35.0	30.3						
17	50.52	.265	75		.592	0.7	S 88 E	4.95	5.79	64.8	44.5	20.3	.095	1.0			.095	1.0
18	53.60	.349	86		.473	0.9	N 83 W	4.27	6.54	63.8	45.0	18.8	.025	1.0			.025	1.0
19	55.02	.336	80		.467	0.2	N 17 E	1.74	1.74	64.2	42.0	22.2						
20	49.02	.247	73		.630	0.4	N 6 W	2.87	4.94	61.0	30.4	30.6						
21	48.25	.233	71		.707	0.3	S 42 E	0.73	1.27	58.8	39.8	29.8	*	*			*	*
22							N 15 W	9.04	9.29	62.8	35.0	27.8						
23	49.68	.239	68		.757	0.2	S 53 E	0.51	0.61	63.4	35.5	27.9						
24	54.98	.301	71		.537	0.4	N 32 W	1.88	3.60	69.1	47.3	21.8	.695	8.0			.695	8.0
25	45.83	.246	88		.713	1.0	S 61 E	5.15	6.54	49.0	40.0	9.0						
26	49.35	.228	76		.595	0.6	N 55 W	18.98	14.43	66.2	30.2	36.4						
27	42.72	.185	52		.950	0.1	N 35 W	10.37	11.23	55.2	29.4	35.8						
28	37.00	.158			.903	0.9	N 85 E	7.83	8.11	43.0	38.5	9.5	*	2.0			*	2.0
29							N 82 E	6.61	6.63	42.2	36.5	5.7	.440	3.5			.440	3.5
30	47.00	.283	89		.470	1.0	N 64 E	1.20	2.79	57.2	39.0	18.2	.070	0.5			.070	0.5
	42.43	0.208	75		29.654	0.5	N 36 W	3.99	7.57	52.93	32.06	20.87	2.030	23.0	1.6	8.0	2.190	31.0

GENERAL METEOROLOGICAL ABSTRACT.—MAY, 1855.

Days.	DAILY MEANS.						WIND.			EXTREMES OF TEMPERATURE.			RAIN.		SNOW.		RAIN AND MELTED SNOW.	
	Temperature of the Air.	Pressure of Vapour.	Relative Humidity.	Barometric Pressure.	Pressure of Dry Air.	Clouded Sky.	Resultant Direction.	Resultant Velocity.	Mean Velocity.	Maximum.	Minimum.	Difference.	Depth in Inches.	Approximate duration in hours.	Depth in Inches.	Approximate duration in hours.	Depth in Inches.	Approximate duration in hours.
1	57.35	0.350	76	29.698	29.348	0.4	N 20 E	4.96	4.96	69.0	44.8	24.2						
2	51.72	.251	68	.795	.544	0.8	N 74 E	9.12	9.37	59.2	46.8	12.4						
3	52.20	.219	56	.763	.544	0.3	N 54 E	7.57	7.57	63.6	41.2	22.4						
4	62.05	.188	51	.784	.596	0.0	N 7 W	5.89	5.89	63.4	39.0	24.4						
5	53.38	.221	57	.761	.540	0.0	N 16 W	14.80	14.98	65.8	37.6	28.2						
6							N 17 W	9.72	10.72	64.0	37.0	27.0	1.030	14.0	4.0	4.0	1.030	14.0
7	38.07	.141	68	.524	.383	0.2	N 17 W	9.60	10.63	49.0	33.0	10.0	.300	12.0	0.3	3.0	.300	12.0
8	37.68	.202	90	.476	.274	0.5	N 22 E	4.73	6.09	47.4	33.2	14.2			0.6			
9	45.38	.182	61	.770	.588	0.1	N 10 E	7.59	8.23	57.9	33.0	24.9						
10	50.12	.201	58	.816	.615	0.1	N 20 W	3.87	5.69	62.2	35.2	27.0						
11	51.97	.200	63	.651	.451	0.6	N 69 W	1.85	3.88	70.6	41.0	29.6	*	1.5			*	1.5
12	54.33	.304	74	.598	.294	0.6	S 12 W	3.97	6.01	67.5	41.5	26.0	*	1.0			*	1.0
13							S 87 W	1.29	1.66	71.3	43.4	27.8	.285	3.5			.285	3.5
14	56.17	.330	75	.607	.277	0.7	S 28 E	1.68	4.42	67.2	39.4	27.8						
15	59.85	.396	79	.350	.984	0.7	S 61 W	1.42	1.92	62.6	40.4	22.2						
16	51.62	.276	74	.466	29.210	0.4	N 39 W	6.28	8.00	69.2	52.0	17.2						
17	53.82	.215	54	.750	.535	0.1	N 19 W	8.85	8.85	66.1	36.4	29.7	4.0	4.0			4.0	4.0
18	55.00	.232	54	.648	.416	0.6	N 68 E	8.94	4.63	67.2	38.4	28.8						
19	53.13	.303	76	.485	.182	1.0	N 75 E	6.73	6.89	65.2	47.0	18.2						
20							N 33 E	5.31	7.27	61.6	47.0	14.6						
21	53.28	.231	60	.526	.206	0.4	S 28 E	1.21	1.32	62.6	29.8	33.7						
22	56.53	.251	57	.512	.261	0.6	S 60 E	0.80	1.66	62.6	39.8	22.6						
23	56.17	.295	66	.528	.232	0.4	S 50 E	0.85	0.80	65.7	43.4	22.3						
24							N 48 W	2.40	3.03	76.0	47.0	18.4	.160	0.3			.160	0.3
25	54.90	.261	62	.801	.540	0.0	N 8 W	4.34	4.34	76.0	36.6	39.4						
26	53.22	.184	48	.833	.649	0.0	N 14 W	11.08	11.10	65.2	35.0	30.2						
27							S 80 W	4.73	11.31	61.8	40.2	21.6						
28	56.00	.261	60	.766	.503	1.0	S 91 E	1.01	1.82	64.8	40.5	24.3						
29	57.97	.268	58	.754	.486	0.4	S 73 E	1.41	1.48	68.6	38.4	30.2						
30	57.73	.344	74	.709	.338	0.8	S 57 E	1.10	2.82	73.2	42.3	30.9						
31	60.25	.400	78	.533	.133	0.9	S 18 W	2.56	2.89	73.6	47.0	25.6	.480	1.6			.480	1.6
								5.82	6.01	72.0	57.0	15.0						
	53.07	0.266	65	29.651	29.393	0.5	N 1° W	2.76	6.93	65.40	41.42	23.98	2.565	30.9	0.9	7.0	2.655	37.9

GENERAL METEOROLOGICAL ABSTRACT,—JUNE, 1855.

Days	DAILY MEANS						WIND			EXTREMES OF TEMPERATURE			RAIN		SNOW		RAIN AND MELTED SNOW	
	Temperature of the Air.	Pressure of Vapour.	Halative Humidity	Barometric Pressure.	Pressure of Dry Air.	Clouded Sky.	Resultant Direction.	Resultant Velocity.	Mean Velocity.	Maximum.	Minimum.	Difference.	Depth in Inches.	Approximate duration in hours.	Depth in Inches.	Approximate duration in hours.	Depth in Inches.	Approximate duration in hours.
1	59.13	0.461	93	29.289	28.828	1.0	N 54 W	0.92	4.57	65.0	48.2	16.8	0.315	6.0				
2	54.80	.346	81	.371	29.025	0.9	N 27 W	2.13	4.39	69.2	45.5	23.7	.025	1.2				
3																		
4	48.96	.252	74	.499	.237	0.9	N 86 W	2.79	4.14	60.0	37.6	22.4						
5	54.40	.306	73	.490	.184	0.2	S 81 W	3.51	4.23	55.2	42.5	12.7						
6	55.73	.314	71	.533	.219	0.5	N 75 W	5.22	6.00	63.0	32.2	30.8	*	1.5				
7	52.05	.351	91	.326	28.975	0.9	N 8 W	1.38	1.87	69.5	47.0	22.5	.290	9.0				
8	54.37	.319	76	.376	29.057	0.3	N 37 W	1.83	2.97	58.0	45.2	12.8	.010	0.2				
9	56.50	.382	73	.331	28.999	0.7				63.8	42.2	22.6	.490	6.0				
10										71.0	49.6	21.4	.205	5.0				
11	48.65	.245	73	.384	29.139	0.6	N 60 W	8.94	10.01	64.0	42.6	21.8						
12	50.28	.250	69	.649	.399	0.5	N 49 W	5.37	7.22	58.8	36.2	20.8						
13	58.37	.259	56	.736	.477	0.4	N 63 W	8.35	9.65	63.8	43.0	20.8						
14	64.08	.345	50	.608	.263	0.5	N 75 W	7.78	9.24	67.2	41.8	25.4	.015	1.0				
15	63.58	.373	67	.427	.054	1.0	N 61 W	1.19	3.95	75.4	53.0	22.2						
16	61.43	.393	74	.463	.070	0.7	N 62 E	3.74	4.49	69.2	50.6	18.6						
17										61.5	41.0	20.5	.175	3.0				
18	50.20	.328	66	.731	.403	0.2	N 78 E	6.72	7.03	67.5	53.0	14.5	.335	11.0				
19	53.33	.369	98	.503	.134	1.0	N 54 E	6.21	6.38	55.6	50.4	5.2						
20	55.87	.384	86	.501	.117	0.6	S 1 W	2.85	2.85	63.4	49.0	14.4	.580	10.0				
21	58.23	.422	80	.446	.020	1.0	N 84 E	4.13	5.30	67.0	54.0	13.0						
22	05.47	.483	78	.462	28.979	0.6	N 19 W	7.02	7.77	76.0	58.0	18.0						
23	64 00	.454	78	.640	29.186	0.8	N 67 W	3.32	5.03	72.0	59.0	13.0	.875	10.0				
24										67.0	58.5	8.5	.045	3.0				
25	64.55	.457	76	.510	.053	0.8	N 3 E	8.62	10.36	72.5	57.2	15.3	.060	2.5				
26	62.87	.437	87	.636	.149	0.7	S 77 W	2.32	4.54	74.2	57.0	17.2	.110	1.5				
27	67.62	.561	86	.454	.033	0.9	S 15 W	5.26	5.57	76.6	63.0	13.6	.495	2.6				
28	72.23	.631	83	.690	.059	0.4	S 4 E	1.46	3.50	80.2	66.0	14.2						
29	78.72	.722	70	.604	28.882	0.2	S 39 W	3.86	5.11	91.8	70.0	21.5						
30	77.32	.704	76	.502	.798	0.4	S 20 W	5.65	5.83	86.0	67.4	18.6	.045	0.6				
	59.93	0.406	78	29.513	29.108	0.7	N 69 W	1.33	5.70	68.89	50.08	18.21	4.070	74.1				

GENERAL METEOROLOGICAL ABSTRACT,—JULY, 1855.

Days.	DAILY MEANS.						WIND.			EXTREMES OF TEMPERATURE.			RAIN.		SNOW.		RAIN AND MELTED SNOW	
	Temperature of the Air.	Pressure of Vapour.	Relative Humidity.	Barometric Pressure.	Pressure of Dry Air.	Clouded Sky.	Resultant Direction.	Resultant Velocity.	Mean Velocity.	Maximum.	Minimum.	Difference.	Depth in Inches.	Approximate duration in hours.	Depth in Inches.	Approximate duration in hours.	Depth in Inches.	Approximate duration in hours.
	°						°	Miles.	Miles.	°	°	°						
1	65.32	0.433	75	29.529			S 18 W	8.32	9.24	81.4	62.2	19.2						
2	60.20	.356	77	.661	29.096	0.6	S 81 W	9.20	11.37	76.4	54.8	21.6						
3	68.23	.511	76	.475	.274	0.7	N 94 E	8.10	8.79	65.4	56.0	9.4	.005	0.1				
4	62.32	.413	70	.733	.964	0.1	N 75 W	6.30	8.69	80.2	53.2	27.0						
5	64.25	.422	71	.686	.321	0.6	N 19 W	4.08	6.41	72.5	51.5	21.0						
6	59.93	.336	43	.759	.422	0.2	S 19 W	3.95	6.55	75.0	55.2	19.8						
7			67				N 42 E	4.15	5.92	69.8	49.2	20.6						
8	64.90	.471	79	.616	.146	1.0	S 34 E	5.92	8.97	71.4	57.0	14.4	.010	1.0				
9	68.00	.488	83	.570	.082	0.5	S 4 E	6.29	8.01	72.0	57.9	14.2	*	*				
10	68.65	.496	73	.533	.037	0.2	N 62 W	4.66	5.82	80.8	52.2	28.6	.410	5.5				
11	68.38	.554	82	.427	28.873	0.5	S 25 W	3.12	5.40	79.2	63.0	16.2	.255	3.0				
12	62.88	.459	82	.449	28.990	0.9	S 15 W	1.52	4.07	61.0	50.2	18.8						
13	64.50	.303	62	.644	29.281	0.6	N 33 E	3.77	6.27	72.6	50.2	22.4						
14						0.2	S 41 E	2.29	5.05	73.8	57.0	16.8						
15							S 32 E	4.00	5.09	78.4	59.5	18.9						
16	76.05	.675	78	.742	.067	0.1	S 26 W	7.58	9.11	88.2	59.8	28.4	.295	4.5				
17	78.73	.689	74	.688	28.998	0.3	S 78 W	4.59	5.98	91.6	65.0	26.6	.090	3.0				
18	76.50	.718	81	.616	.903	0.4	S 19 W	8.08	8.41	85.6	71.0	14.6						
19	79.45	.675	70	.492	.817	0.6	N 62 W	9.34	13.06	92.8	33.0							
20	60.67	.428	83	.723	29.295	0.6	N 23 E	5.70	6.17	64.2	59.0	0.2						
21	60.65	.396	77	.768	.371	1.0	S 82 E	7.19	8.41	67.0	55.0	12.0	.085	0.5				
22						0.5	S 26 W	5.21	6.20	68.2	60.0	8.2	.325	3.5				
23	64.85	.511	96	.712	.201	1.0	N 74 E	6.20	4.55	73.0	61.8	11.2	.065	1.5				
24	64.92	.533	88	.669	.136	1.0	S 88 E	4.13	5.98	71.0	62.0	9.0	.905	4.0				
25	68.69	.592	87	.661	.069	1.0	N 69 E	3.37	5.41	72.8	62.8	10.4	*	*				
26	70.35	.662	92	.540	28.578	0.7	S 40 E	1.21	2.45	78.2	64.6	15.4	.315	6.0				
27	73.38	.690	86	.464	28.764	0.6	S 34 E	1.05	2.49	90.2	69.4	12.8	.195	2.5				
28	72.97	.665	85	.459	28.705	0.5	S 48 E	4.02	6.63	82.2	64.5	16.9	.040	1.5				
29							S 58 W	2.14	4.23	61.4	64.5	15.2						
30	70.30	.623	87	.612	28.990	0.6	N 26 E	1.72	5.33	81.2	66.0	12.6						
31	71.58	.598	79	.672	29.074	0.8	S 86 E	1.43	4.00	77.2	64.6	12.8						
							N 70 E	1.56	3.67	78.8	66.0							
	67.95	0.580	79	29.611	29.081	0.6	S 19 W	0.73	6.47	76.75	60.05	16.70	3.242	36.6				

TORONTO METEOROLOGICAL OBSERVATIONS.

GENERAL METEOROLOGICAL ABSTRACT,—AUGUST, 1855.

Days	DAILY MEANS						WIND			EXTREMES OF TEMPERATURE			RAIN		SNOW		RAIN AND MELTED SNOW	
	Temperature of the Air	Pressure of Vapour	Relative Humidity	Barometric Pressure	Pressure of Dry Air	Clouded Sky	Resultant Direction	Resultant Velocity	Mean Velocity	Maximum	Minimum	Difference	Depth in Inches	Approximate duration in hours	Depth in Inches	Approximate duration in hours	Depth in Inches	Approximate duration in hours
1	70.88	0.608	83	29.686	29.083	0.5	N 64 E	2.77	4.12	79.8	65.6	14.2	...	...	...	...	...	...
2	71.77	.627	83	.715	.088	0.1	N 77 E	3.35	4.78	71.5	54.0	17.5	...	...	...	...	...	...
3	74.67	.665	81	.685	.020	0.3	S 19 W	3.58	4.74	83.5	68.8	14.7	.015	0.5	...	...	...	...
4	72.75	.681	87	.593	28.912	0.7	S 10 E	0.37	4.45	81.8	63.2	18.6	.380	0.7	...	...	...	...
5	68.77	.409	70	.575	29.106	0.3	N 17 E	3.78	6.14	76.0	60.0	16.0	...	...	...	...	...	...
6	65.23	.434	72	.673	.238	0.4	N 43 W	1.64	6.88	77.0	54.2	23.4	...	...	...	...	...	...
7	65.58	.509	83	.501	28.992	1.0	N 58 E	3.66	9.47	77.0	60.0	17.0	.020	0.5	...	...	...	...
8	60.78	.510	79	.204	28.694	0.4	N 78 E	6.37	7.86	72.6	63.8	8.8	.005	1.0	...	...	...	...
9	60.82	.520	82	.502	28.994	0.2	N 98 W	16.49	16.95	73.0	53.0	26.2	...	...	...	...	...	...
10	62.68	.432	77	.658	29.182	0.4	N 54 W	6.17	6.79	71.5	50.0	21.5	...	...	...	...	...	...
11	...	...	...	...	.226	...	S 79 E	5.66	8.21	72.2	56.8	16.4	...	...	...	...	...	...
12	66.13	.408	63	.796	.378	0.2	N 9 W	1.24	6.67	77.2	61.2	18.0	.615	4.5	...	...	...	...
13	64.40	.395	67	.793	.398	0.6	S 17 E	5.49	5.27	71.0	52.8	18.0	...	...	...	...	...	...
14	67.78	.617	78	.533	.016	0.6	N 73 W	2.80	5.13	76.8	64.6	12.2	.295	0.5	...	...	...	...
15	69.10	.497	71	.377	28.890	1.0	W	4.73	9.06	82.0	47.8	34.2	...	...	...	...	...	...
16	56.93	.260	59	.560	29.300	0.6	N 55 W	15.29	15.45	67.8	42.8	25.0	.035	0.4	...	...	...	...
17	53.92	.263	66	.878	.614	0.3	S 49 E	7.97	8.39	66.2	40.0	26.2	...	...	...	...	...	...
18	...	...	...	...	...	0.0	S 6 E	2.87	4.45	67.2	45.6	21.6	...	...	...	...	...	...
19	61.75	.409	76	.846	.437	0.0	S 13 W	4.31	4.92	74.2	51.8	22.4	...	...	...	...	...	...
20	66.47	.493	70	.730	.237	0.9	S 82 W	6.20	6.00	78.2	63.8	19.4	...	...	...	...	...	...
21	62.8	.513	84	.640	.127	0.7	N 44 W	2.75	3.71	76.8	59.2	17.6	...	...	...	...	...	...
22	65.00	.507	84	.491	28.984	0.1	S 10 W	1.99	3.88	77.0	51.0	26.0	...	...	...	...	...	...
23	64.85	.420	72	.581	29.101	0.3	S 79 E	3.54	5.74	76.4	55.2	21.2	...	...	...	...	...	...
24	64.58	.487	81	.665	.177	0.5	N 14 W	2.73	3.61	76.0	54.4	21.6	...	...	...	...	...	...
25	63.57	...	...	...	...	0.0	N 48 E	4.66	9.94	74.5	46.4	28.1	...	...	...	...	...	...
26	52.93	.256	65	.875	.619	0.0	S 42 E	7.88	7.88	62.8	43.2	19.6	...	...	...	...	...	...
27	55.48	.290	69	.758	.468	0.6	S 85 W	1.05	4.62	67.2	44.8	22.4	...	...	...	...	...	...
28	60.85	.395	75	.566	.171	0.6	N 6 E	6.89	11.63	75.4	49.0	26.4	...	...	...	...	•	•
29	54.28	.274	67	.897	.623	0.6	N 78 E	8.69	7.54	64.2	44.8	19.4	*	*	...	...	...	...
30	56.18	.352	79	.865	.513	0.6	...	4.06	4.64	70.0	47.0	23.0	...	...	...	...	...	...
	64.06	0.444	74	29.653	29.209	0.4	N 63 W	1.04	6.97	74.61	54.09	20.52	1.455	8.1				

GENERAL METEOROLOGICAL ABSTRACT—SEPTEMBER, 1855.

Days	DAILY MEANS.					WIND.			Extremes of Temperature.			RAIN.		SNOW.		RAIN AND MELTED SNOW	
	Temperature of the Air.	Pressure of Vapour.	Relative Humidity.	Barometric Pressure.	Pressure of Dry Air.	Clouded Sky.	Resultant Direction.	Resultant Velocity.	Mean Velocity.	Maximum.	Minimum.	Difference.	Depth in Inches.	Approximate duration in hours.	Depth in Inches.	Approximate duration in hours.	Depth in Inches.	Approximate duration in hours.
	°							Miles	Miles	°	°	°						
1	71.23	0.563	76	29.629	29.066	0.6	S 32 W	6.76	7.18	82.6	60.0	22.6	0.425	1.8				
2	55.00	.352	81	.772	.421	0.7	N 18 W	6.13	11.63	74.2	56.0	18.2	.035	1.5				
3	57.23	.336	73	.875	.539	0.0	N 40 E	5.99	10.38	61.2	48.0	13.2						
4	61.23	.398	78	.943	.546	0.0	N 59 E	6.24	7.81	67.0	51.5	15.5						
5	61.50	.433	82	.938	.505	0.0	N 63 E	4.19	7.50	70.8	52.8	18.0						
6	63.97	.487	84	.843	.356	0.0	N 65 E	1.91	7.04	71.0	49.2	21.8						
7	71.48	.585	78	.660	.075	0.7	S 1 W	5.72	5.83	74.6	58.8	15.8	.186	2.0				
8						0.5	S 32 W	6.36	4.19	81.2	66.8	14.4						
9						0.1	N 29 W	9.79	3.58	82.4	54.2	28.2						
10	64.52	.441	75	.697	.256	0.4	S 17 W	10.77	6.36	74.5	51.0	23.5						
11	70.22	.549	81	.607	.018	0.8	N 89 E	2.47	9.79	81.8	57.8	24.0	.240	5.0				
12	63.38	.626	90	.517		0.4	S 8 W	5.67	3.94	81.5	53.0	28.5						
13	58.93	.311	65	.785	.691	0.7	N 66 W	7.03	6.16	66.8	43.0	23.8						
14	54.67	.301	72	.777	.475	0.3	S 6 W	11.13	12.54	63.5	46.2	17.3						
15	58.02	.391	82	.640	.476	0.1	N 56 E	1.77	11.48	68.8	50.0	18.8						
16						0.2	S 75 E	2.48	8.79	75.8	54.0	21.8	.535	13.0				
17	66.25	.570	91	.527		0.8	S 54 W	0.59	4.56	60.8	46.4	14.0	.275	4.0				
18	53.35	.329	77	.639	.957	0.0	S 8 E	9.00	6.53	72.2	58.2	14.0						
19	44.12	.206	72	30.016	.303	0.0	N 25 E	5.70	4.98	61.5	36.5	25.0						
20	50.88	.250	69	.648	.811	0.4	N 63 E	8.32	9.05	51.5	36.0	15.5	.010	2.0				
21	54.78	.391	98	.779	.252	0.4	N 74 E	1.86	5.70	56.8	45.2	11.6						
22	55.50	.336	79		.442	1.0	N 27 E	6.09	2.52	59.2	47.0	12.2						
23						0.7	N 14 W	7.54	7.19	58.9	46.4	11.7						
24	62.15	.457	84	.806	.340	0.6	N 69 E	4.46	8.68	70.6	55.5	15.1	.550	6.0				
25	65.23	.546	90	.570	.024	0.8	S 49 E	3.79	8.69	69.2	55.5	13.7	.805	1.2				
26	64.02	.428	76	.326	.898	0.5	S 34 E	4.46	5.29	73.8	45.0	28.8	.005	0.1				
27	47.52	.223	69	.665	.442	0.4	S 84 W	10.40	5.57	54.8	33.0	21.8						
28	46.88	.254	80	.838	.584	0.2	N 53 W	12.19	12.10	56.0	39.0	17.0	.385	4.5				
29	55.08	.352	82	.656	.304	0.1	S 78 E	2.34	12.47	61.2	47.0	14.2	.045	2.6				
30						0.7	N 78 W	5.84	4.99	61.6	50.0	14.8						
	59.49	0.406	79	29.721	29.315	0.4	N 20 E	1.29	7.61	63.41	49.94	18.51	5.585	43.6				

TORONTO METEOROLOGICAL OBSERVATIONS.

GENERAL METEOROLOGICAL ABSTRACT,—OCTOBER, 1855.

Days	DAILY MEANS					WIND			EXTREMES OF TEMPERATURE			RAIN		SNOW		HAIL AND MELTED SNOW	
	Temperature of the Air	Pressure of Vapour	Relative Humidity	Barometric Pressure	Pressure of Dry Air	Clouded Sky	Resultant Direction	Resultant Velocity	Mean Velocity	Maximum	Minimum	Difference	Depth in Inches	Approximate duration in hours	Depth in Inches	Approximate duration in hours	Depth in Inches	Approximate duration in hours
	°							Miles	Miles									
1	56.95	0.401	88	29.412	29.012	0.8	N 53 W	1.00	4.55	65.6	50.0	15.6	0.285	3.5	...	...	0.285	3.5
2	55.22	.380	89	.300	28.920	0.9	N 66 W	2.29	4.12	61.6	48.8	12.8	.020	1.0	...	...	.020	1.0
3	53.12	.305	77	.278	28.973	0.6	N 48 W	9.02	10.32	60.6	38.0	22.6	*	*	...	...	*	*
4	53.73	.335	82	.356	29.020	0.0	...	...	...	64.6	45.0	19.6	.430	6.0	...	...	.430	6.0
5	59.83	.447	89	.355	28.908	1.0	...	...	...	65.0	45.2	19.8	.160	3.0	...	...	.160	3.0
6	46.93	.261	81	.310	29.049	0.8	...	...	...	51.0	36.0	15.0	...	...	...	...	...	...
7	42.07	.227	85	.552	.325	0.7	S 69 W	2.85	7.45	51.4	36.4	15.0	.030	1.0	...	...	.030	1.0
8	50.28	.304	83	.618	.314	0.5	N 71 E	7.29	7.55	48.4	33.5	14.9	...	...	...	...	...	...
9	49.72	.289	85	.800	.510	0.4	S 89 W	12.78	13.97	61.8	38.2	23.6	.015	1.0	...	...	.015	1.0
10	48.70	.246	72	.541	.295	0.5	N 72 W	10.32	10.67	55.0	40.8	14.2	*	1.5	0.1	0.8	*	1.5
11	36.22	.146	66	.700	.554	0.6	N 72 W	14.31	14.47	55.8	22.6	33.2	*	0.8	*	2.0	*	0.8
12	36.62	.188	74	.502	.318	1.0	N 10 W	4.39	5.22	44.0	27.8	16.2	.270	6.0	*	*	.270	6.0
13	46.12	.263	84	.560	.297	0.6	West	5.93	7.74	43.0	27.5	15.5	.015	1.5	...	...	.015	1.5
14	36.30	.159	76	.868	.709	0.2	N 69 W	8.11	8.27	48.2	36.8	11.4	...	...	...	...	...	...
15	40.90	.208	73	.776	.573	0.7	S 16 E	4.87	6.32	54.8	28.8	26.0	...	...	...	...	...	...
16	49.90	.299	82	.578	.289	0.8	S 26 E	5.05	5.47	45.6	25.0	20.6	.020	1.0	...	...	.020	1.0
17	51.97	.310	80	.570	.260	0.8	S 13 E	5.09	7.95	49.2	28.8	20.4	...	...	...	...	...	...
18	53.57	.304	76	.646	.342	0.7	N 47 W	9.55	9.91	59.5	36.8	22.7	...	...	...	...	...	...
19	40.40	.178	72	.596	.418	0.6	S 70 E	2.80	13.93	63.0	45.0	18.6	.510	4.3	0.7	7.0	.510	4.3
20	34.83	.166	82	.617	.461	0.9	S 59 W	8.11	9.45	61.2	40.2	21.1	...	...	...	...	...	...
21	30.98	.135	67	.630	.495	0.8	N 58 W	6.28	6.49	55.3	34.4	20.8	.070	7.0	...	...	.070	7.0
22	34.87	.150	77	.571	.421	0.8	N 36 W	23.8	23.8	49.4	28.6	13.6	...	...	...	...	...	...
23	41.40	.171	75	.432	.261	1.0	N 78 W	11.11	12.57	33.8	24.4	9.4	...	...	...	...	...	...
24	43.87	.214	82	.250	.036	0.9	S 29 W	15.29	16.99	27.4	13.0	14.4	.015	1.0	...	...	.015	1.0
25	41.03	.222	77	.580	.358	0.8	S 74 W	12.85	15.16	45.6	30.8	14.8	.250	6.0	...	...	.250	6.0
26	43.77	.148	54	.731	.583	0.3	N 48 W	14.38	15.67	49.8	29.0	20.8	.045	0.5	...	...	.045	0.5
27	44.25	.236	81	.730	.493	1.0	S 32 W	8.68	8.68	52.4	31.0	21.4	...	...	...	...	...	...
28	—	—	—	—	—	—	S 65 W	10.62	11.80	53.0	30.4	22.6	—	—	—	—	—	—
29	—	—	—	—	—	—	S 60 E	6.13	7.92	52.6	36.6	16.0	.420	7.0	—	—	.420	7.0
	45.39	0.247	78	29.551	29.304	0.7	N 82 W	4.91	9.88	52.60	34.55	18.05	2.485	47.3	0.8	9.8	2.565	57.1

GENERAL METEOROLOGICAL ABSTRACT,—NOVEMBER, 1855.

Days.	DAILY MEANS.						WIND.			Extremes of Temperature.			RAIN.		SNOW.		Rain and Melted Snow	
	Temperature of the Air.	Pressure of Vapour.	Relative Humidity.	Barometric Pressure.	Pressure of Dry Air.	Clouded Sky.	Resultant Direction.	Resultant Velocity.	Mean Velocity.	Maximum.	Minimum.	Difference.	Depth in Inches.	Approximate duration in hours.	Depth in Inches.	Approximate duration in hours.	Depth in Inches.	Approximate duration in hours.
	°							Miles.	Miles.									
1	46.92	0.237	73	29.616	29.378	0.8	N 14 W	8.26	10.24	54.0	33.2	20.8	*	*			*	*
2	40.08	.108	67	.905	.642	0.4	N 89 E	6.81	7.24	45.8	26.4	19.4						
3	33.43	.157	77	.829	.672	0.4	N 21 E	6.78	7.23	43.2	23.6	19.6						
4							N 70 E	3.40	5.60	44.5	26.8	17.7						
5	46.03	.254	82	.760	.504	0.9	N 78 E	11.40	11.89	39.0	13.0	13.0	1.030	15.0			1.030	15.0
6	49.62	.295	84	.602	.307	1.0	N 88 E	7.79	7.84	52.8	39.0	9.8	1.005	14.0			1.005	14.0
7	46.58	.328	98	.656	.228	1.0	N 20 W	2.87	6.01	52.0	33.8	10.6						
8	43.15	.214	77	.994	.660	0.1	S 88 W	4.09	6.02	49.5	27.8	11.99						
9	40.95	.193	76	30.059	.866	0.1	East	4.89	6.35	46.0	32.0	14.0						
10	41.53	.223	80	29.790	.557	0.9	N 86 E	3.87	4.53	49.2	36.4	12.8						
11	50.13	.341	95	.500	.249	0.7	N 77 E	18.76	13.89	52.5	42.8	9.7	.020	9.0			.020	9.0
12	45.77	.505	68	.828	.623	0.0	N 16 E	3.14	8.87	54.4	39.0	15.4	.120	10.0			.120	10.0
13	43.97	.190	68	.872	.676	0.3	N 54 W	8.75	9.05	51.0	26.8	24.2						
14	47.02	.269	84	.610	.341	1.0	N 97 W	2.08	3.15	54.6	31.6	23.0						
15	38.35	.181	74	.634	.453	0.7	N 41 E	2.09	3.97	59.2	41.0	19.2	.130	2.0	0.5	2.0	.130	2.0
16	30.70	.147	84	.374	.227	0.9	N 32 W	13.80	16.07	46.4	23.2	23.2	.180	4.0	0.5	5.0	.230	6.0
17							N 70 E	11.09	17.09	37.0	13.0	13.0			*	*	.050	5.0
18							N 97 W	15.21	15.71	37.5	20.5	12.5			2.0	4.0		
19	28.90	.130	80	.895	.755	0.6	N 93 W	12.39	12.91	42.2	19.2	13.0					.020	4.0
20	29.20	.146	69	.906	.760	0.8	N 44 E	6.88	13.07	31.2	13.2	18.0						
21	34.53	.152	73	.506	.350	1.0	N 64 W	15.96	19.88	41.2	21.0	20.2						
22	27.55	.120	72	.946	.826	0.8	S 88 W	7.11	9.50	38.0	20.0	18.0						
23	37.78	.163	72	.484	.158	0.9	S 94 W	18.52	23.21	43.0	19.8	23.2	.005	0.2			.005	0.2
24	28.35	.126	80	.793	.657	0.1	N 72 W	9.18	10.27	37.6	20.0	17.6						
25							N 61 E	8.12	11.93	45.2	34.4	10.8	.100	3.0			.100	3.0
26	35.92	.160	76	.495	.265	0.7	N 83 W	13.07	14.61	42.8	27.8	14.4	*	*	*	*	*	*
27	39.52	.157	65	.226	.069	0.5	N 59 W	13.77	13.83	46.0	30.2	15.8						
28	31.13	.125	68	.187	.012	0.7	N 29 W	15.43	18.10	32.0	15.5	26.5						
29	24.80	.105	77	.526	.422	0.4	N 70 W	10.28	10.93	30.0	21.0	9.0						
30	32.68	.137	73	.586	.449	0.1	S 44 W	10.87	11.39	39.8	32.2	7.6						
	38.58	0.190	77	29.004	29.475	0.6	N 66 W	3.18	10.81	45.50	28.74	16.76	4.590	57.2	3.0	11.0	4.890	68.2

GENERAL METEOROLOGICAL ABSTRACT,—DECEMBER, 1855.

Days.	DAILY MEANS.						WIND.			EXTREMES OF TEMPERATURE.			SNOW.		RAIN.		HAIL AND MELTED SNOW.	
	Temperature of the Air.	Pressure of Vapour.	Relative Humidity.	Barometric Pressure.	Pressure of Dry Air.	Clouded Sky.	Resultant Direction.	Resultant Velocity.	Mean Velocity.	Maximum.	Minimum.	Difference.	Depth in Inches.	Approximate duration in hours.	Depth in Inches.	Approximate duration in hours.	Depth in Inches.	Approximate duration in hours.
	°							Miles.	Miles.									
1	41.78	0.194	76	29.268	29.074	0.6	S 31 W	10.02	10.31	46.4	35.0	11.4	...	...	...	...	0.145	1.5
2	32.88	.146	75	.380	.294	0.3	S 77 W	13.15	14.23	46.2	30.8	15.4	...	*	...	*	*	*
3	34.23	.144	74	.654	.510	0.4	S 84 W	15.34	15.55	37.0	26.8	10.2	...	...	...	...	.030	1.5
4	37.52	.167	75	.698	.531	0.1	S 63 W	9.69	10.05	40.0	26.4	13.6	...	...	...	...	*	*
5	37.89	.179	79	.697	.518	0.6	S 35 W	6.69	6.91	45.6	29.2	16.4	...	...	...	...	.030	1.5
6	32.82	.144	79	.992	.848	0.4	West	8.60	9.02	44.5	29.5	15.0	...	...	...	...	*	*
7	35.97	.175	82	.578	.403	0.7	N 6 W	5.02	7.00	42.8	25.8	17.0	...	...	...	...	1.030	13.5
8						1.0	S 69 E	11.75	11.78	38.2	31.4	6.8	*	*	18.5	13.5	.140	1.1
9	23.98	.108	76	.029	28.926	0.8	N 56 W	10.09	17.84	47.0	26.0	21.0	...	...	1.1	...	*	*
10	21.30	.074	68	.786	.711	0.3	N 61 W	16.85	19.30	28.4	15.6	12.8	...	...	...	...	...	...
11	24.70	.109	80	30.102	.933	0.7	N 61 W	16.14	15.59	26.8	15.4	11.4	0.6	5.5	...	5.5	.060	5.5
12	25.69	.120	84	30.007	.887	1.0	S 88 E	3.02	6.82	29.2	17.0	12.2	...	...	...	...	...	...
13	30.30	.152	87	29.926	.774	1.0	N 1 W	5.39	5.57	31.6	15.0	16.6	...	...	...	...	.485	11.0
14	38.42	.195	94	.626	.431	1.0	S 89 E	13.23	14.15	36.8	23.6	15.2	...	...	...	...	.015	0.2
15						1.0	S 40 W	2.17	4.29	42.0	30.2	11.8	0.1	1.0	...	1.0	.010	1.0
16						1.0	S 56 W	5.07	6.73	42.2	32.4	9.8	...	...	...	...	...	...
17	31.30	.133	73	.477	.345	0.7	S 85 W	17.33	17.94	37.4	25.8	11.6	...	...	...	...	...	...
18	22.05	.081	67	.825	.744	0.7	N 88 W	10.44	10.66	25.8	17.4	8.4	...	...	...	...	...	...
19	22.12	.093	76	.924	.831	0.4	N 41 W	2.65	3.51	32.0	18.2	13.8	4.6	11.0	...	11.0	.460	11.0
20	28.35	.131	80	.866	.735	0.8	S 23 W	5.35	5.78	25.2	14.0	11.2	...	...	...	...	...	...
21	38.67	.165	72	.435	.267	1.0	S 35 W	6.91	9.69	37.0	16.5	20.5	...	...	...	...	...	...
22	32.90	.165	89	.312	.147	1.0	N 36 E	7.42	11.03	42.5	31.6	10.7	...	...	...	...	...	...
23						1.0	S 76 W	12.66	14.23	34.2	22.4	11.8	5.2	12.2	...	...	.520	12.2
24	16.00	.075	76	.985	.910	0.7	N 29 W	4.36	6.58	36.2	14.8	21.4	3.8	9.0	...	9.0	.360	9.0
25						0.4	N 9 E	8.91	9.08	23.5	14.6	8.9	...	...	...	...	...	...
26	11.12	.057	74	.775	.718	0.6	S 80 W	15.82	16.54	19.8	6.7	13.1	0.2	1.0	...	1.0	.020	1.0
27	13.25	.064	75	.017	.953	1.0	N 74 W	16.45	16.59	16.6	5.8	10.8	...	...	...	...	...	...
28	12.28	.064	78	30.598	.834	1.0	N 49 W	6.44	9.28	18.9	5.5	13.3	15.0	15.0	...	15.0	1.500	15.0
29	6.60	.052	77	29.608	.556	0.7	N 29 E	14.82	16.28	20.4	−5.2	25.6	...	...	...	...	...	...
30						0.4	N 29 E	16.37	16.56	10.8	−2.2	13.0	...	...	...	...	...	...
31	17.73	.082	79	.686	.604	...	S 63 W	12.29	12.43	22.0	10.6	11.4	...	...	...	...	...	...
	26.99	0.123	77	29.702	29.579	0.7	S 88 W	5.29	11.38	32.91	18.75	14.16	29.5	54.7	1.845	28.8	4.705	93.5

GENERAL METEOROLOGICAL ABSTRACT.—JANUARY, 1856.

Days	DAILY MEANS.					Sky. Clouded	WIND.			EXTREMES OF TEMPERATURE.			RAIN.		SNOW.		RAIN AND MELTED SNOW.	
	Temperature of the Air.	Pressure of Vapour.	Relative Humidity.	Barometric Pressure.	Pressure of Dry Air.		Resultant Direction.	Resultant Velocity.	Mean Velocity.	Maximum.	Minimum.	Difference.	Depth in Inches.	Approximate duration in hours.	Depth in Inches.	Approximate duration in hours.	Depth in Inches.	Approximate duration in hours.
								Miles.	Miles.									
1	18.05	0.085	81	29.918	29.833	0.6	S 80 W	4.57	4.64	22.4	10.8	11.6						
2	21.82	.097	79	.843	.746	0.5	S 87 E	0.90	2.16	30.0	12.5	17.2						
3	21.52	.093	75	.685	.592	0.0	West	12.53	13.63	31.6	3.4	28.2			*	18.2	.200	18.2
4	11.98	.057	72	30.179	30.122	1.0	N 73 E	4.32	6.53	18.2	7.4	10.8						
5	13.60	.070	91	29.833	29.763	1.0	N 33 E	12.34	14.73	18.9	7.5	11.3			2.0	6.0	.100	6.0
6							S 33 W	2.96	6.55	23.0	6.0	17.0						
7	24.78	.121	87	.484	.314	0.9	S 43 W	12.75	17.82	32.4	-1.8	34.0			1.0	0.5	*	*
8	1.87	.032	72	.530	.499	0.1	S 76 W	24.14	24.19	1.8	-12.0	13.8						
9	−4.03	.033	65	.630	.597	0.0	S 76 W	20.46	20.56	6.5	-12.0	18.5						
10	15.02	.074	78	.853	.779	0.3	S 80 W	15.81	16.29	25.0	5.2	19.8			4.4	10.3	.440	10.3
11	9.62	.060	85	30.060	.990	0.6	S 67 W	5.10	7.25	19.0	-4.1	23.1			2.8	10.5	.280	10.5
12	22.60	.116	89	29.770	.654	0.1	N 2 E	10.93	11.64	25.2	5.7	19.8			0.1	4.0	.010	4.0
13							N 25 W	10.00	11.17	12.5	-6.9	19.4						
14	18.58	.088	84	.510	.422	1.0	N 71 W	7.14	8.71	24.1	-2.6	23.7			0.5	5.8	.050	5.8
15	17.43	.081	79	.528	.447	0.6	S 66 W	14.98	15.54	17.2	8.6	8.4						
16	23.03	.103	80	.250	.147	1.0	S 67 W	8.66	8.73	25.3	12.5	15.5			*	1.0	*	1.0
17	20.30	.139	85	.312	.173	1.0	N 39 W	3.37	7.47	33.3	22.8	8.1						
18	20.95	.142	85	.485	.293	2.0	N 5 E	18.34	18.50	34.4	10.8	19.5						
19	10.40	.057	74	.711	.654	0.6	N 4 W	9.19	9.37	13.0	-1.2	12.8			1.2	8.0	.120	8.0
20						0.4	N 24 W	8.73	9.43	24.0	2.0	16.5						
21	9.15	.052	72	.590	.578	0.8	N 64 W	2.53	2.59	20.2	0.8	19.4			*	0.6	*	0.6
22	18.05	.090	84	.696	.545	0.4	S 63 W	12.47	12.65	26.0	13.0	13.0						
23	19.25	.085	78	.707	.622	0.7	S 69 W	13.39	17.48	27.0	-2.0	26.0						
24	16.80	.071	71	.716	.645	0.0	N 42 W	8.56	9.20	11.6	-3.8	15.6						
25	2.42	.035	63	30.234	30.199	0.2	N 69 W	3.56	3.81	20.9	10.0	10.9						
26	10.15	.058	74	30.109	30.051		N 6 W	10.10	10.19									
27						1.0	N 34 E	2.80	2.96	20.3	8.2	11.0			1.1	11.0	.110	11.0
28	21.93	.098	81	29.200	29.192	0.9	N 27 W	2.33	2.96	23.8	8.8	15.0			0.3	7.5	.030	7.5
29	21.33	.094	78	.399	.305	0.8	S 69 W	8.05	8.23	23.8	8.2	15.6			*	4.0	.020	4.0
30	16.52	.071	74	.385	.313	0.7	S 74 W	16.74	16.85	26.8	9.8	16.2			0.2	4.0		
31	15.08	.071	77	.502	.431	1.0	S 58 W	3.58	3.91	20.2	9.2	11.0			*	1.0		
	16.02	0.080	78	29.670	29.589	0.7	N 75 W	5.24	10.00	22.65	6.03	16.03			13.6	88.4	1.300	88.4

GENERAL METEOROLOGICAL ABSTRACT.—FEBRUARY, 1856.

TORONTO METEOROLOGICAL OBSERVATIONS.

Days	DAILY MEANS.						WIND.			Extremes of Temperature.			RAIN.		SNOW.		Rain and Melted Snow.	
	Temperature of the Air.	Vapour. Pressure of	Relative Humidity.	Barometric Pressure.	Pressure of Dry Air.	Clouded Sky.	Resultant Direction.	Resultant Velocity.	Mean Velocity.	Maximum.	Minimum.	Difference.	Depth in Inches.	Approximate duration in hours.	Depth in Inches.	Approximate duration in hours.	Depth in Inches.	Approximate duration in hours.
								Miles.	Miles.									
1	21.50	0.104	84	29.171	29.067	0.5	S 74 W	12.84	14.12	30.5	4.6	25.9	...	...	0.4	6.3	.040	6.3
2	2.70	.042	77	.356	.314	0.3	N 68 W	15.05	15.17	16.8	−7.0	23.8	...	...	...	...	...	...
3	8.20	.046	69	.515	.468	0.6	S 85 W	11.88	12.59	10.2	−5.8	16.0	...	...	...	...	...	...
4	9.27	.054	76	.580	.526	0.4	S 79 W	18.38	18.44	12.0	3.0	9.0	...	...	1.6	7.0	.160	7.0
5	9.85	.057	76	.929	.872	0.9	S 73 W	13.03	18.06	16.0	−1.5	17.5	...	...	0.3	3.0	.030	3.0
6	25.23	.119	85	.450	.331	0.8	S 54 W	2.68	7.01	25.0	0.2	25.0	...	...	*		*	
7	6.73	.047	74	.610	.563	0.4	N 67 W	7.35	11.00	30.6	4.0	26.6	...	...	...	...	...	...
8	9.80	.054	73	.684	.630	0.6	N 25 W	5.09	5.94	16.0	−0.2	16.2	...	...	...	...	...	...
9							S 88 W	6.84	7.08	19.2	−1.8	21.0	...	...	2.3	2.3		
10							S 56 W	9.32	9.53	29.5	9.4	20.1	...	...	5.0	17.0	.500	17.0
11	28.90	.145	90	.175	.080	1.0	N 43 W	7.95	11.64	33.4	8.0	25.4	...	...	*		*	
12	0.10	.032	62	.342	.310	0.4	N 65 W	8.21	18.59	10.0	−18.7	28.7	...	...	...	...	...	...
13	−0.88	.027	77	.832	.805	0.1	N 88 W	6.13	6.47	5.8	−18.7	24.5	...	...	...	...	...	...
14	1.82	.035	66	.664	.629	0.2	S 75 W	10.22	10.46	12.2	−10.8	23.0	...	...	...	...	...	...
15	19.00	.091	88	.129	.038	1.0	S 46 W	13.65	13.88	26.4	9.2	17.2	...	...	0.3	6.5	.030	6.5
16	21.17	.090	83	.897	.798	0.8	N 52 W	12.88	15.37	31.8	5.5	26.3	...	...	2.0	8.0	.200	8.0
17							N 65 W	18.40	14.37	12.5	−0.5	13.0	...	...	0.1	0.5	.010	0.5
18	3.80	.038	68	.600	.562	0.0	N 50 W	14.55	15.67	11.2	−1.0	12.2	...	...	...	...	...	...
19	16.32	.069	62	.721	.651	0.5	S 68 W	12.38	13.93	24.8	4.0	20.8	...	...	...	...	...	...
20	29.87	.134	77	.414	.280	0.9	N 88 W	11.98	12.40	34.8	14.5	20.3	...	...	...	...	...	...
21	25.22	.110	80	.400	.290	0.4	S 83 W	4.81	5.10	27.8	13.6	24.2	...	...	...	...	...	...
22	25.33	.116	81	.369	.253	0.6	S 33 W	0.28	3.21	36.8	12.2	24.6	...	...	...	...	...	...
23	27.06	.110	78	.222	.112	0.5	N 42 W	13.13	14.23	36.3	10.5	25.8	...	...	...	...	...	...
24							N G4 W	6.07	7.80	28.2	12.8	15.4	...	...	...	...	...	...
25	19.30	.082	75	.371	.289	0.5	N 70 W	4.45	6.17	29.0	6.2	22.8	...	...	...	...	...	...
26	18.65	.077	72	.582	.505	0.1	N 31 W	2.92	6.28	29.5	6.2	23.3	...	...	...	...	...	...
27	21.05	.089	75	.563	.474	0.6	N 42 B	9.01	10.81	29.1	10.5	18.0	...	...	...	...	...	...
28	22.60	.097	76	.657	.560	0.6	N 3 E	1.42	4.97	30.0	12.8	17.2	...	...	...	...	...	...
29	25.87	.114	80	.772	.658	1.0	N 57 W	2.86	5.37	32.8	20.0	12.8	...	...	...	...	...	...
	15.09°	0.080	76	29.488	29.409	0.6	N 81 W	7.70	10.71	24.22	3.57	20.65	...	...	9.7	50.6	0.970	50.6

GENERAL METEOROLOGICAL ABSTRACT,—MARCH, 1856.

Days	DAILY MEANS.					WIND.			EXTREMES OF TEMPERATURE.			RAIN.		SNOW.		RAIN AND MELTED SNOW	
	Temperature of the Air.	Pressure of Vapour.	Relative Humidity.	Barometric Pressure.	Pressure of Dry Air.	Clouded Sky.	Resultant Direction.	Resultant Velocity.	Mean Velocity.	Maximum.	Minimum.	Difference.	Depth in Inches.	Approximate duration in hours.	Depth in Inches.	Approximate duration in hours.	Depth in Inches.	Approximate duration in hours.
1	24.15	0.113	84	29.591	29.478	1.0	N 66 E	14.63	15.00	28.2	20.0	8.2			4.5	17.5	0.450	17.5
2	19.57	.081	73	.591	.528	0.4	N 76 W	13.28	15.7	28.6	11.6	17.0			0.3	3.0	.030	3.0
3	24.72	.111	82	.009	.303	0.5	S 69 W	8.90	11.01	25.5	7.4	18.1			3.4	3.0	.340	3.0
4	22.22	.090	73	.414	.370	0.7	S 82 W	17.11	20.85	33.2	11.5	21.7			0.4	5.0	.040	5.0
5	16.40	.071	72	.460	.384	0.4	S 56 W	12.41	13.02	27.6	13.4	14.2			0.2	3.5	.020	3.5
6	15.02	.076	83	.425	.370	0.8	N 64 W	14.93	15.36	24.5	2.0	22.5						
7	1.08	.035	69	.446	.370	0.1	S 70 W	11.45	14.24	−2.5	−26.9	24.4						
8				.694	.659		N 67 W	14.04	14.33	−2.4	−10.8							
9							N 59 W	7.66	8.71	6.8	−14.0	20.4			1.9	4.0	.190	4.0
10	6.55	.052	78	.627	.575	0.1	S 73 W	18.75	19.15	20.2	−12.2	32.4						
11	14.40	.053	65	.363	.304	0.3	N 84 W	17.35	18.52	22.6	8.2	14.4						
12	18.28	.071	76	.463	.392	0.6	N 69 W	11.96	12.19	24.8	11.0	13.8						
13	21.90	.085	71	.724	.638	0.5	N 34 W	0.64	7.93	30.2	14.4	15.8			0.2	2.5	.020	2.5
14	26.00	.102	70	.721	.619	0.6	S 57 W	6.27	8.61	33.0	15.0	18.0						
15	28.77	.120	75	.718	.597	0.9	S 90 W	8.66	8.88	34.0	21.0	13.0						
16							N 59 W	5.25	5.66	35.2	18.8	16.4						
17	30.65	.115	68	.797	.682	0.3	S 86 W	4.55	5.36	40.0	18.8	20.5			*	3.0	*	3.0
18	28.55	.118	74	.769	.651	0.4	N 64 E	3.37	3.63	39.6	22.5	17.1						
19	31.60	.152	86	.416	.263	1.0	N 26 E	1.52	4.19	35.2	20.8	14.4						
20	29.82	.126	73	.382	.256	0.6	S 69 W	0.97	2.83	39.0	23.0	15.0						
21							N 19 W	2.92	5.36	41.0	25.5	15.5						
22	31.90	.129	72	.595	.397	0.1	N 58 W	2.31	4.43	38.8	18.2	20.5			1.0	5.0	.100	5.0
23							S 15 E	4.36	5.48	38.2	18.5	19.7			3.6	17.0	.360	17.0
24	34.35	.174	88	.252	.078	1.0	N 20 W	8.24	10.70	37.0	29.0	8.0						
25	33.18	.146	77	.542	.396	1.0	N 58 W	11.79	11.79	41.4	27.2	14.2						
26	30.50	.132	78	.466	.334	0.7	N 71 W	10.65	15.90	38.5	22.5	16.0			0.5	9.0	.050	9.0
27	33.98	.086	66	.399	.306	0.7	N 35 W	15.81	21.05	38.0	15.5	12.5			0.2	3.0	.020	3.0
28	20.50	.091	79	.507	.416	1.0	N 49 W	17.21	18.53	24.1	15.0	9.1						
29	21.68	.072	60	.660	.588	0.1	N 63 W	15.65	15.91	31.8	13.0	18.5						
30	20.90						N 28 W	11.15	12.12	31.8	10.8	21.0						
31		.076	64	.022	.947	0.0	N 36 W	3.49	5.63	31.8	10.2	21.6						
	23.06	0.099	74	29.559	29.460	0.5	N 71 W	7.68	11.39	30.47	12.87	17.60			16.2	75.5	1.620	75.5

GENERAL METEOROLOGICAL ABSTRACT,—APRIL, 1856.

Days.	DAILY MEANS.						WIND.			Extremes of Temperature.			RAIN.		SNOW.		Rain and Melted Snow	
	Temperature of the Air.	Pressure of Vapour.	Relative Humidity.	Barometric Pressure.	Pressure of Dry Air.	Clouded Sky.	Resultant Direction.	Resultant Velocity.	Mean Velocity.	Maximum.	Minimum.	Difference.	Depth in Inches.	Approximate duration in hours.	Depth in Inches.	Approximate duration in hours.	Depth in Inches.	Approximate duration in hours.
	°						°	Miles.	Miles.			°						
1	27.55	0.124	80	29.961	29.837	0.1	S 76 E	1.75	2.51	35.8	14.2	21.6						
2	34.92	.172	85	.431	.259	0.9	S 76 E	4.50	4.95	37.3	32.0	5.3	0.550	9.0			0.550	9.0
3	37.95	.196	86	.250	.054	1.0	S 42 W	6.17	6.35	43.2	33.5	9.7	.175	9.5			.175	9.5
4	34.45	.163	82	.474	.311	1.0	N 43 W	6.93	7.37	37.6	29.8	7.8	.010	2.5	0.1	2.5	.010	2.5
5	36.72	.168	70	.636	.473	0.7	N 39 W	5.81	6.21	45.0	31.5	13.5						
6						0.4	S 37 W	1.07	2.42	45.8	22.0	15.6						
7	40.92	.171	69	.709	.538	0.1	S 45 W	1.19	1.19	51.5	29.5	22.0	*	0.5	*		*	0.5
8	41.72	.169	60	.695	.666	0.3	N 68 E	1.31	2.37	54.2	33.5	20.7						
9	45.07	.206	62	.669	.463	0.2	N 54 W	7.23	11.89	58.8	29.4	20.4						
10	35.75	.129	71	.944	.815	1.0	S 68 E	2.51	4.42	46.0	28.0	17.4	.230	3.0			.230	3.0
11	39.58	.172	83	.611	.439	0.8	N 6 W	1.75	2.17	50.0	30.9	19.1	.545	9.5			.545	9.5
12	36.67	.183		.325	.142	0.8	S 45 W	12.87	13.21	43.4	23.2	20.2						
13							S 2 W	2.72	5.33	34.8	22.8	12.0						
14			75	.602	.441	1.0	N 89 E	0.84	1.44	40.5	33.2	7.3	*	*	*		*	*
15	39.95	.161	83	.501	.296	1.0	N 84 E	15.31	15.44	43.2	36.2	7.0	.705	10.8			.705	10.8
16	44.13	.203	87	.496	.247	0.5	S 81 W	5.25	6.01	53.5	37.8	15.7						
17	46.27	.249	82	.427	.170	1.0	S 65 W	0.88	1.82	53.4	37.8	15.6	.015	0.5			.015	0.5
18	46.08	.257	80	.391	.147	0.9	N 23 E	2.15	3.94	48.3	32.2	16.1	.115	1.3			.115	1.3
19	44.20	.244	64	.645	.462	0.3	N 7 E	6.00	8.91	50.6	32.2	18.3						
20		.188					S 7 E	13.86	14.16	47.8	31.5	16.3						
21	43.35	.227	81	.466	.239	1.0	N 18 E	7.09	8.31	51.2	34.2	17.0	.315	9.0			.315	9.0
22	37.22	.202	91	.237	.035	0.7	S 46 E	1.45	2.94	42.4	29.8	12.6	.070	5.5			.070	5.5
23	41.25	.209	81	.417	.208	0.4	S 84 E	2.08	2.69	52.8	32.7	20.1						
24	49.55	.233	81	.535	.302	0.5	N 2 W	1.31	3.48	54.4	36.2	18.2	.035	2.0			.035	2.0
25	45.02	.251	83	.798	.548	0.0	N 81 E	1.35	2.97	63.2	39.0	24.2						
26	52.53	.269	66	.758	.489	0.3	S 80 E	4.22	4.67	63.5	41.6	21.9	.025	2.0			.025	2.0
27						0.5	S 20 E	0.65	2.28	65.2	45.4	19.8						
28	59.83	.271	56	.461	.190	0.2	S 67 W	7.70	10.04	72.2	45.5	26.7						
29	53.10	.249	64	.628	.379	0.2	N 29 W	3.46	7.76	67.4	39.0	28.4						
30	47.75	.212	65	.847	.635	0.7	N 83 E	13.84	14.24	54.6	42.2	12.4						
	42.27	0.208	75	29.579	29.376	0.6	N 29 E	1.64	6.05	50.47	33.39	17.08	2.780	62.6	0.1	2.5	2.790	65.1

GENERAL METEOROLOGICAL ABSTRACT,—MAY, 1856.

Days.	DAILY MEANS.						WIND.			EXTREMES OF TEMPERATURE.			RAIN.		SNOW.		RAIN AND MELTED SNOW	
	Temperature of the Air.	Pressure of Vapour.	Relative Humidity.	Barometric Pressure.	Pressure of Dry Air.	Clouded Sky.	Resultant Direction.	Resultant Velocity.	Mean Velocity.	Maximum.	Minimum.	Difference.	Depth in Inches.	Approximate duration in hours.	Depth in Inches.	Approximate duration in hours.	Depth in Inches.	Approximate duration in hours.
	°							Miles.	Miles.	°	°	°						
1	46.10	0.236	77	29.694	29.458	1.0	N 86 E	20.75	20.89	59.0	37.0	22.0	0.790	13.0				
2	44.08	.262	92	.391	.129	1.0	N 67 E	9.57	10.25	47.6	37.0	10.6	.195	8.2				
3	46.30	.216	70	.547	.331	0.4	N 10 W	8.27	11.91	56.2	31.2	25.0						
4	44.27	.179	62	.892	.713	0.7	N 22 W	15.30	15.62	52.8	34.0	18.8						
5	48.08	.175	53	.814	.639	0.8	N 81 E	3.88	8.77	52.0	32.0	20.0						
6	50.00	.193	55	.671	.378	0.7	N 79 E	12.19	12.47	51.8	38.2	13.6						
7	45.10	.249	94	.513	.264	1.0	N 81 E	9.93	10.47	57.2	42.0	15.2	.330	15.0				
8	43.12	.239	86	.544	.305	1.0	N 66 E	10.82	11.01	46.0	39.0	7.0	.095	6.5				
9	54.47	.264	64	.498	.234	0.2	N 68 E	4.86	5.29	47.6	35.8	11.8						
10							N 29 W	5.34	9.43	65.4	41.5	23.9						
11	49.83	.225	64	.626	.401	0.6	N 56 W	5.99	5.99	71.0	50.0	21.0	.055	1.5				
12	45.28	.219	74	.830	.611	0.7	N 11 W	13.95	14.21	56.4	39.5	16.9						
13	52.73	.217	51	.613	.396	0.8	N 74 E	6.14	6.45	51.6	40.2	11.4						
14	58.62	.317	61	.543	.147	0.8	S 76 E	4.31	4.67	60.4	40.0	20.4	.235	8.5				
15	50.53	.283	81	.658	.388	0.3	S 60 W	5.23	9.14	66.2	45.5	20.7	.125	2.0				
16	54.25	.302	77	.670	.388	0.3	N 11 W	5.85	7.25	62.0	40.0	22.0						
17			72	.486	.184	1.0	N 73 W	8.44	8.88	60.6	45.6	15.0	2.135	12.0				
18							N 32 W	0.84	1.35	59.8	47.8	11.7	.026	1.5				
19	57.85	.361	77	.321		0.4	S 70 W	4.48	9.92	65.8	50.2	15.6						
20	56.50	.297	60	.501	28.960	0.1	N 19 W	13.54	13.84	59.0	39.0	20.0						
21	49.58	.208	60	.701	29.274	0.0	N 28 W	2.59	7.70	60.5	39.5	21.7						
22	53.88	.251	62	.760	.553	0.2	S 17 W	2.56	3.21	64.2	44.0	20.2						
23	63.72	.398	71	.610	.212	0.3	N 41 E	5.78	7.23	75.0	56.0	19.0						
24							N 45 W	13.19	14.98	82.8	42.5	14.2	.110	3.0				
25							N 32 W	17.84	18.46	57.8	42.5	15.3						
26	57.53	.298	66	.613		0.1	N 29 W	5.80	6.65	71.4	43.0	28.4						
27	53.10	.322	82	.305	28.820	0.9	S 65 E	0.88	1.48	61.0	48.0	13.0	.355	8.0				
28	53.48	.306	75	.229	28.973	0.6	N 32 W	12.65	12.93	64.8	41.2	23.6	*	*				
29	42.42	.215	79	.383	28.923	1.0	N 1 W	6.24	9.87	46.0	34.0	12.0	.030	6.2				
30	41.02	.167	67	.620	29.167	0.9	N 41 W	12.56	13.22	46.4	31.2	15.2						
31	51.67	.225	60	.717	.463	0.5	S 86 W	9.00	10.42	62.8	37.2	25.6	.100	4.0				
	50.52	0.259	71	29.592	29.324	0.6	N 0 4 E	3.99	9.81	59.56	40.63	18.93	4.580	89.4	*	*		*

TORONTO METEOROLOGICAL OBSERVATIONS.

GENERAL METEOROLOGICAL ABSTRACT,—JUNE, 1856.

Days.	DAILY MEANS.						WIND.			Extremes of Temperature.			RAIN.		SNOW.		Rain and Melted Snow	
	Temperature of the Air.	Pressure of Vapour.	Relative Humidity.	Barometric Pressure.	Pressure of Dry Air.	Clouded Sky.	Resultant Direction.	Resultant Velocity.	Mean Velocity.	Maximum.	Minimum.	Difference.	Depth in Inches.	Approximate duration hours.	Depth in Inches.	Approximate duration in hours.	Depth in Inches.	Approximate duration in hours.
1	54.80	...	...	...	...	...	N 45 W	1.75	5.39	70.0	42.0	28.0	.035	1.0	...	...	...	...
2	61.02	0.364	86	29.651	29.287	0.6	S 22 E	0.83	5.27	63.2	49.3	13.9	.315	1.5	...	...	...	...
3	...	.477	89	.599	.129	1.0	S 77 E	4.0	5.29	70.4	51.5	18.9	.015	0.7	...	...	...	...
4	57.33	.354	78	.731	.377	1.0	N 82 E	4.08	4.79	65.0	17.0	17.0	.160	4.0	...	...	...	...
5	57.17	.306	92	.699	.308	0.8	S 84 E	6.69	6.84	63.2	51.5	12.8	...	...	...	...	...	...
6	53.97	.372	95	.513	.141	0.9	N 64 E	2.97	6.97	61.5	47.2	14.3	...	...	...	...	...	...
7	...	...	...	...	...	...	N 76 E	5.04	5.04	64.4	47.0	17.4	.445	4.0	...	...	...	...
8	...	...	...	...	...	...	S 59 E	0.66	3.81	61.6	51.2	10.4	.055	3.5	...	...	...	...
9	58.38	.410	85	.433	.023	0.7	S 38 W	2.18	3.45	66.4	48.0	18.4	*	*	...	...	...	...
10	61.13	.490	81	.501	.081	0.2	S 19 E	2.20	2.08	73.0	47.0	26.0	...	...	...	...	...	...
11	61.57	.425	80	.505	.080	0.0	S 66 E	3.20	3.58	72.5	51.8	20.7	...	...	...	...	...	...
12	59.08	.419	86	.431	.012	0.7	N 10 E	4.76	4.76	70.8	50.0	20.8	.120	2.8	...	...	...	...
13	59.10	.383	78	.349	28.966	0.6	S 36 E	2.73	5.95	70.0	50.0	20.0	.090	0.9	...	...	...	...
14	55.18	.357	84	.401	29.044	1.0	S 35 E	6.58	7.23	62.8	49.6	13.2	.025	0.4	...	...	...	...
15	...	...	...	...	...	...	S 19 E	6.51	6.29	61.8	44.4	17.4	...	...	...	...	...	...
16	58.15	.348	74	.661	.313	0.1	S 8 W	3.66	3.69	67.8	44.0	23.8	...	...	...	...	...	...
17	60.55	.352	77	.606	.254	0.6	N 89 E	5.02	5.97	69.2	50.4	18.8	...	3.0	...	...	...	...
18	60.43	.430	83	.624	.094	0.4	S 78 E	3.85	4.50	70.6	51.8	18.8	.335	2.7	...	...	...	...
19	65.35	.487	77	.598	.077	0.3	S 27 W	2.08	3.06	68.6	52.6	16.0	...	...	...	...	...	...
20	71.13	.566	70	.564	.032	0.3	S 36 W	5.64	6.10	78.0	58.0	20.0	...	...	...	...	...	...
21	74.57	.575	...	.598	...	0.1	S 34 W	6.28	6.60	80.5	60.0	20.5	...	...	...	...	...	...
22	...	...	...	.677	.102	...	S 31 W	4.43	4.75	83.8	66.0	17.8	...	...	...	...	...	...
23	...	...	...	...	...	...	S 61 E	4.17	5.27	87.8	61.0	26.8	...	...	...	...	...	...
24	59.42	.364	73	.750	.386	0.3	N 84 E	2.93	3.01	66.2	48.5	17.7	.310	...	...	...	...	...
25	60.45	.376	74	.569	.193	0.7	S 84 W	3.71	5.52	67.0	55.8	11.2	...	...	...	...	...	...
26	66.92	.544	84	.493	28.940	0.5	S 50 W	2.08	3.85	78.4	57.5	20.9	...	...	...	...	...	...
27	69.48	.534	76	.488	28.954	0.3	N 43 W	2.85	4.27	78.8	55.4	23.4	...	...	...	...	...	...
28	64.42	.360	62	.623	29.263	0.1	S 27 E	0.59	2.74	72.5	53.8	19.2	...	...	...	...	...	...
29	73.08	.582	73	.351	28.769	0.1	S 35 W	4.59	4.85	83.0	67.0	16.0	.295	3.5	...	...	...	...
30	67.82	.409	71	.444	28.975	0.3	S 49 W	5.24	5.55	59.2	04.0	25.2	...	...	...	...	...	...
							N 65 W	14.60	16.03	79.8	51.0	28.8	...	...	...	...	...	...
	62.11	0.432	70	29.548	29.117	0.5	S 21 W	0.90	5.80	71.59	52.39	19.20	3.200	27.9	...	...	...	...

GENERAL METEOROLOGICAL ABSTRACT.—JULY, 1856.

TORONTO METEOROLOGICAL OBSERVATIONS.

Days	DAILY MEANS.						WIND.			EXTREMES OF TEMPERATURE.			RAIN.		SNOW.		RAIN AND MELTED SNOW	
	Temperature of the Air.	Pressure of Vapour.	Relative Humidity.	Barometric Pressure.	Pressure of Dry Air.	Clouded Sky.	Resultant Direction.	Resultant Velocity.	Mean Velocity.	Maximum.	Minimum.	Difference.	Depth in Inches.	Approximate duration in hours.	Depth in Inches.	Approximate duration in hours.	Depth in Inches.	Approximate duration in hours.
	°							Miles	Miles	°	°	°						
1	60.03	0.354	70	29.818	29.464	0.1	S 64 E	0.16	3.94	67.4	51.0	16.4	...	...	...	...	...	...
2	60.18	.342	68	.660	.318	0.5	S 65 E	1.72	2.39	70.2	52.4	17.8	...	...	...	...	...	...
3	73.52	.505	63	.421	28.917	0.3	N 72 E	3.57	5.70	87.0	60.0	27.0	...	...	...	...	...	...
4	63.50	.394	68	.515	29.121	0.4	S 16 E	0.60	3.05	74.4	49.5	24.9	...	...	...	...	...	...
5	65.82	.439	69	.445	.006	0.2	S 69 W	6.26	7.83	81.2	54.4	26.8	...	...	...	...	...	...
6	...	...	...	...	...	...	N 18 W	10.63	11.37	71.4	50.0	21.4	...	...	...	...	...	...
7	58.78	.318	67	.641	.323	0.3	N 76 E	4.76	6.15	65.0	50.0	15.0	...	1.5	...	...	...	...
8	63.73	.394	68	.643	.246	0.2	N 82 E	7.66	8.10	70.6	57.2	13.4	.375	...	...	...	...	...
9	63.83	.456	72	.600	.144	0.0	N 86 E	3.85	4.54	72.0	57.0	15.0	...	...	...	...	...	...
10	70.57	.511	70	.681	.120	0.2	S 20 E	1.22	1.81	77.0	58.0	19.0	...	...	...	...	...	...
11	68.93	.538	74	.458	28.920	0.6	S 31 W	2.02	3.14	78.8	62.2	16.6	*	*	...	...	...	...
12	...	.560	82	.284	28.724	...	S 53 E	2.54	4.04	75.4	62.0	13.4	...	...	...	...	...	...
13	...	...	...	...	...	0.9	S 92 W	3.81	3.67	81.4	61.4	20.0	.405	2.0	...	...	...	...
14	73.73	.531	79	.528	28.897	0.3	S 33 W	3.42	4.05	84.8	66.0	18.8	...	...	...	...	...	...
15	73.52	.516	75	.586	29.070	0.2	S 29 W	5.21	5.52	81.6	54.6	27.0	...	...	...	...	...	...
16	76.50	.559	67	.631	.042	0.4	S 23 W	5.11	5.52	86.0	63.0	23.0	...	...	...	...	...	...
17	81.77	.691	68	.471	28.790	0.2	S 51 W	7.40	8.88	96.6	69.6	27.0	...	...	...	...	...	...
18	71.00	.423	57	.448	29.024	0.1	N 98 W	13.85	15.86	83.4	58.5	24.9	...	...	...	...	...	...
19	65.90	.415	66	.579	.164	0.5	N 26 W	14.56	14.83	76.4	55.5	20.9	...	...	...	...	...	...
20	...	...	...	...	...	0.5	N 12 W	9.26	10.03	77.8	55.8	22.0	.075	1.0	...	...	...	...
21	66.07	.412	66	.805	.393	0.1	N 56 W	2.71	3.52	79.0	57.0	24.0	...	...	...	...	...	...
22	69.90	.395	58	.804	.409	0.5	S 45 W	3.75	4.41	82.0	57.0	25.0	.115	1.5	...	...	...	...
23	71.38	.542	72	.778	.236	0.2	S 12 W	3.76	4.28	84.2	61.0	23.2	...	...	...	...	...	...
24	75.82	.529	64	.750	.230	0.1	N 10 W	3.71	3.56	88.5	63.5	24.1	...	...	...	...	...	...
25	76.78	.548	63	.662	.114	0.0	S 50 W	4.42	5.37	88.4	64.0	24.4	...	...	...	...	...	...
26	79.30	.537	57	.617	.080	0.7	S 56 W	2.77	4.11	90.2	68.2	22.0	...	...	...	...	...	...
27	...	...	...	...	...	...	S 50 W	5.30	6.00	87.0	67.6	19.4	.085	1.7	...	...	...	...
28	74.70	.007	74	.614	.007	0.6	S 51 W	8.48	3.83	86.5	67.0	19.5	.050	0.6	...	...	...	...
29	70.97	.641	87	.482	28.791	0.6	S 12 W	3.76	4.14	90.2	63.0	17.2	.015	1.5	...	...	...	...
30	73.27	.487	63	.471	28.994	0.5	N 49 W	7.58	7.92	85.7	57.0	28.7	...	...	...	...	...	...
31	67.97	.440	68	.603	29.163	0.7	S 54 E	2.01	4.03	80.0	57.0	23.0	...	...	...	...	...	...
	69.90	0.489	69	29.591	29.102	0.4	N 79 W	1.57	5.84	80.36	59.04	21.32	1.120	9.8				

TORONTO METEOROLOGICAL OBSERVATIONS.

GENERAL METEOROLOGICAL ABSTRACT,—AUGUST, 1856.

Date	DAILY MEANS.						WIND.			Extremes of Temperature.			RAIN.		SNOW.		Rain and Melted Snow	
	Temperature of the Air.	Vapour. Pressure of	Relative Humidity.	Barometric Pressure.	Pressure of Dry Air.	Sky. Clouded	Direction. Resultant	Resultant Velocity.	Mean Velocity.	Maximum.	Minimum.	Difference.	Depth in Inches.	Approximate duration in hours.	Depth in Inches.	Approximate duration in hours.	Depth in Inches.	Approximate duration in hours.
1	71.20	0.485	67	29.689	29.164	0.2	S 70 E	Miles. 3.11	Miles. 5.00	82.2	57.6	24.6	...	...	...	...	...	...
2	72.60	.559	73	.464	28.925	0.6	N 80 E	0.97	6.42	82.7	63.0	19.7	.145	2.0	...	...	...	...
3	...	...	...	...	...	...	N 8 E	3.50	5.69	78.8	58.0	20.8	...	...	...	...	...	...
4	67.17	.454	71	.616	29.162	0.4	S 14 E	1.21	4.35	77.0	55.5	21.5	...	...	...	...	...	...
5	70.63	.454	61	.646	.192	0.1	N 62 W	1.67	5.94	80.0	60.8	19.2	...	...	...	...	...	...
6	70.58	.459	62	.608	.149	0.2	N 12 W	2.67	7.36	79.6	57.0	22.6	.090	2.0	...	...	...	...
7	66.50	.486	77	.436	28.950	0.7	N 83 W	3.43	5.60	73.2	59.0	14.2	.085	0.2	...	...	...	...
8	68.83	.444	72	.448	29.006	0.9	N 83 W	5.96	7.01	72.0	53.8	18.2	*	...	...	...	...	...
9	64.77	.472	78	.562	.090	0.6	N 56 W	6.54	7.61	76.4	55.3	20.7	...	...	...	...	...	...
10	...	...	...	...	...	0.3	S 40 W	5.38	6.38	81.0	55.2	25.5	.020	0.5	...	...	...	...
11	67.63	.379	61	.412	.063	0.6	N 83 W	7.16	7.81	81.0	55.5	25.5	.020	1.0	...	...	...	...
12	63.52	.450	78	.376	28.926	0.3	N 80 W	5.75	7.87	78.0	46.5	31.5	.040	0.5	...	...	...	...
13	63.67	.418	74	.405	.967	0.1	N 85 W	1.49	6.93	74.8	52.8	22.4	...	...	...	...	...	...
14	68.10	.360	66	.525	.165	0.3	N 59 W	4.63	9.31	78.4	50.2	28.2	.050	1.0	...	...	...	...
15	59.88	.383	76	.625	.243	0.4	N 48 W	5.76	6.86	71.0	49.0	22.0	.085	0.5	...	...	...	...
16	60.73	.361	71	.707	.346	0.4	N 31 W	6.15	8.39	70.2	51.6	18.6	...	...	...	...	...	...
17	...	...	...	...	...	...	S 33 W	5.56	5.00	74.6	55.0	19.6	...	...	...	...	...	...
18	...	...	...	...	.090	0.8	S 86 E	5.81	6.65	69.0	56.4	12.6	.405	12.2	...	...	...	...
19	62.17	.419	77	.509	...	1.0	S 87 E	7.26	7.50	64.8	56.5	8.3	...	...	...	...	...	...
20	61.13	.463	88	.204	28.742	0.7	N 34 W	15.22	15.92	74.2	57.0	17.2	...	...	...	...	...	...
21	64.27	.446	76	.218	.772	0.5	N 3 W	5.11	6.86	68.5	53.0	15.5	...	...	...	...	...	...
22	62.52	.436	79	.411	.976	0.6	N 28 W	2.56	4.90	75.4	56.2	19.2	.735	3.0	...	...	...	...
23	65.10	.466	73	.528	29.062	0.6	N 82 W	6.14	8.63	79.4	58.5	20.9	...	...	...	...	...	...
24	66.45	.516	82	.450	.934	0.7	N 15 W	10.46	10.63	75.0	46.0	29.0	.020	0.5	...	...	...	...
25	...	...	...	...	...	0.6	S 11 W	9.03	9.09	60.5	41.5	19.0	...	...	...	...	...	...
26	50.88	.253	70	.636	29.384	0.4	N 29 W	2.77	3.41	66.5	44.8	21.7	...	...	...	...	...	...
27	56.58	.299	68	.743	.444	0.3	S 1 W	2.50	2.80	71.5	45.0	26.5	...	...	...	...	...	...
28	59.17	.374	77	.707	.333	1.0	S 87 W	3.08	5.47	74.8	52.2	22.6	.055	0.2	...	...	...	...
29	63.88	.423	74	.605	.082	0.6	S 87 W	8.57	8.78	63.8	45.0	18.8	...	...	...	...	...	...
30	57.73	.328	71	.501	.173	0.6	N 65 W	4.13	6.60	68.0	45.0	23.0	...	...	...	...	...	...
31	57.60	.304	66	.639	.335	0.0	N 1 E	8.32	8.62	68.2	43.4	24.8	...	...	...	...	...	...
	63.59	0.419	73	29.521	29.102	0.5	N 50 W	2.88	7.09	73.74	52.95	20.79	1.680	23.6				

GENERAL METEOROLOGICAL ABSTRACT,—SEPTEMBER, 1856.

Days.	DAILY MEANS.					WIND.			EXTREMES OF TEMPERATURE.			RAIN.		SNOW.		RAIN AND MELTED SNOW.	
	Temperature of the Air.	Vapour of Pressure.	Relative Humidity.	Barometric Pressure.	Pressure of Dry Air.	Clouded Sky.	Resultant Direction.	Resultant Velocity.	Mean Velocity.	Maximum.	Minimum.	Difference.	Depth in Inches.	Approximate duration hours.	Depth in Inches.	Approximate duration in hours.	Depth in Inches.	Approximate duration in hours.
1	58.87	0.295	74	29.959	29.664	0.0	East	4.06	6.22	63.2	41.5	21.7	...	...	...	...	...	...
2	56.37	.208	63	.908	.695	0.1	N 89 E	2.47	5.38	72.0	45.0	27.0	...	...	...	...	...	...
3	58.73	.335	70	.915	.580	0.2	S 69 E	3.46	4.46	69.0	46.2	22.8	...	...	...	...	...	...
4	63.47	.402	72	.820	.418	0.0	S 70 E	3.82	3.82	76.5	48.0	28.5	...	...	...	...	...	...
5	63.10	.493	87	.778	.294	1.0	N 20 E	1.64	3.07	70.4	55.0	15.0	0.240	...	...	...	...	...
6	63.55	.595	88	.721	.126	1.0	S 27 W	2.82	5.86	75.4	61.2	14.2	...	8.7	...	...	...	...
7	...	...	...	...	...	...	...	...	...	64.0	54.0	10.0	.505	7.5	...	...	...	...
8	68.35	.454	81	.714	.260	0.4	S 83 E	5.05	8.70	64.8	51.5	13.3	...	...	...	...	...	...
9	66.35	.495	86	.663	.229	0.1	S 52 W	5.65	5.99	76.4	53.5	22.9	...	...	...	...	...	...
10	71.83	.646	77	.406	.759	1.0	S 8 W	3.72	3.72	78.2	53.5	14.7	.725	2.8	...	...	...	...
11	64.70	.357	61	.475	.118	0.2	S 64 W	9.71	10.03	78.3	48.8	29.5	...	...	...	...	...	...
12	57.50	.357	77	.521	.164	0.6	N 60 W	3.52	13.10	73.5	44.0	29.5	.225	3.0	...	...	...	...
13	59.53	.359	73	.485	.126	0.2	S 19 E	6.25	6.25	64.8	46.2	18.6	.020	0.3	...	...	...	...
14	...	...	...	...	...	...	N 62 W	2.33	12.59	69.6	44.0	25.6	...	...	...	...	...	...
15	60.82	.377	72	.564	.187	0.3	S 8	2.63	4.24	68.5	44.0	24.5	...	...	...	...	...	...
16	57.22	.330	72	.736	.406	0.6	N 56 W	8.89	9.75	76.6	48.8	27.8	.640	8.2	...	...	...	...
17	60.62	.429	83	.543	.114	1.0	S 57 W	1.24	5.57	65.6	47.4	18.2	.050	2.0	...	...	...	...
18	60.27	.363	72	.404	.036	0.7	N 79 E	4.44	5.78	71.0	44.0	17.0	...	...	...	...	...	...
19	57.28	.250	56	.404	.307	0.3	S 42 W	8.15	11.83	76.6	51.2	25.4	...	...	...	...	...	...
20	52.32	.248	66	.691	.443	0.4	S 60 W	9.40	10.26	62.0	38.0	24.0	...	...	...	...	...	...
21	...	...	...	...	...	...	N 28 W	1.99	3.97	58.8	35.2	23.6	.020	1.0	...	...	...	...
22	47.67	.240	74	.686	.396	0.4	N 32 W	4.12	4.12	56.9	35.0	21.9	...	...	...	...	...	...
23	47.37	.232	73	.586	.304	0.8	N 33 W	1.15	2.77	56.0	37.5	18.5	...	...	...	...	...	...
24	44.43	.218	77	.472	.255	0.2	N 48 W	4.53	6.50	53.2	37.0	16.2	.015	0.5	...	...	...	...
25	48.47	.260	69	.381	.121	0.6	S 79 W	6.26	6.33	57.0	39.0	18.0	...	0.1	...	...	...	...
26	52.65	.290	75	.477	.187	0.3	S 18 E	4.82	5.15	67.0	40.0	27.0	...	...	...	...	...	...
27	52.32	.285	74	.665	.380	0.7	S 59 E	1.52	4.34	61.4	41.2	20.2	...	...	...	...	...	...
28	...	...	...	...	...	...	N 28 E	2.77	8.48	64.4	46.6	17.8	.015	*	...	...	...	...
29	46.90	.307	87	.472	.165	1.0	S 30 W	1.57	1.57	54.0	42.0	12.0	1.195	13.9	...	...	...	...
30	46.93	.297	90	.205	.918	1.0	S 84 W	5.05	5.58	53.4	39.0	15.4	.455	12.0	...	...	...	...
	57.15	0.351	75	29.600	29.249	0.5	S 79 W	1.99	6.53	66.69	45.66	21.03	4.105	55.0	...	...	...	...

GENERAL METEOROLOGICAL ABSTRACT,—OCTOBER, 1856.

Days.	Temperature of the Air.	Pressure of Vapour.	Relative Humidity.	Barometric Pressure.	Pressure of Dry Air.	Clouded Sky.	Resultant Direction.	Resultant Velocity.	Mean Velocity.	Maximum.	Minimum.	Difference.	Rain Depth in Inches.	Rain Approximate duration in hours.	Snow Depth in Inches.	Snow Approximate duration in hours.	Rain and Melted Snow Depth in Inches.	Rain and Melted Snow Approximate duration in hours.
1	44.68	0.213	73	29.281	29.067	0.6	S 38 W	9.89	10.06	53.0	37.6	15.4						
2	47.47	.217	68	.441	.224	0.6	S 50 W	8.24	9.59	55.0	37.0	18.0						
3	48.53	.217	66	.738	.521	0.2	S 47 W	3.68	4.79	59.5	36.8	22.7						
4	50.95	.265	78	.783	.499	0.2	N 71 E	2.83	3.04	59.2	40.0	19.2	*	*			*	*
5							N 58 W	2.52	4.11	66.0	39.4	26.6						
6	54.78	.283	69	.900	.627	0.2	N 30 E	7.24	7.48	63.2	39.4	23.8						
7	46.07	.249	81	.936	.689	0.1	N 73 E	2.37	2.73	53.2	37.2	16.0						
8	49.67	.295	84	.849	.554	0.3	S 32 E	0.58	0.76	61.0	37.0	24.0						
9	56.72	.337	77	.815	.478	0.1	S 62 E	0.59	0.82	71.4	43.2	28.2						
10	54.83	.314	76	.767	.453	0.0	S 62 E	0.45	0.51	69.2	44.0	25.2						
11	56.42	.281	65	.799	.518	0.4	N 19 W	7.96	9.13	67.4	43.5	23.9	.115	1.5			.115	1.5
12							S 79 E	0.86	1.08	58.2	42.8	15.4	*	*			*	*
13	48.07	.223	65	.696	.473	0.6	S 20 E	12.49	13.54	59.5	31.0	28.5						
14	36.32	.119	55	30.020	.901	0.2	N 10 E	9.74	9.96	41.4	26.0	15.4						
15	35.17	.140	69	30.132	.992	0.0	N 43 W	0.22	2.50	45.5	25.5	20.0						
16	38.57	.177	75	29.962	.785	0.0	S 83 W	1.49	3.48	40.5	25.0	24.5						
17	44.90	.248	83	.790	.542	0.8	N 49 E	5.83	6.40	56.0	33.5	22.5	.365	9.0			.365	9.0
18	47.05	.291	91	.644	.353	1.0	N 32 W	3.47	4.46	48.8	42.4	6.4	.225	10.0			.225	10.0
19							S 60 W	0.72	0.77	56.0	35.6	19.2	.010	*			.010	*
20	44.05	.267	93	.917	.650	0.6	S 33 W	0.04	0.04	54.6	35.4	19.0						
21	46.70	.283	89	.789	.506	0.4	N 66 W	0.13	0.14	61.2	43.0	18.2						
22	55.17	.366	85	.661	.195	1.0	N 25 W	4.40	4.63	48.0	23.0	18.2	.025	0.3			.025	0.3
23	40.97	.167	64	.755	.588	0.3	N 83 W	9.82	10.40	46.0	23.0	23.0						
24	31.52	.121	60	.851	.830	0.3	N 83 W	3.28	4.36	30.2	23.8	15.4	.010	1.0			.010	1.0
25	40.60	.167	67	.741	.573	0.6	S 82 E	1.85	2.45	44.7	33.0	11.7						
26							S 54 W	4.38	7.39	53.0	35.0	18.0						
27	45.47	.281	93	.420	.139	1.0	S 73 W	15.12	15.17	48.0	35.8	12.2	.105	6.0			.105	6.0
28	41.90	.176	68	.384	.208	0.6	S 73 W	11.45	11.45	47.2	35.0	12.2	.020	*			.020	*
29	45.45	.233	78	.405	.172	1.0	S 43 W	9.33	11.45	51.4	38.5	12.9			*	1.5	*	1.5
30	38.22	.166	72	.302	.136	0.8	S 76 W	13.99	14.17	49.2	28.8	14.4			.1		.010	*
31	34.13	.132	68	.397	.265	0.7	S 75 W	13.09	14.89	40.8	28.5	12.3						
	45.34	0.231	75	29.707	29.475	0.5	N 76 W	2.15	6.07	54.04	35.22	18.82	0.875	27.8	0.1	1.5	0.885	29.3

GENERAL METEOROLOGICAL ABSTRACT.—NOVEMBER, 1856.

	DAILY MEANS.					WIND.			EXTREMES OF TEMPERATURE.			RAIN.		SNOW.		RAIN AND MELTED SNOW	
Date.	Temperature of the Air.	Pressure of Vapour.	Relative Humidity.	Barometric Pressure.	Pressure of Dry Air.	Clouded Sky.	Resultant Direction.	Resultant Velocity.	Mean Velocity.	Maximum.	Minimum.	Difference.	Depth in Inches.	Approximate duration in hours.	Depth in Inches.	Approximate duration in hours.	Depth in Inches.	Approximate duration in hours.
1	44.05	0.200	69	29.191	28.991	0.7	S 54 W	9.42	10.75	56.0	38.2	17.8						
2	49.98	.314	92	.418	.174	...	S 40 W	2.20	3.74	52.5	40.2	12.3	0.175	6.0	...	...	0.175	6.0
3	46.02	.256	76	.178	28.922	1.0	N 8 E	3.83	3.93	52.0	45.0	7.0	.205	7.0	...	...	.205	7.0
4	27.92	.098	64	.822	29.724	0.8	N 78 W	14.96	20.93	56.4	24.0	32.4	...	...	...	...	...	...
5	35.43	.157	75	.935	...	0.6	N 65 W	10.49	10.95	34.2	18.8	15.4	...	...	...	...	...	...
6	47.72	.251	77	.694	.443	0.7	S 5 E	.928	8.70	43.0	20.8	22.2	...	...	...	...	...	...
7	39.32	.204	78	.631	.427	1.0	S 1 E	6.17	6.59	43.0	39.4	13.6	...	...	*	*	...	...
8						0.6	S 96 W	10.77	13.85	53.2	25.8	27.4	.180	4.0	.1	...	.180	4.0
9						...	N 76 W	5.33	5.64	33.0	24.0	9.0	.045	5.0	...	...	.045	5.0
10	33.15	.133	70	.874	.740	1.0	S 33 E	5.03	6.37	40.0	23.5	16.5	...	...	.5	.5	.010	0.5
11	40.35	.187	76	.781	.594	1.0	S 72 W	2.42	8.74	42.0	24.0	10.2	...	...	.5	3.8	.340	9.4
12	38.70	.171	73	.861	.690	0.9	N 69 W	8.82	9.05	44.0	30.0	14.0	.290	5.6	.6	5.5	.105	5.8
13	36.03	.137	69	.789	.602	1.0	N 88 E	3.00	5.48	39.0	30.0	9.0	.055	0.3	...	...	.015	0.2
14	35.67	.171	83	.719	.548	0.9	N 6 E	9.74	10.78	39.2	23.0	16.2	.015	0.2	...	...	.010	2.0
15	33.70	.153	78	.558	.404	0.5	N 25 W	6.61	8.22	41.2	22.0	19.2	...	...	.6	2.0	.060	2.0
16						...	S 89 W	9.73	10.58	43.8	25.5	18.3	...	...	.1	1.5	.010	1.5
17	29.77	.123	81	.512	.379	0.9	N 65 W	10.91	11.08	33.5	25.0	8.5	...	...	...	...	...	...
18	32.05	.143	76	.764	.622	0.8	N 74 W	8.73	9.05	37.0	25.0	12.0	...	...	...	...	...	...
19	32.03	.136	76	.888	.753	0.5	N 88 W	0.12	1.39	42.0	24.0	18.0	...	...	...	...	...	...
20	34.85	.160	79	.972	.812	1.0	N 80 E	5.73	5.79	37.8	31.7	6.1	...	...	...	...	...	...
21	41.55	.219	83	.515	.296	1.0	S 55 E	6.83	16.64	49.2	34.0	15.2	.195	3.7	...	...	.195	3.7
22	39.68	.171	70	.693	.522	0.7	S 62 W	10.07	10.09	45.0	27.0	18.0	...	...	...	...	...	...
23						...	S 67 E	4.89	5.33	42.4	30.2	12.2	...	...	...	...	...	...
24	39.52	.192	80	.705	.513	0.8	N 10 E	0.78	1.07	45.4	31.0	14.4	...	...	...	...	...	...
25	40.59	.228	91	.472	.244	1.0	N 83 E	9.46	13.53	45.2	37.0	8.2	.215	9.5	...	...	.215	9.5
26	41.87	.194	75	.505	.311	0.5	S 80 W	13.06	13.18	45.4	35.0	10.4	*	1.0	...	...	*	1.0
27	35.90	.136	67	.590	.454	0.9	S 80 W	10.16	10.29	40.8	26.8	14.0	...	...	3.5	3.0	.350	3.0
28	33.13	.148	78	.574	.426	0.8	N 74 E	7.69	9.17	35.2	25.0	10.2	...	...	4.2	14.0	.420	14.0
29	26.57	.130	88	.848	.219	...	N 1 W	6.02	8.19	29.5	10.4	10.1	...	...	*	*	*	*
30						...	N 72 W	7.32	8.71	36.8	27.0	9.8	...	...	...	...	...	...
	37.89	0.179	78	29.642	29.463	0.8	S 85 W	2.95	8.75	49.02	28.74	14.27	1.375	49.3	9.5	30.2	2.325	72.5

GENERAL METEOROLOGICAL ABSTRACT,—DECEMBER, 1856.

Days.	DAILY MEANS.						WIND.			Extremes of Temperature.			RAIN.		SNOW.			Rain and Melted Snow	
	Temperature of the Air.	Pressure of Vapour.	Relative Humidity.	Barometric Pressure.	Pressure of Dry Air.	Clouded Sky.	Resultant Direction.	Resultant Velocity.	Mean Velocity.	Maximum.	Minimum.	Difference.	Depth in Inches.	Approximate duration in hours.	Depth in Inches.	Approximate duration in hours.	Depth in Inches.	Approximate duration in hours.
1	28.57	0.120	81	29.765	29.635	0.8	N 28 E	5.25	6.57	34.5	17.5	17.0	...	...	1.0	4.0	0.100	4.0
2	26.72	.122	83	.511	.389	1.0	N 52 E	14.43	17.60	36.0	20.2	15.8	...	...	5.8	9.5	.580	9.5
3	30.48	.139	79	28.910	28.771	0.9	S 79 W	16.56	21.01	37.8	21.0	16.8	...	0.5	0.2	1.5	.020	2.0
4	26.55	.113	79	29.616	.503	1.0	N 76 W	10.25	10.91	31.5	13.5	18.0	...	...	...	*	*	*
5	24.93	.104	75	.818	.714	0.5	S 66 W	9.33	9.66	30.8	14.8	16.0	...	...	...	...	...	...
6	23.45	.100	78	.814	.714	0.4	S 71 W	14.27	14.28	29.7	13.0	16.0	...	...	...	...	...	...
7	...	...	...	...	...	...	S 77 W	6.95	8.11	27.6	13.0	10.3	...	...	...	4.0	.030	4.0
8	20.40	.096	83	.684	.788	0.6	N 48 W	3.77	4.18	27.6	13.6	14.6	...	...	0.3	3.0	.010	3.0
9	25.73	.115	81	30.014	30.014	0.8	S 56 E	3.21	4.42	25.2	13.4	11.8	...	...	0.1	...	...	...
10	31.47	.135	76	.129	29.747	0.3	S 82 E	6.78	7.41	30.0	17.8	12.2	.330	1.5	...	0.5	.330	1.5
11	37.80	.206	91	.882	.028	0.5	S 33 W	11.13	18.57	42.2	32.6	9.6	.855	9.3	...	3.0	.855	9.3
12	33.88	.145	76	.229	.448	0.9	S 65 W	10.46	10.62	36.2	28.5	7.7	*	...	2.6	0.5	.200	0.5
13	34.05	.155	80	.548	.576	1.0	S 56 E	4.44	4.91	35.9	31.0	4.9	.465	5.0	0.4	3.0	.505	9.0
14	...	...	...	.731	...	...	S 70 W	19.76	28.06	40.2	19.7	20.5	...	...	0.1	4.5	.010	2.5
15	19.35	.083	76	.615	.633	0.8	N 75 W	8.87	9.67	21.0	17.7	3.3	...	...	0.3	1.2	.010	1.2
16	18.00	.080	76	.740	.660	0.9	N 81 W	7.04	10.20	21.9	5.5	16.4	...	...	...	...	.030	*
17	3.45	.048	94	30.097	.049	0.4	N 15 W	8.17	8.27	-8.8	-8.8	18.0	...	...	...	...	...	...
18	-2.08	.040	96	.379	.379	0.2	N 52 E	9.42	9.77	-15.4	-9.1	24.5	.090	4.0	1.0	3.0	.100	6.0
19	24.00	.112	82	.419	30.379	1.0	S 67 E	13.82	14.72	38.0	15.4	22.6	.060	5.0	0.2	2.0	.100	6.5
20	29.85	.153	85	29.855	.748	0.6	S 59 W	19.03	19.96	39.2	13.7	25.5	...	...	...	1.5	.060	6.5
21	...	...	...	.392	.239	...	S 48 W	10.19	11.87	24.2	13.2	11.0	...	...	...	...	...	...
22	18.45	.095	89	.492	.397	1.0	N 75 E	1.07	8.18	22.0	5.0	17.0	...	...	3.0	13.8	.300	13.8
23	8.37	.057	88	.778	.721	0.2	N 33 W	9.21	9.38	12.4	0.5	11.9	...	...	...	...	...	...
24	13.12	.070	88	.552	.482	0.5	N 62 W	16.19	16.34	18.0	6.0	12.0	...	...	...	...	...	...
25	...	...	...	...	...	1.0	N 85 W	15.18	15.78	23.5	14.0	9.5	...	1.0	0.1	1.0	.010	2.0
26	25.80	.122	87	.677	.555	0.9	N 7 E	10.49	14.47	29.8	13.5	16.3	...	...	0.5	3.0	.030	3.0
27	19.08	.094	87	.801	.707	...	S 62 W	8.37	9.42	24.2	14.9	9.3	...	...	0.1	1.0	.010	1.0
28	...	...	...	...	...	1.0	N 2 E	2.27	32.0	19.0	13.0	...	...	...	...	...	...
29	26.33	.123	84	.622	.499	1.0	S 62 W	8.55	8.70	30.2	23.6	6.6	...	...	...	...	.060	*
30	24.13	.113	85	.730	.617	1.0	S 78 W	2.96	3.13	26.2	21.0	5.2	...	...	0.6	3.5	.060	3.5
31	23.92	.117	99	.886	.769	0.9	North	5.22	6.70	27.0	19.0	8.0	...	...	...	*	*	*
	22.88	0.110	82	29.711	29.601	0.8	S 87 W	4.62	11.56	28.74	15.55	13.19	1.790	26.8	16.3	62.0	3.420	86.3

GENERAL METEOROLOGICAL ABSTRACT,—JANUARY, 1857.

Days	Temperature of the Air	DAILY MEANS. Pressure of Vapour.	Relative Humidity.	Barometric Pressure.	Pressure of Dry Air.	Clouded Sky.	WIND. Resultant Direction.	Resultant Velocity.	Mean Velocity.	EXTREMES OF TEMPERATURE. Maximum.	Minimum.	Difference.	RAIN. Depth in Inches.	Approximate duration in hours.	SNOW. Depth in Inches.	Approximate duration in hours.	RAIN AND MELTED SNOW. Depth in Inches.	Approximate duration in hours.
1	24.37	0.124	92	29.963	29.839	0.9	N 37 E	8.06	8.31	27.8	20.5	7.3			3.5	16.5	0.350	17.5
2	29.92	.145	89	.635	.490	1.0	S 57 E	9.23	10.86	33.8	22.0	13.6			0.3	5.0	.030	5.0
3	28.77	.138	87	.355	.217		N 80 W	11.41	14.04	31.5	21.0	10.5			*	5.0	*	5.0
4						0.7	N 74 W	10.12	10.37	25.2	14.5	10.7						
5	10.33	.066	85	.848	.843	0.5	N 19 W	7.65	7.79	17.0	−7.5	24.2		1.0				
6	1.42	.043	80	30.049	30.006	0.6	N 56 W	5.20	5.39	7.5	−8.8	16.3						
7	1.00	.042	81	29.900	29.900	0.4	N 68 W	12.85	13.64	16.4	−11.8	28.2			0.2	1.5	.020	1.5
8	0.42	.044	87	.942	.926	1.0	N 75 W	5.51	7.15	12.5	−12.0	24.5						
9	17.08	.089	88	30.070	30.026	1.0	S 58 W	13.80	13.86	21.5	11.5	10.0			5.5	10.6	.550	10.6
10	20.38	.105	92	29.903	29.605		N 13 W	7.43	8.17	23.5	7.0	16.5						
11				.290	.175		N 41 W	12.77	13.66	8.9	3.0	5.9						
12	13.37	.077	90	.778	.701	0.8	N 62 W	10.45	10.52	17.0	7.5	9.5			0.2	2.2	.020	2.2
13	18.40	.096	86	.536	.440	1.0	S 71 W	6.65	6.78	23.5	11.8	11.7			0.9	3.5	.090	3.5
14	15.42	.082	86	.539	.457	0.9	N 16 W	9.32	9.38	20.5	−3.0	23.5						
15	2.32	.046	86	.961	.915	0.1	N 54 W	5.35	6.30	9.0	−4.5	13.5			0.3	3.0	.030	3.0
16	13.58	.061	92	.745	.684	1.0	S 58 W	14.42	15.09	21.2	4.2	17.0			0.1	1.5	.010	1.5
17	1.60	.049	83	.896	.788	0.3	N 36 W	13.33	14.78	17.5	−17.4	34.9						
18							N 4 W	9.32	9.50	0.0	−18.0	18.0						
19	9.78	.072	93	.065	.593	0.7	N 38 W	9.32	10.37	19.5	−3.2	22.7			0.2	1.0	.020	1.0
20	16.43	.064	86	.431	.347	0.8	N 83 W	14.18	14.69	22.2	11.6	10.6			1.0	19.0	.100	19.0
21	13.72	.078	86	.468	.386	0.7	N 22 W	13.66	15.87	22.0	−12.8	34.8				0.7	*	0.7
22	9.18	.025	98	.734	.709	0.1	N 09 W	4.28	6.71	−11.2	−20.1	8.9						
23	5.07	.028	87	.822	.794	0.4	S 52 W	12.61	13.80	6.0	−17.0	23.0						
24		.054	91	.690	.636	0.7	N 89 W	9.31	9.63	10.0	−5.0	15.0	2.0					
25							S 21 E	3.20	3.76	12.2	−4.5	16.7						
26	16.82	.101	94	.844	.743	1.0	N 53 W	0.18	9.56	33.8	−1.2	35.0			0.2	3.0	.020	3.0
27	25.27	.131	89	.885	.754	0.4	N 27 E	7.2	5.52	37.2	5.7	31.5			1.0	1.5	.100	1.5
28	16.48	.080	88	30.046	.958	0.6	N 52 W	4.49	5.52	26.4	3.2	23.2	*		*	3.5	*	5.5
29	19.27	.094	86	29.904	.810	0.3	N 52 W	1.36	3.12	26.4	8.7	19.7						
30	18.88	.099	91	.906	.807	1.0	N 80 E	15.26	16.01	27.0	13.6	13.5		3.5	5.0	4.0	.500	4.0
31	28.28	.150	94	.291	.141	0.8	S 10 W	6.42	14.75	33.4	7.2	26.2			4.2	6.3	.420	9.8
	12.75	.083	89	29.786	29.653	0.7	N 70 W	4.96	10.31	19.46	0.85	18.61	*	6.5	21.8	87.8	2.190	94.3

GENERAL METEOROLOGICAL ABSTRACT,—FEBRUARY, 1857.

Days.	DAILY MEANS.						WIND.			EXTREMES OF TEMPERATURE.			RAIN.		SNOW.		RAIN AND MELTED SNOW	
	Temperature of the Air.	Pressure of Vapour.	Relative Humidity.	Barometric Pressure.	Pressure of Dry Air.	Clouded Sky.	Resultant Direction.	Resultant Velocity.	Mean Velocity.	Maximum.	Minimum.	Difference.	Depth in Inches.	Approximate duration in hours.	Depth in Inches.	Approximate duration in hours.	Depth in Inches.	Approximate duration in hours.
	°						°	Miles.	Miles.									
1	3.72	0.046	82	29.812	29.766	0.3	S 64 W	11.00	11.29	11.8	−1.0	12.8	...	...	...	...	...	...
2	17.62	.089	81	.810	.721	0.8	N 71 W	7.51	7.92	12.0	−5.9	17.9	...	...	...	...	1.0	1.0
3	31.43	.153	86	.758	.606	1.0	S 66 E	5.40	7.01	33.1	1.1	32.0	...	...	2.0	4.5	.200	4.5
4	30.98	.171	93	.668	.497	1.0	N 20 E	6.19	8.61	38.2	26.0	12.2	...	...	0.2	0.7	.770	15.5
5	39.95	.222	91	.691	.469	1.0	N 76 E	6.23	7.08	43.3	25.6	17.4	.750	14.8	...	...	.020	0.6
6	47.08	.239	75	.436	.197	0.9	N 71 E	2.39	3.07	43.8	36.0	7.8	.020	0.6	...	...	.020	0.6
7							S 7 E	8.17	8.78	51.3	40.2	11.1	.080	4.0	...	...	.080	4.0
8							S 82 W	17.47	19.08	41.0	15.1	25.9	.090	3.0	*	...	.090	4.5
9	21.33	.068	74	30.109	30.021	0.6	S 22 W	16.28	17.80	28.2	14.4	13.8	...	...	0.5	1.5	.050	1.0
10	6.72	.053	81	.166	.113	0.4	N 76 W	18.79	20.57	15.0	−2.0	17.0	...	...	...	1.0	...	1.0
11	4.38	.050	85	.317	.267	0.7	N 70 W	5.79	5.79	11.0	−4.5	15.5	...	...	*	*	...	*
12	22.18	.112	86	.317	.207	0.9	S 58 E	8.57	11.50	37.2	8.4	28.8	...	...	*	*	...	*
13	36.02	.152	72	.067	.635	0.4	S 76 E	9.08	11.50	43.3	20.3	20.3	...	...	...	...	...	2.4
14	31.83	.170	93	29.787	.605	0.7	N 80 E	4.76	8.90	41.0	21.0	20.0	.055	2.4	...	...	.055	21.5
15				.775			S 51 E	0.45	3.35	44.2	37.0	7.2	1.620	21.5	...	...	1.620	10.0
16						1.0	S 7 E	1.10	1.11	44.8	35.0	9.8	.210	10.0	...	...	.210	0.1
17	40.98	.248	97	.572	.324	0.8	S 72 W	1.76	4.70	52.4	35.0	17.4	.005	0.1	...	...	.005	9.9
18	44.35	.277	95	.528	.251	0.9	N 10 W	7.14	8.06	43.2	26.5	16.7	.115	6.7	2.2	4.2	.335	13.5
19	38.02	.197	87	.664	.457	1.0	N 32 E	2.47	2.67	30.3	26.0	4.3	...	...	1.5	13.5	.150	5.4
20	28.17	.136	87	.786	.650	1.0	N 38 E	10.58	14.35	32.5	25.0	7.5	...	...	5.0	5.4	.570	13.4
21	28.93	.143	88	.550	.407	0.7	N 38 E	6.40	7.69	37.8	27.2	10.6	.070	8.0	...	...	...	...
22	31.35	.148	84	.680	.531	...	S 72 W	12.48	12.63	31.5	27.5	4.0	...	...	...	...	...	...
23	35.98	.179	86	.500	.321	0.5	S 30 W	4.94	5.23	46.0	30.5	14.5	...	8.0	...	...	...	8.0
24	42.77	.219	90	.293	.074	0.8	S 41 W	8.15	10.30	52.2	33.5	18.7	...	...	...	...	.035	...
25	33.85	.155	78	.619	.464	0.3	N 37 W	10.30		42.0	21.8	20.2	.085	3.0	...	...	.035	3.0
26	21.77	.088	72	30.045	.957	0.6	N 85 W	17.83	18.31	27.5	16.8	10.7	...	...	0.3	1.5	.030	1.5
27	23.72	.106	84	29.676	.570	0.9	N 53 W	14.42	15.32	29.8	15.5	14.3	...	...	...	...	...	...
28	22.57	.088	71	.358	.270	0.2	S 84 W	11.02	12.22	31.5	13.0	18.5	...	...	...	...	...	...
	° 28.53	0.147	84	29.736	29.689	0.7	S 78 W	3.68	9.82	35.66	20.42	15.25	3.050	78.1	11.7	34.3	4.220	107.4

GENERAL METEOROLOGICAL ABSTRACT,—MARCH, 1857.

Days	DAILY MEANS.						WIND.			EXTREMES OF TEMPERATURE.			RAIN.		SNOW.		RAIN AND MELTED SNOW	
	Temperature of the Air.	Pressure of Vapour.	Relative Humidity.	Barometric Pressure.	Pressure of Dry Air.	Clouded Sky.	Resultant Direction.	Resultant Velocity.	Mean Velocity.	Maximum	Minimum	Difference	Depth in Inches.	Approximate duration in hours.	Depth in Inches.	Approximate duration in hours.	Depth in Inches.	Approximate duration in hours.
1	1.10	...	...	29.884	29.789	0.1	N 25 W	13.26	16.22	32.5	−4.5	37.0	...	...	2.5	12.5	0.250	12.5
2	16.48	.045	90	.670	.486	0.7	N 42 W	11.58	11.64	8.6	−5.5	14.1	...	...	0.2	4.0	.020	4.0
3	28.08	.118	81	.569	.476	0.5	S 61 W	11.10	12.00	25.6	−2.8	28.4	...	...	0.2	1.0	...	1.0
4	34.22	.172	73	.339	.167	1.0	S 12 E	4.02	9.76	29.2	8.1	21.1	...	...	...	...	.020	1.5
5	17.63	.070	87	.411	.341	0.4	S 75 W	6.39	12.79	38.8	17.5	21.3	...	...	0.2	1.5	.020	1.5
6	12.25	.062	71	.791	.729	0.6	N 75 W	23.23	23.76	24.4	7.0	17.4	...	...	...	...	...	...
7	...	...	77	...	...	...	N 74 W	12.18	12.37	17.0	5.3	11.7	...	...	...	...	...	...
8	21.22	.106	86	.383	.277	0.7	N 15 W	6.79	7.22	24.2	4.8	19.4	...	...	1.9	3.0	.190	3.0
9	11.15	.070	87	.655	.585	0.8	N 61 W	13.20	16.23	31.8	1.2	30.6	...	...	2.2	10.0	.220	10.0
10	18.33	.078	74	.644	.566	0.6	N 68 W	6.19	6.88	21.6	0.9	20.7	...	...	*	0.3	*	0.3
11	13.35	.059	70	.926	.867	0.0	N 63 W	6.06	7.02	29.2	3.5	25.7	...	...	0.1	1.5	.010	1.5
12	24.83	.096	70	.804	.708	0.6	West	9.55	10.67	24.0	4.0	20.0	...	...	...	...	...	...
13	31.58	.128	71	.572	.449	0.8	S 31 W	7.35	7.56	32.5	10.0	22.5	...	...	...	...	...	...
14	...	...	...	...	...	...	N 83 W	7.39	7.96	39.4	15.5	23.9	...	...	...	...	...	...
15	...	...	...	...	...	...	S 18 E	0.92	1.80	32.4	16.2	16.2	...	...	...	...	...	...
16	31.68	.154	86	.518	.364	0.7	S 43 W	2.52	3.07	40.2	27.8	12.4	.145	1.0	0.5	10.0	.195	1.0
17	33.72	.163	82	.627	.474	0.6	S 61 E	3.02	5.57	27.8	0.3	11.0	.090	4.2	*	*	.090	4.2
18	37.37	.194	87	.380	.186	0.8	N 9 W	3.70	5.98	48.8	30.0	18.8	...	...	3.0	10.0	.300	10.0
19	28.88	.141	83	.311	.170	1.0	N 35 W	23.01	23.35	32.1	23.0	9.1	...	...	0.2	1.5	.020	1.5
20	31.68	.135	76	.472	.337	0.4	S 03 W	2.01	8.83	39.5	23.8	16.7	...	...	0.2	1.5	.020	1.5
21	36.73	.153	72	.600	.447	0.5	N 90 W	12.99	13.22	44.4	28.0	16.4	...	...	...	...	*	...
22	...	...	...	...	...	...	N 81 E	8.64	9.06	57.0	43.0	15.0	...	...	...	...	...	...
23	44.13	.195	70	.551	.356	0.9	N 74 W	4.60	7.17	38.2	14.2	23.4	...	..	...	...	.100	6.4
24	36.33	.191	90	.514	.323	1.0	N 81 W	4.04	5.18	38.2	32.2	6.0	.100	5.9	0.5	0.5	.010	1.3
25	30.92	.134	77	.540	.406	0.8	N 46 W	20.66	21.10	34.5	21.8	12.7	...	...	0.1	1.3	...	...
26	32.20	.131	73	.653	.522	0.3	N 36 W	12.64	12.79	39.2	26.5	11.8	...	...	...	...	...	...
27	34.60	.138	70	.623	.485	0.6	N 41 W	9.61	9.71	41.0	29.2	10.0	...	...	...	...	...	...
28	36.58	.137	64	.639	.502	0.9	N 23 W	12.20	12.37	43.0	33.0	10.0	...	...	...	...	...	...
29	...	...	...	...	...	...	N 30 W	13.44	13.59	42.2	28.8	13.4	...	...	...	...	...	...
30	38.73	.120	54	.853	.763	0.0	...	...	...	49.8	28.0	21.8	...	...	...	...	...	...
31	39.73	.161	67	.856	.695	0.6	...	...	...	50.6	28.0	22.6	...	...	...	...	...	...
	27.82	0.124	77	29.596	29.472	0.6	N 63 W	6.69	10.84	35.25	17.79	17.46	0.335	11.1	11.3	48.6	1.465	59.7

GENERAL METEOROLOGICAL ABSTRACT,—APRIL, 1857.

Days.	DAILY MEANS.							WIND.			Extremes of Temperature.			RAIN.		SNOW.		RAIN AND MELTED SNOW	
	Temperature of the Air.	Pressure of Vapour.	Relative Humidity.	Barometric Pressure.	Pressure of Dry Air.	Clouded Sky.		Resultant Direction.	Resultant Velocity.	Mean Velocity.	Maximum.	Minimum.	Difference.	Depth in Inches.	Approximate duration in hours.	Depth in Inches.	Approximate duration in hours.	Depth in Inches.	Approximate duration in hours.
1	26.08	0.118	77	29.491	29.372	0.6		N 26 W	22.36	23.03	42.5	10.0	32.5	*	1.0	0.3	3.0	0.030	4.0
2	20.35	.073	65	.933	.861	0.1		N 32 W	9.11	9.25	31.2	5.9	25.3						
3	28.28	.117	75	.784	.667	0.4		S 51 E	3.12	5.61	36.8	18.5	18.3		*				*
4	43.40	.217	78	.549	.330	0.6		N 48 W	1.89	5.72	51.9	17.0	17.0	.020	14.0			.020	16.0
5								N 77 W	3.05	9.44	47.0	31.0	16.0	.390		2.0	2.0	.590	5.1
6	26.90	.121	81	.179	.058	0.7		S 72 W	12.77	13.74	22.2	17.7	14.5			2.7	5.1	.270	1.0
7	27.65	.113	73	.632	.519	0.8		N 48 W	9.84	13.87	33.8	18.8	15.0			1.9	1.0	.030	3.2
8	35.60	.178	86	.608	.430	1.0		S 21 W	0.94	6.39	42.0	30.2	11.8	*	*		8.2	.190	
9	34.52	.159	79	.735	.576	0.8		S 85 E	3.88	7.27	41.0	28.8	12.2						
10								N 36 E	3.04	7.87	42.8	30.2	12.6						
11	36.00	.168	79	.465	.298	0.4		N 43 W	5.26	7.87	44.2	29.8	14.4						
12								S 48 W	4.20	5.27	44.2	26.2	18.0		0.1	0.5	4.5	.050	0.1
13	36.48	.156	73	.594	.438	0.5		S 67 W	6.02	5.55	46.0	27.5	18.5			0.2	5.0	.020	4.5
14	38.55	.189	82	.233	.044	0.6		N 65 E	14.90	11.93	46.0	33.5	12.5						5.0
15	34.47	.161	82	.996	28.835	0.6		S 62 W	6.02	15.48	37.8	28.8	9.0						
16	33.55	.158	83	28.996	29.114	0.8		S 54 W	8.75	10.11	38.8	27.4	11.4	.565	5.0			.745	
17	33.17	.122	65	29.272	.371	0.2		S 55 W	6.08	10.53	40.6	26.0	14.6		3.0	1.8	6.5	.150	3.0
18	35.83	.152	72	.503		0.5		N 73 E	8.20		40.5	27.2	13.3		9.0	1.5	7.5	.150	15.5
19					.522	0.9		N 53 W	2.36	7.51	37.8	27.8	10.0	.095	2.0	0.2	0.6	.115	7.5
20						1.0		N 32 W	20.36	20.52	42.0	28.0	14.0						2.6
21	35.17	.147	73	.469	.342	0.7		S 9 W	6.67	8.11	47.4	32.6	14.8						
22	38.45	.194	84	.362	.168	0.2		N 21 W	12.64	12.83	51.0	33.0	18.0						
23	42.58	.163	61	.462	.298	0.2		N 30 W	12.38	12.61	48.6	32.2	16.4						
24	39.15	.165	70	.537	.372	0.6		N 76 W	3.63	6.57	49.8	29.0	20.8	.670	3.0			.820	3.5
25	40.10	.171	69	.584	.417	0.4		S 52 W	9.30	7.89	27.5	32.0	12.5	.015	9.0	1.5		.015	12.5
26	30.55	.159	66	.614	.455	0.2		S 86 E	5.07	9.85	44.5	32.0	12.4		1.5				1.5
27	39.27	.196	83	.221	.025	0.9		S 86 W	15.84	19.09	44.6	32.2	12.4						
28	37.93	.166	73	.666	.500	0.1		N 62 W	11.77	12.14	48.0	27.2	20.8						
29	39.50	.172	69	.840	.609	0.2		N 85 W	0.87	6.49	50.0	30.2	19.8						
30	40.55	.158	64	.894	.726	0.3		N 80 E	10.28	10.60	47.5	33.2	14.3						
	35.36	0.156	74	29.530	29.374	0.5		N 60 W	4.15	10.24	43.36	27.24	16.12	1.755	39.6	12.9	41.9	3.045	81.5

GENERAL METEOROLOGICAL ABSTRACT,—MAY, 1857.

Days	DAILY MEANS.						WIND.			EXTREMES OF TEMPERATURE.			RAIN.		SNOW.		RAIN AND MELTED SNOW	
	Temperature of the Air.	Pressure of Vapour.	Relative Humidity.	Barometric Pressure.	Pressure of Dry Air.	Clouded Sky.	Resultant Direction.	Resultant Velocity.	Mean Velocity.	Maximum.	Minimum.	Difference.	Depth in Inches.	Approximate duration in hours.	Depth in Inches.	Approximate duration in hours.	Depth in Inches.	Approximate duration in hours.
	°							Miles.	Miles.	°	°	°						
1	43.42	0.231	83	29.566	29.335	1.0	S 78 E	5.11	5.50	48.4	38.8	9.6	0.345	13.8	...	...	0.345	13.8
2	41.23	.296	88	.489	.263	1.0	N 38 W	8.13	8.96	40.4	35.0	11.4	.420	7.0	...	...	.420	7.0
3	41.62	.228	57	.466	.239	1.0	N 53 E	2.49	5.89	48.8	36.0	12.8	...	...	...	...	...	...
4	43.75	.205	84	.285	.020	1.0	N 46 W	12.30	13.27	46.2	37.8	7.4	1.375	19.2	...	...	1.375	19.2
5	40.82	.210	83	.520	.310	1.0	N 75 W	0.11	4.61	50.2	37.8	12.4	.245	20.0	...	...	.245	20.0
6	43.52	.227	81	.688	.461	1.0	S 9 E	4.53	5.16	44.7	34.5	10.2	*	2.5	...	...	*	2.5
7	46.48	.216	60	.775	.559	0.5	S 22 W	1.20	3.44	53.0	34.4	18.0	.020	0.4	...	...	.020	0.4
8	55.73	.329	75	.446	.117	0.3	N 85 E	4.85	5.42	54.2	37.2	17.0	...	...	...	...	...	...
9						0.9	S 46 W	8.06	9.97	67.8	41.5	26.3	.315	3.6	...	...	.315	3.6
10						0.6	N 58 W	20.65	22.39	53.0	27.8	25.2	*	...	*	0.5	*	...
11	31.95	.134	74	.830	.696	0.6	N 49 E	3.45	8.05	38.0	26.0	12.0	...	...	...	...	...	...
12	39.72	.161	67	.849	.688	0.0	S 28 E	1.22	4.73	49.0	31.5	17.5	...	...	...	...	...	...
13	45.40	.175	60	.740	.674	0.2	N 70 E	1.34	6.80	53.2	34.5	18.7	...	...	...	...	...	...
14	46.25	.220	71	.353	.133	1.0	N 68 E	16.98	17.25	50.4	41.8	8.6	.250	7.0	...	...	.250	7.0
15	45.57	.254	84	.304	.050	1.0	N 53 E	1.62	9.01	49.0	39.0	10.0	.305	7.0	...	...	.305	7.0
16	43.22	.216	77	.528	.312	0.6	N 73 W	13.45	15.09	58.2	33.4	24.8	.140	0.7	...	...	.140	0.7
17						0.2	N 62 W	6.07	7.06	50.4	33.2	17.2	...	...	...	...	...	...
18	47.35	.235	73	.776	.541	0.7	N 53 E	6.48	8.59	54.2	39.2	15.0	...	...	...	...	...	...
19	52.37	.227	58	.690	.463	0.7	N 32 E	9.51	11.85	60.0	44.0	16.0	...	...	...	...	...	...
20	48.65	.212	65	.624	.411	0.5	N 12 E	5.35	8.29	67.0	35.5	26.5	...	...	...	...	...	...
21	59.68	.271	55	.547	.275	0.3	N 38 W	10.46	11.11	71.8	45.0	26.8	...	...	...	...	...	...
22	56.28	.328	74	.457	.159	0.5	S 22 W	3.80	6.01	68.0	42.2	22.2	...	...	...	...	...	...
23	60.48	.293	57	.491	.198	0.2	S 49 W	2.24	4.71	72.5	46.0	26.5	...	...	...	...	...	...
24							S 22 E	2.52	3.46	69.8	50.0	19.8	...	...	...	...	...	...
25	63.85	.360	63	.404	.104	0.2	N 33 E	5.06	6.16	74.8	51.5	23.3	...	...	...	...	...	...
26	59.88	.371	75	.435	.084	0.7	S 77 E	4.31	5.34	68.2	53.6	14.6	*	1.0	...	...	*	1.0
27	55.15	.381	85	.366	.084	0.6	S 10 W	6.30	6.84	67.0	47.7	19.3	.220	5.0	...	...	.220	5.0
28	52.15	.312	82	.281	28.969	0.5	S 20 W	6.73	7.95	66.5	44.0	22.5	.295	...	...	...	.295	...
29	51.42	.275	74	.367	29.092	0.9	S 78 W	7.64	8.10	56.2	45.0	11.2	...	...	...	...	...	...
30	54.78	.292	70	.533	.241	0.7	S 60 E	1.50	2.75	61.5	48.8	12.7	.135	5.8	...	...	.135	5.8
31							N 74 E	7.28	7.38	60.0	51.0	9.0	.080	1.8	...	...	.080	1.8
	8.87	0.254	74	29.535	29.282	0.6	N 23 W	1.14	8.13	57.17	40.24	16.94	4.145	94.8	*	0.5	4.145	95.3

TORONTO METEOROLOGICAL OBSERVATIONS. 43

GENERAL METEOROLOGICAL ABSTRACT.—JUNE, 1857.

	DAILY MEANS.						WIND.			EXTREMES OF TEMPERATURE.			RAIN.		SNOW.		RAIN AND MELTED SNOW	
Days.	Temperature of the Air.	Pressure of Vapour.	Relative Humidity.	Pressure Barometric	Pressure of Dry Air.	Clouded Sky.	Resultant Direction.	Resultant Velocity.	Mean Velocity	Maximum.	Minimum.	Difference.	Depth in Inches.	Approximate duration in hours.	Depth in Inches.	Approximate duration in hours.	Depth in Inches.	Approximate duration in hours.
	°							Miles.	Miles.									
1	57.62	0.391	84	29.237	28.846	0.7	S 19 W	2.73	3.62	66.5	40.5	17.0	0.110	4.8	...	...	...	...
2	52.83	.284	72	.258	28.974	0.9	S 65 W	6.96	7.44	59.8	46.5	13.3	.025	1.0	...	...	!	...
3	53.02	.319	81	.292	28.973	0.8	S 88 W	5.30	7.21	65.0	42.2	22.8	.440	4.0	...	...	...	...
4	49.10	.220	64	.646	29.326	0.6	N 75 W	5.46	7.85	58.0	35.0	23.0	...	...	...	...	...	...
5	48.35	.215	64	.581	.366	0.4	N 77 W	6.52	7.06	59.0	40.0	19.0	.010	1.0	...	...	...	...
6	55.08	.260	63	.403	.143	0.9	N 71 W	7.29	8.07	68.2	49.8	24.4	.060	1.7	...	...	...	...
7							N 77 E	5.39	6.08	62.5	48.8	13.7		0.6				
8						1.0	N 68 E	2.36	10.46	59.4	49.0	10.4	.350	2.0	...	...	...	...
9	65.33	.380	88	.419	.039	1.0	S 79 E	3.45	3.45	60.0	51.2	8.8	.035	0.7	...	...	...	...
10	55.08	.397	93	.528	.131	1.0	N 80 E	2.96	6.04	59.2	55.0	14.2	...	9.5	...	...	...	...
11	60.48	.449	87	.409	28.900	0.8	N 48 W	2.96	6.52	64.4	47.2	17.2	.605	1.2	...	...	...	...
12	57.32	.363	78	.022	28.659	0.7	N 39 W	5.46	6.52	66.0	50.0	16.0	.230	4.0	...	...	...	...
13	57.08	.365	79	.145	28.780	0.7	N 78 W	9.17	10.87	72.2	50.0	22.2	*	0.1	...	...	...	...
14	60.97	.382	65	.380	28.998	0.3	S 85 W	2.14	6.23	67.5	46.0	21.5						
15	54.45					1.0	N 70 R	6.34	8.54	60.0	49.0	11.0	.030	1.2	...	...	...	...
16	52.67	.288	69	.655	29.367	1.0	N 75 E	17.22	17.22	56.5	48.9	7.6	.195	6.8	...	...	...	...
17	54.85	.322	73	.472	.150	0.9	N 75 E	7.77	8.00	67.4	52.2	15.2	.005	1.5	...	...	...	...
18	55.03	.383	90	.395	.013	0.9	S 66 E	3.64	6.24	61.2	47.0	14.2	.085	4.0	...	...	...	...
19	55.83	.398	91	.389	28.951	0.4	N 78 W	10.00	10.18	64.5	46.5	18.0	...	...	...	...	...	...
20	53.58	.362	81	.339	28.996	0.8	S 8 W	3.00	4.03	60.0	49.0	11.0	...	...	...	...	...	...
21			90	.396	29.034	1.0	N 89 E	1.10	4.50	65.8	51.8	14.0	.030	6.5	...	...	...	...
22	55.25	.372	87	.411	.039	0.3	S 22 E	13.70	14.52	60.8	40.6	20.2	.145	2.5	...	...	...	...
23	56.88	.316	71	.617	.301	0.4	N 34 W	14.52	6.75	67.0	46.2	20.8	.395	7.3	...	...	...	...
24	58.98	.388	69	.661	.323	0.3	N 02 W	5.07	4.50	67.0	47.0	20.0	...	...	...	...	...	...
25	64.32	.305	68	.632	.242	0.1	S 75 W	2.52	5.16	68.0	47.0	21.0	...	0.2	...	...	...	...
26	68.42	.422	68	.632	.210	0.4	N 20 W	1.90	2.95	75.8	52.5	15.3	.105	...	...	...	...	...
27	66.47	.501	83	.595	.094	0.6	N 72 E	1.92	3.58	75.5	60.0	15.5	...	...	...	...	...	...
28							S 30 W	2.47	4.44	76.0	58.8	17.5	.265	3.0	...	...	...	...
29	64.52	.467	77	.394	28.937	0.6	N 36 W	10.45	10.86	73.8	53.5	20.3	1.070	7.0	...	...	...	...
30	56.43	.307	69	.381	29.074	0.6	S 82 W	8.12	9.60	63.8	50.6	13.2	...	...	...	...	...	...
	56.92	0.358	77	29.427	29.074	0.7	N 49 W	1.15	7.60	65.48	48.99	16.49	5.060	66.0				

GENERAL METEOROLOGICAL ABSTRACT,—JULY, 1857.

	DAILY MEANS.						WIND.			EXTREMES OF TEMPERATURE.			RAIN.		SNOW.		RAIN AND MELTED SNOW	
Date.	Temperature of the Air.	Pressure of Vapour.	Relative Humidity.	Barometric Pressure.	Pressure of Dry Air.	Clouded Sky.	Resultant Direction.	Resultant Velocity.	Mean Velocity.	Maximum.	Minimum.	Difference.	Depth in Inches.	Approximate duration in hours.	Depth in Inches.	Approximate duration in hours.	Depth in Inches.	Approximate duration in hours.
								Miles.	Miles.									
1	54.65	0.390	86	29.406	29.137	1.0	N 66 E	6.06	14.08	60.7	51.0	9.7	0.030	2.1	...	...	...	...
2	56.45	.329	74	.704	.375	0.6	N 76 E	6.15	6.15	62.5	47.0	15.5	...	0.1	...	...	...	...
3	61.68	.359	67	.640	.281	0.3	S 53 W	1.45	3.93	69.8	53.2	16.6	...	...	...	...	...	...
4	63.83	.451	78	.687	.236	0.1	N 74 W	2.73	5.48	75.8	50.8	24.4	...	...	...	...	...	...
5	...	...	...	...	...	...	S 30 W	1.91	3.41	73.0	54.0	19.0	*	0.2	...	...	...	...
6	64.12	.408	70	.701	.299	0.3	S 69 E	2.64	2.09	73.4	56.0	17.4	...	...	...	...	...	...
7	67.78	.537	82	.604	.067	0.9	N 60 W	3.21	7.14	78.5	57.8	20.7	.215	0.6	...	...	...	...
8	64.92	.421	70	.735	.311	0.4	S 27 W	1.41	4.71	72.2	53.4	18.8	...	...	...	...	...	...
9	66.42	.370	59	.823	.352	0.0	N 57 E	3.97	5.15	75.2	58.0	17.2	...	...	...	...	...	...
10	68.50	.463	68	.814	.332	0.0	S 41 E	1.91	2.43	78.0	58.0	20.0	...	...	...	...	...	...
11	72.77	.696	77	.767	.171	0.3	N 13 W	1.59	2.45	83.2	63.5	19.7	...	...	...	...	...	...
12	...	...	...	...	...	...	S 26 W	1.50	2.43	86.2	64.5	21.7	...	...	...	...	...	...
13	75.43	.649	74	.614	28.965	0.0	S 25 E	2.88	3.05	86.6	64.4	22.2	*	3.5	...	...	...	...
14	75.06	.829	75	.686	28.907	0.2	N 74 E	2.10	2.65	83.0	65.0	18.0	.515	0.1	...	...	...	...
15	73.68	.609	76	.526	28.917	0.5	S 65 E	0.37	1.57	83.0	66.2	16.8	*	0.1	...	...	...	...
16	71.15	.618	84	.548	28.928	0.6	N 98 E	1.91	2.46	78.6	63.5	15.1	...	...	...	...	...	...
17	72.90	.637	78	.540	28.883	0.5	N 70 E	1.36	1.50	80.8	64.7	16.1	...	...	...	...	...	...
18	76.25	.679	78	.467	28.788	0.5	S 14 W	2.63	2.93	85.4	65.0	20.4	...	...	...	...	...	...
19	...	...	...	...	...	0.7	S 44 W	4.78	7.50	85.0	62.8	22.2	.050	3.5	...	...	...	...
20	67.40	.533	62	.362	28.749	0.5	N 31 W	2.52	5.07	78.2	59.2	19.0	.330	4.5	...	...	...	...
21	64.77	.475	80	.308	28.533	0.7	N 81 E	3.28	5.05	73.0	59.0	14.0	.065	2.0	...	...	...	...
22	65.98	.488	80	.497	28.949	1.0	N 81 E	4.22	5.94	73.5	59.0	14.5	...	...	...	...	...	...
23	65.93	.533	86	.650	29.017	0.7	N 23 E	6.75	7.83	70.0	61.8	8.2	.665	10.0	...	...	...	...
24	65.22	.551	91	.653	.002	0.7	S 9 W	1.81	3.38	71.4	57.2	14.2	.115	7.0	...	...	...	...
25	69.73	.605	85	.719	.114	0.1	S 10 E	3.05	3.25	78.5	61.0	17.5	...	...	...	...	...	...
26	...	...	...	...	...	0.5	S 61 E	2.78	3.29	81.5	62.0	19.5	...	...	...	...	...	...
27	76.15	.700	81	.567	28.567	0.0	S 21 W	8.61	8.61	84.5	68.0	16.5	...	...	...	...	...	...
28	68.33	.523	77	.689	29.016	0.0	N 48 W	8.35	9.05	74.2	56.0	18.2	.240	2.5	...	...	...	...
29	67.37	.477	73	.710	.233	0.5	S 79 E	8.12	4.37	73.0	60.9	12.1	...	...	...	...	...	...
30	67.25	.519	79	.577	.064	0.7	N 79 E	4.58	4.74	73.5	62.0	11.5	...	...	...	...	...	...
31	63.27	.521	86	.445	29.024	0.3	S 97 W	2.93	4.66	78.8	54.0	24.5	1.260	7.0	...	...	...	...
	67.76	0.520	78	29.598	29.068	0.5	S 68 E	0.81	4.74	76.79	59.32	17.47	3.475	43.2	...	...	...	...

GENERAL METEOROLOGICAL ABSTRACT.—AUGUST, 1857.

TORONTO METEOROLOGICAL OBSERVATIONS.

Date	DAILY MEANS.						WIND.			EXTREMES OF TEMPERATURE.			RAIN.		SNOW.		RAIN AND MELTED SNOW	
	Temperature of the Air.	Pressure of Vapour.	Relative Humidity.	Barometric Pressure.	Pressure of Dry Air.	Clouded Sky.	Resultant Direction.	Resultant Velocity.	Mean Velocity.	Maximum.	Minimum.	Difference.	Depth in Inches.	Approximate duration in hours.	Depth in Inches.	Approximate duration in hours.	Depth in Inches.	Approximate duration in hours.
	°							Miles.	Miles.	°	°	°						
1	65.60	0.487	72	29.487	29.060	0.5	N 76 W	4.84	5.62	75.8	55.0	20.8	...	...	...	...	...	...
2	68.20	.488	73	.621	.138	.2	S 86 W	3.31	4.74	78.4	54.8	23.6	...	...	...	...	...	...
3	68.60	.555	82	.532	28.977	0.8	S 57 W	2.27	4.35	76.8	57.0	19.8	...	...	...	...	...	...
4	66.85	.505	64	.593	29.198	0.2	N 14 W	5.19	6.70	77.2	59.8	17.4	.020	1.0	...	...	...	...
5	66.58	.468	74	.725	.257	0.0	N 15 W	1.02	7.82	77.4	54.5	22.9	...	...	...	...	...	...
6	69.80	.519	75	.756	.237	0.4	N 63 E	1.95	2.87	76.6	57.5	19.1	...	...	...	...	...	...
7	73.68	.530	67	.724	.201	0.4	N 64 E	2.51	2.85	80.0	57.5	22.5	...	*	...	...	...	...
8		.511	77	.362	28.550	.7	N 25 W	5.04	7.91	85.2	62.2	23.0	...	*	...	...	...	...
9	67.43	.367	61	.457	29.089	0.3	N 88 E	4.07	4.97	75.2	59.8	15.4	...	...	...	...	...	...
10	65.30	.512	89	.575	.063	1.0	S 83 W	2.33	5.37	71.4	58.5	15.9	...	...	...	...	...	...
11	63.25	.698	80	.402	28.764	0.6	N 35 W	6.00	7.17	75.2	52.0	23.2	...	11.8	...	...	...	...
12	76.38	.601	82	.482	.881	0.9	S 61 E	2.44	5.20	72.0	55.2	16.8	.890	1.5	...	...	...	...
13	70.17	.601	82	.482	.881	0.9	N 42 W	9.30	9.57	89.2	69.0	19.2	.890	1.5	...	...	...	...
14	62.78	.402	71	.628	29.226	0.4	N 73 W	4.45	6.59	83.0	54.6	28.0	...	...	...	...	...	...
15							N 44 W	4.81	7.58	74.4	55.6	19.8	.940	...	...	...	...	...
16				.007	.162	1.0	N 70 E	7.66	8.11	67.2	56.0	11.2	1.110	9.5	...	...	...	...
17	59.43	.446	90	.678	.286	0.6	N 22 E	2.41	6.23	62.2	55.5	6.7	.275	7.2	...	...	...	...
18	61.92	.392	84	.645	.192	0.1	S 46 E	6.05	7.07	68.3	55.4	12.7	.240	4.3	...	...	...	...
19	61.63	.454	64	.753	.406	0.6	N 76 W	7.07	7.07	71.0	52.5	18.5	.055	0.9	...	...	...	...
20	62.97	.347	77	.731	.325	0.6	N 41 W	7.52	7.97	71.5	47.2	24.3	...	...	...	...	...	...
21	61.18	.406	82	.327	28.851	0.9	N 46 E	5.51	7.24	69.2	48.8	20.4	.125	3.0	...	...	...	...
22	63.95	.476					S 5 W	8.82	10.05	71.4	56.8	14.6	.146	5.5	...	...	...	...
23		.353	76	.701	29.348	0.0	S 75 W	10.63	12.92	70.8	46.0	25.0	.150	4.5	...	...	...	...
24	57.93	.448	79	.829	.381	0.2	S 67 W	4.33	5.67	70.8	48.8	22.0	...	...	...	...	...	...
25	68.35	.436	76	.707	.381	0.9	S 25 W	5.74	3.52	73.2	52.4	20.8	...	...	...	...	...	...
26	64.33	.568	87	.391	28.823	0.7	East	2.96	4.73	75.0	52.8	22.2	.915	10.1	...	...	...	...
27	67.52	.568	87	.391	28.823	0.7	S 23 E	8.84	6.27	75.0	61.0	14.0	.500	8.0	...	...	...	...
28	65.02	.492	81	.294	28.902	0.0	S 63 W	5.34	6.27	76.5	56.5	20.0	...	...	...	...	...	...
29	60.18	.396	78	.509	29.118	0.6	N 36 W	8.25	4.83	69.2	48.0	21.2	...	...	...	...	...	...
30							S 67 W	4.27	4.83	72.0	49.8	22.2	...	...	...	...	...	...
31	63.55	.454	80	.803	.949	0.0	S 42 W	4.17	4.30	74.6	53.5	21.1	...	...	...	...	...	...
	65.31	0.467	77	29.594	29.127	0.5	N 77 W	1.51	6.30	74.46	54.95	19.50	5.265	67.3				

GENERAL METEOROLOGICAL ABSTRACT.—SEPTEMBER, 1857.

Days.	DAILY MEANS.						WIND.			EXTREMES OF TEMPERATURE.			RAIN.		SNOW.		RAIN AND MELTED SNOW	
	Temperature of the Air.	Pressure of Vapour.	Relative Humidity.	Barometric Pressure.	Pressure of Dry Air.	Clouded Sky.	Resultant Direction.	Resultant Velocity.	Mean Velocity.	Maximum.	Minimum.	Difference.	Depth in Inches.	Approximate duration in hours.	Depth in Inches.	Approximate duration in hours.	Depth in Inches.	Approximate duration in hours.
	°						°	Miles.	Miles.	°	°	°						
1	65.30	0.488	81	29.919	29.431	0.1	S 84 E	2.16	2.16	76.5	54.0	22.5	...	...	...	...	...	...
2	66.67	.527	63	.915	.888	0.3	S 85 E	1.32	2.71	76.2	57.5	18.7	...	...	...	...	...	...
3	67.43	.496	77	.989	.443	0.5	N 71 E	2.26	3.19	75.5	60.0	15.5	...	...	...	...	...	...
4	67.83	.528	80	.852	.324	0.3	S 15 W	0.50	0.58	77.8	57.8	20.0	...	7.0	...	...	...	...
5	65.25	.513	83	.701	.188	0.5	N 74 W	3.68	5.97	76.5	48.0	28.5	.213	...	...	...	...	...
6	...	...	...	...	...	...	...	...	...	65.5	49.2	16.3	...	...	...	...	...	...
7	54.75	.265	64	30.042	.778	0.1	N 31 W	3.41	5.01	61.4	45.0	16.4	...	...	...	...	...	...
8	57.30	.341	75	29.918	.576	0.1	S 62 E	2.54	3.55	68.4	44.0	24.4	...	...	...	...	...	...
9	61.18	.423	80	.753	.329	0.4	S 22 W	1.51	1.54	72.2	45.4	26.8	...	...	...	...	...	...
10	68.60	.553	82	.584	.026	0.3	S 30 W	1.03	1.03	79.0	55.5	23.5	...	0.5	...	...	...	...
11	70.92	.601	81	.016	.013	1.0	S 89 E	5.55	5.59	82.0	60.0	22.0	.002	...	...	...	...	...
12	63.45	.499	85	.697	.129	0.5	S 88 E	7.69	7.69	67.0	60.0	7.0	...	...	...	...	...	...
13	...	...	...	...	...	...	...	2.63	2.72	75.2	59.8	15.4	...	2.5	...	...	...	...
14	67.42	.559	84	.522	.963	0.0	N 56 W	5.14	6.00	76.4	53.5	22.9	.135	...	...	...	...	...
15	59.68	.329	69	.759	.430	0.1	S 35 W	10.23	10.23	68.5	50.0	18.5	...	...	...	...	...	...
16	57.75	.361	78	.780	.378	0.9	S 56 E	3.91	4.07	62.2	49.5	12.7	.225	5.0	...	...	...	...
17	63.90	.512	88	.383	.013	0.7	S 46 W	6.52	8.01	75.0	51.8	23.2	.215	2.0	...	...	...	...
18	52.15	.275	72	.744	.370	0.5	N 50 W	7.24	8.70	58.2	44.5	13.7	...	...	...	...	...	...
19	48.27	.273	82	.628	.460	1.0	N 36 B	9.39	10.70	52.6	45.4	7.2	.430	9.0	...	...	...	...
20	...	...	...	...	...	...	...	0.48	6.07	57.5	39.8	17.7	...	...	...	...	...	...
21	52.87	.277	70	.748	.471	0.5	N 45 E	4.49	5.37	59.0	40.2	18.8	.210	4.0	...	...	...	...
22	52.45	.307	79	.445	.138	0.6	N 87 W	4.99	6.07	61.2	39.8	21.4	.015	0.5	...	...	...	...
23	48.58	.248	73	.485	.237	0.4	S 74 W	7.13	7.27	60.6	45.4	15.4	...	...	...	...	...	...
24	56.25	.375	84	.595	.220	0.0	S 20 W	5.42	5.62	60.8	39.8	27.2	...	...	...	...	...	...
25	61.52	.411	77	.640	.238	0.0	S 15 W	5.08	5.66	67.0	49.3	18.7	...	...	...	...	...	...
26	57.50	.361	79	.805	.441	0.0	S 45 W	1.32	3.27	66.2	47.0	19.2	...	...	...	...	...	...
27	...	...	...	...	...	...	...	5.85	7.52	74.0	49.8	24.2	.100	0.5	...	...	...	...
28	52.68	.309	78	.611	.301	0.8	S 78 W	12.81	13.11	64.5	35.0	29.6	.085	0.7	...	...	...	...
29	41.32	.178	71	.796	.018	0.4	N 37 W	0.86	7.09	49.8	35.1	14.7	...	...	...	...	...	...
30	43.78	.195	71	.743	.548	0.6	N 73 W	4.57	4.09	54.0	34.2	19.8	.010	0.2	...	...	...	...
	58.64	0.393	78	29.712	29.319	0.4	N 68 W	1.61	5.55	67.48	48.14	19.34	2.640	31.9	...	...	...	...

GENERAL METEOROLOGICAL ABSTRACT,—OCTOBER, 1857.

Days	DAILY MEANS.						WIND.			EXTREMES OF TEMPERATURE.			RAIN.			SNOW.			RAIN AND MELTED SNOW.		
	Temperature of the Air.	Pressure of Vapour.	Relative Humidity.	Barometric Pressure.	Pressure of Dry Air.	Clouded Sky.	Resultant Direction.	Resultant Velocity.	Mean Velocity.	Maximum.	Minimum.	Difference.	Depth in Inches.	Approximate duration in hours.		Depth in Inches.	Approximate duration in hours.		Depth in Inches.	Approximate duration in hours.	
1	46.47	0.278	87	29.650	29.377	1.0	N 42 E	3.98	5.04	51.8	39.2	12.6	0.080	7.0					0.080	7.0	
2	43.98	.175	62	.856	.681	0.5	N 49 E	5.77	6.28	51.2	38.8	12.4									
3	47.17	.266	82	.947	.681	1.0	N 64 E	2.97	3.09	52.2	38.2	14.0									
4						0.7	N 81 E	1.32	1.38	56.2	49.2	7.0									
5	53.08	.349	87	.855	.506	0.2	S 25 E	0.79	0.99	60.2	44.0	16.2									
6	54.20	.340	83	.740	.400	0.5	N 29 W	6.49	6.63	64.0	42.0	22.0									
7	48.47	.274	82	.739	.465	0.0	S 16 W	1.27	2.46	58.2	37.8	20.4									
8	62.43	.311	81	.644	.388	0.1	S 51 W	1.79	2.62	63.8	37.6	26.2									
9	54.42	.354	95	.732	.378	0.9	N 52 E	1.33	1.36	60.2	45.0	15.2									
10	49.97	.268	76	.811	.543	0.0	N 72 E	5.90	6.09	54.8	40.0	14.8									
11	57.03	.411	89	.692	.281	0.9	N 85 E	3.40	3.92	58.0	42.0	16.0	.385	7.5					.385	7.5	
12	55.53	.353	81	.766	.413	0.4	S 11 W	2.43	3.79	60.8	49.5	11.3	.010	1.5					.010	1.5	
13	50.47	.277	77	.714	.437	0.7	N 27 E	2.72	4.23	61.8	40.0	21.8									
14	50.68	.294	81	.414	.120	1.0	N 81 E	3.47	4.13	57.0	49.0	8.0									
15	46.18	.211	68	.374	.163	0.5	N 3 W	6.28	6.49	53.0	45.0	8.0	*	0.5					*	0.5	
16	45.03	.204	69	.646	.442	0.5	N 30 W	10.67	10.96	52.0	31.2	20.8									
17						0.0	S 61 W	5.38	6.26	52.4	34.8	16.6									
18						0.7	N 29 W	2.50	4.96	49.5	40.0	9.5									
19	46.32	.236	74	.466	.230	0.5	S 86 W	13.11	13.89	52.2	31.2	21.0	.240	8.0					.240	8.0	
20	32.82	.122	66	.726	.604	0.2	S 61 W	16.71	17.04	39.5	26.5	13.0	.055	4.0					.055	4.0	
21	35.60	.143	71	.994	.750	0.5	N 75 W	6.55	6.61	45.0	26.8	18.2									
22	38.42	.192	82	.933	.741	0.8	N 79 E	2.59	4.10	46.8	27.4	19.4									
23	43.50	.236	85	.824	.588	0.8	S 37 E	2.60	3.59	51.0	38.2	12.8									
24	46.3	.253	91	.608	.325	1.0	N 63 E	4.30	4.44	49.6	41.2	8.4	.235	8.0					.235	8.0	
25						0.5	N 11 W	13.06	13.00	49.6	38.6	11.0	.020	3.5		0.2			.020	3.5	
26	39.77	.160	66	.478	.318	0.4	N 14 W	27.08	27.08	46.2	30.0	16.2									
27	37.67	.128	57	.578	.449	1.0	N 25 W	6.78	9.83	44.2	30.0	14.2									
28	36.13	.150	72	.539	.388	1.0	N 51 E	3.83	3.76	39.3	32.2	7.1						6.0	.020	6.0	
29	36.47	.183	85	.452	.269	0.7	N 36 E	1.61	1.62	38.8	30.0	8.8		0.5				5.0	*	5.0	
30	38.15	.182	79	.438	.256	0.7	S 84 W	0.64	1.97	45.0	29.5	15.5	*	0.5					*	0.5	
31	40.20	.192	78	.496	.304	0.9	S 88 W	3.50	5.18	45.6	35.8	9.7	.015	1.5					.015	1.5	
	45.42	0.243	78	29.667	29.424	0.6	N 19 W	2.93	6.24	51.93	37.47	14.45	1.040	42.0		0.2	11.0		1.000	53.0	

GENERAL METEOROLOGICAL ABSTRACT,—NOVEMBER, 1857.

Date	DAILY MEANS.					WIND.			Extremes of Temperature.			RAIN.		SNOW.		Rain and Melted Snow	
	Temperature of the Air.	Pressure of Vapour.	Relative Humidity.	Barometric Pressure.	Pressure of Dry Air.	Clouded Sky.	Resultant Direction.	Resultant Velocity.	Mean Velocity.	Maximum.	Minimum.	Difference.	Depth in Inches.	Approximate duration in hours.	Depth in Inches.	Approximate duration in hours.	Depth in Inches.	Approximate duration in hours.
	°							Miles.	Miles.									
1	39.92	.180	74	......	.077	0.4	S 42 W	8.17	8.71	46.4	35.5	10.9	*		......	......	*	0.2
2	38.22	.190	70	29.557	.535	0.6	S 77 W	12.07	12.51	48.8	35.0	13.8	*	0.2	......	......	*	0.8
3	39.15	.190	79	.675	.485	0.7	West	9.57	9.93	43.5	33.8	9.7		0.8				
4	45.57	.275	90	.296	.021	0.8	N 69 E	4.59	5.43	44.5	33.2	11.3	.005	0.4			.005	0.4
5	40.02	.200	57	.268	.067	0.8	S 61 E	3.44	10.08	54.0	38.8	15.2	.415	6.5			.415	6.5
6	42.70	.213	51	.493	.276	0.9	S 64 W	7.38	8.42	58.0	36.4	21.6						
7							N 64 E	9.35	10.06	49.0	37.8	11.2	.145	9.0			.145	9.0
8							S 85 E	4.17	8.88	58.2	45.0	13.2	.370	15.0	0.7	1.5	.370	15.0
9	45.05	.275	91	.410	.135	1.0	S 67 W	8.17	8.62	50.4	33.2	17.2	1.020	18.0			1.020	18.0
10	37.72	.144	64	.834	.690	0.3	S 55 W	9.58	9.82	43.4	30.0	13.4						
11	37.08	.144	67	30.082	.888	0.5	S 63 W	6.79	6.86	43.4	33.0	10.4	.030	4.5			.030	4.5
12	39.75	.198	81	29.602	.404	1.0	S 46 W	6.42	7.34	44.0	33.0	11.0	*		*		*	1.5
13	35.22	.139	67	.547	.408	0.8	N 77 W	9.41	11.85	39.0	21.5	17.5						
14	25.08	.091	65	.943	.852	0.1	N 32 W	7.03	7.25	30.0	20.5	9.5						
15							S 55 W	4.20	4.49	38.5	22.5	16.0	.215	3.0	0.2	5.5	.215	8.5
16	39.02	.164	87	.504	.340	0.8	S 33 W	2.54	3.19	38.0	30.0	8.0	.025	0.2	2.0	13.0	.025	0.2
17	34.97	.159	78	.131	29.971	0.8	S 52 W	12.06	12.15	36.8	31.2	5.6	.140	4.0			.140	4.0
18	37.10	.143	67	28.980	28.732	0.7	S 21 W	7.10	10.39	42.4	31.5	10.9	.075	3.0	0.2	1.0	.075	3.0
19	33.53	.169	84	28.671	28.503	0.8	S 45 W	16.18	19.60	44.0	27.0	17.0	.055	2.0	2.0	5.0	.050	5.0
20	22.68	.101	80	28.953	28.853	0.6	S 57 W	19.59	19.63	27.0	17.2	9.8			2.0	13.0	.200	13.0
21	27.75	.127	82	29.165	29.038	1.0	S 44 W	17.69	19.90	32.2	24.8	7.4			0.5	6.0	.050	6.0
22							N 73 W	7.91	8.64	29.2	18.2	10.8			2.5	8.5	.250	8.5
23	24.08	.109	81	.245	.136	0.6	N 75 W	7.42	9.59	29.5	13.2	16.3			0.5	2.5	.050	2.5
24	14.25	.071	75	.579	.508	0.7	N 87 W	8.60	11.13	20.8	-2.8	23.8			*	0.2	.050	0.2
25	11.00	.062	76	30.156	30.094	0.7	S 75 W	9.00	9.33	20.2	-3.5	23.7						
26	20.43	.086	77	30.191	30.105	0.4	S 64 W	6.89	6.99	26.2	16.4	10.8						
27	27.82	.121	77	30.075	29.954	0.3	S 42 W	6.89	19.99	35.4	15.5	19.9						
28	34.45	.151	75	30.015	.864	0.4	S 26 W	1.60	1.95	41.0	29.8	12.2	.140	3.0			.140	3.0
29							N 67 E	7.22	7.44	41.5	33.8	7.7	.745	10.0			.745	10.0
30	42.07	.248	94	29.680	.391	1.0	S 29 E	1.06	4.03	43.0	37.2	5.8						
	33.54	0.157	77	29.534	29.367	0.7	S 61 W	5.45	9.25	30.94	26.55	13.89	3.235	76.6	6.9	43.2	3.925	119.8

GENERAL METEOROLOGICAL ABSTRACT,—DECEMBER, 1857.

Days.	DAILY MEANS.					WIND.			EXTREMES OF TEMPERATURE.			RAIN.		SNOW.		RAIN AND MELTED SNOW.	
	Temperature of the Air.	Pressure of Vapour.	Relative Humidity.	Barometric Pressure.	Pressure of Dry Air.	Clouded Sky.	Resultant Direction.	Resultant Velocity.	Mean Velocity.	Maximum.	Minimum.	Difference.	Depth in Inches.	Approximate duration in hours.	Depth in Inches.	Approximate duration in hours.	Depth in Inches.	Approximate duration in hours.
1	36.85	0.168	78	29.729	29.561	0.7	S 52 W	3.65	8.68	38.6	30.0	8.6	...	...	...	...	...	...
2	37.55	.107	74	.572	.405	0.8	S 64 W	7.68	9.13	41.5	30.2	11.3	...	...	...	...	...	...
3	30.40	.116	68	.766	.650	0.8	N 85 W	12.14	12.29	32.3	24.8	7.5	...	...	*	2.0	.040	2.0
4	29.47	.121	74	.784	.663	0.6	S 76 E	0.64	4.76	32.4	24.0	8.4	...	...	0.4	8.0	.050	3.0
5	28.95	.134	83	.696	.562	1.0	N 77 E	12.23	12.89	33.9	26.5	7.4	...	...	0.5	2.0	.050	3.0
6	...	...	...	...	...	0.4	S 78 E	3.79	7.99	40.5	32.5	8.0	.325	12.0	...	...	.325	12.0
7	37.22	.178	81	.611	.433	0.7	S 61 W	3.13	4.15	43.8	33.5	10.3	.165	5.0	...	...	.165	5.0
8	39.75	.180	75	.677	.497	0.9	N 79 E	2.97	7.00	46.0	35.2	10.8	.190	3.5	...	...	.190	3.5
9	40.37	.220	88	.266	.046	0.8	S 63 W	1.63	11.65	42.5	35.0	7.5	1.055	15.5	...	...	1.055	15.5
10	32.48	.135	72	.489	.355	0.3	S 88 W	1.81	13.16	37.2	20.8	16.4	...	...	1.5	4.8	.150	4.8
11	23.32	.103	83	.014	.911	0.1	S 25 W	1.97	2.11	30.7	14.5	15.7	...	...	...	...	...	...
12	23.33	.107	83	30.014	30.072	...	S 74 W	1.74	1.92	30.0	15.0	16.3	...	...	...	...	...	...
13	...	...	...	30.179	...	0.2	S 45 W	9.32	9.56	40.8	30.0	14.0	...	...	...	...	...	...
14	37.68	.181	81	29.799	29.618	1.0	S 72 W	1.44	2.19	38.5	30.2	8.3	...	...	...	...	...	...
15	36.85	.191	88	.913	.723	1.0	N 77 E	3.02	3.25	38.5	29.4	9.1	...	...	...	...	...	...
16	38.87	.183	95	.838	.655	1.0	N 56 E	0.12	0.13	39.3	30.0	9.3	...	...	...	...	...	...
17	35.15	.191	94	.606	.417	1.0	N 61 E	6.19	5.36	40.5	25.8	14.7	...	...	...	...	...	...
18	35.50	.182	86	.308	.126	1.0	N 54 W	13.12	17.42	27.0	21.2	5.8	.530	8.2	*	0.6	.530	8.2
19	24.97	.104	76	.938	.894	0.9	S 32 W	7.63	7.70	27.0	21.2	7.0	.405	10.5	*	*	.405	11.1
20	...	...	...	...	...	...	S 36 W	1.41	1.56	31.0	17.0	14.0	...	...	...	...	...	...
21	31.03	.146	83	.694	.548	0.7	N 46 E	2.24	2.96	37.0	23.0	12.0	...	...	3.5	6.5	.350	6.5
22	31.43	.143	80	.293	.150	0.8	N 76 W	10.93	3.57	34.5	22.5	12.0	...	...	0.5	2.5	.050	2.5
23	29.07	.118	72	.155	.086	0.8	S 74 W	15.69	11.76	34.5	23.2	10.3	...	...	...	...	...	...
24	22.92	.081	71	.673	.582	0.7	N 58 W	6.55	16.52	29.8	10.2	19.6	...	...	...	...	...	...
25	...	...	...	...	...	...	S 92 E	4.14	6.96	22.0	18.5	3.5	...	...	...	...	...	...
26	20.47	.085	75	550	.465	1.0	S 17 W	9.35	5.29	23.2	4.7	18.4	...	...	0.3	10.0	.090	10.0
27	...	...	...	...	...	0.8	S 58 W	11.54	11.54	38.4	21.2	29.8	...	...	0.5	7.3	.050	7.3
28	33.12	.150	79	.667	.417	0.6	N 13 E	2.46	3.29	34.6	22.0	12.6	...	...	*	0.5	*	0.5
29	28.25	.125	79	.632	.508	1.0	S 59 E	2.49	3.23	34.5	32.0	4.8	...	...	0.3	2.0	.030	2.0
30	35.50	.197	95	.248	.051	1.0	N 13 E.	0.41	0.51	37.0	32.2	4.8	.635	9.5	0.5	6.0	.585	6.0
31	32.57	.156	84	.088	29.932	0.6	S 74 W	8.94	9.76	35.0	28.8	6.2	...	...	0.5	4.0	.050	4.0
	31.86	0.149	80	29.619	29.470	0.7	N 89 W	2.51	6.84	35.75	24.20	11.55	3.205	64.2	9.0	52.2	4.105	116.4

7

GENERAL METEOROLOGICAL ABSTRACT.—JANUARY, 1858.

TORONTO METEOROLOGICAL OBSERVATIONS.

Days	DAILY MEANS.						WIND.			EXTREMES OF TEMPERATURE.			RAIN.		SNOW.		RAIN AND MELTED SNOW	
	Temperature of the Air.	Vapour, Pressure of	Relative Humidity.	Barometric Pressure.	Pressure of Dry Air.	Clouded Sky.	Resultant Direction.	Resultant Velocity.	Mean Velocity.	Maximum.	Minimum.	Difference.	Depth in Inches.	Approximate duration in hours.	Depth in Inches.	Approximate duration in hours.	Depth in Inches.	Approximate duration in hours.
								Miles.	Miles.									
1	29.48	0.135	77	29.535	29.410	0.5	N 81 W	4.40	5.47	35.4	24.2	11.2	...	...	0.1	2.5	0.010	2.5
2	27.77	.105	71	.694	.589	0.1	S 64 W	7.11	7.27	35.4	20.0	15.4	...	...	...	...	...	...
3	40.18	.170	68	.199	.029	0.4	S 53 W	13.66	13.96	40.0	19.2	20.8	...	...	...	...	...	...
4	29.97	.128	78	.493	.365	0.7	N 52 E	7.08	7.17	44.4	34.0	10.4	...	...	2.0	6.5	.200	6.5
5	20.53	.089	82	.505	.416	0.7	N 38 W	5.75	7.12	35.0	29.2	5.8	...	...	1.0	11.5	.100	11.5
6	20.37	.078	71	30.055	.977	0.3	N 55 W	2.23	4.77	29.2	15.6	13.6	...	...	...	...	...	...
7	21.25	.084	73	30.213	30.129	0.5	S 10 E	8.08	8.29	24.2	18.5	5.7	...	...	...	...	...	...
8	32.70	.121	63	29.712	29.591	0.4	N 85 E	3.82	4.63	35.0	11.6	23.4	...	...	...	...	...	...
9							S 69 W	7.13	7.67	38.2	21.0	17.2	.517	7.5	.2	5.2	.517	7.5
10							N 69 W	8.50	8.74	39.7	14.2	25.5	.090	5.0	...	...	.090	5.0
11	41.05	.205	79	.153	28.949	0.8	S 69 W	18.59	15.87	46.2	31.6	14.6	...	...	.2	7.0	...	...
12	33.77	.129	68	.825	29.696	0.3	N 68 E	8.28	9.92	45.8	38.5	3.3	...	...	.2	6.0	...	...
13	35.82	.148	70	.669	.521	0.2	N 81 W	5.49	9.12	42.0	28.8	13.2	...	...	.3	...	...	...
14	31.90	.152	84	.931	.779	0.4	East	3.76	5.83	38.5	26.2	12.3	.330	7.8	...	...	.350	13.0
15	36.05	.175	82	.506	.331	1.0	S 88 E	8.42	8.55	38.2	31.0	7.2	...	...	...	...	.020	...
16	32.32	.160	86	.314	.164	1.0	N 36 W	15.50	15.98	39.4	32.8	6.6	...	...	...	...	.020	...
17						...	N 71 W	8.05	4.24	28.2	21.2	7.0	...	...	...	...	.030	...
18	28.98	.138	86	.678	.540	1.0	N 68 W	2.75	3.86	32.5	24.0	8.5	...	...	...	...	...	...
19	27.27	.116	79	.734	.618	1.0	N 32 W	1.36	2.31	33.2	23.6	9.6	...	...	...	...	...	...
20	39.17	.132	81	.807	.675	0.8	S 47 W	4.13	4.45	31.4	18.2	13.2	...	...	...	...	...	...
21	33.90	.143	74	.859	.716	1.0	N 50 W	2.46	5.10	42.4	25.0	17.4	...	...	...	...	...	...
22	21.30	.094	82	30.250	30.157	0.8	N 57 E	10.46	10.87	34.0	15.8	18.2	...	...	...	...	...	...
23	27.97	.126	82	30.091	29.965	0.5	S 79 E	2.68	2.77	38.8	27.0	11.8	...	...	...	...	...	...
24						1.0	N 76 E	1.77	1.85	45.0	35.5	9.5	.125	7.0	.2	1.5	.125	1.5
25	41.80	.246	93	29.755	.509	0.8	S 62 E	1.22	10.77	47.4	40.8	6.6	.075	3.5	.2	...	.075	...
26	42.82	.210	75	.385	.175	0.3	N 32 W	9.75	7.72	33.4	29.8	3.6	.015	2.5	...	...	.015	...
27	29.02	.121	78	.502	.381	1.0	N 14 W	7.63	6.16	26.2	18.0	8.2	...	...	...	...	...	...
28	23.65	.109	84	.455	.346	1.0	N 25 W	5.10	12.89	25.8	23.2	2.6	...	...	...	...	...	*
29	24.57	.101	76	.581	.481	0.6	N 39 W	12.02	13.16	15.5	...	10.3	...	...	*	*	*	3.0
30	17.37	.075	76	.706	.631	...	S 9 E	18.01	18.18	24.4	6.5	17.9	...	...	*	2.0	*	2.0
31						...		0.70	1.43									
	30.08	0.134	78	29.675	29.541	0.6	N 71 W	2.33	7.40	35.27	23.73	11.54	1.152	38.3	4.0	45.2	1.552	78.5

GENERAL METEOROLOGICAL ABSTRACT,—FEBRUARY, 1858.

Days	DAILY MEANS.						WIND.			Extremes of Temperature.			RAIN.		SNOW.		Rain and Melted Snow	
	Temperature of the Air.	Pressure of Vapour.	Relative Humidity.	Barometric Pressure.	Pressure of Dry Air.	Clouded Sky.	Resultant Direction.	Resultant Velocity.	Mean Velocity.	Maximum.	Minimum.	Difference.	Depth in Inches.	Approximate duration in hours.	Depth in Inches.	Approximate duration in hours.	Depth in Inches.	Approximate duration in hours.
	°						°	Miles.	Miles.									
1	27.63	0.120	78	29.577	29.457	0.9	N 80 E	15.63	16.05	32.8	16.0	16.8			6.0	8.0	0.600	8.0
2	31.97	.156	86	.137	.981	1.0	S 70 W	7.49	9.35	34.2	26.2	8.0			0.5	4.5	.050	5.0
3	27.52	.129	82	.612	.483	0.5	S 69 W	11.67	12.00	33.0	28.4	4.6			0.5	1.0	.050	1.0
4	15.40	.063	71	.743	.680	0.3	S 70 W	4.21	4.29	25.5	9.3	15.7						
5	13.65	.058	64	.696	.638	0.9	S 75 W	8.19	8.30	24.2	0.5	23.7						
6	24.57	.109	81	.697	.588	1.0	S 30 W	9.75	9.75	32.2	15.0	17.2			0.4	2.0	.040	2.0
7															0.2	1.5	.020	1.5
8	20.10	.083	77	.808	.725	1.0	S 82 W	11.91	12.83	32.5	24.8	7.7			0.4	4.0	.040	4.0
9	24.37	.118	89	.197	.079	1.0	N 16 W	1.88	2.08	24.0	18.0	6.0			5.0	14.0	.500	14.0
10	11.58	.062	82	.340	.278	0.7	S 73 E	0.67	8.40	32.2	15.2	17.0	0.5		0.5	4.5	.050	4.5
11	2.77	.043	84	.753	.710	1.0	S 86 W	21.21	21.80	23.0	9.8	13.2						
12	11.80	.057	77	.867	.809	0.7	S 76 W	4.63	5.57	6.5	0.8	5.7						
13	9.67	.052	72	.804	.752	0.2	N 12 W	2.87	3.22	21.4	15.2	6.2						
14						1.0	N 58 E	16.68	17.23	13.5	−4.2	17.7			6.0	17.0	.600	17.0
15	15.67	.067	76	.802	.869	0.4	N 8 E	6.00	6.96	19.8	7.8	12.4			2.5	10.5	.250	10.5
16	7.52	.047	75	.843	.706	0.4	N 66 W	4.48	5.16	14.2	11.0	3.2						
17	1.60	.037	73	.082	.945	0.2	N 39 W	12.10	12.26	10.8	−7.3	18.1						
18	6.15	.039	67	.886	.847	0.8	N 50 W	3.97	4.38	11.0	−0.8	11.8			3.0	7.0	.300	7.0
19	6.75	.050	84	.745	.694	0.9	N 3 E	6.93	7.37	12.0	0.5	11.5			0.5	7.5	.050	7.5
20	13.33	.068	81	.512	.444	0.8	N 44 E	16.30	16.68	21.0	8.0	13.0			0.2	3.5	.020	3.5
21						0.8	N 80 W	2.79	6.70	27.2	8.6	18.4						
22	12.43	.059	77	.822	.763	0.8	N 51 W	9.79	11.04	20.1	10.2	9.9						
23	11.50	.060	77	.991	.931	0.6	S 75 W	2.34	3.64	27.2	8.0	19.0			0.1	3.0	.010	3.0
24	20.55	.084	74	.598	.514	0.8	S 60 W	3.52	3.52	27.5	19.0	19.0						
25	26.48	.103	73	.520	.417	0.8	S 45 W	9.04	9.61	32.4	19.2	13.2						
26	26.53	.109	73	.545	.436	0.9	N 60 W	6.44	7.18	33.2	11.5	21.7			0.1	1.0	.010	1.0
27	38.07	.152	66	.302	.150	0.2	S 26 W	4.54	11.28	42.4	29.5	12.9			0.8	7.0	.080	7.0
28						0.7	N 25 W	7.14	7.55	34.2	30.0	4.2						
	16.98	0.080	77	29.660	29.580	0.7	N 72 W	3.22	9.12	24.11	10.85	13.26	0.5		26.7	96.0	2.670	96.5

GENERAL METEOROLOGICAL ABSTRACT,—MARCH, 1858.

Days.	DAILY MEANS.					WIND.			Extremes of Temperature.			RAIN.		SNOW.		RAIN AND MELTED SNOW	
	Temperature of the Air.	Pressure of Vapour.	Relative Humidity.	Barometric Pressure.	Pressure of Dry Air.	Clouded Sky.	Resultant Direction.	Resultant Velocity.	Mean Velocity.	Maximum.	Minimum.	Difference.	Depth in Inches.	Approximate duration in hours.	Depth in Inches.	Approximate duration in hours.	Depth in Inches.	Approximate duration in hours.
1	18.28	0.074	74	29.490	29.416	0.9	N 44 W	Miles. 12.93	Miles. 13.25	25.5	21.0	4.5	...	...	...	...	...	...
2	7.92	.043	70	.518	.475	0.4	N 60 W	8.34	8.50	15.8	5.2	10.6	...	...	0.2	3.0	.020	3.0
3	7.07	.050	79	.669	.619	0.5	N 69 W	6.76	7.22	17.8	0.5	17.3	...	...	...	...	...	...
4	4.95	.038	69	.915	.877	0.3	N 25 W	5.55	5.69	17.2	−4.8	17.2	...	...	...	...	...	...
5	2.12	.037	75	.918	.891	0.0	N 41 W	20.69	20.88	12.4	−5.5	17.9	...	...	*	*	*	...
6	9.73	.043	62	.631	.588	0.4	N 56 W	5.85	6.11	7.8	1.9	...	...	...	...	...	...	...
7	...	...	...	...	...	...	N 71 W	4.21	4.41	10.8	1.0	...	...	...	...	...	...	...
8	14.05	.062	73	.264	.202	0.5	N 63 W	4.28	5.04	23.0	2.5	20.5	...	...	...	...	...	...
9	17.32	.067	71	.173	.106	0.9	N 61 W	7.09	7.69	25.2	0.8	24.4	...	...	*	*	*	...
10	29.83	.119	72	.271	.152	0.5	S 22 W	5.65	6.88	23.2	10.5	12.7	.015	1.8	...	...	.015	1.8
11	33.80	.137	68	.337	.249	0.5	N 77 W	16.92	17.12	39.3	16.8	22.5	.012	1.0	...	1.0	.012	1.0
12	29.47	.090	57	.842	.752	0.3	N 88 W	8.58	10.09	39.3	16.8	9.3	.305	2.0	...	...	.305	2.0
13	28.58	.115	72	30.011	.896	0.7	N 72 E	3.34	3.90	42.2	16.8	25.4	.120	4.5	...	...	.120	4.5
14	...	...	...	...	...	...	N 66 W	0.58	1.25	32.9	21.4	11.5	.230	8.3	...	...	.230	8.3
15	37.00	.213	96	29.750	.537	1.0	N 80 E	1.72	1.72	45.8	29.2	16.6	.078	2.0	...	...	.078	2.0
16	41.77	.253	95	.537	.284	1.0	N 81 E	0.01	0.47	46.0	29.0	17.0	...	...	...	...	...	...
17	46.70	.275	86	.132	.907	0.8	S 45 W	8.23	9.47	48.2	34.0	14.2	...	...	...	...	...	...
18	43.12	.189	66	.549	.361	0.5	N 86 W	14.35	14.00	55.4	38.5	16.9	...	...	...	...	...	...
19	34.89	.161	79	.970	.809	0.6	N 35 E	2.84	5.83	47.8	42.2	5.6	...	...	...	...	...	...
20	36.42	.168	76	.558	.389	0.0	N 84 E	6.62	7.55	30.8	23.0	6.8	...	...	...	...	...	...
21	...	...	...	...	...	0.7	N 87 W	22.69	23.62	46.0	29.0	17.0	.125	8.0	*	0.5	.125	8.0
22	32.07	.104	57	.696	.532	0.5	N 49 W	10.77	12.14	52.5	35.6	16.9	.010	1.5	...	...	.010	1.5
23	29.07	.112	70	.736	.624	0.1	S 74 E	3.06	3.67	37.0	31.2	5.8	...	...	...	...	...	0.5
24	33.78	.113	59	.720	.607	0.0	S 8 W	1.14	1.37	34.8	18.4	16.4	...	...	...	...	...	...
25	39.23	.142	62	.458	.316	0.8	N 28 W	12.91	13.88	42.0	24.4	17.6	.020	1.0	*	0.5	.020	1.0
26	34.89	.086	49	.086	.800	0.2	N 35 W	10.84	10.97	31.0	13.0	18.8	.002	1.4	...	...	.002	1.4
27	30.17	.117	69	.517	.400	0.9	N 33 E	3.78	4.61	41.2	26.2	15.0	...	...	...	...	*	...
28	...	...	...	...	...	0.1	N 49 W	8.47	8.91	41.0	27.7	13.3	...	...	...	...	...	...
29	41.52	.162	63	.785	.573	0.0	N 31 W	12.22	12.35	47.2	29.0	18.2	...	...	...	...	...	0.5
30	42.60	.115	41	.815	.700	0.0	N 23 W	8.57	9.05	51.2	30.0	21.2	...	...	...	...	...	...
31	43.27	.130	46	.798	.668	0.2	N 77 E	6.90	7.36	53.2	34.8	18.4	...	...	...	...	...	...
	28.44	0.119	69	29.630	29.501	0.5	N 58 W	5.45	8.56	50.9	31.5	10.4						
										37.01	21.93	15.08	0.917	31.6	0.2	11.0	0.937	42.5

TORONTO METEOROLOGICAL OBSERVATIONS. 53

GENERAL METEOROLOGICAL ABSTRACT,—APRIL, 1858.

Days	DAILY MEANS.					WIND.			EXTREMES OF TEMPERATURE.			RAIN.		SNOW.		RAIN AND MELTED SNOW	
	Temperature of the Air.	Pressure of Vapour.	Relative Humidity.	Barometric Pressure.	Pressure of Dry Air.	Sky. Clouded	Resultant Direction.	Resultant Velocity.	Mean Velocity.	Maximum.	Minimum.	Difference.	Depth in Inches.	Approximate duration in hours.	Depth in Inches.	Approximate duration in hours.	Depth in Inches.	Approximate duration in hours.
1	45.78	0.181	60	29.695	29.514	0.7	N 86 E	3.95	4.25	54.0	35.5	18.5	...	...	...	...	...	...
2	43.48	.200	59	.530	.330	0.6	S 46 E	1.71	2.93	58.8	34.0	24.8	...	...	...	...	...	...
3	42.37	.147	54	.419	.272	...	N 78 E	5.70	6.10	57.0	33.8	23.2	...	...	...	...	...	...
4	30.88	.103	61	.792	.689	0.7	S 23 E	1.96	7.57	43.0	18.6	...	0.035	0.8	...	...	.035	0.8
5	31.07	.092	53	.917	.825	0.6	S 87 W	12.42	14.79	53.2	35.5	17.7	...	...	...	...	...	...
6	36.73	.174	79	.529	.355	0.7	N 51 W	13.40	13.85	35.4	32.2	3.2	...	...	...	...	...	...
7	49.53	.213	63	.271	.058	0.1	S 45 E	0.34	5.56	40.0	21.8	18.2	...	...	...	...	...	...
8	42.52	.172	63	.673	.501	0.7	N 77 E	16.02	16.06	41.0	28.0	13.0	...	...	...	...	...	...
9	...	...	...	...	...	1.0	S 83 W	9.42	11.49	57.2	34.0	23.2	.055	4.5	...	...	.055	4.5
10	...	...	...	...	...	0.4	N 11 W	7.32	11.79	47.2	40.0	7.2	.010	2.0	...	...	.010	2.0
11	...	...	...	...	.194	1.0	N 76 E	11.84	12.04	38.0	33.2	4.8	...	...	...	...	...	...
12	...	...	75	.366	.888	1.0	N 76 E	22.65	22.57	38.6	34.2	4.4	...	...	...	...	...	...
13	...	.172	93	.117	.894	0.7	N 64 E	3.99	4.82	42.2	36.0	6.2	.630	16.5	...	...	.630	16.5
14	...	.229	87	.138	29.076	0.8	S 12 W	2.29	3.28	50.8	36.8	14.0	.135	15.0	...	...	.135	15.0
15	...	.254	73	.299	.345	0.8	S 86 W	6.78	10.10	52.0	38.2	13.8	.087	1.6	.1	1.6	.087	1.6
16	...	.223	53	.474	.564	0.2	S 85 W	6.32	9.00	53.5	33.5	20.0	*	0.1	*	1.0	*	0.1
17	...	.129	51	.681	...	0.0	N 56 W	2.76	5.58	29.5	19.1	19.1	...	...	...	...	...	...
18	...	.117	...	...	...	...	N 57 E	2.24	4.46	47.4	27.6	19.8	...	...	...	...	...	...
19	38.03	.141	56	.833	.692	1.0	N 80 E	17.46	17.51	42.2	36.8	5.4	.075	12.5	...	...	.075	12.5
20	39.80	.236	91	.253	.017	1.0	N 46 E	6.67	11.88	44.0	38.2	5.8	.390	18.0	...	...	.390	18.0
21	44.42	.254	68	.336	.132	0.9	N 84 W	9.79	10.00	51.0	39.0	12.0	.015	1.5	...	...	.015	1.5
22	45.77	.270	74	.244	28.974	0.6	S 20 E	2.38	9.62	55.0	36.8	18.2	.095	3.0	...	...	.095	3.0
23	40.25	.142	56	.450	29.309	1.0	N 84 W	15.51	15.58	44.2	39.8	4.4	...	...	...	...	...	...
24	32.40	.128	70	.601	.473	1.0	N 79 W	12.51	13.83	38.4	31.0	7.4	*	*	...	...	*	*
25	...	...	...	...	...	...	N 34 W	4.98	6.09	38.0	27.5	10.5	...	...	...	...	...	...
26	35.10	.121	60	.800	.739	0.1	S 1 E	2.96	6.59	41.2	26.5	14.7	...	...	...	...	...	...
27	38.40	.113	50	.751	.638	0.3	N 51 W	3.15	8.92	46.2	28.5	17.7	...	...	...	...	...	...
28	43.20	.148	54	.624	.476	0.1	N 59 W	0.81	9.19	55.0	33.5	21.5	.165	5.3	...	...	.165	5.3
29	43.15	.178	64	.363	.185	0.1	N 78 E	2.91	4.08	49.8	36.4	18.4	*	*	...	...	*	*
30	62.12	.304	78	.253	28.949	0.6	N 43 W	7.31	8.23	65.2	41.0	24.2	...	...	...	...	...	...
	41.46	0.176	66	29.499	29.323	0.7	N 14 W	1.64	9.57	49.32	34.15	14.10	1.042	80.8	0.1	2.5	1.652	63.3

TORONTO METEOROLOGICAL OBSERVATIONS.

GENERAL METEOROLOGICAL ABSTRACT,—MAY, 1858.

Days.	DAILY MEANS.					WIND.			Extremes of Temperature.			RAIN.		SNOW.		Rain and Melted Snow	
	Temperature of the Air.	Pressure of Vapour.	Relative Humidity.	Barometric Pressure.	Pressure of Dry Air.	Clouded Sky.	Resultant Direction.	Resultant Velocity. Miles.	Mean Velocity. Miles.	Maximum.	Minimum.	Difference.	Depth in Inches.	Approximate duration in hours.	Depth in Inches.	Approximate duration in hours.	Depth in Inches.	Approximate duration in hours.
1	44.72	0.199	67	29.773	29.574	0.6	N 22 W	4.34	6.74	53.0	39.0	14.0	...	...	...	...	...	...
2	44.30	.110	39	30.029	.919	0.8	S 77 E	1.52	3.02	47.4	34.2	13.2	...	...	...	...	...	...
3	50.30	.253	69	29.647	.394	0.9	N 76 E	11.55	11.63	48.6	35.5	13.1	.085	6.0	...	...	...	...
4	51.08	.310	83	.439	.129	0.7	N 72 E	6.62	7.09	56.0	42.6	13.4	*	0.5	...	...	...	...
5	57.15	.228	51	.451	.222	0.5	N 54 E	6.13	7.41	58.0	46.0	12.0	...	...	...	...	...	...
6	55.12	.227	53	.640	.413	0.1	North.	8.97	9.19	64.2	48.6	15.6	...	...	...	...	...	...
7	53.52	.266	66	.581	.315	0.9	S 19 E	1.52	3.21	63.0	48.8	12.2	...	...	...	...	...	...
8							S 50 E	2.04	2.54	64.2	42.2	22.0	...	...	...	...	...	...
9	44.87	.158	53	.652	.494	1.0	N 68 W	10.66	13.16	69.8	50.0	19.8	.085	1.5	...	...	...	...
10	43.97	.243	84	.213	28.970	1.0	N 64 E	3.48	6.78	51.0	38.1	12.9	.590	13.5	...	...	...	...
11	45.78	.234	70	.353	.119	0.7	N 73 E	15.24	19.68	47.5	43.4	4.1	1.590	4.5	...	...	...	...
12	49.70	.236	64	.747	.511	0.5	N 76 W	11.84	12.07	51.8	40.0	11.8	.083	...	...	...	...	...
13	48.72	.226	65	.572	.346	0.5	N 70 E	1.18	8.18	58.4	37.8	20.6	...	...	...	...	...	...
14	50.15	r188	51	.591	.403	0.4	N 67 E	8.25	9.03	53.4	43.0	10.4	...	...	...	...	...	...
15							N 42 E	12.65	14.40	63.2	42.5	20.7	...	...	...	...	...	...
16							S 8 W	2.89	5.80	49.8	31.0	18.8	...	...	...	...	...	...
17	40.92	.217	85	.506	.289	1.0	N 60 E	11.37	11.97	42.8	36.8	6.0	.540	12.0	...	...	...	...
18	44.28	.232	80	.623	.391	0.7	N 65 W	6.51	6.69	47.0	34.0	13.0	.010	1.2	...	...	...	...
19	47.33	.208	64	.027	.419	0.8	N 15 W	3.30	6.53	51.4	34.0	17.4	.040	1.0	...	...	...	...
20	46.52	.211	79	.652	.211	1.0	N 65 W	10.13	10.67	55.0	39.0	16.0	*	0.5	...	...	...	...
21	46.28	.170	54	.706	.535	1.0	N 49 W	18.08	13.55	58.5	38.0	20.5	...	...	...	...	...	...
22	49.15	.218	61	.837	.619	0.1	S 6 W	3.62	5.00	63.5	38.0	25.5	...	...	...	...	...	...
23							N 46 W	1.84	8.29	63.5	38.5	25.0	.160	8.5	...	...	...	...
24	55.63	.309	70	.899	.090	0.9	N 31 W	3.46	7.81	60.2	45.0	15.2	.1050	14.5	...	...	...	...
25	50.78	.277	75	.442	.165	1.0	N 76 E	18.18	18.10	51.0	44.5	6.5	1.190	20.0	...	...	...	...
26	45.88	.282	93	.331	.049	1.0	N 67 E	13.13	13.15	47.5	44.8	2.7	.1190	1.0	...	...	...	...
27	40.15	.201	81	.635	.354	1.0	N 70 E	10.00	10.06	52.8	42.0	10.8	*	...	...	...	...	...
28	50.70	.257	70	.780	.523	0.6	N 83 E	11.31	11.46	56.4	45.0	11.4	.310	11.0	...	...	...	...
29	50.10	.255	71	.632	.378	0.8	East	58.8	8.0	53.8	45.8	8.0	.106	2.0	...	...	...	...
30							N 79 E	6.99	7.10	63.8	44.4	14.4	.150	1.0	...	...	...	...
31	56.77	.389	83	.520	.031	0.7	S 21 W	2.65	7.01	68.0	50.0	18.0						
	48.90	0.229	69	29.584	29.345	0.7	N 42 E	3.33	9.30	55.74	41.68	14.06	6.367	108.7				

GENERAL METEOROLOGICAL ABSTRACT.—JUNE, 1858.

Days	Temperature of the Air	Pressure of Vapour	Relative Humidity	Barometric Pressure	Pressure of Dry Air	Clouded Sky	Wind Resultant Direction	Wind Resultant Velocity	Wind Mean Velocity	Max Temp	Min Temp	Diff	Rain Depth (Inches)	Rain Duration (hours)	Snow Depth	Snow Duration	Rain+Snow Depth	Rain+Snow Duration
1	61.05	0.309	60	29.685	29.376	0.2	S 82 W	3.15	4.82	72.2	46.8	25.4	...	...				
2	62.68	.318	57	.806	.488	0.4	N 7 E	0.69	3.93	72.6	46.2	26.4	.155	3.0				
3	58.90	.300	61	.697	.397	0.6	N 74 E	8.51	8.61	64.5	54.9	9.6	.516	8.0				
4	58.95	.476	80	.803	.327	0.7	N 69 W	5.06	8.53	73.2	50.8	22.4	.185	2.5				
5	60.10	.355	68	.554	.199	0.9	S 7 W	4.11	5.80	69.0	52.9	16.1	.210	2.7				
6	...	...	...	...	...	...	...	2.35	4.96	68.0	48.5	19.5	*	0.2				
7	63.53	.348	58	.635	.287	0.7	S 58 W	5.43	11.19	74.0	52.9	21.1	...	...				
8	58.58	.271	56	.821	.550	0.6	S 62 W	1.00	3.84	65.5	48.5	17.0	...	...				
9	54.30	.315	75	.632	.317	1.0	S 72 W	6.74	6.92	65.7	52.0	4.8	.363	11.0				
10	58.40	.418	85	.302	28.884	1.0	N 29 N	8.67	8.67	65.7	52.0	14.0	.785	9.5				
11	55.85	.264	59	.607	29.343	0.9	N 1 W	9.12	9.27	62.0	52.9	9.1	...	...				
12	53.08	.246	61	.602	.356	1.0	N 61 E	9.87	10.73	57.5	46.0	11.5	.325	5.5				
13	...	...	...	...	...	...	N 20 W	8.22	8.10	55.2	47.0	8.2	.005	1.5				
14	56.68	.320	69	.505	.245	0.0	S 7 W	4.22	4.45	68.2	45.2	23.0	...	...				
15	58.25	.320	67	.542	.222	0.4	S 55 E	2.20	3.27	68.2	45.5	22.7	*	...				
16	63.38	.411	71	.610	.199	0.7	N 1 W	2.04	2.23	71.8	50.0	21.8	0.1	...				
17	68.62	.496	71	.669	.172	0.2	S 17 W	4.45	4.85	76.8	54.7	22.1	...	...				
18	71.05	.555	73	.686	.031	0.2	South	5.15	5.22	79.8	55.8	24.0	*	...				
19	73.72	.636	77	.530	28.944	0.6	S 18 W	2.21	3.98	81.9	63.7	18.2	0.1	...				
20	...	...	...	...	...	...	S 49 W	2.41	4.36	83.5	64.2	19.3	...	...				
21	71.60	.613	80	.587	29.974	0.2	S 61 W	2.31	4.69	81.1	64.6	16.5	...	...				
22	70.42	.527	71	.096	29.169	0.1	N 71 E	4.28	4.59	76.2	60.2	16.0	...	...				
23	72.70	.617	77	.091	-.074	0.2	S 87 E	2.26	2.33	82.4	61.9	20.5	...	...				
24	77.85	.692	73	.600	28.908	0.3	S 65 E	4.40	4.73	87.0	65.6	21.4	.450	2.7				
25	78.70	.736	75	.653	.816	0.7	S 16 W	3.78	5.16	90.2	70.8	19.4	...	...				
26	79.98	.760	75	.587	.827	0.3	S 34 W	2.88	3.37	85.8	69.1	16.7	...	...				
27	...	...	...	...	...	...	S 33 W	1.39	2.82	86.4	69.8	16.6	...	...				
28	77.08	.617	65	.623	29.005	0.1	N 71 W	2.36	4.95	85.2	66.6	18.6	...	...				
29	77.20	.641	68	.590	.949	0.1	N 52 E	1.27	3.15	84.6	65.6	19.0	...	...				
30	72.30	.580	67	.641	.110	0.2	N 87 E	5.64	6.17	75.7	69.4	6.3	...	...				
	66.15	0.465	69	29.606	29.141	0.5	S 20 E	0.25	5.53	73.94	56.41	17.54	2.943	46.8				

GENERAL METEOROLOGICAL ABSTRACT.—JULY, 1858.

Days.	Temperature of the Air.	Pressure of Vapour.	Relative Humidity.	Barometric Pressure.	Pressure of Dry Air.	Clouded Sky.	WIND Resultant Direction.	WIND Resultant Velocity.	WIND Mean Velocity.	Extremes of Temperature Maximum.	Extremes of Temperature Minimum.	Extremes of Temperature Difference.	RAIN Depth in Inches.	RAIN Approximate duration in hours.	SNOW Depth in Inches.	SNOW Approximate duration in hours.	RAIN AND MELTED SNOW Depth in Inches.	RAIN AND MELTED SNOW Approximate duration in hours.
	°							Miles	Miles	°	°	°						
1	62.10	0.326	58	29.033	29.308	0.9	N 67 E	7.87	7.93	67.5	60.0	7.5	*	1.0	..	..	..	..
2	66.45	.448	69	.460	.021	0.4	N 83 E	4.12	4.26	71.2	60.2	11.0	.087	2.0	..	..	..	..
3	73.78	.644	79	.346	28.702	0.7	N 50 W	7.56	9.49	84.8	63.1	21.7	.013	2.0	..	..	..	..
4						0.0	N 27 W	10.39	10.90	80.8	65.8	15.0	..	..	..	..	..	..
5	63.45	.336	58	.874	29.538	0.1	S 88 E	4.05	6.64	70.2	58.7	11.5	..	..	..	..	..	..
6	67.32	.454	68	.633	.888	0.2	S 66 E	1.42	2.84	76.0	52.0	24.0	..	..	..	..	..	..
7	75.45	.588	73	.502	.384	0.5	S 3 W	3.80	4.65	84.2	60.6	23.6	..	..	..	..	..	..
8	67.32	.653	81	.587	.050	0.5	S 73 E	2.67	2.86	85.0	69.8	16.2	.300	1.5	..	..	..	..
9	75.78	.591	79	.568	28.996	0.8	N 76 E	2.64	2.67	76.0	65.6	10.4	..	..	..	..	..	..
10	75.13	.690			28.873		N 76 W	3.52	6.07	82.8	66.2	16.6	.265	1.2	..	..	..	..
11						0.9	N 22 E	9.39	9.60	63.5	63.5	2.1	1.005	15.0	..	..	..	..
12	58.25	.426	88	.525	29.100	0.6	N 14 E	5.88	6.25	61.4	56.4	5.0	.147	5.5	..	..	..	..
13	63.90	.465	78	.010	.146	0.4	N 71 W	2.03	3.88	73.2	56.6	17.6	..	..	..	..	..	..
14	67.63	.474	71	.767	.283	0.2	N 47 E	1.50	3.52	76.4	60.0	16.4	..	..	..	..	..	..
15	69.43	.521	74	.758	.237	0.3	N 47 E	2.11	2.15	77.8	59.0	19.4	..	..	..	..	..	..
16	71.98	.616	81	.666	.050	0.7	S 22 W	3.45	5.35	77.8	61.2	16.6	*	0.6	..	..	..	..
17	69.30	.523	74	.726	.302	0.8	N 32 W	2.31	4.43	73.0	67.3	5.7	.075	..	..	..	..	..
18						..	S 81 E	3.57	4.81	72.4	60.4	12.0	..	..	..	..	..	..
19	67.40	.389	59	.841	.452	0.1	N 78 E	2.56	4.14	76.2	56.0	20.2	..	..	..	..	..	..
20	67.70	.428	64	.591	.163	0.5	N 53 E	1.08	1.65	76.5	57.0	19.5	..	0.2	..	..	..	..
21	67.57	.494	72	.878	.884	0.2	N 72 W	5.41	8.26	82.6	59.3	23.3	.060	..	..	..	..	..
22	66.85	.526	74	.461	.105	0.4	N 85 W	8.12	8.33	77.6	62.0	15.5	..	..	..	..	..	..
23	63.63	.326	52	.655	.246	0.1	N 13 W	7.99	8.44	72.6	55.7	16.9	..	..	..	..	..	..
24	62.63	.360	55	.725	.365	0.3	N 56 E	3.54	5.44	70.0	54.6	15.4	..	..	..	..	..	..
25			64			0.6	S 75 E	4.97	5.17	69.6	54.2	15.3	..	..	..	..	..	..
26	72.70	.581	73	.689	28.953	0.7	S 20 W	5.37	7.20	79.6	66.4	23.2	..	..	..	..	..	..
27	70.90	.321	44	.582	29.261	1.0	N 76 W	10.96	11.10	82.2	64.6	17.6	..	0.7	..	..	..	..
28	64.17	.445	74	.708	.264	0.8	S 83 E	3.65	4.27	69.4	53.7	15.7	.120	0.2	..	..	..	..
29	68.82	.596	83	.440	28.844	0.8	S 88 E	5.26	5.20	79.8	61.9	17.0	*	1.5	..	..	..	..
30	63.85	.507	86	.456	28.949	0.8	N 42 E	1.50	3.32	70.0	60.5	9.5	*		..	..	..	..
31	67.50	.471	69	.647	29.077	0.4	N 60 W	1.74	4.18	75.4	59.8	15.6	..	..	..	..	..	..
	67.86	0.481	70	29.606	29.126	0.5	N 15 E	1.13	5.76	75.44	59.98	15.46	3.072	31.4	..	..	..	..

TORONTO METEOROLOGICAL OBSERVATIONS. 57

GENERAL METEOROLOGICAL ABSTRACT,—AUGUST, 1858.

Days	DAILY MEANS.						WIND.			Extremes of Temperature.			RAIN.		SNOW.		Rain and Melted Snow.	
	Temperature of the Air.	Pressure of Vapour.	Relative Humidity.	Barometric Pressure.	Pressure of Dry Air.	Clouded Sky.	Resultant Direction.	Resultant Velocity.	Mean Velocity.	Maximum.	Minimum.	Difference.	Depth in Inches.	Approximate duration in hours.	Depth in Inches.	Approximate duration in hours.	Depth in Inches.	Approximate duration in hours.
	°							Miles.	Miles.	°	°	°						
1	69.60	0.527	73	29.570	...	...	N 76 E	3.66	4.51	75.4	59.8	15.6	...	...	...	...	...	...
2	71.22	.603	80	.579	.062	0.8	N 83 E	10.98	11.17	74.0	62.2	11.8	1.010	4.0	...	...	...	...
3	72.98	.546	70	.405	.502	0.5	N 26 W	4.94	7.75	80.4	65.0	15.4	.330	5.5	...	...	...	...
4	72.47	.471	61	.439	.898	0.4	S 73 W	5.86	6.79	81.8	66.6	15.2	.420	2.2	...	...	...	...
5	73.75	.453	55	.582	.111	0.2	N 67 W	8.19	8.36	83.6	64.2	19.4	...	...	...	...	...	...
6	70.65	.543	73	.662	.209	0.0	N 26 W	10.51	10.76	82.8	61.9	17.2	...	...	...	...	...	...
7	...	...	...	.739	.196	0.4	S 9 W	1.17	1.88	78.2	61.9	16.3	...	...	...	...	...	...
8	...	...	...	...	...	...	S 64 E	1.32	1.51	79.4	67.6	11.8	...	...	...	...	...	...
9	75.72	.631	71	.658	.027	0.3	N 3 E	1.52	3.14	84.0	66.7	17.3	...	...	...	...	...	...
10	77.07	.657	71	.591	.934	0.2	S 5 E	0.49	3.97	83.8	63.2	20.6	...	1.0	...	...	...	...
11	72.18	.612	78	.612	.965	0.6	N 24 W	4.90	5.22	79.4	66.8	12.6	•	...	...	...	...	...
12	72.20	.550	69	.577	.249	0.1	N 74 E	2.69	5.39	78.5	67.6	10.9	...	...	...	...	...	...
13	69.95	.493	67	.910	.425	0.0	N 78 E	4.02	5.25	76.0	61.3	14.7	*	...	...	...	...	...
14	73.00	.565	70	.747	.182	0.4	S 38 E	2.56	3.92	80.8	63.8	17.0	...	...	...	...	...	...
15	...	...	...	...	...	...	N 52 E	4.46	6.35	82.2	61.6	20.6	...	...	...	...	...	...
16	...	...	...	...	.247	0.1	S 75 E	1.82	1.90	75.4	62.8	12.6	.205	1.5	...	...	...	...
17	68.38	.509	73	.756	.073	0.2	S 24 W	4.72	5.36	78.4	41.0	31.2	...	...	...	...	...	...
18	73.06	.564	70	.637	.017	0.8	S 11 E	7.49	10.31	78.4	66.0	12.4	...	...	...	...	...	...
19	65.47	.459	74	.476	.295	0.4	N 47 W	4.15	4.28	63.8	45.2	26.6	...	...	...	...	...	...
20	56.60	.283	62	.578	.155	0.4	N 25 W	7.84	8.65	76.8	46.2	30.6	...	1.0	...	...	...	...
21	65.15	.344	57	.500	.295	0.4	S 80 W	8.97	21.6	52.4	51.2	9.4	...	...	...	...	...	...
22	60.32	.335	54	.630	...	...	N 63 W	14.95	15.40	76.0	46.0	17.2	...	...	...	...	...	...
23	55.90	.251	58	.835	.683	0.0	N 54 W	5.36	7.83	65.0	46.0	20.0	...	...	...	...	...	...
24	60.32	.275	56	.788	.513	0.2	N 84 W	6.06	6.47	75.2	41.0	31.2	...	...	...	...	...	...
25	61.47	.356	66	.890	.524	0.0	S 50 E	2.28	5.49	72.4	45.8	26.6	...	9.7	...	...	...	...
26	64.03	.481	81	.672	.19	1.0	S 67 E	6.14	7.00	63.8	53.8	14.2	.535	17.5	...	...	...	...
27	67.93	.545	80	.364	.819	0.9	S 8 W	7.93	8.05	59.8	45.4	14.2	...	...	...	...	...	...
28	61.50	.487	89	.291	28.804	1.0	N 60 W	3.69	4.32	71.0	60.8	6.4	1.015	11.5	...	...	...	...
29	...	...	...	...	...	...	N 30 W	7.16	7.16	67.2	56.3	2.1	.270	2.5	...	...	...	...
30	60.02	.467	90	.416	28.940	1.0	N 70 W	2.44	4.08	64.2	53.8	10.4	.105	...	...	...	...	...
31	61.07	.412	76	.586	29.173	0.6	S 55 W	2.03	3.90	68.6	58.5	10.1	...	...	...	...	...	...
	67.61	0.478	70	29.619	29.142	0.4	N 69 W	1.57	6.50	75.35	59.21	16.17	3.890	56.4	...	...	...	...

GENERAL METEOROLOGICAL ABSTRACT,—SEPTEMBER, 1858.

	DAILY MEANS.					WIND.			EXTREMES OF TEMPERATURE.			RAIN.		SNOW.		RAIN AND MELTED SNOW.	
Days.	Temperature of the Air.	Pressure of Vapour.	Relative Humidity.	Barometric Pressure.	Pressure of Dry Air.	Clouded Sky.	Resultant Direction.	Resultant Velocity.	Mean Velocity.	Maximum.	Minimum.	Difference.	Depth in Inches.	Approximate duration in hours.	Depth in Inches.	Approximate duration in hours.	Depth in Inches.	Approximate duration in hours.
	°							Miles.	Miles.	°	°	°						
1	61.42	0.430	79	29.639	29.209	0.3	S 12 E	2.05	3.44	70.2	53.1	17.1	...	...	...	...	...	...
2	63.48	.496	85	.464	28.968	0.5	S 70 E	3.50	3.88	69.0	54.2	14.8	0.025	1.0	...	...	...	...
3	64.52	.487	79	.388	.901	0.6	S 38 W	3.20	4.33	61.8	55.6	12.2	...	...	...	...	...	...
4	63.77	.429	78	.355	28.926	0.7	S 17 W	6.29	6.46	71.5	55.6	15.9	...	...	...	...	...	...
5	...	...	...	...	...	0.0	S 78 W	7.32	7.79	72.4	61.0	11.4	...	...	...	...	...	...
6	62.58	.433	77	.741	29.308	0.0	S 1 E	2.84	3.65	72.0	49.2	22.8	...	...	...	...	...	...
7	67.48	.486	73	.747	.263	0.4	S 1 W	3.38	3.52	78.8	56.6	22.2	...	...	...	...	...	...
8	70.23	.527	73	.666	.139	0.5	N 23 W	5.63	5.65	81.4	59.5	21.7	...	...	...	...	...	...
9	70.98	.596	79	.606	.008	0.5	S 17 W	3.95	4.16	81.4	61.6	16.8	...	...	...	...	...	...
10	67.33	.549	81	.451	28.902	0.4	S 17 W	7.33	9.56	76.4	65.8	10.6	.060	2.0	...	...	...	...
11	59.27	.326	67	.513	29.187	0.2	S 42 W	7.42	8.64	65.0	54.0	15.0	.070	2.5	...	...	...	...
12	...	...	...	...	...	0.5	N 68 W	9.69	9.74	65.0	47.0	18.0	...	...	...	...	...	...
13	55.83	.298	67	.869	.571	0.1	S 22 E	2.89	4.33	63.5	46.2	17.3	...	...	...	...	...	...
14	59.35	.380	75	.758	.378	0.1	S 78 E	4.06	5.02	66.0	46.8	19.2	...	...	...	...	...	...
15	53.13	.415	77	.468	.023	0.4	N 89 E	5.42	7.01	69.0	56.0	13.0	...	...	...	...	...	...
16	57.88	.305	64	.247	28.942	0.6	N 53 W	12.36	13.42	65.5	56.1	9.4	...	0.4	...	...	...	...
17	52.52	.260	67	.676	29.416	0.4	N 74 W	10.38	10.67	62.8	46.9	15.9	.015	...	...	...	...	...
18	52.38	.321	81	.947	.626	0.5	W 37 W	0.82	2.73	60.8	39.8	21.0	...	...	...	...	...	...
19	...	...	...	...	...	0.3	N 81 E	4.06	4.23	65.8	50.0	15.8	...	...	...	...	...	...
20	66.23	.481	76	.730	.240	0.7	S 24 W	3.86	3.95	90.0	51.0	29.0	...	...	...	...	...	...
21	56.45	.344	73	.691	.347	0.1	N 36 W	11.25	11.89	67.0	55.4	11.6	...	10.5	...	...	...	...
22	53.18	.173	57	.855	.682	0.1	S 11 W	6.76	6.85	54.4	42.2	12.2	.315	0.1	...	...	...	...
23	53.13	.247	71	.775	.528	0.7	N 3 W	3.82	3.90	57.8	35.6	21.9	*	...	...	...	...	...
24	50.98	.256	68	.711	.455	0.6	N 61 E	6.55	6.62	57.8	42.0	15.8	...	...	...	...	...	...
25	47.58	.221	67	.965	.744	0.1	N 97 E	1.46	2.85	56.5	40.4	16.1	...	...	...	...	...	...
26	...	...	...	...	...	0.0	S 87 E	0.97	3.00	58.5	39.5	19.0	...	0.4	...	...	...	...
27	52.87	.302	75	.997	.695	0.7	S 77 E	2.60	2.78	59.5	40.5	19.0	...	5.0	...	...	...	...
28	55.18	.367	84	.766	.399	0.0	S 27 W	1.58	1.62	62.4	46.8	15.6	*	...	...	...	...	...
29	54.37	.475	78	.423	28.948	0.5	N 15 E	3.32	4.30	71.2	52.9	18.3	.250	...	...	...	...	...
30	55.05	.359	81	.450	29.091	0.8		2.86	3.64	64.8	51.6	13.2	...	...	...	...	...	...
	59.11	0.384	74	29.650	29.266	0.4	S 74 W	1.58	5.69	67.52	50.79	16.73	0.735	21.9				

GENERAL METEOROLOGICAL ABSTRACT,—OCTOBER, 1858.

Days.	DAILY MEANS.							WIND.			EXTREMES OF TEMPERATURE.			RAIN.		SNOW.		RAIN AND MELTED SNOW	
	Temperature of the Air.	Pressure of Vapour.	Relative Humidity.	Barometric Pressure.	Pressure of Dry Air.	Clouded Sky.	Resultant Direction.	Resultant Velocity.	Mean Velocity.	Maximum.	Minimum.	Difference.	Depth in Inches.	Approximate duration in hours.	Depth in Inches.	Approximate duration in hours.	Depth in Inches.	Approximate duration in hours.
1	48.45	0.250	73	29.527	29.277	0.6	N 23 W	7.75	8.13	54.4	48.2	6.2	0.010	4.5	...	...	0.110	4.5
2	52.38	.300	75	.591	.291	0.6	S 28 E	5.03	5.53	58.5	39.0	19.5	...	...	...	...	...	...
3	52.90	.276	66	.437	.161	0.7	S 60 W	7.24	7.70	76.3	53.8	22.5	.035	3.0	...	...	.035	3.0
4	53.23	.226	62	.762	.536	0.1	N 77 W	4.29	4.85	54.7	53.6	5.1	.065	1.5	...	...	.065	1.5
5	51.65	.253	66	.690	.497	0.4	N 55 W	6.75	7.04	59.8	54.7	24.0	...	...	...	...	...	...
6	49.78	.277	73	.141	28.864	0.7	S 82 E	6.33	6.62	64.0	40.0	18.6	.155	3.0	...	...	.155	3.0
7	41.52	.161	61	.173	29.013	0.6	S 81 W	13.74	14.67	56.6	38.0	10.8	.240	3.1	...	...	.240	3.1
8	43.68	.211	74	.517	.306	0.5	S 69 W	11.75	11.93	63.2	52.4	12.2	.032	4.9	*	0.2	.032	4.9
9	...	...	...	...	...	...	S 56 W	7.06	7.50	47.4	35.2	16.3	.050	1.5	...	...	.050	1.5
10	45.40	.209	69	.847	.638	1.0	N 83 W	3.79	3.98	53.5	39.0	14.0	...	...	...	...	...	...
11	49.23	.292	82	.632	.340	1.0	S 84 E	7.56	7.82	49.6	39.8	9.8	.080	0.5	...	...	.080	0.5
12	51.97	.322	83	.426	.104	0.8	S 33 W	4.60	4.96	53.8	44.2	9.6	.500	2.0	...	...	.500	2.0
13	46.00	.226	72	.508	.282	0.5	S 55 W	6.73	6.83	56.2	49.6	6.6	...	5.7	...	...	...	5.7
14	44.97	.226	75	.826	.600	0.4	S 82 W	0.42	1.14	49.8	42.0	7.8	...	...	...	...	...	...
15	48.42	.275	81	.984	.709	1.0	S 67 E	4.47	4.53	53.8	39.1	14.7	.030	2.7	...	...	.030	2.7
16	...	...	...	...	...	...	S 10 W	2.11	2.12	52.0	39.8	12.2	...	...	...	...	...	...
17	...	...	...	...	...	...	S 19 W	3.51	3.51	62.5	45.8	16.7	...	...	...	...	...	...
18	52.57	.302	77	.895	.596	0.1	N 10 W	5.50	5.91	63.2	42.8	20.4	...	...	...	...	...	...
19	54.68	.328	76	.829	.502	0.7	N 71 E	7.00	7.35	65.7	47.0	18.7	...	...	...	...	...	...
20	53.78	.309	74	.815	.506	0.7	N 77 E	3.65	3.69	58.0	48.0	9.2	.390	6.6	...	...	.390	6.6
21	51.13	.321	86	.788	.467	1.0	S 15 W	1.77	3.33	53.0	44.4	5.0	.020	1.0	...	...	.020	1.0
22	51.03	.298	80	.679	.380	0.8	N 23 W	3.57	5.09	55.8	43.1	10.6	...	...	...	...	...	...
23	48.70	.235	69	.731	.496	0.9	N 40 E	4.54	5.62	52.0	40.2	12.7	...	...	...	...	...	...
24	...	...	...	...	...	...	N 61 E	6.34	7.04	48.0	40.8	5.8	...	...	...	...	...	...
25	43.78	.157	55	.956	.801	0.1	N 57 E	5.04	5.64	46.9	31.5	7.2	...	...	...	...	...	...
26	39.87	.133	54	.961	.828	0.2	N 55 E	2.35	2.74	51.2	35.2	15.4	...	...	...	...	...	...
27	49.23	.154	54	.964	.810	0.1	N 58 E	11.57	11.78	52.0	38.6	16.0	.020	1.2	...	...	.020	1.2
28	48.15	.218	63	.889	.671	0.6	S 87 E	13.41	13.46	52.8	47.2	5.6	.145	5.5	...	...	.145	5.5
29	50.65	.385	90	.643	.308	1.0	S 46 W	2.09	2.11	57.8	50.6	7.2	.025	2.5	...	...	.025	2.5
30	52.47	.353	88	.499	.146	0.8	S 67 W	3.31	3.49	53.6	43.8	9.8	*	0.2	...	...	*	0.2
31	...	...	...	...	...	...	...	...	...	...	...	...	...	...	...	...	...	...
	48.79	0.256	72	29.681	29.426	0.6	N 84 W	0.36	5.96	55.79	43.41	12.37	1.797	49.2	*	0.2	1.797	49.4

GENERAL METEOROLOGICAL ABSTRACT,—NOVEMBER, 1858.

Date.	DAILY MEANS.						WIND.			Extremes of Temperature.			RAIN.		SNOW.		Rain and Melted Snow	
	Temperature of the Air.	Pressure of Vapour.	Relative Humidity.	Barometric Pressure.	Pressure of Dry Air.	Clouded Sky.	Resultant Direction.	Resultant Velocity.	Mean Velocity.	Maximum.	Minimum.	Difference.	Depth in Inches.	Approximate duration in hours.	Depth in Inches.	Approximate duration in hours.	Depth in Inches.	Approximate duration in hours.
1	47.93	0.260	77	29.931	29.671	1.0	N 69 E	9.07	10.06	53.0	46.8	6.2						0.2
2	43.88	.219	77	.853	.634	1.0	N 70 E	19.40	19.53	46.2	42.0	4.2	.977	9.5			.977	9.5
3	44.43	.208	92	.788	.470	1.0	N 89 E	9.39	9.52	45.8	42.0	3.8	.565	20.0			.565	20.0
4	46.37	.277	57	.639	.362	1.0	N 49 E	0.54	0.77	47.6	43.4	4.2	.020	5.5			.020	5.5
5	45.53	.266	67	30.013	.847	1.0	N 76 E	5.67	6.06	49.0	41.2	7.8	.210	7.0			.210	7.0
6	41.40	.223	85	.376	.153	1.0	N 51 E	7.06	7.19	46.0	41.4	4.0	.842	17.0			.842	17.0
7							N 24 W	0.63	0.99	44.6	35.6	9.0	.025	5.5			.025	5.5
8	38.73	.195	82	.400	.265	1.0	N 6 B	7.12	7.37	42.9	37.1	5.8		0.5				0.5
9	34.02	.144	74	.554	.410	1.0	N 1 E	5.40	5.57	37.0	32.2	4.8			0.1	2.2	.010	2.2
10	29.38	.129	78	.710	.581	0.6	N 74 E	4.59	4.76	33.2	28.0	5.2			*	0.1	*	0.1
11	26.65	.097	67	.803	.706	0.6	N 74 E	2.15	2.62	32.6	20.5	12.1						
12	34.53	.147	73	.603	.456	0.7	s 26 E	5.09	8.23	39.8	25.7	14.1	.365	9.5	0.2	1.0	.365	9.5
13	30.30	.143	61	.435	.292	0.7	N 61 W	9.84	10.98	39.0	33.0	6.0	.070	2.5	0.2	5.0	.090	3.5
14							N 82 W	3.62	3.77	39.0	29.9	9.1			0.2	4.0	.020	5.0
15	23.47	.097	78	.680	.533	0.6	N 54 W	9.04	9.31	27.0	15.3	11.7			0.1	7.5	.010	4.0
16	28.70	.124	79	.563	.469	0.8	N 75 W	12.53	12.86	33.3	20.5	12.8					.010	7.5
17	33.10	.120	65	.683	.563	0.6	N 75 W	10.56	10.89	39.0	26.2	12.8			*		*	0.2
18	33.65	.139	71	.618	.479	0.8	s 88 W	13.51	13.63	29.4	23.2	6.2				0.2		2.0
19	28.85	.090	57	.734	.644	0.1	N 82 W	11.70	13.01	27.0	22.5	4.8			0.2	2.0		
20	32.05	.131	74	.608	.477	0.6	N 42 W	3.39	6.64	33.3	21.3	17.3						
21							N 41 E	4.95	4.97	39.0	31.2	7.8	.680	7.2	1.5	18.5	.680	7.2
22	35.40	.157	76	.529	.372	0.7	N 78 E	12.49	13.66	41.2	25.0	16.2	.125	0.5	0.2	2.5	.274	14.0
23	32.95	.170	91	.335	.165	1.0	N 43 E	7.87	8.33	35.0	31.8	3.2					.020	2.5
24	30.17	.120	81	.504	.368	0.9	N 32 W	14.77	14.94	32.2	27.8	4.4						
25	30.18	.154	91	.703	.549	1.0	N 52 W	12.09	12.33	28.2	24.1	3.8						
26	30.73	.139	81	.983	.729	1.0	N 50 W	18.64	18.64	32.0	27.0	5.0			0.8	5.5	.080	5.5
27	29.37	.137	82	.771	.634	0.9	s 39 W	1.66	3.05	33.2	21.3	11.9						
28							N 41 E	6.38	6.90	34.4	30.6	3.8						
29	30.25	.136	81	.853	.217	1.0	s 55 W	7.33	11.03	35.3	24.4	10.9	.020	2.0	0.2	2.0	.020	2.0
30	25.97	.121	84	.645	.525	0.6	N 71 W	11.88	12.72	29.2	25.0	4.2	.060	2.5	0.6	2.5	.060	2.5
	34.16	0.162	79	29.637	29.464	0.8	N 25 W	3.14	8.87	37.29	30.30.06	7.87	3.578	64.9	4.0	48.0	4.278	132.9

GENERAL METEOROLOGICAL ABSTRACT,—DECEMBER, 1858.

Date	DAILY MEANS.					WIND.			EXTREMES OF TEMPERATURE.			RAIN.		SNOW.		RAIN AND MELTED SNOW	
	Temperature of the Air.	Pressure of Vapour.	Relative Humidity.	Barometric Pressure.	Pressure of Dry Air.	Clouded Sky.	Resultant Direction.	Resultant Velocity.	Mean Velocity.	Maximum.	Minimum.	Difference.	Depth in Inches.	Approximate duration in hours.	Depth in Inches.	Approximate duration in hours.	Depth in Inches.	Approximate duration in hours.
1	24.20	0.110	80	29.963	29.853	0.8	S 79 E	7.62	0.06	37.1	9.8	27.3	...	...	0.5	3.0	...	3.0
2	37.13	.158	69	.695	.542	1.0	S 66 W	3.88	4.42	39.2	25.9	13.3	...	...	1.5	8.0	.050	8.0
3	26.93	.120	87	.795	.660	1.0	N 9 W	5.61	6.55	32.2	26.4	5.8	...	...	1.2	10.5	.150	10.5
4	21.57	.097	84	.697	.600	1.0	N 44 E	10.97	11.35	27.4	17.4	10.0	...	...	0.1	1.0	.120	1.0
5						0.9	N 3 02 W	7.09	16.23	44.0	19.3	24.7	.440	3.0			.450	
6	31.08	.131	76	.847	.716	0.8	N 29 E	1.08	7.18	34.5	30.9	3.6					*	*
7	37.33	.161	71	.502	.341	0.8	N 70 W	4.30	9.76	40.4	26.7	13.7			*	*		
8	20.98	.052	71	.685	.603	0.6	S 86 W	19.36	19.54	26.0	23.8	2.2						
9	16.53	.066	71	30.057	.991	0.5	N 77 W	14.14	14.80	20.3	10.7	10.1						
10	26.55	.114	70	29.817	.703	1.0	N 20 W	5.07	6.92	33.5	13.5	20.0			*	*		
11	25.62	.101	74	.860	.768	0.6	N 56 W	16.46	17.02	32.1	27.9	4.2	.015	1.0	0.2	0.8	.015	1.8
12						0.8	N 21 W	2.71	4.54	38.6	16.2	22.4	.260	5.5	0.5		.260	5.5
13	40.09	.236	95	.485	.248	1.0	S 6 E	3.90	4.65	43.0	25.1	17.9	.245	12.5			.245	12.5
14	40.63	.236	92	.307	.071	1.0	N 33 W	4.08	4.17	45.4	38.0	7.4			0.2	3.0	.020	3.0
15	31.58	.150	80	.496	.346	0.7	S 87 W	6.33	8.68	34.4	31.2	3.2			0.5	1.6	.050	1.6
16	29.32	.134	82	.558	.382	0.7	N 9 E	4.91	5.12	32.5	22.6	9.9			*	0.5	*	0.5
17	19.10	.081	78	.717	.963	0.8	N 58 E	8.97	10.27	22.2	18.0	4.2			0.2	0.8	.020	0.8
18	11.98	.067	89	30.090	30.023	1.0	N 30 W	2.33	5.87	25.4	5.7	19.7	.050	1.5	*	*	.050	1.8
19						0.7	N 50 E	7.67	8.17	37.0	12.1	21.9	.110	2.0	.050	1.5	.050	2.5
20	38.88	.158	81	29.532	29.374	0.9	N 34 W	4.6	13.76	35.0	30.4	4.6	.080	5.0	.110	2.5	.110	2.5
21	33.05	.164	87	.188	.974	0.7	N 56 W	10.19	14.82	34.6	32.8	1.8			*	*	.080	5.0
22	26.23	.109	76	.627	.518	1.0	N 39 E	7.58	8.05	30.2	26.6	3.6						
23	19.98	.093	84	.524	.432	1.0	N 26 W	3.65	3.71	28.0	17.2	10.8	.057	0.5	1.0	14.0	.100	14.5
24	11.27	.061	81	.111	30.050	0.3	S 68 W	0.31	0.31	22.0	9.1	12.9				0.2	*	0.2
25							N 53 W	4.2	23.9	28.1								
26	35.25	.151	73	29.732	29.581	0.7	S 69 W	5.69	6.50	36.4	19.4	17.0	.057	1.5	*	*	.057	1.5
27	29.12	.123	75	.809	.686	1.0	N 83 W	3.55	3.59	37.2	32.2	5.0			0.2	0.5	.020	0.5
28	19.13	.088	65	.651	.563	1.0	N 51 E	6.66	7.36	33.2	28.6	4.6			3.0	2.0	.300	2.0
29	28.45	.147	03	.543	.400	1.0	N 62 E	17.17	17.26	23.6	14.9	8.7	.370	10.0	2.0	23.0	.570	23.0
30	35.43	.176	85	.395	.219	1.0	S 54 W	15.80	16.81	37.0	17.2	19.8				5.0		5.0
31								6.62	7.75	38.0	28.8	9.2	.030	1.5			.030	1.5
	27.40	0.128	81	29.694	29.567	0.8	N 18 W	1.66	9.36	33.19	21.37	11.82	1.057	44.0	10.4	74.4	2.607	118.4

GENERAL METEOROLOGICAL ABSTRACT.—JANUARY, 1859.

Days	DAILY MEANS.					WIND.			EXTREMES OF TEMPERATURE.			RAIN.		SNOW.		RAIN AND MELTED SNOW.	
	Temperature of the Air.	Pressure of Vapour.	Relative Humidity.	Barometric Pressure.	Pressure of Dry Air.	Clouded Sky.	Resultant Direction.	Resultant Velocity.	Mean Velocity.	Maximum.	Minimum.	Difference.	Depth in Inches	Approximate duration in hours.	Depth in Inches	Approximate duration in hours.	Depth in Inches	Approximate duration in hours.
	°							Miles	Miles	°	°	°						
1	31.52	0.152	85	29.663	29.510	0.8	N 63 W	5.57	6.48	36.1	30.4	5.7	...	...	...	...	...	0.6
2	33.73	.150	78	.780	.630	0.8	N 68 E	5.78	6.52	31.4	23.5	7.9	...	...	...	...	...	2.0
3	32.63	.150	81	.638	.488	1.0	S 23 E	7.54	8.20	36.0	23.7	12.3	...	...	0.1	1.5	0.010	1.5
4	34.47	.153	78	.570	.417	0.7	S 88 W	8.96	9.27	34.7	31.2	3.5	...	...	0.2	1.3	.020	1.3
5	29.83	.148	86	.096	.553	0.9	S 62 W	7.70	7.85	40.1	27.0	13.1	...	...	...	...	...	...
6	24.00	.122	88	.175	.053	0.7	N 52 E	2.96	5.58	33.3	27.0	6.3	...	...	2.0	10.2	.200	10.2
7	6.13	.045	77	.571	.526	0.4	N 32 W	14.06	15.29	33.3	26.4	6.9	...	...	2.0	11.5	.200	12.0
8	...	...	...	...	...	...	N 60 W	6.48	11.45	8.0	2.9	5.1	0.5	...	0.5	5.5	.050	6.5
9	...	...	...	...	...	...	N 4 E	7.66	7.78	−8.0	−10.8	2.8	...	...	0.3	4.0	.050	4.0
10	−8.65	.028	70	30.173	30.145	0.6	N 83 E	3.67	7.08	13.3	−26.5	39.8	...	0.5	0.5	18.0	.050	18.0
11	14.45	.072	85	29.655	29.568	1.0	N 50 E	5.65	6.12	18.2	−8.1	26.3	...	...	4.5	9.5	.450	9.5
12	19.67	.098	86	.543	.450	1.0	N 61 E	3.43	5.24	29.2	12.1	10.1	...	0.6	0.1	0.5	.010	1.0
13	33.15	.171	90	.539	.368	1.0	S 42 W	2.12	2.18	36.5	19.0	17.5	...	...	...	...	...	...
14	34.95	.192	95	.233	.041	1.0	N 68 E	7.57	8.78	36.0	32.0	4.0	.655	22.5	0.4	4.0	.655	22.5
15	31.14	.153	86	.110	28.957	1.0	N 68 W	14.41	16.26	36.5	32.1	4.4	.017	1.0	2.2	14.0	.057	5.0
16	...	...	...	...	...	0.7	S 45 W	5.67	6.31	33.0	25.0	8.0	...	...	0.1	4.2	.220	4.2
17	20.47	.106	89	.906	29.699	0.5	N 24 W	6.14	6.34	32.5	24.0	8.5	...	...	*	0.5	.010	0.5
18	17.17	.090	80	.998	.914	0.3	S 50 W	8.79	9.40	30.0	0.0	30.0	...	...	...	...	*	...
19	32.67	.155	83	.743	.588	0.7	S 21 W	5.58	5.63	38.5	19.1	19.4	...	...	...	...	...	...
20	37.98	.194	84	.478	.284	0.7	N 39 W	7.52	7.98	43.2	25.2	18.0	.185	7.5	...	...	.185	7.5
21	31.95	.135	72	.502	.367	1.0	N 64 W	6.30	9.39	36.8	34.5	2.3	...	...	0.2	2.5	.020	2.5
22	13.02	.060	75	.881	.821	0.5	N 70 W	8.76	12.01	18.8	11.1	7.7	...	...	0.2	4.0	.020	4.0
23	...	...	...	...	...	...	S 52 W	13.86	14.17	22.7	7.7	15.0	...	...	...	...	...	...
24	28.23	.111	71	.977	.866	0.2	S 30 W	15.08	15.13	31.9	14.7	17.2	...	...	...	...	...	...
25	32.72	.185	74	.858	.722	0.7	N 40 W	8.81	9.08	36.4	27.0	9.4	...	...	...	...	...	...
26	33.18	.184	73	.987	.852	0.3	S 42 E	6.51	6.04	36.2	29.5	6.7	...	...	...	...	...	10.1
27	30.33	.145	83	.906	.661	0.7	N 77 E	15.60	15.92	37.5	19.5	18.0	.592	7.5	8.0	2.6	.392	2.6
28	36.37	.164	75	.501	.397	0.7	N 63 W	6.84	7.67	40.0	29.5	10.5	...	...	...	...	...	...
29	30.20	.135	74	.729	.604	1.0	N 87 W	9.05	9.75	33.0	27.6	5.4	...	...	0.1	4.5	.010	4.5
30	...	...	...	...	...	...	S 83 W	6.10	6.20	29.0	19.9	9.1	...	...	...	...	...	...
31	27.20	.106	72	.996	.890	0.7	S 43 W	4.21	4.32	31.2	18.9	12.3	...	...	...	...	...	...
	26.44	0.126	81	29.677	29.551	0.7	S 81 W	3.17	8.76	30.46	18.55	11.91	1.449	39.5	16.4	65.9	3.089	105.4

GENERAL METEOROLOGICAL ABSTRACT,—FEBRUARY, 1859.

Days.	DAILY MEANS.						WIND.			Extremes of Temperature.			RAIN.		SNOW.		RAIN AND MELTED SNOW	
	Temperature of the Air.	Pressure of Vapour.	Relative Humidity.	Barometric Pressure.	Pressure of Dry Air.	Clouded Sky.	Resultant Direction.	Resultant Velocity.	Mean Velocity.	Maximum.	Minimum.	Difference.	Depth in Inches.	Approximate duration in hours.	Depth in Inches.	Approximate duration in hours.	Depth in Inches.	Approximate duration in hours.
1	31.22	0.128	70	29.781	29.658	1.0	N 72 E	4.41	5.14	34.0	23.2	10.8	...	...	0.4	6.2	0.040	6.2
2	19.23	.081	77	.584	.502	1.0	N 48 E	10.78	11.11	22.3	18.8	3.5	...	...	2.0	15.0	.200	15.0
3	15.20	.077	89	.287	.210	0.9	N 10 E	3.35	3.79	18.2	12.7	5.5	...	...	0.2	0.5	.020	0.5
4	19.43	.079	76	.419	.340	0.8	S 68 W	8.83	8.94	23.8	9.5	14.3	...	...	2.5	11.0	.250	11.0
5	20.38	.089	82	.826	.737	1.0	N 49 W	1.15	6.42	23.2	12.7	10.5	...	...	0.1	1.5	.010	1.5
6							N 20 W	9.15	9.28	25.2	17.0	8.2	...	...	...	...	...	...
7	20.98	.092	81	.870	.778	0.8	S 55 E	3.79	6.34	27.0	10.9	16.1	...	...	0.2	1.5	.020	4.0
8	30.95	.137	78	.557	.420	0.7	S 1 E	3.66	3.78	35.8	21.8	14.0	...	...	0.5	4.0	.050	1.5
9	26.42	.111	71	.433	.322	0.8	N 20 W	12.07	13.45	35.0	28.8	6.2	...	...	0.5	1.5	.050	3.0
10	9.27	.057	84	.826	.769	0.7	N 24 W	5.56	6.43	14.4	5.0	9.4	...	...	...	...	...	...
11	17.07	.070	75	.925	.855	1.0	N 10 W	2.07	2.53	21.5	3.7	17.8	...	...	0.2	2.5	.020	2.5
12	15.07	.069	82	.883	.814	0.6	N 11 W	3.94	4.03	21.0	13.1	7.9	...	...	...	...	...	...
13							S 51 W	7.64	8.01	24.0	2.1	21.9	...	...	...	...	...	...
14	26.10	.120	84	.657	.538	0.9	S 33 W	5.90	6.03	35.7	19.8	15.9	.035	3.5	...	...	.035	3.5
15	35.87	.196	93	.346	.150	1.0	S 58 W	1.84	2.43	38.0	24.5	13.5	...	...	...	...	...	...
16	31.08	.126	73	.698	.572	0.0	N 85 W	1.30	2.56	27.1	11.7	11.7	...	4.0	...	...	...	4.0
17	33.05	.157	88	.681	.524	1.0	S 81 E	4.18	5.15	38.0	24.0	14.0	.075		...	...	.075	
18	37.18	.187	85	.624	.437	0.3	S 39 W	2.68	2.87	44.5	33.8	10.7	...	5.0	...	...	.290	5.0
19	35.25	.179	86	.379	.200	0.8	S 86 E	3.96	4.49	42.6	25.5	17.1	.290	0.5	*	3.0	*	3.5
20							S 88 W	26.86	28.05	46.2	36.8	9.4	*		*	1.0	*	1.0
21	25.57	.093	67	.632	.540	0.5	N 68 W	17.08	17.33	30.0	22.8	7.2	*	0.2	*	...	*	0.2
22	31.53	.140	77	.620	.480	0.8	S 18 W	1.36	2.70	38.5	20.4	18.1	.055	3.5	...	...	.065	3.5
23	37.55	.171	76	.533	.362	0.8	N 41 W	5.55	6.64	43.0	31.0	12.0	...	...	...	...	...	...
24	25.63	.103	73	.817	.714	0.3	N 2 E	12.52	14.70	31.2	23.2	8.0	...	...	1.0	8.5	.100	8.5
25	20.43	.073	64	.745	.678	0.8	N 81 E	20.69	21.23	28.8	13.9	14.9	...	...	0.5	7.5	.050	7.5
26	30.48	.147	85	.368	.221	0.7	N 83 W	7.15	9.73	35.8	22.0	13.8	...	...	...	...	...	...
27							N 46 W	6.82		40.0	18.9	21.1	...	...	...	...	...	...
28	29.45	.131	79	.676	.546	0.6	N 68 W	12.79	14.11	35.4	28.8	6.6	...	...	0.2	2.0	.020	2.0
	26.04	0.117	79	29.632	29.515	0.7	N 54 W	2.72	8.50	31.65	19.71	12.15	0.455	16.7	8.3	67.2	1.285	88.9

GENERAL METEOROLOGICAL ABSTRACT,—MARCH, 1859.

Days	DAILY MEANS.							WIND.			EXTREMES OF TEMPERATURE.			RAIN.		SNOW.		RAIN AND MELTED SNOW.	
	Temperature of the Air.	Pressure of Vapour.	Relative Humidity.	Barometric Pressure.	Pressure of Dry Air.	Clouded Sky.		Resultant Direction.	Resultant Velocity.	Mean Velocity.	Maximum.	Minimum.	Difference.	Depth in Inches.	Approximate duration in hours.	Depth in Inches.	Approximate duration in hours.	Depth in Inches.	Approximate duration in hours.
1	18.32	0.060	62	30.002	30.082	0.2		N 11 W	7.50	7.87	25.0	15.1	9.9						
2	21.33	.079	67	30.120	30.041	0.0		N 81 E	7.95	8.52	30.0	20.2	9.8						
3	33.12	.173	90	29.322	29.150	1.0		S 83 E	8.87	8.89	37.0	22.5	14.5						
4	35.87	.186	88	28.900	28.774	1.0		S 36 W	7.20	7.52	42.0	33.4	8.6	.465	8.3			.465	8.3
5	36.50	.165	76	29.406	29.241	0.6		N 78 W	8.11	8.21	42.0	33.4	8.6	.040	1.0			.040	1.0
6									2.09	2.10	38.2	32.3	5.9						
7	36.33	.177	52	.475	.298	1.0		N 74 E	16.08	16.06	39.4	30.0	9.4	.220	8.0			.220	8.0
8	36.17	.188	86	.317	.129	0.7		N 77 E	3.80	3.89	41.4	35.0	6.4	.012	6.0			.012	6.0
9	35.50	.158	76	.693	.525	0.2		S 77 E	0.67	0.82	40.3	31.6	9.2						
10	36.77	.152	70	.685	.533	0.3		N 69 E	9.95	10.03	40.8	31.6	9.2						
11	42.47	.205	74	.394	.189	0.7		N 83 E	7.69	10.77	44.2	38.8	5.4	.090	4.5			.090	4.5
12	40.47	.198	79	.455	.257	0.9		S 47 W	9.99	10.77	40.2	36.5	5.5						
13								N 11 W	1.23	1.77	47.0	32.8	14.2						
14	41.52	.223	81	.378	.155	0.8		N 73 E	7.84	7.84	51.2	30.4	20.8	.385	6.7	0.1		.385	6.7
15	37.45	.155	69	.272	.117	1.0		S 78 W	17.86	18.91	42.0	36.5	5.5		0.2				0.2
16	36.40	.156	73	.799	.643	0.2		S 61 W	6.70	8.62	45.2	29.6	12.8						
17	41.37	.106	15	.586	.420	0.8		N 80 E	6.66	7.06	48.2	36.6	18.6	.285	7.1	1.0		.285	7.1
18	46.03	.301	95	28.787	28.486	1.0		N 12 W	8.89	14.55	52.0	39.2	12.8	1.615	19.3	3.9		1.625	19.3
19	31.73	.128	70	28.692	28.704	0.9		N 68 W	31.11	31.16	32.6	30.2	2.4	.020	3.9			.020	3.9
20								N 70 W	11.99	12.57	40.5	27.8	12.7						
21	32.70	.133	72	29.657	29.534	0.9		N 73 E	9.09	9.29	36.0	24.2	11.8	.250	3.0	0.2		.250	3.0
22	37.08	.208	90	.465	.262	0.7		N 41 W	1.35	4.65	45.0	33.0	12.0	.197	2.8	2.2		.197	2.8
23	40.55	.159	63	.564	.405	0.0		S 71 E	2.77	6.50	50.4	29.5	20.9	.285	2.5	3.0		.285	2.5
24	46.45	.252	80	.154	28.902	0.5		S 37 W	3.42	9.36	54.2	37.6	16.6	.025	1.8			.025	1.8
25	37.22	.165	73	.257	29.092	1.0		West	11.46	12.79	44.0	37.2	6.8						
26	30.98	.112	65	.447	.385	0.7		S 80 W	4.59	6.84	36.8	27.4	9.4						0.2
27								N 77 E	3.79	4.13	37.0	26.8	10.2			*			2.2
28	38.78	.208	87	.150	28.942	0.6		N 73 E	11.47	11.60	49.2	29.6	19.6	.020	3.0	0.2		.020	3.0
29	41.57	.184	67	28.888	28.704	0.9		S 64 W	14.98	19.92	49.1	30.5	18.6	.028	8.5			.028	8.5
30	34.47	.119	61	21.337	29.218	0.5		S 78 W	12.84	13.21	43.0	30.1	12.9	.157	1.1	1.1		.157	1.1
31	33.38	.131	69	.597	.456	0.5		N 89 W	14.31	14.75	38.8	28.5	10.3	.020	1.5	1.5		.020	1.5
	36.34	0.168	75	29.413	29.245	0.7		N 64 W	1.96	10.39	42.10	30.48	11.62	4.054	76.1	1.0	18.0	4.154	89.1

TORONTO METEOROLOGICAL OBSERVATIONS.

GENERAL METEOROLOGICAL ABSTRACT,—APRIL, 1859.

Days	DAILY MEANS							WIND			EXTREMES OF TEMPERATURE			RAIN		SNOW		RAIN AND MELTED SNOW	
	Temperature of the Air	Pressure of Vapour	Relative Humidity	Barometric Pressure	Pressure of Dry Air	Clouded Sky	Resultant Direction	Resultant Velocity	Mean Velocity	Maximum	Minimum	Difference	Depth in Inches	Approximate duration in hours	Depth in Inches	Approximate duration in hours	Depth in Inches	Approximate duration in hours
	°							Miles	Miles	°	°	°						
1	34.70	0.150	75	29.837	29.687	0.2	N 49 E	4.68	6.05	42.2	27.0	15.2			*			
2	35.35	.136	61	.587	.461	0.8	N 78 E	16.03	16.13	37.1	31.2	5.9	0.055	7.9		0.7	0.055	7.9
3													*	0.1	0.3		*	0.1
4	30.27	.101	59	.338	.237	1.0	S 76 W	19.85	20.78	47.5	32.8	14.7			0.2	1.6	.030	1.6
5	29.13	.108	64	.418	.316	0.5	N 78 W	16.91	17.07	33.0	27.0	6.0				4.5		4.5
6	34.22	.116	64	.515	.399	0.7	N 74 W	13.90	14.32	33.8	25.2	8.6	.020	0.5		0.5	.020	0.5
7	37.88	.171	76	.455	.284	0.7	N 85 W	9.96	10.22	40.0	26.8	13.2				3.5		4.9
8	31.50	.106	61	.730	.622	0.5	S 88 W	9.08	11.12	44.8	29.8	15.0	.115	1.4	0.3		.115	1.4
9	31.85	.112	68	.956	.844	0.5	N 45 W	14.64	15.13	38.4	30.0	8.4						
10							S 71 E	4.60	8.53	37.2	22.6	14.6						
11	41.20	.228	92	.132	28.904	1.0	N 78 E	21.28	21.30	39.0	32.2	6.8	1.145	10.2			1.145	10.2
12	46.25	.189	75	.556	29.369	0.7	N 65 E	7.00	9.37	44.8	34.8	10.0	.250	5.7			.250	5.7
13	41.88	.179	67	.631	.452	1.0	N 66 W	5.28	8.91	57.4	39.5	17.9						
14	42.92	.179	63	.172	28.993	1.0	N 77 E	14.24	14.32	46.8	33.6	13.2	.215	2.1			.215	2.1
15	39.08	.157	65	.128	.971	0.5	S 16 W	3.81	17.02	54.0	36.8	17.2	.685	5.0			.685	5.0
16	37.68	.132	58	.356	29.224	0.9	S 49 W	11.65	13.85	46.8	36.2	10.6						
17						0.6	N 87 W	11.70	12.09	44.0	31.2	12.8						
18	40.65	.147	58	.683	.536	0.4	N 56 W	3.59	7.19	43.6	31.0	12.8			*	*	*	*
19	40.90	.190	75	.614	.423	0.7	S 27 W	7.09	7.31	48.4	28.5	19.9						
20	42.93	.190	69	.555	.365	1.0	N 33 W	5.60	7.55	40.4	26.2	14.2	*	0.5		0.5	*	0.5
21	43.78	.180	63	.451	.271	1.0	S 67 E	0.99	1.54	49.6	34.5	15.1						
22						1.0	N 70 E	3.98	4.65	48.4	38.8	9.6						
23	37.55	.147	67	.138	28.991	0.8	N 37 E	9.11	11.00	51.0	39.2	11.8						
24						0.6	N 28 W	22.57	24.15	43.5	34.8	8.7						
25	39.82	.175	73	.598	29.424	0.1	N 70 W	11.79	12.40	53.6	34.2	19.4	.010	0.5	0.1		.010	0.5
26	43.28	.192	68	.510	.318	0.1	S 30 E	2.67	3.97	48.8	29.0	19.8	.030	10.0	0.3	10.0	.030	10.0
27	37.05	.126	57	.720	.594	0.0	N 73 E	1.75	5.86	49.0	37.3	11.8						
28	44.00	.086	31	.845	.759	0.1	N 65 E	5.60	7.78	43.4	33.7	9.7						
29	51.23	.173	46	.744	.570	0.0	N 88 E	4.57	5.21	52.5	33.5	19.0	.092	4.5			.092	4.5
30	54.67	.180	42	.705	.526	0.0	N 66 E	2.20	3.57	62.2	35.0	27.2						
							N 94 E	4.16	5.18	64.8	46.2	18.6						
	39.53	0.154	63	29.535	29.381	0.6	N 36 W	2.33	10.79	46.54	32.92	13.62	2.527	36.7	1.2	21.3	2.647	58.0

GENERAL METEOROLOGICAL ABSTRACT,—MAY, 1859.

Days.	DAILY MEANS.						WIND.			Extremes of Temperature.			RAIN.		SNOW.		Rain and Melted Snow.	
	Temperature of the Air.	Pressure of Vapour.	Relative Humidity.	Barometric Pressure.	Pressure of Dry Air.	Clouded Sky.	Resultant Direction.	Resultant Velocity.	Mean Velocity.	Maximum.	Minimum.	Difference.	Depth in Inches.	Approximate duration in hours.	Depth in Inches.	Approximate duration in hours.	Depth in Inches.	Approximate duration in hours.
1	52.33	0.155	40	29.863	29.708	0.1	N 86 E	4.44	4.77	59.0	44.4	14.6	...	...	...	...	...	...
2	40.62	.156	49	.988	.782	0.1	N 82 E	7.02	7.50	58.0	40.0	18.0	...	...	...	...	...	...
3	55.75	.266	44	.838	.672	0.3	N 76 E	9.21	9.37	64.0	48.0	18.8	0.1	...	...	...	...	...
4	59.68	.321	59	.758	.437	0.5	N 64 E	3.88	5.06	64.0	46.9	17.1	...	...	...	...	...	...
5	64.47	.385	67	.674	.299	0.3	S 46 B	2.29	3.28	71.4	50.5	20.9	...	...	...	...	...	...
6	65.92	.434	65	.529	.095	0.3	S 28 W	1.81	2.57	75.1	51.8	23.3	.215	...	...	...	...	...
7	...	...	71	...	...	0.3	N 35 W	3.47	4.52	76.4	51.8	24.6	.585	...	...	...	...	...
8	45.48	.263	86	.511	.249	1.0	N 58 E	2.15	5.18	79.6	54.2	25.4	...	9.4	...	...	...	...
9	49.55	.182	51	.680	.448	0.0	N 78 E	5.01	5.83	49.4	45.0	4.4	...	10.0	...	...	...	...
10	50.75	.263	60	.713	.450	0.3	N 85 E	6.32	7.50	56.0	42.5	13.5	...	...	...	...	...	...
11	55.67	.350	70	.706	.357	0.4	S 88 B	8.18	8.22	56.5	39.5	17.0	...	...	...	...	...	...
12	56.22	.278	59	.793	.514	0.7	N 30 W	4.92	4.99	63.0	44.0	19.0	...	...	...	...	...	...
13	60.22	.158	43	.949	.791	0.3	N 29 E	7.39	9.36	71.8	51.8	20.0	...	...	...	...	...	...
14	...	...	...	...	...	...	S 15 E	1.35	0.00	57.6	40.0	17.6	.945	10.6	...	...	...	...
15	53.63	.291	70	.514	.223	0.7	S 63 E	3.47	5.30	60.0	42.2	18.0	...	...	...	...	...	...
16	55.05	.377	87	.306	28.926	0.4	S 77 E	2.64	6.65	64.8	44.8	20.0	...	...	...	...	...	...
17	59.07	.421	83	.365	28.942	0.5	N 39 E	3.75	3.65	66.8	51.0	15.8	...	...	...	...	...	...
18	58.47	.297	71	.681	29.384	0.6	N 8 W	4.03	7.25	63.2	45.0	18.2	...	...	...	...	...	...
19	54.00	.294	70	.704	.410	0.2	N 89 W	4.17	4.64	59.0	50.0	9.0	.595	3.5	...	...	...	...
20	55.15	.376	85	.426	.050	0.8	N 62 W	1.61	4.28	57.2	47.2	11.8	.085	1.5	...	...	...	...
21	...	...	...	...	...	...	N 53 W	6.04	7.35	59.2	44.8	15.6	...	...	...	...	...	...
22	52.10	.245	63	.767	.523	0.0	S 26 E	2.43	2.78	59.2	44.1	14.4	...	...	...	...	...	...
23	56.23	.280	62	.746	.466	0.1	S 89 B	2.70	2.87	60.4	43.0	17.4	...	...	...	...	...	...
24	62.27	.334	60	.732	.348	0.7	N 53 W	3.67	3.70	64.0	45.2	18.8	.030	0.2	...	...	...	...
25	64.73	.406	69	.614	.148	0.6	S 83 B	0.21	2.05	66.8	51.0	15.8	.035	1.0	...	...	...	...
26	58.59	.392	75	.298	28.897	0.9	S 39 W	11.69	13.16	72.6	57.0	15.6	.215	4.2	...	...	...	...
27	55.00	.301	81	.463	29.161	0.6	S 70 W	6.9	6.9	66.0	50.8	15.2	.735	9.9	...	...	...	...
28	...	...	...	...	...	...	N 43 W	6.64	8.63	64.4	49.2	15.2	*	0.2	...	...	...	...
29	48.50	.160	48	.918	.758	0.1	S 83 B	7.36	8.92	61.9	49.8	12.1	...	...	...	...	...	...
30	51.58	.263	68	.782	.519	0.5	N 68 E	3.67	3.96	55.2	41.5	13.7	...	...	...	...	...	...
31								5.08	6.37	59.4	42.6	15.6						
	55.16	0.298	67	29.660	29.361	0.4	N 72 E	1.59	5.70	63.40	47.13	16.26	3.410	50.6				

TORONTO METEOROLOGICAL OBSERVATIONS.

GENERAL METEOROLOGICAL ABSTRACT—JUNE, 1859.

Days	DAILY MEANS.							WIND.			EXTREMES OF TEMPERATURE.			RAIN.		SNOW.		RAIN AND MELTED SNOW	
	Temperature of the Air.	Pressure of Vapour.	Relative Humidity.	Barometric Pressure.	Pressure of Dry Air.	Clouded Sky.	Resultant Direction.	Resultant Velocity.	Mean Velocity.	Maximum.	Minimum.	Difference.	Depth in Inches.	Approximate duration in hours.	Depth in Inches.	Approximate duration in hours.	Depth in Inches.	Approximate duration in hours.
1	56.85	0.399	87	29.696	29.297	0.5	S 76 E	3.63	5.02	63.0	48.8	14.2	0.320	3.3			0.320	3.8
2	64.28	.368	68	.532	.144	0.5	S 67 W	7.87	8.23	76.5	53.7	22.8	.035	0.5			.035	0.5
3	52.22	.263	62	.668	.416	0.6	N 52 W	15.79	17.81	63.2	54.8	8.4	*	*	1.0	1.0	*	1.0
4	8.13	.142	62	.930	.788	0.5	N 53 W	4.76	8.10	47.4	36.4	11.0			1.0	1.0		1.0
5							S 1 E	2.21	5.67	60.0	32.2	27.9						
6	53.27	.218	50	.857	.639	0.1	S 67 E	2.75	3.19	64.5	36.8	27.7	.135	3.5			.135	3.5
7	57.77	.311	65	.644	.333	0.6	N 63 W	4.40	6.02	63.2	43.5	19.7	.090	0.4			.090	0.4
8	55.50	.324	73	.477	.153	0.6	S 68 W	11.63	14.84	72.0	56.3	15.7	.050	2.5			.050	2.5
9	54.32	.201	68	.028	.837	0.6	N 63 W	4.96	8.78	63.0	42.6	20.4	.050	1.0			.050	1.0
10	44.85	.160	56	.719	.559	0.6	N 48 W	11.71	12.27	52.4	43.0	9.4	.080				.080	
11	45.62	.200	66	.916	.716	0.1	S 10 E	4.38	7.04	54.5	34.0	20.5						
12							S 58 E	4.75	6.38	58.2	38.0	20.2						
13	61.90	.504	90	.513	.009	0.8	S 82 W	3.38	7.06	72.0	51.2	18.6	.293	2.5			.293	2.5
14	56.53	.399	89	.658	.258	0.8	N 86 E	4.04	4.75	61.2	52.3	8.9	1.575	5.6			1.575	5.6
15	62.37	.463	81	.360	.892	0.8	S 71 W	3.95	7.02	73.4	52.1	21.3						
16	54.62	.285	66	.550	.265	0.6	N 38 W	4.86	5.58	63.5	53.8	9.7	.965	1.8			.965	1.8
17	54.27	.273	64	.548	.275	0.8	N 24 E	4.56	6.74	60.8	46.2	14.6						
18	59.27	.236	47	.569	.333	0.2	N 39 W	4.82	7.57	68.5	47.8	20.7						
19							S 72 E	2.79	4.07	69.4	44.0	25.4						
20	57.72	.413	86	.359	.947	0.9	N 70 E	4.36	5.33	64.8	53.7	11.1	.050	0.5			.050	0.5
21	57.40	.385	81	.358	.973	0.4	S 87 W	6.25	21.4	69.4	54.5	11.5	.422	5.7			.422	5.7
22	60.67	.387	78	.498	.111	0.5	N 55 W	8.06	21.4	59.4	47.0	17.0						
23	62.10	.347	69	.705	.358	0.2	N 43 W	1.69	4.46	69.4	51.8	17.0	*	0.2			*	0.2
24	63.42	.390	68	.705	.315	0.4	N 11 E	4.06	4.58	69.4	54.9	15.9						
25	66.03	.373	65	.706	.333	0.6	N 31 W	2.12	4.52	75.0	57.2	17.8						
26							S 81 E	3.52	3.65	74.2	54.0	20.2						
27	74.08	.530	69	.612	.082	0.4	S 9 W	5.92	7.32	81.4	62.7	18.7	.015	0.5			.015	0.5
28	75.08	.674	78	.627	.953	0.5	N 28 W	6.33	6.59	80.8	69.0	11.8	.060	0.3			.060	0.3
29	73.05	.583	63	.512	.970	0.6	N 71 W	13.80	17.83	86.4	70.0	16.4	.045	0.3			.045	0.3
30	55.20	.286	65	.764	.478	0.0	S 71 W	2.08	5.56	64.5	50.0	14.5						
	58.30	0.355	69	29.620	29.265	0.5	N 77 W	1.95	7.19	66.98	49.82	17.11	4.085	28.6	*	2.0	4.085	30.6

GENERAL METEOROLOGICAL ABSTRACT.—JULY, 1859.

Days.	Temperature of the Air.	Pressure of Vapour.	Relative Humidity.	Barometric Pressure.	Pressure of Dry Air.	Clouded Sky.	WIND Resultant Direction.	WIND Resultant Velocity.	WIND Mean Velocity.	Extremes of Temperature Maximum.	Extremes of Temperature Minimum.	Extremes of Temperature Difference.	RAIN Depth in Inches.	RAIN Approximate duration in hours.	SNOW Depth in Inches.	SNOW Approximate duration in hours.	RAIN AND MELTED SNOW Depth in Inches.	RAIN AND MELTED SNOW Approximate duration in hours.
	°							Miles	Miles	°	°	°						
1	60.98	0.301	73	29.575	29.184	0.7	S 29 E	2.32	2.89	69.5	45.2	24.3	.471	11.0				
2	70.25	.604	82	.266	28.662	0.6	S 50 W	7.04	10.72	81.4	59.2	22.2	.109	3.5				
3	55.08	.269	62	30.024	29.754	0.0	N 26 W	11.77	11.89	60.4	49.8	10.6		1.5				
4	60.52	.323	63	.048	.725	0.3	S 35 E	2.73	5.07	60.4	44.4	15.7						
5	59.37	.398	83	29.938	.539	1.0	S 4 E	2.56	8.67	68.5	46.8	21.7						
6	62.27	.452	81	.888	.386	0.9	S 23 W	2.17	3.51	64.8	56.6	8.2	.045	4.0				
7	66.83	.473	72	.807	.334	0.5	S 56 E	1.99	3.91	68.2	57.2	11.0						
8	68.05	.366	53	.800	.405	0.0	S 53 E	2.22	2.86	75.2	59.2	16.0						
9							N 88 E	4.60	4.97	78.6	61.1	17.5						
10	75.05	.633	73	.721	.059	0.7	S 36 W	3.25	3.94	78.8	58.8	20.0						
11	79.89	.637	68	.708	.065	0.2	S 79 W	1.49	3.01	84.2	61.0	23.2						
12	77.03	.678	72	.706	.028	0.5	S 71 E	3.10	4.45	88.0	68.4	19.6						
13	73.13	.501	61	.707	.205	0.7	N 77 E	8.86	9.12	83.4	69.4	14.0	.191	1.5				
14	70.33	.028	85	.517	28.889	0.7	N 12 E	2.83	4.87	78.5	71.0	7.5	.127	2.8				
15	74.47	.697	81	.541	.854	0.5	S 89 W	1.32	3.60	81.0	67.0	14.0						
16							N 53 E	1.88	2.48	81.4	67.8	13.6						
17							S 86 E	3.75	4.19	69.2	58.2	10.6	.497	6.0				
18	78.08	.653	84	.507	28.824	0.6	N 84 W	2.09	4.82	69.6	58.0	10.6						
19	73.43	.675	77	.360	.685	0.6	N 27 W	9.36	10.02	74.2	67.0	7.2						
20	67.33	.370	57	.499	.129	0.2	S 28 W	1.16	1.27	71.4	55.5	15.9						
21	65.15	.453	79	.532	.060	1.0	N 72 W	5.68	6.70	77.6	61.2	16.4						
22	68.27	.308	73	.390	28.971	0.2	N G1 W	1.23	2.57	72.0	52.8	19.2	.064	0.3				
23	61.10	.317	52	.545	.228	0.1	S 2 E	1.88	4.07	74.5	53.2	21.3	.083	3.2				
24			59				S 87 W	1.14	1.07	74.5	62.8	11.7	.879	3.4				
25	64.85	.521	85	.538	.017	0.6	N 68 W	16.67	17.30	62.8	58.5	4.3						
26	58.65	.312	64	.516	.204	0.6	N 40 W	12.33	12.38	67.0	54.7	12.3						
27	60.08	.335	67	.592	.257	0.2	N 44 W	5.44	7.40	70.4	53.5	16.9	.061	1.2				
28	62.27	.372	65	.659	.280	0.9	N 18 W	2.27	3.14	73.0	54.7	18.3						
29	63.65	.392	67	.772	.380	0.1	S 13 W	3.24	8.53	72.0	53.8	18.2						
30	64.18	.412	68	.734	.322	0.0	S 34 E	3.57	5.83	75.6	56.0	19.6	.095	2.5				
31																		
	66.87	0.471	70	29.648	29.177	0.5	N 56 W	1.48	5.81	74.65	59.20	15.45	2.611	30.9				

GENERAL METEOROLOGICAL ABSTRACT.—AUGUST, 1859.

Days.	DAILY MEANS.						WIND.			EXTREMES OF TEMPERATURE.			RAIN.		SNOW.		RAIN AND MELTED SNOW	
	Temperature of the Air.	Pressure of Vapour.	Relative Humidity.	Barometric Pressure.	Pressure of Dry Air.	Clouded Sky.	Resultant Direction.	Resultant Velocity.	Mean Velocity.	Maximum.	Minimum.	Difference.	Depth in Inches.	Approximate duration in hours.	Depth in Inches.	Approximate duration in hours.	Depth in Inches.	Approximate duration in hours.
	°							Miles.	Miles.	°	°	°						
1	67.92	0.461	69	29.509	29.048	0.4	N 83 W	2.57	8.76	77.4	64.0	13.4	...	...	...	...	...	...
2	66.40	.381	60	.610	.229	0.3	N 84 E	4.05	4.40	73.8	55.6	18.2	...	...	...	...	...	...
3	67.88	.541	79	.558	.018	0.8	N 67 E	2.88	3.87	75.6	60.6	15.0	1.375	11.2	...	...	...	...
4	67.92	.539	79	.424	28.894	0.5	N 66 W	4.11	3.26	75.8	63.1	12.7	.085	0.5	...	...	...	...
5	64.10	.366	62	.551	.185	0.4	N 59 W	6.21	6.26	74.5	58.6	15.9	...	...	...	...	...	...
6	64.80	.410	67	.598	.188	0.3	S 45 W	4.20	4.82	74.2	51.8	22.4	...	...	...	...	...	...
7							N 40 W	7.24	8.01	82.0	61.7	20.5	...	...	...	...	...	...
8	65.37	.408	65	.701	.293	0.3	N 69 E	2.05	2.69	74.0	55.5	18.5	...	...	...	...	...	...
9	68.03	.497	72	.769	.273	0.0	N 63 E	2.22	3.37	78.2	58.8	19.4	...	...	...	...	...	...
10	70.63	.523	69	.698	.175	0.7	N 78 E	2.51	2.79	78.4	62.1	16.3	...	...	...	...	...	...
11	69.98	.588	80	.694	.006	0.8	N 51 E	0.91	2.90	80.2	64.6	15.6	.080	3.5	...	...	...	...
12	69.80	.614	84	.556	28.942	0.4	N 70 E	4.47	4.81	74.0	64.2	9.8	...	...	...	...	...	...
13	69.87	.577	79	.586	29.009	0.4	S 19 E	2.16	2.91	75.4	67.0	8.4	...	...	...	...	...	...
14							N 80 W	0.94	4.46	82.0	63.5	18.5	...	...	...	...	...	...
15				.617	.026	0.4	N 77 E	4.03	4.97	90.4	68.1	12.3	...	...	...	...	...	...
16	72.90	.590	78	.690	.132	0.3	N 79 E	5.03	5.39	69.0	69.0	9.2	...	0.5	...	...	...	...
17	72.02	.656	82	.715	.128	0.2	S 71 E	3.07	3.88	80.4	65.0	15.4	...	...	...	...	...	...
18	72.23	.588	76	.552	.098	0.6	N 17 W	5.53	9.69	80.0	64.1	15.9	.180	3.1	...	...	...	...
19	68.38	.519	74	.629	.324	0.1	S 5 E	10.16	10.33	75.2	56.6	18.6						
20	64.83	.305	52	.590	.378	0.0	N 88 E	3.60	4.43	75.2	56.1	19.1						
21	66.50	.360	57					3.49	4.00	75.4	54.5	20.9						
22	69.78	.497	69	.631	.134	0.6	S 69 E	6.99	8.05	74.2	58.9	15.3	.170	2.5	...	...	...	...
23	66.85	.545	83	.585	.040	1.0	N 88 E	7.06	8.18	70.8	65.6	5.2	1.655	15.0	...	...	...	...
24	65.97	.550	86	.463	.132	0.5	S 15 E	2.61	3.95	72.2	64.6	7.6	.315	2.2	...	...	...	...
25	65.65	.435	70	.528	.003	0.5	S 43 W	6.55	6.94	74.2	58.0	16.2						
26	66.42	.462	68	.590	.048	0.2	N 68 W	4.68	6.95	74.2	58.0	16.2		0.2				
27	60.15	.333	65	.612	.278	0.1	N 79 W	11.04	11.59	78.2	56.8	21.4						
28							N 34 W	11.53	11.60	68.0	56.8	11.2						
29	56.28	.218	52	.717	.499	0.2	N 39 W	6.57	6.71	63.2	49.8	13.4	.040	1.6	...	...	...	...
30	59.15	.317	65	.518	.201	0.9	S 85 W	5.93	7.20	70.5	47.2	20.8	.140	1.6	...	...	...	...
31	56.68	.298	65	.495	.197	0.4	N 68 W	9.21	9.60	65.8	53.7	12.1		1.0				
	66.61	0.463	70	29.599	29.136	0.4	N 36 W	1.62	5.96	73.01	59.38	15.63	3.990	41.3				

GENERAL METEOROLOGICAL ABSTRACT,—SEPTEMBER, 1859.

Days.	DAILY MEANS.					WIND.			EXTREMES OF TEMPERATURE.			RAIN.		SNOW.		RAIN AND MELTED SNOW.	
	Temperature of the Air.	Pressure of Vapour.	Relative Humidity.	Barometric Pressure.	Pressure of Dry Air.	Clouded Sky.	Resultant Direction.	Resultant Velocity.	Mean Velocity.	Maximum.	Minimum.	Difference.	Depth in Inches.	Approximate duration in hours.	Depth in Inches.	Approximate duration in hours.	Depth in Inches.	Approximate duration in hours.
1	56.62	0.323	70	29.439	29.110	0.8	S 68 W	6.41	8.47	65.8	43.0	22.8	0.075	2.0	...	...	...	...
2	54.88	.256	61	.555	.299	0.8	N 94 W	7.70	8.77	61.8	46.8	15.0	...	...	...	...	...	...
3	59.45	.370	75	.431	.061	0.7	S 44 W	3.75	6.52	68.2	51.6	16.6	.395	1.4	...	...	...	...
4	...	...	...	...	...	...	...	...	...	...	...	...	...	...	...	...	...	...
5	51.07	.299	77	.890	.600	0.6	N 61 W	6.00	6.35	62.8	45.8	17.0	...	...	...	...	...	...
6	52.97	.286	65	.004	.744	0.2	N 76 W	3.84	4.77	59.8	47.0	12.8	.117	0.5	...	...	...	...
7	53.43	.295	70	29.981	.695	0.3	N 67 W	2.01	4.79	62.2	43.8	18.4	...	...	...	...	...	...
8	54.23	.270	67	.976	.697	0.1	N 74 W	1.82	3.68	62.2	46.0	16.2	...	...	...	...	...	...
9	59.10	.317	65	.599	.582	0.5	S 77 W	1.84	2.14	63.2	41.9	21.3	...	...	...	...	...	...
10	63.27	.651	94	.622	.071	1.0	East	3.44	3.81	66.4	47.8	18.6	.665	3.0	...	...	...	...
11	...	...	...	...	...	...	S 26 W	4.39	4.80	68.0	58.1	9.9	.100	3.0	...	...	...	...
12	63.02	.367	65	.149	28.776	0.7	S 89 W	13.34	13.34	75.4	54.4	21.0	.038	1.5	...	...	...	...
13	50.53	.211	57	.284	29.073	0.5	N 64 W	12.40	12.03	74.6	52.7	21.9	...	...	...	...	...	...
14	43.17	.130	50	.395	.078	0.3	N 67 W	16.76	18.00	57.0	52.4	4.6	*	0.2	...	...	...	...
15	43.08	.139	50	.996	.858	0.7	N 55 W	12.94	13.82	51.2	40.4	10.8	...	...	...	...	...	...
16	51.12	.268	70	.748	.479	1.0	N 74 E	5.24	5.65	48.4	35.7	12.7	...	...	...	...	...	...
17	53.93	.362	86	.628	.265	0.6	N 77 W	8.30	8.46	54.2	43.0	11.2	...	...	...	...	...	...
18	...	...	...	...	...	...	N 86 E	1.86	2.62	62.0	52.3	9.7	...	...	...	...	...	...
19	57.97	.422	87	.378	28.956	0.7	N 79 E	2.38	3.15	60.8	45.0	15.8	.110	3.0	...	...	...	...
20	52.07	.294	75	.603	29.309	1.0	N 14 E	3.90	5.02	63.2	49.0	13.6	.008	0.3	...	...	...	...
21	51.90	.352	90	.574	.222	1.0	N 37 E	7.02	7.18	56.0	50.0	6.0	1.185	13.5	...	...	...	...
22	56.82	.425	92	.556	.132	0.8	N 64 E	13.56	13.80	57.2	48.5	8.7	.250	0.5	...	...	...	...
23	58.68	.424	86	.066	.243	0.9	N 73 E	3.61	3.69	61.2	52.9	8.3	*	0.3	...	...	...	...
24	60.70	.447	85	.644	.197	0.8	N 16 E	1.25	2.61	65.0	52.5	12.5	...	...	...	...	...	...
25	...	...	...	...	...	...	S 43 W	0.40	0.65	67.5	56.6	10.0	...	...	...	...	...	...
26	58.87	.428	86	.596	.170	1.0	N 44 W	1.60	1.76	65.0	56.6	8.6	.045	1.7	...	...	...	...
27	61.67	.477	87	.557	.080	1.0	N 21 W	5.30	7.02	65.0	51.2	13.8	.007	0.8	...	...	...	...
28	57.47	.393	83	.830	.437	0.2	N 2 E	5.89	5.89	68.4	60.3	8.1	...	...	...	...	...	...
29	51.33	.290	77	.958	.669	0.4	N 85 E	3.49	6.49	64.9	56.6	8.3	...	...	...	...	...	...
30	58.02	.413	83	.735	.322	0.5	S 88 E	4.08	4.25	59.8	49.8	10.0	.530	4.7	...	...	...	...
								8.16	7.02	63.0	42.0	21.0						
	55.18	0.357	75	29.669	29.331	0.7	N 44 W	1.60	6.36	62.68	49.32	13.36	3.525	36.4	*	*	*	*

GENERAL METEOROLOGICAL ABSTRACT.—OCTOBER, 1859.

	DAILY MEANS.						WIND.			EXTREMES OF TEMPERATURE.			RAIN.			SNOW.			RAIN AND MELTED SNOW	
Days.	Temperature of the Air.	Pressure of Vapour.	Relative Humidity.	Barometric Pressure.	Pressure of Dry Air.	Clouded Sky.	Resultant Direction.	Resultant Velocity.	Mean Velocity.	Maximum.	Minimum.	Difference.	Depth in Inches.	Approximate duration in hours.		Depth in Inches.	Approximate duration in hours.		Depth in Inches.	Approximate duration in hours.
1	56.95	0.388	84	29.649	29.261	0.7	S 87 W	6.61	6.93	60.5	55.2	5.3								
2	56.33	.336	73	.566	.231	0.0	N 78 W	10.57	10.97	60.5	50.8	9.7	*	0.2					*	0.2
3	60.40	.408	78	.546	.138	0.0	S 30 W	7.46	7.70	63.5	37.5	26.0								
4	53.70	.333	81	.537	.204	0.4	S 30 W	4.14	4.20	69.8	55.5	14.3								
5	44.35	.217	74	.702	.485	0.6	N 90 W	8.08	11.72	68.5	51.4	17.1	*	0.2					*	0.2
6	44.95	.235	82	.642	.407	1.0	N 78 W	8.06	8.44	53.2	36.5	16.7	.115	7.5					.115	7.5
7	39.88	.178	72	.690	.512	0.7	N 2 E	4.82	5.95	57.0	36.5	20.5	.050	3.0					.050	3.0
8							N 22 E	7.95	8.53	44.7	37.0	7.7								
9				.*			N 60 E	0.81	4.53	46.4	31.0	15.4								
10	44.07	.208	71	.790	.581	0.2	N 78 W	3.93	4.60	53.0	32.0	21.0								
11	47.50	.220	67	.868	.648	0.7	N 34 W	3.58	4.56	57.4	39.2	18.2								
12	46.58	.251	72	.823	.572	0.7	N 72 E	2.19	2.88	52.2	36.4	15.8								
13	57.42	.367	79	.493	.127	0.8	S 32 W	8.48	10.09	63.8	48.0	15.8	.397	2.2					.397	2.2
14	50.73	.246	78	.505	.260	0.4	N 77 W	10.98	11.37	61.2	51.9	9.3								
15	38.92	.178	68	.792	.614	0.5	N 57 W	4.35	4.58	53.0	37.0	16.0								
16			76				S 71 E	5.15	5.65	50.9	33.2	17.7				*	*		*	
17						1.0	S 40 W	6.43	7.31	61.2	45.8	15.4	*	0.1					*	0.1
18	46.37	.198	59	.413	.216	0.7	N 84 W	20.49	20.73	58.8	43.8	15.0	.318	6.5					.318	6.5
19	37.48	.158	71	.565	.407	0.7	N 36 W	6.56	7.43	43.4	34.7	8.7	.010	1.0					.010	1.0
20	32.12	.105	59	.652	.547	0.4	N 36 W	18.63	18.90	38.0	28.8	9.2	.040	4.0	0.5	*	*		.040	4.5
21	31.82	.119	70	.648	.528	0.2	N 49 W	11.86	12.25	39.2	28.0	11.2			0.5	*	*		*	0.5
22	33.75	.103	88	.525	.362	1.0	N 73 W	1.73	1.73	38.0	26.8	11.2								
23							S 55 W	4.22	4.73	43.5	27.0	16.5								
24	42.73	.223	81	.642	.419	1.0	N 88 W	5.95	7.13	46.5	35.4	11.1	.010	0.9	*	3.0			.010	3.9
25	37.18	.131	59	.495	.364	0.7	N 23 W	10.61	11.31	41.5	36.8	4.7								
26	27.87	.111	72	.399	.288	0.9	N 8 E	3.23	4.11	31.0	22.6	8.4								
27	32.37	.128	69	.370	.243	0.4	N 62 W	10.68	11.27	38.2	22.3	15.9								
28	37.52	.139	63	.483	.344	0.9	N 53 W	12.53	12.73	38.2	30.6	14.2								
29	36.52	.146	68	.746	.600	0.9	N 44 W	8.86	8.51	40.6	33.6	7.0								
30							N 59 W	4.40	4.52	40.8	30.8	10.0								
31	37.25	.169	77	.822	.653	0.8	N 77 W	6.22	6.30	40.7	34.6	6.1								
	42.99	0.214	72	29.615	29.400	0.6	N 68 W	5.04	8.12	50.38	37.05	13.33	0.940	25.8		*	4.0		0.940	29.8

GENERAL METEOROLOGICAL ABSTRACT,—NOVEMBER, 1859.

Days	DAILY MEANS.						WIND.			EXTREMES OF TEMPERATURE.			RAIN.		SNOW.		RAIN AND MELTED SNOW	
	Temperature of the Air.	Pressure of Vapour.	Relative Humidity.	Barometric Pressure.	Pressure of Dry Air.	Clouded Sky.	Resultant Direction.	Resultant Velocity.	Mean Velocity.	Maximum.	Minimum.	Difference.	Depth in Inches.	Approximate duration in hours.	Depth in Inches.	Approximate duration in hours.	Depth in Inches.	Approximate duration in hours.
1	37.27	0.159	72	29.733	29.574	0.9	N 55 W	6.72	7.21	41.0	31.8	9.2	...	...	*	...	*	...
2	35.03	.145	73	.788	.643	0.5	N 71 W	8.68	8.95	48.0	31.0	17.0	...	...	...	...	...	...
3	37.00	.167	75	30.026	.859	0.3	S 74 E	3.59	5.41	42.0	27.0	15.0	...	...	...	...	...	...
4	51.15	.279	72	29.071	.892	0.9	S 41 W	7.21	7.41	61.5	27.5	24.0	...	...	...	...	...	...
5	49.07	.170	49	.587	.668	0.2	N 65 W	10.37	11.98	62.6	50.8	11.8	...	...	...	...	...	...
6	41.05	.194	75	.963	.769	1.0	N 74 E	7.82	8.73	40.5	30.2	10.3	...	0.5	*	...	...	0.1
7	44.90	.242	81	.791	.549	1.0	N 80 E	3.13	3.14	45.4	35.8	9.6	...	...	...	...	...	0.2
8	45.90	.249	80	.657	.408	1.0	S 78 E	2.40	2.47	52.0	35.0	17.0	.360	11.3	*	...	.360	11.3
9	35.72	.191	91	.852	.161	0.9	N 1 W	6.98	7.97	49.8	44.5	5.3	.405	13.5	0.2	2.7	.425	16.2
10	41.83	.134	78	.681	.547	0.9	N 14 W	6.61	8.58	39.2	36.8	2.4	...	...	0.2	1.3	.020	1.3
11	41.68	.250	93	28.991	28.991	1.0	...	...	...	30.0	28.5	20.1	1.135	20.5	0.1	...	1.135	20.5
12	29.58	.123	74	.641	29.518	0.8	S 72 W	18.31	18.80	48.5	29.0	7.8	*	1.0	*	4.0	.010	5.0
13	33.70	.154	80	.916	.761	0.6	S 72 W	9.76	9.84	36.8	28.0	5.6	...	...	...	0.5	...	0.5
14	41.79	.195	73	.810	.621	0.7	S 59 E	1.82	2.77	33.5	27.7	8.7	...	...	...	...	...	...
15	45.23	.238	78	.742	.504	1.0	S 43 E	1.69	1.82	36.4	45.1	12.1	...	...	...	...	...	...
16	46.62	.269	83	.689	.370	0.9	S 20 W	4.11	4.15	48.8	39.5	9.3	...	...	...	...	...	...
17	39.32	.292	86	.234	.002	1.0	N 33 E	7.67	9.16	51.0	39.2	11.8	1.470	10.2	*	2.0	1.470	10.2
18	...	...	...	...	...	...	N 29 W	17.38	18.79	47.6	42.5	5.1	.435	15.0	...	...	.435	15.0
19	...	...	...	...	...	...	N 10 W	7.52	9.15	39.0	26.0	13.0	...	...	...	...	...	...
20	33.14	.173	90	.727	.554	1.0	East	15.60	17.29	43.0	21.8	21.8	.570	8.4	...	...	.570	8.4
21	41.95	.220	83	.499	.279	0.8	S 80 W	12.85	13.43	44.5	32.4	12.1	.088	2.5	0.1	...	.088	2.5
22	34.73	.163	80	.903	.740	0.7	S 60 W	12.93	14.81	40.0	35.8	4.2	...	...	*	...	...	...
23	27.37	.127	84	30.156	.029	1.0	N 26 E	4.09	6.58	31.8	27.0	4.8	...	...	...	...	...	...
24	36.35	.196	89	29.463	.267	0.9	S 42 E	7.33	17.89	40.4	24.0	25.4	.410	10.0	...	1.0	.420	11.0
25	40.12	.172	69	.360	.188	0.9	S 77 W	17.31	17.50	42.2	33.0	9.2	*	0.2	*	...	*	0.2
26	...	...	...	...	...	...	S 75 W	9.07	9.96	37.5	30.2	7.3	...	...	...	1.0	...	1.0
27	32.30	.131	72	.589	.458	0.6	N 86 W	12.09	12.32	37.0	28.8	8.2	...	...	...	...	...	...
28	36.30	.161	74	.594	.433	1.0	S 45 W	8.15	8.27	39.7	29.8	9.9	...	...	.1	...	...	...
29	42.43	.218	80	.539	.321	0.7	S 54 W	6.16	6.30	48.2	38.0	10.2	.370	3.0	...	...	.370	3.0
30																		
	38.90	0.190	78	29.675	29.494	0.8	N 81 W	3.39	9.65	48.95	32.77	11.19	5.193	94.1	0.6	12.8	5.253	106.9

TORONTO METEOROLOGICAL OBSERVATIONS.

GENERAL METEOROLOGICAL ABSTRACT,—DECEMBER, 1859.

Days.	DAILY MEANS.						WIND.			EXTREMES OF TEMPERATURE.			RAIN.		SNOW.		RAIN AND MELTED SNOW.	
	Temperature of the Air.	Pressure of Vapour.	Relative Humidity.	Barometric Pressure.	Pressure of Dry Air.	Clouded Sky.	Resultant Direction.	Resultant Velocity. Miles.	Mean Velocity. Miles.	Maximum.	Minimum.	Difference.	Depth in Inches.	Approximate duration in hours.	Depth in Inches.	Approximate duration in hours.	Depth in Inches.	Approximate duration in hours.
1	44.37	0.281	90	29.448	29.167	1.0	N 79 W	10.32	15.00	54.8	40.8	14.0	0.255	10.5	0.1	2.0	0.265	12.5
2	17.27	.062	84	.927	.845	1.0	N 37 W	12.51	13.02	23.8	17.5	6.3			2.5	14.0	.250	14.0
3	6.80	.049	81	30.272	30.223	0.8	N 12 E	14.00	14.54	17.0	0.8	16.2			2.0	7.0	.200	7.0
4	34.23	.184	92	29.633	29.633	1.0	N 22 E	12.90	13.24	28.0	8.0	20.0		5.0	2.5	18.2	.200	18.0
5	38.08	.218	84	.524	.306	1.0	N 66 E	3.39	8.67	38.2	23.5	14.7	*				*	5.0
6	15.38	.080	82	.745	.665	0.7	N 68 W	4.73	10.51	42.0	34.2	7.8	.780	13.0		6.0	1.130	19.0
7	9.60	.056	82	.946	.890	0.7	S 58 W	8.43	8.59	19.8	2.2	14.6			3.5	8.0	.250	8.0
8	22.25	.107	86	.674	.567	0.7	S 70 W	5.58	5.66	27.0	19.8	6.8			2.5			
9	15.60	.082	87	.904	.822	0.6	S 66 W	13.49	18.46	18.8	4.0	14.8						2.5
10							S 79 W	4.54	7.83	20.5	6.8	20.2			0.5	2.5	.050	2.5
11	8.35	.053	84	.543	.490	0.4	N 74 W	15.29	17.91	37.2	1.0	13.4			0.2	1.5	.020	1.5
12	13.65	.069	84	.869	.800	0.8	N 68 W	5.01	5.70	14.4	1.0	24.7			0.1	0.5	.010	0.5
13	15.80	.080	90	.828	.748	0.8	N 5 E	5.54	6.02	13.4	15.4	26.7			3.0	9.5	.300	9.5
14	17.48	.080	82	.816	.736	0.5	N 9 W	7.29	7.53	20.0	15.4	10.2			9.0	9.0	.020	9.0
15	26.60	.124	85	.798	.674	0.7	S 45 W	1.61	1.67	19.8	15.4	4.4			0.2	0.5		0.5
16	29.03	.150	93	.548	.398	1.0	N 16 E	8.36	4.07	26.8	9.0	17.8			*		*	
17							N 73 E	4.21	11.01	32.2	10.4	21.8			4.0	10.8	.400	10.8
18	32.97	.164	87	.424	.260	0.2	S 69 E	8.05	8.08	32.0	22.2	9.8			8.0	14.5	.600	14.5
19	29.60	.151	82	.293	.142	1.0	N 40 W	5.34	5.84	33.0	29.8	4.0			1.5	3.0	.040	3.0
20	21.68	.099	92	.542	.443	1.0	S 58 W	13.16	13.33	35.0	31.0	4.0			4.0	16.0	.150	16.0
21	17.02	.065	85	.545	.461	0.7	N 88 W	6.78	6.89	35.2	29.8	5.4			0.2	1.6	.020	1.6
22	14.12	.071	89	.408	.337	0.6	N 88 W	13.50	14.88	24.8	19.2	5.6						
23	7.78	.057	90	.640	.583	0.7	N 89 W	9.84	10.19	21.0	15.8	5.2						
24							S 77 W	4.56	4.59	18.3	14.0	4.3			0.3	5.0	.030	5.0
25							N 48 W	10.77	12.21	14.2	-1.9	16.1			0.2	1.5	.020	1.5
26	6.07	.050	84	.985		0.2	N 18 E	11.65	12.18	30.3	7.3	23.0			*	1.0	*	1.0
27	-0.53	.038	88	30.085	30.035	1.0	N 45 E	18.18	18.18	31.3	23.2	8.1						
28	7.02	.055	89	30.073		1.0	N 48 E	18.57	18.90	14.0	5.6	9.3			8.5	13.0	.350	13.0
29	16.05	.074	88	29.599	29.544	0.6	S 73 W	13.09	14.07	2.5	-3.0	5.5			4.0	17.0	.400	17.0
30	-1.08	.085	85	.365		0.1	S 75 W	14.64	14.71	25.0	6.6	18.4						
31				.750						8.0	-6.0	9.0						
	17.89	0.098	87	29.709	29.610	0.7	N 63 W	4.29	10.77	25.26	12.94	12.32	1.035	28.5	37.4	163.4	4.775	191.9

TABLE I.

MONTHLY MEANS OF THE TEMPERATURE OF THE AIR AT EACH OF THE SIX OBSERVATION HOURS, FROM 1854 TO 1859 INCLUSIVE.

	Toronto Astronomical time.	2 h.	4 h.	10 h.	12 h.	18 h.	20 h.	Monthly Means.
JANUARY.	1854	26.18	28.43	22.04	22.49	22.23	22.17	23.57
	1855	30.06	28.46	25.01	24.61	23.73	23.80	25.95
	1856	20.67	20.43	14.60	13.83	13.19	13.42	16.02
	1857	16.04	15.75	12.64	11.66	10.34	10.07	12.75
	1858	33.35	32.56	28.47	28.22	29.00	28.60	30.03
	1859	28.75	28.35	26.20	25.87	24.54	24.93	26.44
	Means.	25.84	25.16	21.64	21.11	20.51	20.50	22.46

	Toronto Astronomical time.	2 h.	4 h.	10 h.	12 h.	18 h.	20 h.	Monthly Means.
FEBRUARY.	1854	25.00	25.49	20.91	19.99	17.39	17.75	21.09
	1855	21.80	20.34	13.91	12.49	11.57	12.24	15.41
	1856	21.82	21.77	14.65	12.84	11.10	11.97	15.69
	1857	31.41	30.97	28.63	28.88	25.28	25.90	28.53
	1858	20.92	21.02	16.54	16.08	13.42	13.92	16.98
	1859	29.12	29.09	26.82	25.23	23.67	23.28	26.04
	Means.	25.03	24.78	20.08	19.25	17.07	17.53	20.62

	Toronto Astronomical time.	2 h.	4 h.	10 h.	12 h.	18 h.	20 h.	Monthly Means.
MARCH.	1854	34.96	34.99	29.14	28.45	27.28	29.23	30.68
	1855	34.11	32.94	26.02	27.18	23.05	25.47	28.46
	1856	28.49	28.15	22.40	21.43	17.77	20.03	23.06
	1857	32.98	33.09	27.40	26.30	22.62	24.46	27.82
	1858	33.54	33.46	27.19	26.13	24.09	26.21	28.44
	1859	39.14	39.68	36.32	35.53	33.10	34.25	36.34
	Means.	33.87	33.72	28.43	27.51	24.65	26.61	29.13

TABLE I.—(Continued.)

MONTHLY MEANS OF THE TEMPERATURE OF THE AIR AT EACH OF THE SIX OBSERVATION HOURS, FROM 1854 TO 1859 INCLUSIVE.

	Toronto Astronomical time.	2 h.	4 h.	10 h.	12 h.	18 h.	20 h.	Monthly Means.
APRIL	1854	46.65	47.07	38.62	37.77	36.29	39.62	41.04
	1855	51.20	49.23	39.39	38.69	35.75	40.34	42.43
	1856	47.81	47.33	40.53	39.34	37.57	41.05	42.27
	1857	40.86	40.62	33.27	32.24	30.90	34.25	35.36
	1858	46.44	46.01	39.72	38.84	37.07	40.66	41.46
	1859	44.04	43.73	38.20	36.84	35.52	38.86	39.53
	Means.	46.17	45.66	38.32	37.29	35.52	39 13	40.35

	Toronto Astronomical time.	2 h.	4 h.	10 h.	12 h.	18 h.	20 h.	Monthly Means.
MAY.	1854	58.67	58.12	48.41	46.74	47.93	53.33	52.20
	1855	61.54	60.39	48.11	46.52	48 78	53.06	53.07
	1856	54.95	54.77	48.95	47.17	46.82	50.49	50.52
	1857	53.77	53 37	47.14	45.51	44 45	48.98	48.87
	1858	53.31	52.88	47.15	46.07	45.86	48.12	48.90
	1859	60.70	60.80	52.72	51.16	50.37	55.23	55.16
	Means.	57.16	56.72	48.75	47.19	47.37	51.54	51.45

	Toronto Astronomical time.	2 h.	4 h.	10 h.	12 h.	18 h.	20 h.	Monthly Means.
JUNE.	1854	71.70	70 78	59.39	58.23	59.86	64.78	64.12
	1855	66.66	65.82	56.43	55.13	55.81	59 75	59.93
	1856	67.76	67.73	59.36	57.69	58.07	62.02	62 11
	1857	61.85	61.60	54.84	53.24	53.52	56.47	56.92
	1858	72.28	71.52	63.53	61.88	61.87	65.84	66.15
	1859	64.25	63.83	55.81	53.17	54.31	58.44	58.30
	Means.	67.42	66.88	58.23	56 56	57 24	61 21	61 26

TABLE I.—(Continued.)

MONTHLY MEANS OF THE TEMPERATURE OF THE AIR AT EACH OF THE SIX OBSERVATION HOURS, FROM 1854 TO 1859 INCLUSIVE.

Toronto Astronomical time.		2 h.	4 h.	10 h.	12 h.	18 h.	20 h.	Monthly Means.
JULY	1854	81.86	80.25	67.10	66.50	67.09	72.99	72.47
	1855	73.78	73.57	64.67	62.98	64.70	67.97	67.95
	1856	77.46	77.08	66.30	64.65	64.27	69.62	69.90
	1857	73.76	72.50	64.69	63.40	63.71	68.53	67.76
	1858	73.55	73.57	65.23	63.80	63.32	67.67	67.86
	1859	72.39	72.05	63.80	62.79	62.70	67.47	66.87
	Means.	75.47	74.84	65.30	63.85	64.30	69.04	68.80

Toronto Astronomical time.		2 h.	4 h.	10 h.	12 h.	18 h.	20 h.	Monthly Means.
AUGUST.	1854	76.24	76.24	63.46	61.84	61.24	67.16	66.03
	1855	71.21	70.76	60.97	58.87	58.21	64.34	64.06
	1856	70.58	70.51	60.48	58.82	57.90	63.27	63.59
	1857	71.96	71.63	62.75	61.29	59.40	64.85	65.31
	1858	73.97	74.20	65.37	63.38	61.82	67.14	67.61
	1859	72.96	73.18	63.71	62.34	60.87	66.60	66.61
	Means.	73.15	72.75	62.79	61.09	59.87	65.56	65.87

Toronto Astronomical time.		2 h.	4 h.	10 h.	12 h.	18 h.	20 h.	Monthly Means.
SEPTEMBER.	1854	70.34	67.79	57.98	56.14	53.73	60.28	61.04
	1855	65.23	65.11	57.13	55.68	55.01	58.80	59.49
	1856	64.33	63.26	54.59	53.61	50.80	56.28	57.15
	1857	65.51	65.07	55.70	54.63	53.13	57.90	58.64
	1858	65.95	65.17	57.15	55.39	52.60	58.38	59.11
	1859	60.18	59.87	53.88	52.60	50.35	54.20	55.18
	Means.	65.26	64.38	56.07	54.67	52.60	57.62	58.43

TABLE I.—(Continued.)

MONTHLY MEANS OF THE TEMPERATURE OF THE AIR AT EACH OF THE SIX OBSERVATION HOURS, FROM 1854 TO 1859 INCLUSIVE.

Toronto Astronomical time.		2 h.	4 h.	10 h.	12 h.	18 h.	20 h.	Monthly Means.
OCTOBER	1854	57.38	54.77	46.89	45.73	44.33	48.04	49.52
	1855	50.58	49.76	44.36	43.06	40.93	43.66	45.39
	1856	51.20	50.54	43.44	42.20	40.83	43.84	45.34
	1857	50.93	50.07	43.88	43.17	41.21	43.28	45.42
	1858	53.78	52.87	47.48	46.06	45.05	47.52	48.79
	1859	48.86	47.44	41.27	40.24	38.78	41.34	42.99
	Means.	52.12	50.91	44.55	43.41	41.85	44.61	46.24

Toronto Astronomical time.		2 h.	4 h.	10 h.	12 h.	18 h.	20 h.	Monthly Means.
NOVEMBER	1854	40.56	38.48	36.69	34.39	35.43	35.50	36.84
	1855	42.68	41.52	37.66	36.41	36.35	36.86	38.58
	1856	40.46	39.38	36.54	36.02	35.58	36.35	37.39
	1857	36.99	36.67	32.82	31.57	31.20	31.97	33.54
	1858	36.58	35.95	33.95	33.58	32.30	32.62	34.16
	1859	42.17	41.10	38.63	38.01	36.43	36.95	38.90
	Means.	39.91	39.03	35.88	35.00	34.55	35.04	36.57

Toronto Astronomical time.		2 h.	4 h.	10 h.	12 h.	18 h.	20 h.	Monthly Means.
DECEMBER	1854	26.76	24.43	20.00	21.18	18.04	18.88	21.88
	1855	30.46	29.41	26.30	25.28	24.77	24.73	26.83
	1856	25.35	24.94	22.09	21.85	21.56	21.52	22.88
	1857	34.97	34.34	30.52	30.08	30.00	30.63	31.86
	1858	29.29	29.00	26.47	26.04	27.12	26.46	27.40
	1859	21.03	20.71	17.23	15.74	16.52	16.12	17.89
	Means.	27.81	27.14	23.93	23.36	23.27	23.22	24.79

TABLE II.

MONTHLY AND ANNUAL MEANS OF THE TEMPERATURE OF THE AIR FURNISHED BY SIX DAILY OBSERVATIONS, FROM 1854 TO 1859 INCLUSIVE.

	January.	February.	March.	April.	May.	June.	July.	August.	September	October.	November.	December.	Year.
1854	23.57	21.09	30.68	41.04	52.20	64.12	72.47	68.03	61.04	49.52	36.84	21.88	45.21
1855	25.95	15.41	28.46	42.43	53.07	59.93	67.95	64.06	59.49	45.39	38.58	26.83	43.96
1856	16.02	15.69	23.06	42.27	50.52	62.11	69.90	63.59	57.15	45.34	37.30	22.88	42.16
1857	12.75	28.53	27.82	35.36	48.87	56.92	67.76	65.31	58.64	45.42	33.54	31.86	42.73
1858	30.03	16.98	28.44	41.46	48.90	66.15	67.86	67.61	59.11	48.79	34.16	27.40	44.74
1859	26.44	26.04	36.34	39.53	55.16	58.30	66.87	66.61	55.18	42.99	38.90	17.89	44.19
Means	22.46	20.62	29.13	40.35	51.45	61.26	68.80	65.87	58.43	46.24	36.57	24.79	43.83

TABLE III.

DIFFERENCE OF THE MONTHLY AND ANNUAL MEANS OF THE TEMPERATURE OF THE AIR FROM 1854 TO 1859 INCLUSIVE, IN EXCESS OR DEFECT FROM THE NORMAL MONTHLY AND ANNUAL MEANS, BOTH BEING DERIVED FROM SIX DAILY OBSERVATIONS.

	January.	February.	March.	April.	May.	June.	July.	August.	September	October.	November.	December.	Year.
1854	− 1.28	+ 2.60	+ 0.45	− 0.18	+ 0.65	+ 3.03	+ 6.14	+ 2.31	+ 3.62	+ 4.53	+ 0.70	− 5.18	+ 1.02
1855	+ 1.10	− 8.28	− 1.77	+ 1.21	+ 1.52	− 1.16	+ 1.62	− 1.66	+ 2.07	+ 0.40	+ 2.44	− 0.23	− 0.23
1856	− 8.83	− 8.00	− 7.17	+ 1.05	− 1.03	+ 1.02	+ 3.57	− 2.13	− 0.27	+ 0.35	+ 1.25	− 4.18	− 2.03
1857	−12.10	+ 4.94	− 2.41	− 5.86	− 2.68	− 4.17	+ 1.43	− 0.41	+ 1.22	+ 0.43	− 2.60	+ 4.80	− 1.46
1858	+ 5.18	− 6.71	− 1.79	+ 0.24	− 2.65	+ 5.00	+ 1.53	+ 1.80	+ 1.69	+ 3.80	− 1.98	+ 0.34	+ 0.55
1859	+ 1.59	+ 2.35	+ 6.11	− 1.69	+ 3.61	− 2.79	+ 0.54	+ 0.89	− 2.24	− 2.00	+ 2.76	− 9.17	0.00
Means	− 2.39	− 3.07	− 1.10	− 0.87	− 0.10	+ 0.17	+ 2.47	+ 0.15	+ 1.01	+ 1.25	+ 0.43	− 2.27	− 0.36

TORONTO METEOROLOGICAL OBSERVATIONS.

TABLE IV.

MONTHLY MEANS OF THE TEMPERATURE OF THE AIR AT EACH OF THE SIX OBSERVATION HOURS, FOR THE PERIOD 1854 TO 1859 INCLUSIVE.

Toronto Astronomical time.	2 h.	4 h.	10 h.	12 h.	18 h.	20 h.	Monthly Means.
January	25.84°	25.16°	21.64°	21.11°	20.51°	20.50°	22.46°
February	25.03	24.78	20.08	19.25	17.07	17.53	20.62
March	33.87	33.72	28.43	27.51	24.65	26.61	29.13
April	46.17	45.66	38.32	37.29	35.52	39.13	40.35
May	57.16	56.72	48.75	47.19	47.37	51.54	51.45
June	67.42	66.88	58.23	56.56	57.24	61.21	61.26
July	75.47	74.84	65.30	63.85	64.30	69.04	68.80
August	73.15	72.75	62.79	61.09	59.87	65.56	65.87
September	65.26	64.38	56.07	54.67	52.60	57.62	58.43
October	52.12	50.91	44.55	43.41	41.85	44.61	46.24
November	39.91	39.03	35.88	35.00	34.55	35.04	36.57
December	27.81	27.14	23.93	23.36	23.27	23.22	24.79
Means	49.10	48.50	42.00	40.86	39.90	42.63	43.83

TABLE V.

DIFFERENCES OF THE MEAN MONTHLY TEMPERATURE AT EACH OBSERVATION HOUR IN EXCESS OR DEFECT FROM THE NORMAL MEAN MONTHLY TEMPERATURE OF THE SAME HOUR, TOGETHER WITH THE MEANS OF THE SIX HOURLY DIFFERENCES.

Toronto Astronomical time.	2 h.	4 h.	10 h.	12 h.	18 h.	20 h.	Means.
January	−2.35°	−2.48°	−2.57°	−2.16°	−2.28°	−2.49°	−2.39°
February	−3.78	−3.45	−2.55	−2.73	−2.72	−3.17	−3.07
March	−1.97	−1.48	−0.15	−0.42	−0.90	−1.69	−1.10
April	−1.34	−1.53	−0.34	−0.62	−0.27	−1.13	−0.87
May	−1.41	−1.93	+0.52	+0.63	+1.27	+0.33	−0.10
June	−0.76	−1.87	+1.00	+0.95	+1.47	+0.24	+0.17
July	+0.73	−0.15	+3.31	+4.02	+4.19	+2.74	+2.47
August	−0.45	−1.01	+0.84	+0.73	+0.66	+0.11	+0.15
September	+0.85	+0.21	+1.55	+1.20	+1.26	+1.02	+1.01
October	+1.18	+0.89	+1.47	+1.57	+1.33	+1.05	+1.25
November	−0.15	+0.02	+0.59	+0.67	+1.05	+0.41	+0.43
December	−2.60	−2.36	−2.69	−2.71	−1.45	−1.81	−2.27
Means	−1.00	−1.26	+0.08	+0.09	+0.30	−0.37	−0.36

TABLE VI.

MONTHLY MEAN DIFFERENCES WITHOUT REGARD TO SIGN BETWEEN THE NORMAL TEMPERATURE OF THE DAY AND HOUR AND THE OBSERVED TEMPERATURE OF THE SAME DAY AND HOUR, FOR EACH MONTH OF THE YEARS 1854 TO 1859 INCLUSIVE.

	January.	February.	March.	April.	May.	June.	July.	August.	September	October.	November.	December.	Mean of the Year.
1854	9.2	9.0	9.6	5.5	4.7	4.9	7.4	5.4	6.9	7.1	5.2	10.8	7.1
1855	7.1	12.4	6.2	6.2	4.7	5.8	5.0	4.9	6.5	6.2	6.5	7.8	6.6
1856	9.8	10.4	7.7	4.9	4.9	4.2	5.6	4.3	4.7	5.5	5.4	7.5	6.2
1857	13.5	11.5	7.0	6.6	5.7	5.4	4.9	3.7	5.6	5.1	6.6	6.4	6.8
1858	7.5	10.0	9.0	5.7	5.3	7.3	4.4	5.4	5.1	5.6	5.0	7.7	6.5
1859	9.4	7.4	7.7	4.2	5.6	6.6	5.9	3.5	6.5	6.7	6.2	12.4	6.8
Means.	9.4	10.1	7.9	5.5	5.1	5.7	5.5	4.5	5.9	6.0	5.8	8.8	6.7

TABLE VII.

MONTHLY MEAN DIFFERENCES WITHOUT REGARD TO SIGN BETWEEN THE NORMAL TEMPERATURE OF THE DAY AND HOUR AND THE OBSERVED TEMPERATURE AT EACH OF THE SIX OBSERVATION HOURS, FOR THE PERIOD 1854 TO 1859 INCLUSIVE.

Toronto Astronomical Time.	2 h.	4 h.	10 h.	12 h.	18 h.	20 h.	Monthly Means.
January	9.0	8.9	9.2	9.5	9.8	9.9	9.4
February	9.1	8.9	10.3	10.5	11.0	10.7	10.1
March	7.3	7.3	7.5	7.8	8.9	8.4	7.9
April	6.9	6.7	4.8	4.9	4.7	5.2	5.5
May	6.1	5.9	4.7	4.7	4.5	5.0	5.1
June	6.4	6.6	5.8	5.3	5.0	5.4	5.7
July	5.8	5.7	5.4	5.6	5.5	5.2	5.5
August	4.3	4.3	4.5	4.9	4.8	4.4	4.5
September	6.2	5.9	5.9	5.9	6.0	5.4	5.9
October	6.1	5.6	5.9	6.0	6.5	6.0	6.0
November	5.6	5.3	5.8	6.1	6.2	6.0	5.8
December	8.3	8.3	8.7	8.8	9.3	9.3	8.8
Means	6.8	6.6	6.5	6.7	6.9	6.7	6.7

TABLE VIII.

MEAN DIFFERENCES WITHOUT REGARD TO SIGN BETWEEN THE TEMPERATURES OBSERVED AT 2 P.M. ON CONSECUTIVE DAYS, FOR EACH MONTH IN THE YEARS 1854 TO 1859 INCLUSIVE, THE EFFECT OF ANNUAL VARIATION BEING ELIMINATED.

Years.	January.	February.	March.	April.	May.	June.	July.	August.	September	October.	November.	December.	Yearly Means.
1854	8.48	9.92	5.83	7.44	4.76	8.09	8.42	7.18	6.89	5.68	6.51	7.73	6.84
1855	6.70	5.14	4.52	6.91	6.01	5.80	4.92	4.61	6.41	5.59	4.88	5.54	5.59
1856	7.16	7.89	3.67	5.29	7.40	5.33	5.55	4.85	5.21	5.04	5.80	5.46	5.73
1857	7.02	8.39	7.54	4.50	5.56	5.14	3.48	4.06	6.33	3.47	4.22	4.35	5.42
1858	6.35	6.09	5.45	6.10	6.10	4.54	6.10	4.44	3.94	5.19	3.30	7.92	5.54
1859	7.67	5.96	4.22	5.35	4.96	6.94	5.61	3.23	3.94	5.49	6.71	10.36	5.87
Means.	7.38	7.24	5.37	5.91	5.82	5.64	5.35	4.73	5.45	5.08	5.09	6.89	5.83
Ratio to Mean of Year.	1.27	1.24	0.92	1.01	1.00	0.97	0.92	0.81	0.93	0.87	0.87	1.18	

TABLE IX.

SHEWING FOR EACH MONTH (FOR THE PERIOD 1854 TO 1859 INCLUSIVE) THE NUMBER OF CASES IN A HUNDRED WHEN THE CHANGE OF TEMPERATURE OBSERVED AT 2 P.M. ON CONSECUTIVE DAYS WAS INCREASING, WITH THE AVERAGE VALUES OF THE INCREASING AND OF THE DECREASING CHANGES.

	January.	February.	March.	April.	May.	June.	July.	August.	September	October.	November.	December
Number in a hundred.	48	57	56	53	56	55	56	55	59	54	48	49
Ratio to mean of year.	0.89	1.06	1.04	0.98	1.04	1.02	1.04	1.02	1.09	1.00	0.89	0.91
Average increase......	7.58	6.39	4.79	5.58	5.10	5.22	4.76	4.22	4.77	4.74	5.27	6.91
Ratio to mean of year.	1.39	1.17	0.88	1.03	0.94	0.96	0.87	0.78	0.88	0.87	0.97	1.27
Average decrease......	7.20	8.36	6.12	6.20	6.72	6.15	6.10	5.35	6.43	5.47	4.92	6.88
Ratio to mean of year.	1.13	1.32	0.97	0.90	1.06	0.97	0.96	0.84	1.01	0.86	0.78	1.09

TABLE X.

GIVING FOR EACH OF THE SIXTEEN POINTS OF THE WINDS DIRECTION, THE MEAN DIFFERENCE OF THE TEMPERATURE OF THE AIR FROM THE NORMAL AT THE HOUR OF OBSERVATION, WITH THE NUMBER OF OBSERVATIONS FROM WHICH THE MEANS ARE DERIVED, FOR THE YEARS 1853-59 INCLUSIVE.

The sign (+) indicates that the observed temperature was in excess, and (—) that it was in defect of the normal.

Years.	N.		N.N.E.		N.E.		E.N.E.		E.		E.S.E.		S.E.		S.S.E.	
	No.	Diff.	No.	Diff.	No.	Diff.	No.	Diff.	No.	Diff.	No.	Diff.	No.	Diff.	No.	Diff.
1853	142	−1.32	148	−1.33	108	+0.47	93	+0.86	90	+2.67	46	+2.54	64	+3.32	64	+3.67
1854	113	−3.32	77	−2.39	87	−2.05	87	+3.65	145	−3.71	103	+1.56	48	−3.57	56	+3.24
1855	108	−2.70	79	−5.65	69	−5.58	74	+2.26	136	+0.70	95	+1.69	42	+2.45	54	−2.54
1856	127	−4.39	61	−4.74	65	−0.67	68	−0.06	123	+0.64	69	−1.48	42	−1.31	39	−1.51
1857	102	−4.55	39	−0.21	60	−0.67	126	−0.41	108	−0.27	57	+0.40	46	+1.56	54	−1.41
1858	120	−0.18	57	−3.18	76	−1.44	175	−0.07	156	+1.90	49	+3.92	45	+1.73	60	+2.03
1859	104	−3.80	68	−5.62	75	−3.66	160	−3.62	179	+1.47	65	+0.42	35	+1.63	47	−2.27
1853–59	876	−2.80	529	−3.18	540	−1.81	783	+1.37	937	+1.73	484	+1.18	322	+1.79	374	+2.28

Years.	S.		S.S.W.		S.W.		W.S.W.		W.		W.N.W.		N.W.		N.N.W.		Calms.	
	No.	Diff.	No.	Diff.	No.	Diff.	No.	Diff.	No.	Diff.	No.	Diff.	No.	Diff.	No.	Diff.	No.	Diff.
1853	123	+4.13	129	+3.78	68	+4.19	95	+0.66	103	−1.28	76	−2.39	115	−3.38	156	−4.02	356	+1.73
1854	79	+3.80	112	+4.00	111	+6.88	109	+1.55	103	−2.10	125	−0.99	112	−3.88	163	−3.57	338	+2.23
1855	74	+3.05	118	−4.59	124	−3.78	137	+0.25	168	−2.76	192	−3.40	134	−1.50	146	−2.27	223	−0.85
1856	69	+2.13	122	−1.03	131	−1.23	191	−3.01	174	−4.91	170	−5.22	121	−4.35	144	−4.69	254	−0.25
1857	71	−2.04	130	−0.98	154	−0.03	160	−3.55	136	−4.74	129	+3.87	149	−4.25	165	−2.43	275	−0.93
1858	88	+3.31	93	+1.66	64	+7.00	111	−1.43	132	+0.29	144	−1.83	147	−3.35	150	−2.43	307	+2.02
1859	75	+0.73	144	+4.95	104	+5.03	123	+0.33	156	−1.79	137	−3.55	130	−4.15	145	−3.33	223	+1.13
1853–50	574	+2.69	857	+3.01	756	+3.45	926	−0.73	971	−2.18	913	−3.17	908	−3.54	1060	−3.58	1971	+1.33

TORONTO METEOROLOGICAL OBSERVATIONS.

TABLE XI.

MONTHLY AND YEARLY MEANS OF THE DIURNAL CHANGE OF TEMPERATURE (EXCLUSIVE OF THAT DUE TO ANNUAL VARIATION) FROM 6 A. M. TO 6 A. M. FOR THE PERIOD 1854 TO 1859 INCLUSIVE, ARRANGED ACCORDING TO THE DAILY RESULTANT DIRECTION OF THE WIND.

	January.	February.	March.	April.	May.	June.	July.	August.	September	October.	November.	December.	Year.
N.	− 5.1	− 4.6	−0.8	−2.7	−2.0	−2.3	−1.6	−4.0	−3.7	−6.2	−3 8	− 1.7	−3.3
N.E.	+ 3.3	+ 1.4	0.0	+2.2	+0.6	+0.7	−0.5	+3.2	+0.2	+1.2	−1.7	+ 4.3	+1.5
E.	+10.5	+ 9.0	+5.6	+2.9	+1.8	+0.3	+1.5	+1.7	+3.8	+3.4	+4.1	+ 4.8	+3.5
S.E.	+ 6.0	−17.8	+7.0	+4.8	+2.5	+2.8	+2.1	+3.7	+5.3	+5.4	+4.3	+10.2	+4.6
S.	+11.7	+ 1.6	+9.2	+2 1	+0.6	+1.6	+2.5	+1.8	+5.1	+3.7	+9.9	+18.0	+3.9
S.W.	+ 3.1	+ 7.4	+4.4	+0.4	+0.8	+1.5	+0.8	+2.6	+1.6	+3.0	+0.7	+ 0.1	+2.2
W.	− 4.1	− 1.8	−3.8	−2.4	−1.7	−0.4	−3.4	−2.0	−4.4	−3.0	−2.9	− 3.4	−2.9
N.W.	− 8.9	− 7.1	−3.6	−3.4	−3.6	−3.6	−4.2	−3.4	−5.4	−2.4	−4.2	− 4.5	−4.5

TABLE XII.

FREQUENCY OF INCREASING CHANGES OF TEMPERATURE—THE TOTAL NUMBER IN EACH MONTH AND DIRECTION BEING EXPRESSED BY 100.

	January.	February.	March.	April.	May.	June.	July.	August.	September	October.	November.	December.	Year.
N.	36	41	33	40	32	22	29	13	33	29	36	48	34
N.E.	67	55	25	71	53	56	30	70	65	55	30	70	57
E.	92	81	93	80	71	50	67	68	74	66	90	84	75
S.E.	100	100	83	85	79	73	70	69	71	75	67	100	77
S.	86	40	87	64	63	75	78	68	83	62	83	100	74
S.W.	68	79	58	50	53	69	68	76	65	66	59	50	63
W.	36	42	30	33	42	48	31	39	32	44	40	31	37
N.W.	25	26	33	42	33	36	26	21	26	36	42	31	31

TABLE XIII.

AGGREGATE OF INCREASING CHANGES FOR EACH DIRECTION, THE JOINT AGGREGATE OF INCREASING AND DECREASING CHANGES FOR ANY ONE MONTH AND DIRECTION BEING EXPRESSED BY 100.

	January.	February.	March.	April.	May.	June.	July.	August.	September	October.	November.	December.	Year.
N.	28	21	44	30	25	15	19	4	15	5	22	40	25
N.E.	74	57	50	71	58	61	34	83	52	61	37	76	63
E.	99	93	97	83	74	55	72	73	85	76	85	85	83
S.E.	100	100	94	91	84	80	84	94	87	85	75	100	88
S.	84	65	94	80	58	74	81	72	90	76	89	100	82
S.W.	67	84	79	55	58	74	62	79	63	71	55	51	67
W.	26	41	21	21	29	46	12	25	20	31	31	31	30
N.W.	13	15	21	22	18	14	8	10	8	30	20	26	18

TABLE XIV.

MONTHLY AND YEARLY MEANS OF THE DIURNAL CHANGE OF TEMPERATURE, WITHOUT REGARD TO SIGN AND EXCLUDING THAT DUE TO ANNUAL VARIATION, FROM 6 A.M. TO 6 A.M. FOR THE PERIOD 1854 TO 1859, ARRANGED ACCORDING TO THE DAILY RESULTANT DIRECTION OF THE WIND.

	January.	February.	March	April.	May.	June.	July.	August.	September.	October.	November.	December.	Year.
N.	11.73	8.02	6.87	0.79	4.04	3.30	2.54	4.43	5.38	0.89	6.01	9.17	0.58
N.E.	6.80	10.44	5.58	5.29	3.82	3.06	1.63	4.75	6.05	5.15	0.68	8.17	5.75
E.	10.75	10.50	5.92	4.30	3.85	3.51	3.48	3.77	5.36	0.40	5.82	6.98	5.32
S.E.	6.00	17.80	7.98	5.92	3.61	4.55	3.10	4.21	7.06	7.79	8.50	10.20	5.93
S.	17.20	5.42	10.50	3.39	3.69	3.43	4.01	4.06	6.35	7.20	12.72	17.98	5.95
S.W.	9.18	10.85	7.69	4.31	4.95	3.01	3.49	4.54	6.41	7.24	7.14	5.21	6.36
W.	8.50	10.00	6.48	4.26	3.99	4.57	4.49	4.04	7.40	8.06	7.53	8.97	7.06
N.W.	12.03	9.95	6.33	5.90	5.67	5.06	5.02	4.21	6.49	6.22	7.00	9.33	6.99
Means	10.28	10.38	7.17	5.02	4.20	3.82	3.47	4.25	6.31	6.87	7.75	9.50	6.24

TABLE XV.

COMPARATIVE CHANGES OF TEMPERATURE IN THE SAME MONTH THAT ARE DUE TO DIFFERENT WINDS, BEING THE NUMBERS IN TABLE XIV. EXPRESSED IN TERMS OF THE ARITHMETIC MEAN CHANGE IN THAT MONTH FOR ALL WINDS.

	January.	February.	March.	April.	May.	June.	July.	August.	September.	October.	November.	December.	Year.
N.	1.14	0.77	0.96	1.35	0.96	0.89	0.73	1.04	0.85	1.00	0.85	0.97	1.05
N.E.	0.66	1.01	0.78	1.05	0.91	0.80	0.47	1.12	0.96	0.75	0.86	0.86	0.92
E.	1.05	1.01	0.83	0.86	0.92	0.92	1.00	0.89	0.85	0.93	0.75	0.73	0.85
S.E.	0.58	1.71	1.11	1.18	0.86	1.19	0.89	0.99	1.12	1.13	1.10	1.07	0.95
S.	1.67	0.52	1.46	0.68	0.88	0.90	1.16	0.96	1.01	1.05	1.64	1.89	0.95
S.W.	0.89	1.05	1.07	0.86	1.18	0.79	1.01	1.07	1.02	1.05	0.92	0.55	1.02
W.	0.83	0.97	0.90	0.85	0.95	1.20	1.29	0.95	1.17	1.17	0.97	0.94	1.13
N.W.	1.17	0.96	0.88	1.18	1.35	1.32	1.45	0.99	1.03	0.91	0.90	0.98	1.12

TABLE XVI.

COMPARATIVE DIURNAL CHANGES OF TEMPERATURE THAT ARE DUE IN DIFFERENT MONTHS TO THE SAME WIND, BEING THE NUMBERS IN TABLE XIV. EXPRESSED IN TERMS OF THE ANNUAL ARITHMETIC MEAN FOR THAT WIND.

	January.	February.	March	April.	May.	June.	July.	August.	September.	October.	November.	December.
N.	1.86	1.27	1.09	1.07	0.64	0.54	0.40	0.70	0.85	1.09	1.05	1.45
N.E.	1.21	1.86	0.99	0.94	0.68	0.55	0.29	0.85	1.08	0.92	1.19	1.45
E.	1.83	1.78	1.01	0.73	0.65	0.60	0.59	0.64	0.91	1.09	0.99	1.10
S.E.	0.83	2.46	1.10	0.82	0.50	0.63	0.43	0.58	0.98	1.08	1.18	1.41
S.	2.15	0.68	1.31	0.42	0.46	0.43	0.50	0.51	0.79	0.90	1.59	2.25
S.W.	1.49	1.76	1.25	0.70	0.80	0.49	0.57	0.74	1.04	1.17	1.16	0.84
W.	1.31	1.54	0.99	0.65	0.61	0.70	0.69	0.62	1.13	1.23	1.15	1.37
N.W.	1.74	1.44	0.91	0.85	0.82	0.73	0.72	0.61	0.94	0.90	1.01	1.35

TORONTO METEOROLOGICAL OBSERVATIONS. 85

TABLE XVII.

MONTHLY MEANS OF THE DAILY MAXIMA, MINIMA, AND RANGES OF TEMPERATURE FOR THE YEARS 1854 TO 1859 INCLUSIVE.

MAXIMA.

Months.	January.	February.	March.	April.	May.	June.	July.	August.	September.	October.	November.	December.
1854	20.31	29.63	36.40	47.82	61.82	74.53	84.79	80.72	72.63	58.97	42.08	29.46
1855	32.83	23.19	36.52	52.93	65.40	68.89	76.75	74.61	68.44	52.60	45.50	32.91
1856	22.65	24.22	30.47	50.47	59.56	71.59	80.36	73.74	66.69	54.04	43.02	28.74
1857	19.46	35.66	35.25	43.36	57.17	65.48	76.79	74.45	67.48	51.93	39.94	35.75
1858	35.27	24.11	37.01	48.32	55.74	73.94	75.44	75.38	67.52	55.79	37.90	33.19
1859	30.46	31.85	42.10	46.54	63.40	66.03	74.65	75.01	62.68	50.38	43.95	25.26
Means.	28.33	28.11	36.20	48.24	60.51	70.23	78.13	75.65	67.57	53.95	42.07	30.88

MINIMA.

	January.	February.	March.	April.	May.	June.	July.	August.	September.	October.	November.	December.
1854	13.53	9.15	22.94	30.69	37.90	49.84	58.46	55.26	49.09	41.32	28.13	14.38
1855	17.54	4.81	19.63	32.06	41.42	50.68	60.05	54.09	49.94	34.55	28.74	18.75
1856	6.02	3.57	12.87	33.39	40.63	52.39	59.04	52.95	45.66	35.22	28.74	15.55
1857	0.85	20.42	17.79	27.24	40.24	48.99	59.32	54.95	48.14	37.47	26.55	24.20
1858	23.73	10.85	21.93	34.15	41.68	56.41	59.98	59.21	50.79	43.41	30.03	21.37
1859	18.55	19.71	30.48	32.92	47.13	49.82	59.20	59.38	49.32	37.05	32.77	12.94
Means.	13.37	11.42	20.94	31.74	41.50	51.35	59.34	55.97	48.82	38.17	29.16	17.87

RANGES.

	January.	February.	March.	April.	May.	June.	July.	August.	September.	October.	November.	December.
1854	15.78	20.47	13.38	17.13	23.92	24.69	26.33	25.46	23.59	17.65	13.94	15.08
1855	15.29	18.38	16.89	20.87	23.98	18.21	16.70	20.52	18.51	18.05	16.76	14.16
1856	16.63	20.65	17.60	17.08	18.93	19.20	21.32	20.79	21.03	18.82	14.27	13.19
1857	18.61	15.25	17.46	16.12	16.94	16.49	17.47	19.50	19.34	14.45	13.39	11.55
1858	11.54	13.26	15.08	14.16	14.06	17.54	15.45	16.17	16.73	12.37	7.87	11.82
1859	11.91	12.15	11.62	13.62	16.26	17.11	15.45	15.63	13.36	13.33	11.19	12.32
Means.	14.96	16.69	15.34	16.50	19.02	18.87	18.79	19.68	18.75	15.78	12.90	13.20

TABLE XVIII.

HIGHEST AND LOWEST TEMPERATURES IN EACH MONTH, AND MONTHLY RANGES OF TEMPERATURE FOR THE YEARS 1854 TO 1859 INCLUSIVE.

MAXIMA.

Months.	January.	February.	March.	April.	May.	June.	July.	August.	September.	October.	November.	December.	Year. Tempr.	Date.
1854	46.4	42.8	55.1	64.5	71.4	92.5	98.0	99.2	93.6	75.4	55.4	44.8	99.2	24th Aug.
1855	49.0	39.0	49.4	69.4	77.5	91.5	92.8	83.5	82.6	68.0	59.2	47.0	92.8	19th July.
1856	34.4	37.8	41.4	72.2	82.2	89.2	96.6	82.7	78.4	71.4	56.4	42.2	96.6	17th July.
1857	37.2	52.4	57.6	52.0	74.8	76.0	86.6	88.2	82.0	64.0	58.2	46.0	88.2	13th Aug.
1858	47.4	42.4	55.4	65.2	69.8	90.2	85.0	84.0	81.4	76.3	53.0	45.4	90.2	26th June
1859	43.2	46.2	54.2	64.8	79.6	86.4	88.0	82.2	75.4	69.8	62.6	54.8	88.0	12th July.
Means.	42.9	43.4	52.2	64.7	75.9	87.6	91.2	86.6	82.2	70.8	57.5	46.7	92.5	24th July.

MINIMA.

	January.	February.	March.	April.	May.	June.	July.	August.	September.	October.	November.	December.	Year. Tempr.	Date.
1854	— 5.4	—10.8	7.4	20.2	26.2	35.3	42.5	45.6	35.8	26.4	13.8	—7.0	—10.8	24th Jan.
1855	— 5.4	—25.4	— 2.9	10.7	33.0	36.2	49.2	40.0	33.0	22.6	15.5	—5.2	—25.4	5th Feb.
1856	—12.0	—18.7	—14.0	14.2	31.2	42.0	49.5	41.5	35.0	23.0	18.8	—9.1	—18.7	12th Feb.
1857	—20.1	— 5.9	— 5.5	5.9	26.0	35.0	47.0	46.0	34.1	26.5	— 3.5	4.7	—20.1	22nd Jan.
1858	6.5	— 7.3	— 5.5	21.8	31.0	42.5	52.0	44.0	35.6	31.5	15.3	4.2	— 7.3	17th Feb.
1859	—26.5	— 2.1	9.8	22.6	39.5	32.2	44.7	45.8	35.7	22.3	21.8	—6.0	—26.5	10th Jan.
Means.	—10.5	—11.0	— 1.8	15.9	31.0	37.2	47.5	43.8	34.9	25.4	13.6	—3.1	—18.1	31st Jan.

MONTHLY RANGES.

	January.	February.	March.	April.	May.	June.	July.	August.	September.	October.	November.	December.	
1854	51.8	53.6	47.7	44.3	46.2	57.3	55.5	53.6	57.8	49.0	41.6	51.8	110.0
1855	54.4	64.4	52.3	58.7	44.5	55.3	43.6	43.5	49.6	45.4	43.7	52.2	118.2
1856	46.4	56.5	55.4	58.0	51.0	47.2	47.1	41.2	43.4	48.4	37.6	51.3	115.3
1857	57.3	58.3	63.1	46.1	48.8	41.0	39.6	42.2	47.9	37.5	61.7	41.3	108.3
1858	40.9	49.7	60.9	43.4	38.8	47.7	33.0	40.0	45.8	44.8	37.7	41.2	97.5
1859	69.7	44.1	44.4	42.2	40.1	54.2	43.3	36.4	39.7	47.5	40.8	60.8	114.5
Means.	53.4	54.4	54.0	48.8	44.9	50.4	43.7	42.8	47.4	45.4	43.9	49.8	110.6

TABLE XIX.

MONTHLY MEANS OF THE BAROMETER AT EACH OF THE SIX OBSERVATION HOURS, FROM 1854 TO 1859 INCLUSIVE

Barometer at 32° = 27 inches + the number in the table.

Toronto Astronomical time.		2 h.	4 h.	10 h.	12 h.	18 h.	20 h.	Monthly Means.
JANUARY.	1854	2.583	2.601	2.624	2.615	2.602	2.617	2.607
	1855	2.630	2.645	2.664	2.655	2.617	2.626	2.639
	1856	2.645	2.653	2.685	2.679	2.669	2.687	2.670
	1857	2.714	2.713	2.734	2.729	2.762	2.765	2.736
	1858	2.648	2.662	2.713	2.714	2.656	2.660	2.675
	1859	2.652	2.665	2.683	2.675	2.689	2.698	2.677
	Means.	2.645	2.656	2.684	2.678	2.666	2.675	2.667

Toronto Astronomical time.		2 h.	4 h.	10 h.	12 h.	18 h.	20 h.	Monthly Means.
FEBRUARY.	1854	2.669	2.667	2.710	2.714	2.697	2.711	2.695
	1855	2.602	2.612	2.644	2.638	2.617	2.636	2.625
	1856	2.457	2.462	2.503	2.507	2.495	2.507	2.488
	1857	2.743	2.728	2.707	2.697	2.760	2.781	2.736
	1858	2.650	2.641	2.651	2.645	2.680	2.695	2.660
	1859	2.624	2.621	2.633	2.622	2.637	2.656	2.632
	Means.	2.624	2.622	2.641	2.637	2.648	2.664	2.639

Toronto Astronomical time.		2 h.	4 h.	10 h.	12 h.	18 h.	20 h.	Monthly. Means.
MARCH.	1854	2.494	2.493	2.530	2.520	2.552	2.557	2.525
	1855	2.485	2.477	2.513	2.516	2.540	2.547	2.513
	1856	2.538	2.543	2.570	2.570	2.562	2.571	2.559
	1857	2.566	2.567	2.618	2.618	2.599	2.606	2.596
	1858	2.607	2.601	2.622	2.612	2.632	2.645	2.620
	1859	2.397	2.393	2.416	2.411	2.425	2.434	2.413
	Means.	2.515	2.512	2.545	2.541	2.552	2.560	2.538

TABLE XIX.—(Continued.)

MONTHLY MEANS OF THE BAROMETER AT EACH OF THE SIX OBSERVATION HOURS, FROM 1854 TO 1859 INCLUSIVE.
Barometer at 32° = 27 inches + the numbers in the table.

Toronto Astronomical time.		2 h.	4 h.	10 h.	12 h.	18 h.	20 h.	Monthly Means.
APRIL	1854	2.621	2.604	2.648	2.654	2.646	2.655	2.638
	1855	2.642	2.636	2.659	2.652	2 664	2.670	2.654
	1856	2.559	2.553	2 587	2.585	2.593	2.597	2.579
	1857	2.512	2.508	2.505	2.500	2.511	2.524	2.530
	1858	2.492	2.477	2.497	2.492	2.514	2.521	2.499
	1859	2.514	2.513	2.554	2.552	2.538	2.540	2.535
	Means.	2.557	2.548	2.585	2.583	2.578	2 584	2.572

Toronto Astronomical time.		2 h.	4 h.	10 h.	12 h.	18 h.	20 h.	Monthly Means.
MAY.	1854	2.548	2.536	2.577	2.577	2.574	2.584	2.566
	1855	2.646	2.633	2.635	2.634	2.675	2.685	2.651
	1856	2.577	2.564	2.576	2.568	2.596	2.612	2.582
	1857	2.528	2.516	2.532	2.523	2.553	2.560	2.535
	1858	2.571	2.568	2.589	2.589	2.587	2.600	2.584
	1859	2.657	2.638	2.647	2.643	2.680	2.694	2.660
	Means.	2.588	2.576	2.593	2.589	2.611	2.622	2.596

Toronto Astronomical Time.		2 h.	4 h.	10 h.	12 h.	18 h.	20 h.	Monthly Means.
JUNE	1854	2.544	2.534	2.551	2.546	2.562	2.573	2.551
	1855	2.502	2.480	2.514	2.500	2.532	2.535	2.513
	1856	2.542	2.524	2.543	2.544	2.565	2.573	2.548
	1857	2.416	2.406	2.430	2.430	2.436	2.442	2.427
	1858	2.586	2.572	2.602	2.603	2.630	2.642	2.606
	1859	2.609	2.600	2.631	2.626	2.620	2.632	2.620
	Means.	2.533	2.521	2.545	2.543	2.558	2.566	2.544

TABLE XIX.—(Continued)

MONTHLY MEANS OF THE BAROMETER AT EACH OF THE SIX OBSERVATION HOURS, FROM 1854 TO 1859 INCLUSIVE.

Barometer at 32° = 27 inches + the numbers in the table.

Toronto Astronomical time.		2 h.	4 h.	10 h.	12 h.	18 h.	20 h.	Monthly Means.
JULY	1854	2.628	2.607	2.629	2.637	2.660	2.672	2.640
	1855	2.603	2.589	2.612	2.615	2.619	2.628	2.611
	1856	2.584	2.562	2.576	2.577	2.619	2.629	2.591
	1857	2.581	2.568	2.589	2.589	2.594	2.608	2.588
	1858	2.598	2.583	2.599	2.597	2.625	2.630	2.605
	1859	2.638	2.628	2.644	2.640	2.667	2.672	2.648
	Means.	2.605	2.589	2.608	2.609	2.632	2.640	2.614

Toronto Astronomical time.		2 h.	4 h.	10 h.	12 h.	18 h.	20 h.	Monthly Means.
AUGUST	1854	2.639	2.623	2.642	2.641	2.660	2.673	2.648
	1855	2.642	2.629	2.650	2.651	2.672	2.675	2.653
	1856	2.507	2.501	2.524	2.525	2.531	2.537	2.521
	1857	2.583	2.574	2.594	2.600	2.604	2.612	2.594
	1858	2.608	2.597	2.620	2.617	2.633	2.642	2.619
	1859	2.591	2.578	2.600	2.600	2.600	2.617	2.599
	Means.	2.595	2.584	2.605	2.606	2.620	2.626	2.606

Toronto Astronomical time.		2 h.	4 h.	10 h.	12 h.	18 h.	20 h.	Monthly Means.
SEPTEMBER	1854	2.688	2.674	2.697	2.695	2.722	2.730	2.701
	1855	2.713	2.696	2.707	2.705	2.751	2.755	2.721
	1856	2.580	2.580	2.606	2.691	2.616	2.618	2.600
	1857	2.696	2.686	2.710	2.707	2.733	2.740	2.712
	1858	2.636	2.620	2.643	2.630	2.677	2.686	2.650
	1859	2.655	2.649	2.672	2.668	2.676	2.692	2.669
	Means.	2.661	2.651	2.672	2.669	2.696	2.703	2.675

TABLE XIX.—(Continued.)

MONTHLY MEANS OF THE BAROMETER, AT EACH OF THE SIX OBSERVATION HOURS, FROM 1854 TO 1859 INCLUSIVE.

Barometer at 32° = 27 inches + the numbers in the table.

	Toronto Astronomical time.	2 h.	4 h.	10 h.	12 h.	18 h.	20 h.	Monthly Means.
OCTOBER.	1854	2.677	2.675	2.703	2.699	2.699	2.719	2.696
	1855	2.535	2.538	2.555	2.540	2.566	2.576	2.551
	1856	2.689	2.684	2.713	2.713	2.715	6.727	2.707
	1857	2.647	2.649	2.671	2.672	2.677	2.686	2.667
	1858	2.668	2.668	2.689	2.681	2.684	2.697	2.681
	1859	2.589	2.596	2.634	2.634	2.609	2.625	2.615
	Means.	2.634	2.635	2.661	2.657	2.658	3.072	2.653

	Toronto Astronomical time.	2 h.	4 h.	10 h.	12 h.	18 h.	20 h.	Monthly Means.
NOVEMBER.	1854	2.426	2.436	2.448	2.443	2.427	2.455	2.439
	1855	2.637	2.630	2.667	2.673	2.677	2.694	2.664
	1856	2.621	2.636	2.659	2.657	2.641	2.639	2.642
	1857	2.487	2.497	2.540	2.544	2.530	2.545	2.524
	1858	2.616	2.622	2.631	2.628	2.622	2.640	2.627
	1859	2.653	2.659	2.666	2.657	2.699	2.713	2.675
	Means.	2.573	2.582	2.602	2.600	2.599	2.614	2.595

	Toronto Astronomical time.	2 h.	4 h.	10 h.	12 h.	18 h.	20 h.	Monthly Means.
DECEMBER.	1854	2.572	2.583	2.600	2.596	2.581	2.591	2.587
	1855	2.697	2.701	2.701	2.695	2.701	2.718	2.702
	1856	2.694	2.707	2.717	2.719	2.706	2.723	2.711
	1857	2.599	2.612	2.649	2.647	2.597	2.609	2.619
	1858	2.668	2.688	2.718	2.715	2.683	2.695	2.694
	1859	2.686	2.693	2.719	2.717	2.711	2.729	2.709
	Means.	2.653	2.664	2.684	2.682	2.663	2.677	2.670

TABLE XX.

MONTHLY AND ANNUAL MEANS OF THE BAROMETER, FURNISHED BY SIX DAILY OBSERVATIONS.
1854 TO 1859 INCLUSIVE.

Barometer at 32° = 27 inches + the numbers in the table.

	January.	February.	March.	April.	May.	June.	July.	August.	September	October.	November.	December.	Year.
1854	2.607	2.695	2.525	2.638	2.566	2.551	2.640	2.648	2.701	2.696	2.439	2.587	2.608
1855	2.639	2.625	2.513	2.654	2.651	2.513	2.611	2.653	2.721	2.551	2.664	2.702	2.625
1856	2.670	2.488	2.559	2.579	2.582	2.548	2.591	2.521	2.600	2.707	2.642	2.711	2.600
1857	2.736	2.736	2.596	2.530	2.535	2.427	2.588	2.594	2.712	2.667	2.524	2.619	2.605
1858	2.675	2.660	2.620	2.499	2.584	2.606	2.605	2.619	2.650	2.681	2.627	2.694	2.627
1859	2.677	2.632	2.413	2.535	2.660	2.620	2.648	2.599	2.669	2.615	2.675	2.709	2.621
Mean.	2.667	2.639	2.538	2.572	2.596	2.544	2.614	2.606	2.675	2.653	2.595	2.670	2.614

TABLE XXI.

DIFFERENCES OF THE MONTHLY AND ANNUAL MEANS OF THE BAROMETER, FOR 1854 TO 1859 INCLUSIVE, IN EXCESS OR DEFECT FROM THE ASSUMED NORMAL MONTHLY AND ANNUAL MEANS, BOTH BEING DERIVED FROM SIX DAILY OBSERVATIONS.

	January.	February.	March.	April.	May.	June.	July.	August.	September	October.	November.	December.	Year
1854	−.017	+.086	−.091	−.008	.000	−.027	+.049	+.014	+.056	+.035	−.184	−.054	−.012
1855	+.015	+.016	−.103	+.008	+.085	−.065	+.020	+.019	+.076	−.110	+.041	+.061	+.005
1856	+.046	−.121	−.057	−.067	+.016	−.030	.000	−.113	−.045	+.046	+.019	+.070	−.020
1857	+.112	+.127	−.020	−.116	−.031	−.151	−.003	−.040	+.067	+.006	−.099	−.022	−.015
1858	+.051	+.051	+.004	−.147	+.018	+.028	+.014	−.015	+.005	+.020	+.004	+.053	+.007
1859	+.053	+.023	−.203	−.111	+.094	+.042	+.057	−.035	+.024	−.046	+.052	+.068	+.001
Mean.	−.043	+.030	−.078	−.074	+.030	−.034	+.023	−.028	+.030	−.008	−.028	+.029	−.006

TABLE XXII.

MONTHLY MEANS OF THE BAROMETER AT EACH OF THE SIX OBSERVATION HOURS, FOR THE PERIOD 1854 TO 1859 INCLUSIVE.

Barometer at 32° — 27 inches + the numbers in the table.

Toronto Astronomical time.	2 h.	4 h.	10 h.	12 h.	18 h.	20 h.	Monthly Means.
January	2.645	2.656	2.684	2.678	2.666	2.675	2.667
February	2.624	2.622	2.641	2.637	2.648	2.664	2.639
March	2.515	2.512	2.545	2.541	2.552	2.560	2.537
April	2.557	2.540	2.585	2.583	2.578	2.584	2.572
May	2.588	2.576	2.593	2.580	2.611	2.622	2.596
June	2.533	2.521	2.545	2.543	2.558	2.566	2.544
July	2.605	2.589	2.608	2.609	2.632	2.640	2.614
August	2.595	2.584	2.605	2.606	2.620	2.626	2.606
September	2.661	2.651	2.672	2.669	2.696	2.703	2.675
October	2.634	2.635	2.661	2.667	2.658	2.672	2.653
November	2.573	2.582	2.602	2.600	2.599	2.614	2.595
December	2.653	2.664	2.684	2.682	2.663	2.677	2.671
	2.590	2.595	2.619	2.616	2.623	2.634	2.614

TABLE XXIII.

DIFFERENCES OF THE MEAN MONTHLY READINGS OF THE BAROMETER AT EACH OBSERVATION HOUR, IN EXCESS OR DEFECT FROM THE ASSUMED NORMAL FOR THE HOUR, TOGETHER WITH THE MEANS OF THE SIX HOURLY DIFFERENCES.

Toronto Astronomical time.	2 h.	4 h.	10 h.	12 h.	18 h.	20 h.	Monthly Means.
January	+0.043	+0.043	+0.053	+0.049	+0.069	+0.033	+0.043
February	+ .028	+ .027	+ .028	+ .043	+ .033	+ .024	+ .031
March	− .085	− .083	− .078	− .078	− .069	− .078	− .079
April	− .082	− .077	− .065	− .049	− .081	− .063	− .073
May	+ .033	+ .036	+ .028	+ .027	+ .029	+ .030	+ .031
June	− .039	− .037	− .027	− .025	− .037	− .030	− .034
July	+ .022	+ .019	+ .022	+ .022	+ .026	+ .025	+ .023
August	− .034	− .030	− .024	− .023	− .025	− .030	− .028
September	+ .025	+ .027	+ .029	+ .033	+ .032	+ .030	+ .029
October	− .011	− .008	− .004	− .006	− .008	− .014	− .009
November	− .085	− .080	− .019	− .026	− .028	− .030	− .028
December	+ .032	+ .082	+ .044	+ .046	+ .013	+ .011	+ .030
	−0.008	−0.007	0.000	+0.001	−0.007	−0.011	−0.005

TABLE XXIV.

MONTHLY MEAN DIFFERENCES WITHOUT REGARD TO SIGN BETWEEN THE OBSERVED READING OF THE BAROMETER AND THE ASSUMED NORMAL PROPER TO THE DAY AND HOUR, FOR EACH MONTH OF THE YEARS 1854 TO 1859 INCLUSIVE.

	January.	February.	March.	April.	May.	June.	July.	August.	September	October.	November.	December.	Mean of the Year.
1854	0.257	0.265	0.274	0.189	0.135	0.127	0.112	0.091	0.157	0.249	0.275	0.225	0.196
1855	.315	.170	.231	.160	.138	.124	.104	.139	.152	.108	.210	.244	.180
1856	.223	.227	.165	.183	.145	.106	.112	.140	.153	.206	.201	.236	.175
1857	.240	.242	.141	.205	.149	.179	.113	.132	.149	.147	.343	.220	.189
1858	.239	.212	.208	.238	.152	.085	.120	.134	.175	.200	.134	.205	.175
1859	.220	.176	316	.203	.188	.138	.163	.081	.187	.129	.208	.216	.185
Means	0.249	0.215	0.223	0.196	0.151	0.126	0.121	0.119	0.162	0.183	0.228	0 225	0.183

TABLE XXV.

MONTHLY MEAN DIFFERENCES WITHOUT REGARD TO SIGN BETWEEN THE OBSERVED READING OF THE BAROMETER AND THE ASSUMED NORMAL FOR THE DAY AND HOUR, AT EACH OF THE SIX OBSERVATION HOURS, FOR THE PERIOD 1854 TO 1859 INCLUSIVE.

Toronto Astronomical time.	2 h.	4 h.	10 h.	12 h.	18 h.	20 h.	Monthly Means.
January	0.255	0.247	0.237	0.237	0.259	0.259	0.249
February	.222	.218	.211	.213	.213	.217	.215
March	.226	.220	.217	.220	.222	.230	.223
April	.202	.195	.179	.179	.206	.216	.196
May	.154	.147	.139	.143	.162	.163	.151
June	.132	.126	.116	.114	.134	.136	.126
July	.125	.120	.112	.114	.127	.128	.121
August	.123	.119	.113	.114	.123	.126	.119
September	.166	.160	.157	.160	.164	.167	.162
October	.185	.179	.173	.179	.190	.192	.183
November	.229	.222	.228	.229	.230	.232	.228
December	.230	.228	.222	.220	.225	.226	.225
Means	.187	.182	.175	.177	.188	.191	.183

TABLE XXVI.

MEAN DIFFERENCES, WITHOUT REGARD TO SIGN, BETWEEN THE HEIGHTS OF THE BAROMETER OBSERVED AT 2 P.M. ON CONSECUTIVE DAYS, FOR EACH MONTH IN THE YEARS 1854 TO 1859 INCLUSIVE.

Years.	January.	February.	March.	April.	May.	June.	July.	August.	September	October.	November.	December.	Yearly Means.
1854	0.302	0.368	0.256	0.225	0.149	0.097	0.142	0.127	0.172	9.216	0.250	0.219	0.210
1855	.246	.165	.278	.104	.107	.135	.111	.141	.158	.120	.249	.311	.185
1856	.236	.243	.187	.222	.154	.106	.110	.106	.128	.153	.199	.365	.184
1857	.261	.205	.231	.207	.146	.126	.097	.145	.106	.134	.256	.286	.188
1858	.303	.238	.237	.193	.222	.139	.145	.135	.167	.168	.158	.208	.200
1859	.265	.228	.333	.221	.155	.155	.133	.086	.169	.120	.270	.271	.201
Means.	0.269	0.241	0.254	0.210	0.155	0.127	0.123	0.124	0.160	0.155	0.230	0.292	0.195
Ratio to Mean of Year.	1.38	1.24	1.30	1.08	0.79	0.65	0.63	0.64	0.82	0.79	1.18	1.50	...

TABLE XXVII.

NUMBER OF CASES IN A HUNDRED IN EACH MONTH (FOR THE PERIOD 1854 TO 1859 INCLUSIVE) WHEN THE HEIGHT OF THE BAROMETER OBSERVED AT 2 P.M. ON CONSECUTIVE DAYS WAS INCREASING, WITH THE AVERAGE VALUES OF THE INCREASING AND OF THE DECREASING CHANGES.

	January.	February.	March.	April.	May.	June.	July.	August.	September.	October.	November.	December.
Number in a hundred..	52	50	52	49	49	49	50	57	46	48	50	53
Ratio to Mean of Year..	1.03	0.99	1.03	0.97	0.97	0.97	0.99	1.13	0.91	0.95	0.99	1.05
Average increase......	0.262	0.243	0.243	0.215	0.158	0.126	0.125	0.114	0.171	0.159	0.238	0.275
Ratio to Mean of Year..	1.35	1.25	1.25	1.11	0.82	0.65	0.65	0.59	0.88	0.82	1.20	1.42
Average decrease......	0.276	0.240	0.266	0.206	0.153	0.127	0.122	0.186	0.151	0.150	0.227	0.310
Ratio to Mean of Year..	1.40	1.22	1.35	1.05	0.78	0.64	0.62	0.69	0.77	0.76	1.15	1.58

TABLE XXVIII.

MEAN DIFFERENCES OF THE READING OF THE BAROMETER FROM THE NORMAL AT THE HOUR OF OBSERVATION, FOR EACH OF THE SIXTEEN POINTS OF THE WIND'S DIRECTION, WITH THE NUMBER OF OBSERVATIONS FROM WHICH THE MEANS ARE DERIVED, FOR THE YEARS 1853-59 INCLUSIVE.

The sign (+) indicates that the observed reading was in excess, and (—) that it was in defect of the normal.

Years.	N.		N.N.E.		N.E.		E.N.E.		E.		E.S.E.		S.E.		S.S.E.	
	No.	Diff.	No.	Diff.	No.	Diff.	No.	Diff.	No.	Diff.	No.	Diff.	No.	Diff.	No.	Diff.
1853	142	+0.069	148	+0.025	108	+0.050	93	+0.024	90	+0.019	46	+0.095	64	+0.072	64	+0.057
1854	113	+ .138	77	+ .139	87	+ .084	87	— .062	145	— .012	103	— .001	48	+ .028	56	+ .027
1855	168	+ .073	79	+ .093	69	+ .058	74	— .068	136	— .047	95	+ .047	42	+ .065	64	+ .063
1856	127	+ .074	61	+ .117	65	+ .013	68	— .022	123	+ .011	69	— .001	42	+ .035	39	+ .055
1857	102	+ .046	39	+ .038	60	— .015	126	— .023	108	— .014	67	+ .004	46	+ .009	39	+ .021
1858	120	+ .060	57	+ .070	76	+ .040	175	— .011	156	+ .033	49	— .014	45	— .101	60	+ .063
1859	104	+ .073	68	+ .106	75	+ .079	160	— .009	179	+ .017	65	+ .078	35	+ .067	47	+ .022
1853-59	876	+ .069	529	+ .079	540	+ .052	783	— .008	937	+ .016	484	+ .031	322	+ .041	374	+ .043

Years.	S.		S.S.W.		S.W.		W.S.W.		W.		W.N.W.		N.W.		N.N.W.		Calms.	
	No.	Diff.	No.	Diff.	No.	Diff.	No.	Diff.	No.	Diff.	No.	Diff.	No.	Diff.	No.	Diff.	No.	Diff.
1853	123	—0.011	129	—0.030	68	—0.097	95	0.000	102	—0.042	76	—0.030	115	—0.027	156	+0.004	356	+0.021
1854	79	+ .039	112	— .068	111	— .163	109	— .131	103	— .069	125	— .049	112	— .035	163	+ .012	333	+ .017
1855	74	+ .010	118	— .062	124	— .115	137	— .083	108	— .068	132	— .060	134	— .033	146	— .022	229	+ .027
1856	69	— .010	122	— .046	131	— .119	191	— .076	174	— .066	170	— .064	121	— .033	144	+ .017	254	+ .021
1857	71	— .018	139	— .062	154	— .098	100	— .086	136	— .035	129	— .012	149	— .008	165	— .025	276	+ .039
1858	83	+ .045	93	— .086	64	— .149	111	— .064	132	— .064	144	— .007	147	— .001	160	+ .030	307	+ .049
1859	75	+ .048	144	— .035	104	— .073	123	— .100	156	— .062	137	— .083	130	— .020	145	+ .089	223	+ .042
1853-59	574	+ .016	857	— .057	756	— .116	926	— .079	971	— .061	913	— .043	908	— .017	1069	+ .019	1971	+ .030

TABLE XXIX.

MONTHLY AND YEARLY MEANS OF THE DIURNAL CHANGE IN THE READINGS OF THE BAROMETER (CORRECTED TO TEMPERATURE 32°) FROM 6 A.M. TO 6 A.M. FOR THE PERIOD 1854 TO 1859 INCLUSIVE, ARRANGED ACCORDING TO THE DAILY RESULTANT DIRECTION OF THE WIND.

	January.	February.	March	April.	May.	June.	July.	August.	September.	October.	November.	December.	Year.
N.	+0.062	+0.079	+0.006	+0.153	+0.095	+0.118	+0.039	+0.109	+0.153	+0.106	+0.161	+0.050	+0.007
N.E.	− .268	− .167	− .154	− .023	− .057	− .066	− .003	− .064	− .001	− .032	− .103	− .249	− .102
E.	− .388	− .331	− .353	− .198	− .101	− .104	− .053	− .094	− .122	− .179	− .217	− .309	− .179
S.E.	− .325	− .390	− .269	− .197	− .101	− .135	− .058	− .172	− .293	− .138	− .347	− .570	− .197
S.	− .283	− .206	− .243	− .058	− .076	− .038	− .065	− .003	− .111	− .058	− .200	− .233	− .009
S.W.	− .050	− .155	− .060	+ .030	+ .008	− .001	− .018	+ .015	− .062	− .054	− .056	+ .015	− .036
W.	+ .213	+ .122	+ .203	+ .140	+ .129	+ .077	+ .093	+ .004	+ .117	+ .118	+ .185	+ .150	+ .144
N.W.	+ .255	+ .172	+ .150	+ .203	+ .157	+ .124	+ .160	+ .102	+ .144	+ .114	+ .252	+ .227	+ .170

TABLE XXX.

FREQUENCY OF INCREASING CHANGES IN EACH MONTH, THE TOTAL NUMBER IN EACH DIRECTION BEING 100.

	January.	February.	March.	April.	May.	June.	July.	August.	September.	October.	November.	December.	Year.
N.	79	64	67	80	68	56	57	80	89	79	93	52	72
N.E.	11	36	38	41	40	33	60	30	41	40	30	15	34
E.	13	6	10	19	31	28	36	30	15	3	3	16	20
S.E.	20	0	0	15	13	18	35	8	0	11	8	0	15
S.	0	20	0	29	24	25	30	40	8	38	33	0	23
S.W.	35	29	35	70	53	57	36	47	44	41	38	56	44
W.	80	72	72	75	76	74	73	82	80	79	84	76	77
N.W.	80	82	81	91	84	76	96	84	83	69	92	83	84

TABLE XXXI.

AGGREGATE OF INCREASING CHANGES FOR EACH DIRECTION, THE JOINT AGGREGATE OF INCREASING AND DECREASING CHANGES IN THE MONTH FOR ANY ONE DIRECTION BEING EXPRESSED BY 100.

	January.	February.	March	April.	May.	June.	July.	August.	September.	October.	November.	December.	Year.
N.	67	70	51	80	79	85	71	87	90	80	92	63	76
N.E.	1	20	23	44	31	18	48	24	50	33	22	12	23
E.	2	2	2	9	19	15	26	14	7	1	1	4	8
S.E.	0	0	0	10	2	6	19	0	0	10	1	0	4
S.	0	5	0	29	20	25	20	27	9	16	12	0	15
S.W.	38	20	37	58	53	50	40	57	28	35	39	55	40
W.	88	75	89	84	88	79	90	87	92	84	91	81	85
N.W.	93	88	90	94	88	90	90	90	92	79	90	89	90

TORONTO METEOROLOGICAL OBSERVATIONS.

TABLE XXXII.

MONTHLY AND YEARLY MEANS OF THE DIURNAL CHANGE, WITHOUT REGARD TO SIGN, IN THE READINGS OF THE BAROMETER (CORRECTED TO TEMPERATURE 32°) FROM 6 A.M. TO 6 A.M., FOR THE PERIOD 1854 TO 1859, ARRANGED ACCORDING TO THE DAILY RESULTANT DIRECTION OF THE WIND.

	January.	February.	March.	April.	May.	June.	July.	August.	September.	October.	November.	December.	Year.
N.	0.186	0.196	0.283	0.252	0.164	0.172	0.095	0.148	0.190	0.177	0.190	0.188	0.187
N.E.	.276	.279	.289	.203	.147	.103	.097	.122	.145	.094	.184	.325	.191
E.	.405	.342	.369	.241	.103	.149	.108	.131	.142	.183	.222	.336	.212
S.E.	.326	.390	.269	.245	.106	.152	.093	.173	.293	.173	.357	.570	.214
S.	.283	.231	.242	.139	.127	.077	.109	.137	.135	.086	.265	.234	.141
S.W.	.244	.257	.238	.180	.147	.090	.087	.105	.116	.183	.251	.151	.176
W.	.277	.249	.256	.205	.170	.131	.117	.125	.139	.174	.229	.243	.207
N.W.	.294	.230	.188	.233	.208	.155	.162	.127	.173	.193	.313	.292	.213
Means.	.286	.272	.267	.212	.154	.129	.108	.134	.167	.158	.251	.292	.193

TABLE XXXIII.

COMPARATIVE DIURNAL CHANGES IN THE HEIGHT OF THE BAROMETER IN THE SAME MONTH THAT ARE DUE TO DIFFERENT WINDS, BEING THE NUMBERS IN TABLE XXXII. EXPRESSED IN TERMS OF THE MEAN CHANGE IN THAT MONTH FOR ALL WINDS.

	January.	February.	March.	April.	May.	June.	July.	August.	September.	October.	November.	December.	Year.
N.	0.65	0.72	1.06	1.19	1.06	1.33	0.88	1.10	1.14	1.12	0.76	0.64	0.97
N.E.	0.97	1.03	1.08	0.96	0.95	0.80	0.90	0.91	0.87	0.59	0.73	1 11	0.99
E.	1.42	1.26	1.38	1.14	1.06	1.16	1.00	0.98	0.85	1.16	0.88	1.15	1.10
S.E.	1.14	1.43	1 01	1.16	0.69	1.18	0.86	1.29	1 75	1.09	1 42	1.95	1.11
S.	0.99	0.85	0.91	0.66	0.82	0.60	1.01	1.02	0.81	0.54	1.06	0.80	0.73
S.W.	0.85	0.94	0.89	0.85	0.95	0.70	0.81	0.78	0.70	1 16	1.00	0.52	0.91
W.	0.97	0 92	0.97	0.97	1.10	1.02	1.08	0.93	0.83	1.10	0.91	0.83	1.07
N.W.	1.03	0.85	0.70	1.10	1.35	1.20	1.50	0.95	1.04	1.22	1.25	1.00	1.11

TABLE XXXIV.

COMPARATIVE DIURNAL CHANGES IN THE HEIGHT OF THE BAROMETER THAT ARE DUE IN DIFFERENT MONTHS TO THE SAME WIND, BEING THE NUMBERS IN TABLE XXXII. EXPRESSED IN TERMS OF THE ANNUAL ARITHMETIC MEAN FOR THAT WIND.

	January.	February.	March.	April.	May.	June.	July.	August.	September.	October.	November.	December.
N.	0.99	1.05	1.51	1.35	0.88	0.92	0.51	0.79	1.02	0.95	1.02	1.01
N.E.	1.46	1.48	1.53	1.07	0.78	0 54	0.51	0.65	0.77	0 50	0.97	1.72
E.	1.74	1.47	1.58	1.03	0.70	0.64	0.46	0.56	0 61	0.78	0.95	1.44
S.E.	1.24	1.49	1.03	0 94	0.40	0.58	0.35	0.66	1 12	0.66	1.36	2.17
S.	1.65	1.34	1.41	0.81	0.74	0.45	0.63	0.80	0 78	0.50	1.54	1.36
S.W.	1.43	1.50	1.39	1.05	0.86	0.53	0 51	0.61	0.68	1.07	1.47	0.88
W.	1.44	1.29	1.34	1.06	0.88	0.08	0.61	0.65	0.72	0.90	1.19	1.20
N.W.	1.37	1 07	0.88	1.09	0.97	0.72	0.76	0.59	0.81	0.90	1.46	1.36

TABLE XXXV.

HIGHEST AND LOWEST READINGS, AND MONTHLY RANGES OF THE BAROMETER IN EACH MONTH FROM 1854 TO 1859 INCLUSIVE.

Barometer at 32° = 27 inches + the numbers in the table.

HIGHEST.

Years.	January.	February.	March.	April.	May.	June.	July.	August.	September.	October.	November.	December.	Year. Barom.	Date.
1854	3.210	3.172	3.098	3.233	2.986	2.955	2.885	2.845	3.142	3.121	3.196	3.245	3.245	23rd Dec.
1855	3.552	3.088	3.079	2.998	2.902	2.811	2.833	3.019	3.092	2.923	3.131	3.201	3.552	8th Jan.
1856	3.280	3.086	3.062	3.099	2.969	2.798	2.844	2.797	3.013	3.200	3.048	3.480	3.480	18th Dec.
1857	3.168	3.361	3.006	3.006	2.896	2.707	2.848	2.860	3.076	2.994	3.281	3.258	3.361	10th Feb.
1858	3.408	3.060	3.159	3.006	3.198	2.891	2.915	2.939	3.098	3.042	2.070	3.351	3.408	8th Jan.
1859	3.311	3.002	3.255	3.046	2.986	2.966	3.141	2.811	3.049	2.902	3.252	3.392	3.392	3rd Dec.
Means.	3.323	3.128	3.113	3.065	2.990	2.855	2.911	2.879	3.078	3.040	3.146	3.321	3.406	

LOWEST.

Years.	January.	February.	March.	April.	May.	June.	July.	August.	September.	October.	November.	December.	Year. Barom.	Date.
1854	1.693	2.002	1.788	2.045	2.066	2.287	2.308	2.384	2.302	1.731	1.685	1.917	1.685	25th Nov.
1855	1.717	2.172	1.792	2.233	2.283	1.942	2.337	2.130	2.247	1.945	1.983	1.459	1.459	9th Dec.
1856	2.186	1.778	1.828	2.081	2.125	2.207	2.241	2.174	2.149	2.217	1.902	1.459	1.459	14th Dec.
1857	2.181	2.152	2.115	1.898	2.199	1.952	2.255	2.155	2.248	2.289	1.452	1.852	1.452	19th Nov.
1858	1.973	1.940	1.849	2.011	2.032	2.147	2.290	2.231	2.167	2.000	2.190	2.008	1.849	21st Mar.
1859	1.934	1.877	1.286	1.993	2.224	2.260	2.159	2.306	2.038	2.018	1.881	2.201	1.286	19th Mar.
Means.	1.947	1.987	1.776	2.044	2.155	2.133	2.265	2.230	2.192	2.033	1.849	1.816	1.532	

MONTHLY RANGES.

Years.	January.	February.	March.	April.	May.	June.	July.	August.	September.	October.	November.	December.	Year
1854	1.526	1.170	1.310	1.188	0.920	0.668	0.577	0.461	0.840	1.390	1.511	1.328	1.560
1855	1.835	0.916	1.287	0.765	0.619	0.869	0.496	0.889	0.845	0.978	1.148	1.742	2.093
1856	1.094	1.308	1.234	1.018	0.844	0.591	0.603	0.623	0.864	0.983	1.146	2.021	2.021
1857	0.987	1.209	0.891	1.108	0.697	0.755	0.593	0.705	0.828	0.705	1.829	1.406	1.900
1858	1.435	1.120	1.310	0.995	1.166	0.744	0.625	0.708	0.931	1.042	0.780	1.343	1.550
1859	1.377	1.125	1.969	1.053	0.762	0.706	0.982	0.505	1.011	0.944	1.371	1.191	2.106
Means.	1.376	1.141	1.337	1.021	0.835	0.722	0.646	0.649	0.886	1.007	1.297	1.505	1.875

TORONTO METEOROLOGICAL OBSERVATIONS.

TABLE XXXVI.

MONTHLY MEANS OF THE PRESSURE OF DRY AIR AT EACH OF THE SIX OBSERVATION HOURS, FOR THE YEARS 1854 TO 1859 INCLUSIVE.

Pressure of Dry Air at 32° = 27 inches + the numbers in the table.

	Toronto Astronomical time.	2 h.	4 h.	10 h.	12 h.	18 h.	20 h.	Monthly Means.
JANUARY.	1854	2.454	2.473	2.502	2.494	2.485	2.499	2.485
	1855	.494	.515	.539	.530	.498	.510	.514
	1856	.551	.564	.607	.604	.596	.613	.589
	1857	.626	.621	.651	.647	.683	.690	.653
	1858	.507	.529	.583	.581	.518	.530	.542
	1859	.530	.546	.559	.548	.554	.569	.551
	Means.	2.527	2.541	2.573	2.567	2.556	2.569	2.556

	Toronto Astronomical time.	2 h.	4 h.	10 h.	12 h.	18 h.	20 h.	Monthly Means.
FEBRUARY.	1854	2.546	2.544	2.601	2.608	2.595	2.611	2.584
	1855	.498	.514	.558	.556	.537	.557	.537
	1856	.362	.370	.423	.435	.424	.436	.409
	1857	.594	.581	.556	.543	.619	.641	.589
	1858	.564	.555	.569	.564	.606	.622	.580
	1859	.509	.502	.512	.499	.522	.547	.515
	Means.	2.512	2.511	2.536	2.534	2.551	2.569	2.536

	Toronto Astronomical time.	2 h.	4 h.	10 h.	12 h.	18 h.	20 h.	Monthly Means.
MARCH.	1854	2.324	2.325	2.379	2.372	2.408	2.407	2.369
	1855	.343	.332	.379	.385	.424	.424	.381
	1856	.433	.438	.469	.470	.471	.480	.460
	1857	.438	.441	.493	.495	.482	.483	.472
	1858	.489	.478	.490	.493	.514	.531	.501
	1859	.227	.228	.243	.241	.259	.271	.245
	Means.	2.376	2.374	2.410	2.409	2.426	2.433	2.405

TABLE XXXVI.—(Continued)

MONTHLY MEANS OF THE PRESSURE OF DRY AIR AT EACH OF THE SIX OBSERVATION HOURS, FOR THE YEARS 1854 TO 1859 INCLUSIVE.

Pressure of Dry Air at 32° = 27 inches + the numbers in the table.

Toronto Astronomical time.		2 h.	4 h.	10 h.	12 h.	18 h.	20 h.	Monthly Means.
APRIL	1854	2.402	2.382	2.439	2.451	2.460	2.440	2.430
	1855	.422	.424	.453	.446	.472	.459	.446
	1856	.336	.337	.392	.396	.402	.396	.376
	1857	.348	.344	.413	.407	.364	.370	.374
	1858	.317	.307	.312	.311	.347	.345	.323
	1859	.355	.362	.308	.400	.381	.391	.381
	Means.	2.363	2.359	2.401	2.402	2.404	2.402	2.388

Toronto Astronomical time.		2 h.	4 h.	10 h.	12 h.	18 h.	20 h.	Monthly Means.
MAY.	1854	2.236	2.216	2.309	2.316	2.308	2.285	2.278
	1855	.360	.357	.386	.383	.428	.437	.393
	1856	.313	.299	.313	.307	.354	.356	.324
	1857	.259	.253	.273	.271	.322	.311	.282
	1858	.326	.329	.348	.348	.353	.364	.345
	1859	.342	.329	.349	.354	.396	.399	.361
	Means.	2.306	2.297	2.330	2.330	2.360	2.359	2.331

Toronto Astronomical time.		2 h.	4 h.	10 h.	12 h.	18 h.	20 h.	Monthly Means.
JUNE	1854	2.067	2.069	2.149	2.140	2.148	2.121	2.217
	1855	.050	.049	.128	.134	.151	.135	.108
	1856	.071	.062	.125	.142	.156	.145	.117
	1857	.042	.028	.095	.098	.095	.084	.074
	1858	.079	.068	.158	.161	.192	.186	.141
	1859	.230	.231	.295	.300	.273	.262	.265
	Means.	2.090	2.084	2.158	2.164	2.169	2.156	2.137

TABLE XXXVI.—(Continued.)

MONTHLY MEANS OF THE PRESSURE OF DRY AIR, AT EACH OF THE SIX OBSERVATION HOURS, FOR THE YEARS 1854 TO 1859 INCLUSIVE.

Pressure of Dry Air at 32° = 27 inches + the numbers in the table.

	Toronto Astronomical time.	2 h.	4 h.	10 h.	12 h.	18 h.	20 h.	Monthly Means.
JULY	1854	2.024	2.025	2.115	2.140	2.152	2.085	2.090
	1855	.032	.033	.107	.132	.094	.088	.081
	1856	.075	.059	.091	.104	.147	.134	.102
	1857	.029	.024	.084	.091	.099	.061	.068
	1858	.084	.074	.128	.138	.169	.154	.125
	1859	.140	.143	.188	.190	.205	.197	.177
	Means.	2.064	2.060	2.119	2.133	2.144	2.123	2.107

	Toronto Astronomical time.	2 h.	4 h.	10 h.	12 h.	18 h.	20 h.	Monthly Means.
AUGUST	1854	2.124	2.109	2.173	2.185	2.238	2.189	2.170
	1855	.156	.157	.215	.237	.268	.222	.209
	1856	.057	.059	.122	.131	.130	.113	.102
	1857	.077	.086	.139	.152	.174	.135	.127
	1858	.103	.113	.142	.156	.187	.150	.142
	1859	.108	.122	.139	.153	.163	.132	.136
	Means.	2.104	2.108	2.155	2.169	2.193	2.157	2.148

	Toronto Astronomical time.	2 h.	4 h.	10 h.	12 h.	18 h.	20 h.	Monthly Means.
SEPTEMBER	1854	2.213	2.198	2.270	2.295	2.349	2.298	2.271
	1855	.290	.275	.290	.311	.360	.355	.315
	1856	.214	.221	.255	.256	.294	.256	.249
	1857	.261	.255	.336	.337	.380	.348	.319
	1858	.235	.220	.258	.261	.326	.292	.266
	1859	.305	.300	.324	.330	.368	.361	.331
	Means.	2.253	2.245	2.289	2.298	2.346	2.318	2.292

TABLE XXXVI.—(Continued.)
MONTHLY MEANS OF THE PRESSURE OF DRY AIR AT EACH OF THE SIX OBSERVATION HOURS, FOR THE YEARS 1854 TO 1859 INCLUSIVE.

Pressure of Dry Air at 32° = 27 inches + the numbers in the table.

Toronto Astronomical time.		2 h.	4 h.	10 h.	12 h.	18 h.	20 h.	Monthly Means.
OCTOBER	1854	2.355	2.361	2.426	2.432	2.442	2.433	2.408
	1855	.273	.281	.303	.296	.338	.334	.304
	1856	.447	.441	.488	.491	.492	.494	.475
	1857	.381	.388	.434	.437	.452	.450	.424
	1858	.406	.409	.436	.431	.433	.439	.426
	1859	.363	.392	.418	.420	.400	.409	.400
	Means.	2.371	2.379	2.417	2.418	2.426	2.426	2.406

Toronto Astronomical time.		2 h.	4 h.	10 h.	12 h.	18 h.	20 h.	Monthly Means.
NOVEMBER	1854	2.240	2.251	2.268	2.268	2.249	2.277	2.259
	1855	.441	.440	.481	.493	.489	.504	.475
	1856	.447	.461	.481	.479	.455	.456	.463
	1857	.326	.332	.386	.390	.375	.392	.367
	1858	.453	.463	.470	.466	.457	.477	.464
	1859	.454	.470	.472	.464	.517	.531	.484
	Means.	2.394	2.403	2.426	2.427	2.424	2.439	2.419

Toronto Astronomical time.		2 h.	4 h.	10 h.	12 h.	18 h.	20 h.	Monthly Means.
DECEMBER	1854	2.457	2.470	2.490	2.487	2.478	2.490	2.479
	1855	.570	.578	.577	.572	.579	.600	.579
	1856	.577	.596	.611	.614	.596	.612	.601
	1857	.439	.455	.506	.505	.450	.463	.470
	1858	.539	.557	.594	.591	.553	.567	.567
	1859	.576	.585	.625	.629	.614	.632	.610
	Means.	2.526	2.540	2.567	2.566	2.545	2.561	2.551

TABLE XXXVII.

MONTHLY AND ANNUAL MEANS OF THE PRESSURE OF DRY AIR FURNISHED BY SIX DAILY OBSERVATIONS FOR 1854 TO 1859 INCLUSIVE.

Pressure of Dry Air at 32° = 27 inches + the numbers in the table.

	January.	February.	March.	April.	May.	June.	July.	August.	September	October.	November.	December.	Year.
1854	2.485	2.584	2.369	2.430	2.278	2.117	2.090	2.170	2.271	2.408	2.259	2.470	2.328
1855	.514	.537	.381	.446	.393	.108	.081	.209	.315	.304	.475	.579	.362
1856	.589	.409	.460	.376	.324	.117	.102	.102	.249	.475	.463	.601	.356
1857	.653	.589	.472	.374	.282	.074	.068	.127	.319	.424	.367	.470	.352
1858	.541	.580	.501	.323	.345	.141	.125	.142	.266	.426	.464	.567	.368
1859	.551	.515	.245	.381	.361	.265	.177	.136	.331	.400	.484	.610	.371
Means	2.556	2.536	2.405	2.388	2.331	2.137	2.107	2.148	2.292	2.406	2.410	2.551	2.356

TABLE XXXVIII.

MONTHLY MEANS OF THE PRESSURE OF DRY AIR AT EACH OF THE SIX OBSERVATION HOURS, FOR THE PERIOD 1854 TO 1859 INCLUSIVE.

Pressure of Dry Air at 32° = 27 inches + the numbers in the table.

Toronto Astronomical time.	2 h.	4 h.	10 h.	12 h.	18 h.	20 h.	Monthly Means.
January	2.527	2.541	2.573	2.567	2.556	2.569	2.556
February	.512	.511	.536	.534	.551	.569	.536
March	.376	.374	.410	.400	.426	.433	.405
April	.363	.359	.401	.402	.404	.402	.388
May	.308	.297	.330	.330	.360	.359	.331
June	.090	.084	.158	.164	.169	.156	.137
July	.064	.060	.119	.133	.144	.123	.107
August	.104	.108	.155	.169	.193	.157	.148
September	.253	.245	.289	.298	.348	.318	.292
October	.371	.379	.417	.418	.426	.426	.406
November	.394	.403	.426	.427	.424	.439	.419
December	.526	.540	.567	.566	.545	.561	.551
Means	2.324	2.325	2.365	2.368	2.379	2.376	2.356

TABLE XXXIX.

MONTHLY MEANS OF THE PRESSURE OF VAPOUR AT EACH OF THE SIX OBSERVATION HOURS, FOR THE YEARS 1854 TO 1859 INCLUSIVE.

Toronto Astronomical time.		2 h.	4 h.	10 h.	12 h.	18 h.	20 h.	Monthly Means.
JANUARY.	1854	0.129	0.128	0.122	0.121	0.116	0.116	0.122
	1855	.130	.129	.126	.125	.119	.117	.125
	1856	.093	.089	.078	.075	.073	.074	.080
	1857	.088	.088	.083	.082	.079	.075	.083
	1858	.141	.133	.129	.132	.138	.130	.134
	1859	.123	.119	.124	.127	.135	.128	.126
	Means.	0.118	0.114	0.110	0.110	0.110	0.107	0.112

Toronto Astronomical time.		2 h.	4 h.	10 h.	12 h.	18 h.	20 h.	Monthly Means.
FEBRUARY.	1854	0.118	0.124	0.108	0.106	0.102	0.104	0.110
	1855	.104	.090	.086	.081	.080	.079	.088
	1856	.094	.092	.079	.072	.070	.070	.080
	1857	.149	.147	.151	.154	.142	.139	.147
	1858	.086	.086	.081	.082	.074	.073	.080
	1859	.115	.119	.121	.123	.115	.109	.117
	Means.	0.111	0.111	0.104	0.103	0.097	0.096	0.104

Toronto Astronomical time.		2 h.	4 h.	10 h.	12 h.	18 h.	20 h.	Monthly Means.
MARCH.	1854	0.170	0.168	0.151	0.149	0.144	0.151	0.156
	1855	.143	.145	.134	.131	.116	.123	.132
	1856	.105	.105	.102	.100	.092	.092	.099
	1857	.128	.127	.125	.123	.117	.123	.124
	1858	.117	.123	.123	.110	.117	.114	.119
	1859	.171	.165	.173	.170	.167	.162	.168
	Means.	0.139	0.139	0.135	0.132	0.126	0.127	0.133

TORONTO METEOROLOGICAL OBSERVATIONS.

TABLE XXXIX.—(*Continued.*)

MONTHLY MEANS OF THE PRESSURE OF VAPOUR AT EACH OF THE SIX OBSERVATION HOURS, FOR THE YEARS 1854 TO 1859 INCLUSIVE.

	Toronto Astronomical time.	2 h.	4 h.	10 h.	12 h.	18 h.	20 h.	Monthly Means.
APRIL	1854	0.219	0.222	0.209	0.203	0.187	0.206	0.207
	1855	.220	.212	.206	.207	.192	.211	.208
	1856	.223	.216	.195	.190	.191	.201	.203
	1857	.164	.164	.152	.153	.147	.154	.156
	1858	.175	.170	.184	.182	.166	.176	.176
	1859	.159	.151	.156	.152	.157	.149	.154
	Means.	0.193	0.189	0.184	0.181	0.173	0.183	0.184

	Toronto Astronomical time.	2 h.	4 h.	10 h.	10 h.	18 h.	20 h.	Monthly Means.
MAY.	1854	0.312	0.320	0.269	0.260	0.266	0.299	0.288
	1855	.277	.275	.249	.252	.247	.248	.258
	1856	.264	.265	.263	.261	.242	.256	.259
	1857	.270	.263	.259	.252	.230	.249	.254
	1858	.243	.239	.242	.241	.234	.236	.239
	1859	.315	.309	.298	.289	.284	.296	.298
	Means.	0.280	0.278	0.263	0.259	0.251	0.264	0.266

	Toronto Astronomical time.	2 h.	4 h.	10 h.	12 h.	18 h.	20 h.	Monthly Means.
JUNE.	1854	0.476	0.465	0.401	0.397	0.414	0.451	0.434
	1855	.452	.440	.386	.375	.381	.401	.406
	1856	.471	.461	.418	.402	.409	.428	.432
	1857	.374	.378	.335	.332	.341	.358	.353
	1858	.507	.504	.444	.442	.437	.456	.465
	1859	.379	.369	.336	.327	.347	.370	.355
	Means.	0.443	0.436	0.387	0.379	0.388	0.411	0.407

TABLE XXXIX.—(*Continued.*)

MONTHLY MEANS OF THE PRESSURE OF VAPOUR AT EACH OF THE SIX OBSERVATION HOURS, FOR THE YEARS 1854 TO 1859 INCLUSIVE.

Toronto Astronomical time.		2 h.	4 h.	10 h.	12 h.	18 h.	20 h.	Monthly Means.
JULY	1854	0.603	0.582	0.515	0.497	0.518	0.587	0.550
	1855	.571	.557	.504	.483	.525	.540	.530
	1856	.510	.503	.485	.473	.472	.495	.489
	1857	.552	.544	.505	.497	.495	.527	.520
	1858	.514	.509	.470	.459	.456	.476	.481
	1859	.498	.485	.456	.450	.461	.476	.471
	Means.	0.541	0.530	0.489	0.476	0.488	0.517	0.507

Toronto Astronomical time.		2 h.	4 h.	10 h.	12 h.	18 h.	20 h.	Monthly Means.
AUGUST	1854	0.516	0.514	0.469	0.456	0.431	0.484	0.478
	1855	.486	.471	.436	.414	.403	.453	.444
	1856	.450	.442	.402	.395	.401	.424	.419
	1857	.506	.488	.455	.447	.431	.476	.467
	1858	.505	.484	.478	.461	.446	.493	.478
	1859	.483	.456	.461	.447	.446	.484	.463
	Means.	0.491	0.476	0.450	0.437	0.426	0.469	0.458

Toronto Astronomical time.		2 h.	4 h.	10 h.	12 h.	18 h.	20 h.	Monthly Means.
SEPTEMBER	1854	0.475	0.476	0.426	0.399	0.373	0.431	0.430
	1855	.423	.421	.417	.394	.382	.400	.406
	1856	.366	.359	.351	.345	.322	.361	.351
	1857	.435	.431	.375	.370	.353	.393	.393
	1858	.401	.399	.384	.378	.350	.394	.384
	1859	.350	.349	.348	.338	.308	.330	.337
	Means.	0.408	0.406	0.383	0.371	0.348	0.385	0.384

TABLE XXXIX.—(*Continued.*)

MONTHLY MEANS OF THE PRESSURE OF VAPOUR AT EACH OF THE SIX OBSERVATION HOURS, FOR THE YEARS 1854 TO 1859 INCLUSIVE.

	Toronto Astronomical time.	2 h.	4 h.	10 h.	12 h.	18 h.	20 h.	Monthly Means.
OCTOBER.	1854	0.323	0.315	0.277	0.268	0.256	0.286	0.288
	1855	.262	.257	.251	.244	.228	.241	.247
	1856	.242	.243	.225	.222	.222	.231	.231
	1857	.267	.261	.236	.235	.225	.236	.243
	1858	.262	.260	.252	.250	.252	.258	.256
	1859	.226	.204	.216	.214	.209	.216	.214
	Means.	0.264	0.257	0.243	0.239	0.232	0.245	0.247

	Toronto Astronomical time.	2 h.	4 h.	10 h.	12 h.	18 h.	20 h.	Monthly Means.
NOVEMBER.	1854	0.186	0.185	0.180	0.175	0.175	0.178	0.180
	1855	.196	.199	.186	.180	.188	.190	.190
	1856	.174	.174	.178	.179	.186	.183	.179
	1857	.161	.160	.154	.154	.155	.153	.157
	1858	.163	.159	.161	.162	.165	.163	.162
	1859	.199	.189	.194	.193	.183	.182	.190
	Means.	0.180	0.179	0.175	0.174	0.175	0.175	0.176

	Toronto Astronomical time.	2 h.	4 h.	10 h.	12 h.	18 h.	20 h.	Monthly Means.
DECEMBER.	1854	0.115	0.113	0.110	0.110	0.101	0.101	0.109
	1855	.127	.123	.124	.123	.121	.118	.123
	1856	.117	.110	.107	.106	.112	.110	.110
	1857	.160	.157	.143	.142	.147	.145	.149
	1858	.129	.131	.124	.123	.130	.128	.128
	1859	.110	.108	.094	.088	.097	.097	.099
	Means.	0.126	0.124	0.117	0.115	0.118	0.117	0.120

TABLE XL.

MONTHLY MEANS OF THE RELATIVE HUMIDITY AT EACH OF THE SIX OBSERVATION HOURS, FOR THE YEARS 1854 TO 1859 INCLUSIVE.

Toronto Astronomical time.		2 h.	4 h.	10 h.	12 h.	18 h.	20 h.	Monthly Means.
JANUARY.	1854	82	84	86	86	85	83	84
	1855	76	78	85	86	86	83	82
	1856	76	73	79	79	81	80	78
	1857	84	86	90	91	91	89	89
	1858	71	70	79	82	83	80	78
	1859	73	72	81	84	90	85	81
	Means.	77	77	83	85	86	83	82

Toronto Astronomical time.		2 h.	4 h.	10 h.	12 h.	18 h.	20 h.	Monthly Means.
FEBRUARY.	1854	83	82	86	87	80	86	86
	1855	76	76	82	83	83	80	80
	1856	69	70	80	79	81	78	76
	1857	77	78	85	85	91	87	84
	1858	71	71	81	82	80	78	77
	1859	69	70	81	85	86	82	79
	Means.	74	74	83	84	85	82	80

Toronto Astronomical time.		2 h.	4 h.	10 h.	12 h.	18 h.	20 h.	Monthly Means.
MARCH.	1854	79	78	88	89	89	86	85
	1855	72	76	85	86	86	83	81
	1856	64	65	78	79	82	76	74
	1857	67	65	78	80	86	85	77
	1858	55	58	75	74	79	71	69
	1859	68	65	77	78	85	70	75
	Means.	68	68	80	81	84	80	77

TABLE XL.—(Continued.)

MONTHLY MEANS OF THE RELATIVE HUMIDITY AT EACH OF THE SIX OBSERVATION HOURS, FOR THE YEARS 1854 TO 1859 INCLUSIVE.

	Toronto Astronomical time.	2 h.	4 h.	10 h.	12 h.	18 h.	20 h.	Monthly Means.
APRIL	1854	69	68	86	87	86	83	80
	1855	56	59	83	84	85	80	75
	1856	68	68	77	78	83	77	75
	1857	63	63	79	82	82	77	74
	1858	54	54	73	74	73	67	66
	1859	53	52	66	69	75	62	63
	Means.	61	61	77	79	81	74	72

	Toronto Astronomical time.	2 h.	4 h.	10 h.	12 h.	18 h.	20 h.	Monthly Means.
MAY.	1854	64	66	79	81	79	74	74
	1855	51	53	74	79	72	62	65
	1856	64	63	75	78	75	70	71
	1857	66	66	78	82	78	71	74
	1858	59	59	74	76	74	70	69
	1859	58	57	72	74	75	66	67
	Means.	60	61	75	78	76	69	70

	Toronto Astronomical time.	2 h.	4 h.	10 h.	12 h.	18 h.	20 h.	Monthly Means.
JUNE	1854	64	64	80	82	81	75	74
	1855	69	70	83	84	84	77	78
	1856	71	69	84	85	86	79	79
	1857	69	71	79	82	83	79	77
	1858	60	62	73	77	75	68	60
	1859	60	59	72	77	77	71	69
	Means.	66	66	78	81	81	75	74

TABLE XL.—(Continued)

MONTHLY MEANS OF THE RELATIVE HUMIDITY, AT EACH OF THE SIX OBSERVATION HOURS, FOR THE YEARS 1854 TO 1859 INCLUSIVE.

Toronto Astronomical time.	2 h.	4 h.	10 h.	12 h.	18 h.	20 h.	Monthly Means.
JULY. 1854	56	57	78	80	79	74	71
1855	70	67	82	84	87	81	79
1856	56	56	76	78	79	69	69
1857	67	70	83	86	85	77	78
1858	62	61	74	76	77	70	70
1859	61	60	75	76	78	69	70
Means.	62	62	78	80	81	73	73

Toronto Astronomical time.	2 h.	4 h.	10 h.	12 h.	18 h.	20 h.	Monthly Means.
AUGUST. 1854	55	58	80	82	80	74	72
1855	64	63	81	82	82	75	74
1856	62	61	77	80	85	74	73
1857	64	65	81	83	86	78	77
1858	59	57	75	77	79	72	70
1859	59	55	76	78	82	72	70
Means.	61	60	78	80	82	74	73

Toronto Astronomical time.	2 h.	4 h.	10 h.	12 h.	18 h.	20 h.	Monthly Means.
SEPTEMBER. 1854	63	69	87	87	87	81	79
1855	67	67	86	86	86	79	79
1856	61	62	81	82	85	79	76
1857	67	68	83	85	86	80	78
1858	60	62	79	83	84	77	74
1859	65	66	81	82	82	76	75
Means.	64	66	83	84	85	79	77

TORONTO METEOROLOGICAL OBSERVATIONS.   111

TABLE XL.—(*Continued.*)

MONTHLY MEANS OF THE RELATIVE HUMIDITY AT EACH OF THE SIX OBSERVATION HOURS, FOR THE YEARS 1854 TO 1859 INCLUSIVE.

	Toronto Astronomical time.	2 h.	4 h.	10 h.	12 h.	18 h.	20 h.	Monthly Means.
OCTOBER	1854	68	73	85	85	87	84	80
	1855	69	69	83	85	85	81	78
	1856	63	65	77	80	85	79	75
	1857	70	71	80	81	84	80	78
	1858	62	63	75	77	80	75	72
	1859	59	57	78	81	82	77	72
	Means.	65	66	80	81	84	79	76

	Toronto Astronomical time.	2 h.	4 h.	10 h.	12 h.	18 h.	20 h.	Monthly Means.
NOVEMBER	1854	71	74	83	85	83	83	80
	1855	69	73	78	80	82	82	77
	1856	68	71	80	82	85	82	78
	1857	71	73	77	80	80	78	77
	1858	72	72	79	81	86	83	79
	1859	72	72	80	81	83	81	78
	Means.	71	73	79	81	83	82	78

	Toronto Astronomical time.	2 h.	4 h.	10 h.	12 h.	18 h.	20 h.	Monthly Means.
DECEMBER	1854	74	77	83	84	83	80	80
	1855	70	71	80	82	81	80	77
	1856	79	78	83	82	86	85	82
	1857	76	77	82	82	83	82	80
	1858	75	76	82	82	83	84	81
	1859	83	84	87	88	89	90	87
	Means.	76	78	83	83	84	83	81

TABLES XLI. AND XLII.

MONTHLY AND ANNUAL MEANS OF THE PRESSURE OF VAPOUR AND RELATIVE HUMIDITY FURNISHED BY SIX DAILY OBSERVATIONS, FOR 1854 TO 1859 INCLUSIVE.

PRESSURE OF VAPOUR.

	January.	February.	March.	April.	May.	June.	July.	August.	September.	October.	November.	December.	Year.
1854	0.122	0.110	0.156	0.207	0.288	0.434	0.550	0.478	0.430	0.288	0.180	0.109	0.279
1855	.125	.088	.132	.208	.258	.406	.530	.444	.406	.247	.190	.123	.263
1856	.080	.080	.099	.203	.250	.432	.489	.419	.351	.231	.179	.110	.244
1857	.083	.147	.124	.156	.254	.353	.520	.467	.393	.243	.157	.149	.254
1858	.134	.060	.119	.176	.230	.465	.481	.478	.384	.256	.162	.128	.259
1859	.126	.117	.168	.154	.298	.355	.471	.463	.337	.214	.190	.009	.249
Means.	0.112	0.104	0.133	0.184	0.266	0.407	0.507	0.458	0.384	0.247	0.176	0.120	0.258

RELATIVE HUMIDITY.

	January.	February.	March.	April.	May.	June.	July.	August.	September.	October.	November.	December.	Year.
1854	84	86	85	80	74	74	71	72	79	80	80	80	79
1855	82	80	81	75	65	78	79	74	79	78	77	77	77
1856	78	76	74	75	71	79	69	73	75	75	78	82	75
1857	89	84	77	74	74	77	78	77	76	78	77	80	79
1858	78	77	69	66	69	69	70	70	74	72	79	81	73
1859	81	79	75	63	67	69	70	70	75	72	78	87	74
Means	82	80	77	72	70	74	73	73	77	76	78	81	76

TABLES XLIII. AND XLIV.
MONTHLY MEANS OF THE PRESSURE OF VAPOUR, AND RELATIVE HUMIDITY AT EACH OF THE SIX OBSERVATION HOURS, FOR THE PERIOD 1854 TO 1859 INCLUSIVE.

Toronto Astronomical time.	2 h.	4 h.	10 h.	12 h.	18 h.	20 h.	Monthly Means.
January	0.118	0.114	0.110	0.110	0.110	0.107	0.112
February	.111	.111	.104	.103	.097	.096	.104
March	.139	.139	.135	.132	.126	.127	.133
April	.193	.189	.184	.181	.173	.183	.184
May	.280	.278	.263	.259	.251	.264	.266
June	.443	.436	.387	.379	.388	.411	.407
July	.541	.530	.489	.476	.488	.517	.507
August	.491	.476	.450	.437	.426	.469	.458
September	.408	.406	.383	.371	.348	.385	.384
October	.264	.257	.243	.239	.232	.245	.247
November	.180	.179	.175	.174	.175	.175	.176
December	.126	.124	.117	.115	.118	.117	.120
Means	0.275	0.270	0.253	0.248	0.244	0.258	0.258

Toronto Astronomical time.	2 h.	4 h.	10 h.	12 h.	18 h.	20 h.	Monthly Means.
January	77	77	83	85	86	83	82
February	74	74	83	84	85	82	80
March	68	68	80	81	84	80	77
April	61	61	77	79	81	74	72
May	60	61	75	78	76	69	70
June	66	66	78	81	81	75	74
July	62	62	78	80	81	73	73
August	61	60	78	80	82	74	73
September	64	66	83	84	85	79	77
October	65	66	80	81	84	79	76
November	71	73	79	81	83	82	78
December	76	78	83	83	84	83	81
Means	67	68	80	81	83	78	76

TABLE XLV.

MONTHLY MEANS OF THE EXTENT OF SKY CLOUDED, AT EACH OF THE SIX OBSERVATION HOURS, (THE HEMISPHERE BEING UNITY), FOR THE YEARS 1854 TO 1859 INCLUSIVE.

Toronto time.	\multicolumn{7}{c}{JANUARY.}	\multicolumn{7}{c}{FEBRUARY.}
	2 h.	4 h.	10 h.	12 h.	18 h.	20 h.	Monthly Means.	2 h.	4 h.	10 h.	12 h.	18 h.	20 h.	Monthly Means.
1854	0.80	0.85	0.72	0.69	0.80	0.85	0.78	0.78	0.73	0.65	0.70	0.65	0.72	0.71
1855	.83	.81	.83	.76	.81	.73	.79	.77	.68	.63	.71	.76	.73	.71
1856	.69	.68	.62	.59	.66	.73	.66	.60	.64	.39	.41	.60	.63	.55
1857	.63	.73	.64	.65	.71	.74	.68	.75	.72	.61	.68	.77	.79	.72
1858	.57	.53	.48	.47	.82	.78	.61	.75	.69	.69	.62	.70	.68	.69
1859	.79	.86	.60	.59	.69	.77	.72	.76	.83	.66	.61	.75	.81	.74
Means.	.72	.74	.67	.62	.75	.77	.71	.73	.72	.60	.62	.71	.73	.69

	\multicolumn{7}{c}{MARCH.}	\multicolumn{7}{c}{APRIL.}
1854	0.61	0.65	0.61	0.50	0.67	0.66	0.62	0.64	0.67	0.57	0.61	0.61	0.69	0.63
1855	.78	.74	.63	.59	.68	.61	.67	.49	.51	.52	.52	.53	.48	.51
1856	.56	.56	.47	.50	.51	.50	.52	.65	.60	.50	.47	.68	.71	.60
1857	.63	.60	.52	.60	.66	.64	.61	.67	.62	.42	.44	.50	.57	.54
1858	.59	.54	.46	.46	.47	.48	.50	.72	.70	.59	.63	.60	.67	.65
1859	.66	.66	.53	.54	.77	.76	.65	.65	.61	.52	.52	.60	.66	.59
Means.	.64	.63	.54	.53	.63	.61	.60	.64	.62	.52	.53	.59	.63	.59

	\multicolumn{7}{c}{MAY.}	\multicolumn{7}{c}{JUNE.}
1854	0.50	0.57	0.26	0.22	0.39	0.36	0.38	0.57	0.67	0.40	0.35	0.47	0.48	0.49
1855	.49	.52	.37	.33	.53	.55	.46	.70	.71	.50	.59	.68	.69	.64
1856	.60	.61	.60	.67	.58	.55	.59	.58	.43	.36	.46	.46	.51	.47
1857	.75	.80	.50	.51	.55	.58	.61	.75	.72	.55	.57	.70	.83	.69
1858	.77	.83	.52	.51	.75	.75	.69	.57	.55	.46	.45	.40	.42	.48
1859	.44	.38	.27	.44	.49	.45	.41	.55	.46	.42	.42	.57	.55	.50
Means.	.59	.62	.42	.43	.55	.54	.52	.62	.59	.45	.47	.55	.58	.55

TABLE XLV.—(*Continued.*)

MONTHLY MEANS OF THE EXTENT OF SKY CLOUDED, AT EACH OF THE SIX OBSERVATIONS, FOR THE YEARS 1854 TO 1859 INCLUSIVE.

Toronto time.	JULY.							AUGUST.						
	2 h.	4 h.	10 h.	12 h.	18 h.	20 h.	Monthly Means.	2 h.	4 h.	10 h.	12 h.	18 h.	20 h.	Monthly Means.
1854	0.38	0.46	0.29	0.31	0.35	0.33	0.35	0.47	0.47	0.43	0.31	0.46	0.51	0.44
1855	.63	.57	.47	.51	.63	.72	.59	.58	.59	.35	.34	.34	.46	.44
1856	.47	.49	.24	.36	.45	.34	.39	.63	.55	.25	.35	.59	.53	.48
1857	.51	.55	.30	.33	.55	.51	.46	.53	.49	.35	.48	.55	.42	.47
1858	.57	.52	.42	.43	.53	.54	.50	.49	.43	.35	.29	.45	.49	.42
1859	.48	.48	.47	.44	.51	.36	.46	.44	.39	.32	.35	.45	.48	.40
Means.	.51	.51	.37	.40	.50	.47	.46	.52	.49	.34	.35	.47	.48	.44

	SEPTEMBER.							OCTOBER.						
1854	0.44	0.45	0.45	0.34	0.56	0.58	0.47	0.59	0.59	0.48	0.56	0.73	0.71	0.61
1855	.49	.47	.39	.40	.47	.46	.45	.69	.65	.61	.60	.72	.79	.68
1856	.55	.55	.50	.48	.47	.41	.49	.52	.53	.42	.40	.48	.47	.47
1857	.49	.49	.30	.37	.45	.45	.43	.64	.64	.61	.54	.66	.61	.62
1858	.50	.49	.30	.31	.41	.47	.41	.65	.59	.56	.57	.61	.63	.60
1859	.70	.72	.61	.63	.61	.65	.65	.68	.65	.55	.48	.73	.77	.64
Means.	.53	.53	.42	.42	.50	.50	.48	.63	.61	.54	.53	.65	.66	.60

	NOVEMBER.							DECEMBER.						
1854	0.81	0.78	0.72	0.62	0.79	0.77	0.75	0.84	0.70	0.77	0.82	0.81	0.82	0.79
1855	.72	.65	.50	.49	.60	.62	.60	.72	.74	.59	.62	.64	.70	.67
1856	.85	.83	.74	.76	.78	.91	.81	.77	.77	.67	.74	.82	.80	.76
1857	.83	.78	.61	.52	.63	.66	.67	.71	.75	.67	.69	.77	.78	.73
1858	.91	.84	.80	.83	.71	.77	.81	.87	.87	.79	.83	.79	.82	.83
1859	.86	.81	.79	.79	.83	.75	.81	.75	.80	.64	.66	.75	.76	.73
Means.	.83	.78	.69	.67	.72	.75	.74	.78	.77	.69	.73	.76	.78	.75

TABLE XLVI.

MONTHLY AND ANNUAL MEANS OF THE EXTENT OF THE SKY CLOUDED FROM SIX DAILY OBSERVATIONS, FOR 1854 TO 1859 INCLUSIVE.

	January.	February.	March.	April.	May.	June.	July.	August.	September.	October.	November.	December.	Year.
1854	0.78	0.71	0.62	0.63	0.38	0.49	0.35	0.44	0.47	0.61	0.75	0.79	0.59
1855	.79	.71	.67	.51	.46	.54	.59	.44	.45	.68	.60	.67	.60
1856	.66	.55	.52	.60	.59	.47	.39	.48	.49	.47	.81	.76	.57
1857	.68	.72	.61	.54	.61	.69	.46	.47	.43	.62	.67	.73	.60
1858	.61	.69	.50	.65	.69	.48	.50	.42	.41	.60	.81	.83	.60
1859	.72	.74	.65	.59	.41	.50	.46	.40	.65	.64	.81	.73	.61
Means...	0.71	0.69	0.60	0.59	0.52	0.55	0.46	0.44	0.48	0.60	0.74	0.75	0.59

TABLE XLVII.

MONTHLY MEANS OF THE EXTENT OF SKY CLOUDED AT EACH OBSERVATION HOUR, FOR THE PERIOD 1854 TO 1859 INCLUSIVE.

Toronto Astronomical time.	2 h.	4 h.	10 h.	12 h.	18 h.	20 h.	Monthly Means.
January............	0.72	0.74	0.67	0.62	0.75	0.77	0.71
February............	.73	.72	.60	.62	.71	.73	.69
March............	.64	.63	.54	.53	.63	.61	.60
April............	.64	.62	.52	.53	.59	.63	.59
May............	.59	.62	.42	.43	.55	.54	.52
June............	.62	.59	.45	.47	.55	.58	.55
July............	.51	.51	.37	.40	.30	.47	.40
August............	.52	.49	.34	.35	.47	.48	.44
September............	.53	.53	.42	.42	.50	.50	.48
October............	.63	.61	.54	.53	.65	.66	.60
November............	.83	.78	.69	.67	.72	.75	.74
December............	.76	.77	.69	.73	.76	.78	.75
Means............	0.65	0.63	0.52	0.52	0.62	0.62	0.59

TABLE XLVIII.

MEAN CLOUDED SKY FOR EACH OF THE SIXTEEN POINTS OF THE WIND'S DIRECTION, WITH THE NUMBER OF OBSERVATIONS FROM WHICH THE MEANS ARE DERIVED, FOR THE YEARS 1853-69 INCLUSIVE.

Year.	N.		N.N.E.		N.E.		E.N.E.		E.		E.S.E.		S.E.		S.S.E.	
	No.	Clouded Sky.	No.	Clouded Sky.	No.	Clouded Sky.	No.	Clouded Sky.	No.	Clouded Sky.	No.	Clouded Sky.	No.	Clouded Sky.	No.	Clouded Sky.
1853	142	0.53	148	0.65	106	0.83	93	0.77	90	0.65	46	0.55	64	0.65	64	0.40
1854	113	0.43	77	0.62	87	0.71	87	0.83	145	0.69	103	0.65	48	0.59	56	0.43
1855	168	0.48	79	0.59	69	0.68	74	0.80	136	0.74	95	0.74	42	0.08	54	0.58
1856	127	0.44	61	0.69	65	0.70	68	0.73	123	0.84	89	0.57	42	0.08	39	0.57
1857	102	0.51	39	0.67	60	0.80	126	0.91	108	0.70	57	0.70	46	0.65	54	0.58
1858	120	0.55	57	0.70	78	0.60	176	0.84	166	0.72	49	0.68	45	0.46	60	0.45
1859	104	0.59	68	0.62	75	0.77	160	0.73	179	0.62	65	0.55	35	0.49	47	0.50
1853-59	876	0.50	529	0.65	540	0.74	783	0.80	937	0.70	484	0.64	322	0.57	374	0.49

Year.	S.		S.S.W.		S.W.		W.S.W.		W.		W.N.W.		N.W.		N.N.W.		Calms.	
	No.	Clouded Sky.	No.	Clouded Sky.	No.	Clouded Sky.	No.	Clouded Sky.	No.	Clouded Sky.	No.	Clouded Sky.	No.	Clouded Sky.	No.	Clouded Sky.	No.	Clouded Sky.
1853	123	0.49	129	0.66	68	0.54	95	0.70	102	0.54	76	0.49	116	0.63	166	0.46	356	0.52
1854	79	0.39	112	0.59	111	0.70	109	0.68	103	0.69	125	0.50	112	0.63	163	0.48	333	0.56
1855	74	0.57	118	0.56	124	0.68	137	0.59	168	0.59	132	0.60	134	0.61	146	0.53	223	0.57
1856	69	0.46	122	0.59	131	0.67	191	0.64	174	0.49	170	0.50	121	0.74	144	0.46	254	0.50
1857	71	0.55	139	0.55	154	0.68	160	0.61	136	0.52	129	0.47	149	0.48	165	0.44	275	0.61
1858	83	0.46	93	0.56	64	0.61	111	0.66	132	0.61	144	0.55	147	0.66	150	0.50	307	0.53
1859	75	0.45	144	0.65	104	0.74	123	0.66	156	0.60	137	0.58	130	0.55	145	0.52	223	0.66
1853-59	574	0.48	857	0.58	756	0.67	926	0.64	971	0.57	913	0.53	908	0.53	1069	0.48	1971	0.55

TABLE XLIX.

COMPARATIVE VIEW OF THE ANNUAL VARIATIONS OF CERTAIN METEOROLOGICAL ELEMENTS DERIVED FROM THE SERIES 1842-48, AND FROM THE SERIES 1854-59.

Months.	Temperature.		Barometer.		Pressure of Dry Air.		Pressure of Vapour.		Relative Humidity.	
	1842 1848	1854 1859	1842 1848	1854 1859	1842 1848	1854 1859	1842 1848	1854 1859	1842 1848	1854 1859
January	−19.00	−21.44	−.003	+.053	+.139	+.200	−.142	−.146	+ 5	+ 6
February	−21.05	−23.09	−.007	+.025	+.149	+.180	−.156	−.154	− 2	+ 4
March	−14.51	−14.58	+.001	−.076	+.131	+.049	−.130	−.125	− 3	+ 1
April	− 1.68	− 3.47	+.036	−.042	+.093	+.032	−.057	−.074	− 6	− 4
May	+ 8.59	+ 7.52	−.056	−.018	−.089	−.025	+.033	+.006	− 5	− 6
June	+16.37	+17.35	−.044	−.070	−.182	−.219	+.138	+.149	− 2	− 2
July	+21.67	+24.88	−.032	.000	−.235	−.249	+.204	+.249	− 4	− 3
August	+21.42	+22.08	+.017	−.006	−.213	−.208	+.230	+.200	+ 1	− 3
September	+13.27	+14.65	+.026	+.061	−.092	−.064	+.118	+.120	+ 2	+ 1
October	− 0.12	+ 2.42	+.042	+.039	+.064	+.050	−.022	−.011	+ 4	0
November	− 8.08	− 7.26	+.005	−.019	+.083	+.003	−.078	−.082	+ 6	+ 2
December	−16.89	−19.03	+.022	+.056	+.155	+.195	−.133	−.138	+ 3	+ 5

TABLE L.

COMPARATIVE VIEW OF THE ANNUAL MEANS OF THE DIURNAL VARIATIONS AT THE SIX OBSERVATION HOURS FOR THE SAME TWO SERIES.

Hours.	Temperature.		Barometer.		Pressure of Dry Air.		Pressure of Vapour.		Relative Humidity.	
	1842 1848	1854 1859	1842 1848	1854 1859	1842 1848	1854 1859	1842 1848	1854 1859	1842 1848	1854 1859
2	+ 5.90	+ 5.25	−.013	−.015	−.040	−.032	+.026	+.017	− 9	− 9
4	+ 5.56	+ 4.65	−.018	−.019	−.041	−.031	+.024	+.012	− 9	− 8
10	− 2.30	− 1.85	−.001	+.005	+.011	+.009	−.012	−.005	+ 3	+ 4
12	− 3.42	− 3.99	−.005	+.002	+.012	+.012	−.017	−.010	+ 5	+ 5
18	− 4.56	− 3.95	+.010	+.009	+.032	+.023	−.022	−.014	+ 7	+ 7
20	− 1.21	− 1.22	+.025	+.020	+.025	+.020	.000	.000	+ 2	+ 2

TORONTO METEOROLOGICAL OBSERVATIONS.

TABLES LI.

RESULTANT DIRECTION, RESULTANT VELOCITY, AND MEAN VELOCITY OF THE WIND FOR EACH MONTH.

RESULTANT DIRECTION.

	January.	February.	March.	April.	May.	June.	July.	August.	September.	October.	November.	December.	Year.
1854	N 77 W	N 7 E	N 53 W	N 50 E	N 90 E	N 24 E	N 131 W	N 64 W	N 22 W	N 45 W	N 90 W	N 44 W	N 45 W
1855	N 73 W	N 40 W	N 88 W	N 36 W	N 1 W	N 69 W	N 161 W	N 63 W	N 20 E	N 82 W	N 66 W	N 92 W	N 64 W
1856	N 75 W	N 81 W	N 71 W	N 29 E	N 4 E	N 159 W	N 79 W	N 50 W	N 101 W	N 76 W	N 95 W	N 93 W	N 71 W
1857	N 70 W	N 102 W	N 63 W	N 60 W	N 23 W	N 49 W	N 112 E	N 77 W	N 68 W	N 19 W	N 119 W	N 89 W	N 74 W
1858	N 71 W	N 72 W	N 58 W	N 14 W	N 42 E	N 100 E	N 15 E	N 69 W	N 106 W	N 34 W	N 25 W	N 18 W	N 41 W
1859	N 99 W	N 54 W	N 64 W	N 36 W	N 72 E	N 77 W	N 56 W	N 36 W	N 44 W	N 68 W	N 81 W	N 53 W	N 61 W
1854 TO 1859	N 77 W	N 67 W	N 70 W	N 23 W	N 20 E	N 73 W	N 66 W	N 58 W	N 61 W	N 62 W	N 85 W	N 70 W	N 62 W

RESULTANT VELOCITY.

	January.	February.	March.	April.	May.	June.	July.	August.	September.	October.	November.	December.	Year.
1854	2.44	1.73	3.39	2.57	0.40	0.71	0.37	1.76	1.33	1.52	3.44	4.30	1.47
1855	1.91	4.34	4.76	3.99	2.70	1.33	0.73	1.04	1.29	4.91	3.18	5.29	2.47
1856	5.24	7.70	7.68	1.64	3.99	0.90	1.57	2.88	1.98	2.15	2.95	4.62	3.03
1857	4.96	3.68	6.63	4.15	1.14	1.15	0.81	1.51	1.61	2.93	5.45	2.51	2.54
1858	2.33	3.22	5.45	1.64	3.33	0.25	1.13	1.57	1.53	0.36	3.14	1.66	1.59
1859	3.17	2.72	1.96	2.33	1.59	1.95	1.48	1.62	1.60	5.04	3.39	4.29	2.24
1854 TO 1859	3.20	3.45	4.89	2.14	1.91	0.69	0.41	1.68	1.16	2.60	3.13	3.42	2.18

MEAN VELOCITY.

	January.	February.	March	April.	May.	June.	July.	August.	September.	October.	November.	December.	Year.
1854	6.91	6.91	8.03	6.81	5.38	4.15	4.03	4.60	4.04	4.57	7.54	8.56	5.96
1855	7.26	8.17	9.95	7.57	5.93	5.70	6.47	6.97	7.01	9.88	10.81	11.38	8.14
1856	10.69	10.71	11.39	6.05	9.81	5.30	5.84	7.03	6.53	6.07	8.75	11.56	8.31
1857	10.31	9.82	10.84	10.24	8.13	7.60	4.74	6.36	5.55	6.24	9.25	6.84	7.99
1858	7.40	9.12	8.56	9.57	9.30	5.53	5.76	6.50	5.69	5.96	8.87	9.36	7.64
1859	8.76	8.50	10.39	10.79	5.70	7.19	5.81	5.96	6.36	8.12	9.65	10.77	8.17
1854 TO 1859	8.56	8.87	9.86	8.50	7.37	5.91	5.44	6.24	5.96	6.81	9.15	9.75	7.70

TABLE LII.

MONTHLY AND ANNUAL RESULTANT DIRECTIONS OF THE WIND AT EACH HOUR OF TORONTO ASTRONOMICAL TIME, FOR THE PERIOD 1854 TO 1859 INCLUSIVE.

Hours Commencing.	January.	February.	March.	April.	May.	June.	July.	August.	September.	October.	November.	December.	Year.
0	N 84 W	N 83 W	N 83 W	N 111 W	N 107 E	N 158 W	N 180 W	N 142 W	N 146 W	N 86 W	N 91 W	N 73 W	N 103 W
1	N 86 W	N 82 W	N 84 W	N 110 W	N 108 E	N 164 W	N 175 W	N 139 W	N 142 W	N 87 W	N 90 W	N 79 W	N 103 W
2	N 87 W	N 81 W	N 83 W	N 97 W	N 80 E	N 168 W	N 175 W	N 123 W	N 135 W	N 84 W	N 90 W	N 81 W	N 101 W
3	N 82 W	N 79 W	N 80 W	N 75 W	N 49 E	N 154 W	N 176 W	N 105 W	N 120 W	N 77 W	N 88 W	N 82 W	N 90 W
4	N 79 W	N 72 W	N 76 W	N 51 W	N 19 E	N 118 W	N 153 W	N 79 W	N 92 W	N 70 W	N 83 W	N 82 W	N 77 W
5	N 82 W	N 70 W	N 74 W	N 45 W	N	N 87 W	N 94 W	N 56 W	N 78 W	N 70 W	N 84 W	N 80 W	N 70 W
6	N 82 W	N 64 W	N 72 W	N 47 W	N 3 W	N 52 W	N 55 W	N 49 W	N 61 W	N 66 W	N 83 W	N 80 W	N 64 W
7	N 76 W	N 62 W	N 66 W	N 34 W	N 1 W	N 39 W	N 52 W	N 41 W	N 55 W	N 60 W	N 83 W	N 81 W	N 59 W
8	N 79 W	N 61 W	N 68 W	N 25 W	N 6 E	N 24 W	N 36 W	N 38 W	N 44 W	N 59 W	N 78 W	N 81 W	N 56 W
9	N 81 W	N 56 W	N 64 W	N 20 W	N	N 16 W	N 32 W	N 32 W	N 35 W	N 51 W	N 77 W	N 76 W	N 51 W
10	N 76 W	N 58 W	N 61 W	N 13 W	N 1 E	N 16 W	N 29 W	N 30 W	N 30 W	N 52 W	N 80 W	N 70 W	N 48 W
11	N 73 W	N 62 W	N 58 W	N 9 W	N 3 E	N 18 W	N 28 W	N 29 W	N 21 W	N 51 W	N 79 W	N 68 W	N 46 W
12	N 72 W	N 58 W	N 56 W	N 2 W	N 6 E	N 18 W	N 18 W	N 24 W	N 22 W	N 44 W	N 79 W	N 66 W	N 43 W
13	N 71 W	N 55 W	N 54 W	N 2 W	N 6 E	N 17 W	N 14 W	N 22 W	N 20 W	N 51 W	N 81 W	N 62 W	N 40 W
14	N 70 W	N 56 W	N 54 W	N 3 W	N 2 E	N 16 W	N 11 W	N 26 W	N 20 W	N 52 W	N 80 W	N 57 W	N 40 W
15	N 74 W	N 59 W	N 53 W	N 2 W	N 10 E	N 21 W	N 9 W	N 25 W	N 17 W	N 43 W	N 79 W	N 54 W	N 39 W
16	N 70 W	N 61 W	N 50 W	N 2 W	N 15 E	N 18 W	N 11 W	N 20 W	N 15 W	N 43 W	N 83 W	N 56 W	N 39 W
17	N 73 W	N 62 W	N 53 W	N 2 W	N 15 E	N 24 W	N 15 W	N 18 W	N 14 W	N 39 W	N 84 W	N 56 W	N 38 W
18	N 73 W	N 64 W	N 53 W	N 1 W	N 16 E	N 29 W	N 15 W	N 30 W	N 21 W	N 39 W	N 86 W	N 62 W	N 40 W
19	N 71 W	N 66 W	N 52 W	N 10 W	N 27 E	N 42 W	N 14 W	N 38 W	N 36 W	N 45 W	N 82 W	N 56 W	N 42 W
20	N 68 W	N 65 W	N 53 W	N 9 W	N 20 E	N 67 W	N 19 W	N 55 W	N 49 W	N 50 W	N 83 W	N 59 W	N 48 W
21	N 69 W	N 68 W	N 62 W	N 12 W	N 36 E	N 126 W	N 140 W	N 74 W	N 78 W	N 58 W	N 87 W	N 59 W	N 63 W
22	N 75 W	N 72 W	N 72 W	N 40 W	N 61 E	N 145 W	N 171 E	N 112 W	N 121 W	N 66 W	N 86 W	N 62 W	N 80 W
23	N 82 W	N 76 W	N 78 W	N 80 W	N 84 E	N 157 W	N 173 E	N 138 W	N 145 W	N 70 W	N 92 W	N 67 W	N 96 W
Period of 24 hours	N 77 W	N 67 W	N 70 W	N 23 W	N 29 E	N 73 W	N 66 W	N 58 W	N 61 W	N 62 W	N 85 W	N 70 W	N 62 W

TORONTO METEOROLOGICAL OBSERVATIONS. 121

TABLE LIII.

MONTHLY AND YEARLY RESULTANT VELOCITIES OF THE WIND FOR EACH HOUR OF TORONTO ASTRONOMICAL TIME, FOR THE PERIOD 1854 TO 1859 INCLUSIVE, THE VELOCITIES BEING IN MILES PER HOUR.

Hours.	January.	February.	March.	April.	May.	June.	July.	August.	September.	October.	November.	December.	Year.
0	4.71	4.34	5.97	1.17	1.49	2.35	2.97	2.67	2.35	3.54	4.40	4.39	2.61
1	4.69	4.17	6.14	1.50	1.17	2.45	2.90	2.92	2.10	3.29	4.75	4.46	2.71
2	4.45	3.94	6.26	1.68	0.98	2.34	2.73	2.73	2.05	3.34	4.15	4.24	2.70
3	3.92	3.98	6.26	1.92	1.03	1.70	1.97	2.29	1.75	3.21	4.07	3.94	2.56
4	3.48	3.76	6.27	1.99	1.37	1.42	1.16	1.96	1.70	3.39	3.77	3.89	2.60
5	3.02	2.94	5.99	2.45	1.89	0.96	0.75	2.50	1.43	2.85	3.10	3.75	2.48
6	3.10	3.13	5.48	2.68	2.29	0.86	0.69	2.50	1.38	2.47	2.83	3.82	2.44
7	3.05	3.29	5.10	2.47	2.27	1.14	0.69	2.21	1.47	2.47	2.59	3.92	2.38
8	3.02	3.28	4.93	2.84	2.04	1.19	0.80	2.30	1.58	2.45	2.53	4.00	2.35
9	2.55	3.12	5.15	3.38	1.95	1.50	1.05	2.37	1.60	2.34	2.44	3.98	2.38
10	2.73	2.92	4.60	3.17	2.02	1.66	1.46	2.24	1.92	2.15	2.53	3.88	2.36
11	2.88	2.80	4.39	2.79	2.23	1.58	1.64	2.03	1.82	2.00	2.38	3.80	2.28
12	2.77	2.92	4.24	3.01	2.21	1.68	1.81	2.08	1.60	1.92	2.61	3.53	2.25
13	2.73	3.42	4.29	3.07	2.30	1.73	2.05	2.25	1.80	2.04	2.52	2.94	2.32
14	2.92	3.35	3.95	3.01	2.69	1.53	2.05	2.15	1.96	2.23	2.64	2.76	2.33
15	2.81	3.23	3.92	2.84	2.43	1.40	2.01	2.31	1.90	2.21	2.75	2.67	2.25
16	2.71	3.34	3.97	2.95	2.24	1.16	1.93	2.12	1.73	2.06	2.62	2.55	2.15
17	2.74	3.23	3.75	3.10	2.47	1.31	1.79	2.10	1.61	2.16	2.43	2.44	2.11
18	2.74	3.73	3.80	3.25	3.52	1.34	1.74	2.26	1.58	2.10	2.66	2.41	2.23
19	3.02	3.57	4.21	3.09	3.54	0.97	1.54	2.09	1.72	2.43	2.58	2.27	2.22
20	3.30	3.53	4.50	2.63	3.39	0.84	0.69	2.25	1.43	3.09	2.75	2.85	2.22
21	3.77	4.00	5.09	1.92	2.56	1.12	0.57	1.95	1.24	3.14	3.52	3.11	2.24
22	3.90	3.98	5.38	1.17	1.82	1.62	1.82	1.77	1.41	3.18	4.17	3.87	2.15
23	4.45	4.30	5.71	0.92	1.49	2.08	2.48	2.49	2.01	3.33	4.43	3.93	2.37
Period of 24 hours.	3.29	3.45	4.89	2.14	1.91	0.69	0.41	1.68	1.16	2.60	3.13	3.42	2.18

TABLE LIV.

MONTHLY AND YEARLY MEAN VELOCITIES OF THE WIND FOR EACH HOUR OF TORONTO ASTRONOMICAL TIME, FOR THE PERIOD 1854 TO 1859 INCLUSIVE, THE VELOCITIES BEING IN MILES PER HOUR.

Hours.	January.	February.	March.	April.	May.	June.	July.	August.	September.	October.	November.	December.	Year.
0	10.43	10.69	12.09	11.29	10.33	8.80	8.76	8.99	9.27	10.33	11.57	10.97	10.29
1	10.54	10.54	12.29	11.12	10.28	9.06	8.52	9.45	8.94	10.22	11.79	11.05	10.32
2	10.45	10.13	12.50	10.99	10.05	8.89	8.74	9.72	9.21	9.98	11.86	10.69	10.27
3	9.86	9.95	12.28	10.66	9.67	8.85	8.18	9.52	8.80	9.39	10.94	10.02	9.84
4	9.23	9.72	12.56	10.43	9.41	8.57	7.63	9.11	7.86	8.50	10.28	9.97	9.44
5	8.63	8.54	11.18	9.13	8.02	7.25	6.39	7.84	6.09	6.65	9.06	9.60	8.20
6	8.06	8.57	10.24	8.15	6.90	5.98	5.01	6.41	5.09	5.87	8.83	9.04	7.45
7	6.73	8.88	9.87	7.17	6.23	4.88	3.68	5.16	4.64	5.77	8.27	9.63	6.91
8	8.38	8.99	9.41	7.22	5.91	4.41	3.31	4.95	4.45	5.73	8.31	9.63	6.72
9	7.74	8.08	9.22	7.06	5.26	4.19	3.39	4.63	4.68	5.29	8.02	9.23	6.40
10	7.91	7.69	8.53	6.82	5.06	4.17	3.82	4.62	4.66	5.42	7.98	9.44	6.34
11	7.76	7.73	8.28	6.58	5.13	3.94	3.61	4.08	4.29	5.08	7.93	9.70	6.18
12	7.90	7.84	8.12	6.58	4.92	4.11	4.00	3.98	4.09	4.92	7.95	9.63	6.17
13	7.65	8.19	8.04	6.50	4.99	3.84	3.82	4.16	4 40	5.00	7.82	9.21	6.14
14	7.48	8.11	7.85	6.82	5.34	3.82	4.07	4.18	4.48	5.41	7.80	9.43	6.24
15	7.42	7.86	7.93	6.71	5.03	3.77	3.83	4.29	4.39	5.25	8.13	9.48	6.17
16	7.49	8.13	8.32	6.67	4.97	3.93	3.65	4.15	4.16	5.09	8.26	9.14	6.16
17	7.32	7.99	8.12	7.06	5.42	4.01	3.58	4.24	4.19	5.17	8.09	9.22	6.30
18	7.94	8.02	8.36	7.50	7.27	4.61	4.01	4.56	4.29	4.91	8 08	9.25	6.62
19	7.65	8 06	8.64	8.44	8.03	5.10	4.72	4.79	5.11	5 50	7.91	8.49	6.87
20	8.08	8 57	9.45	9.31	9.02	6.17	5.73	6.43	6.04	6.87	8.70	9.57	7.83
21	8.83	9.55	10.44	9.77	9.47	7.01	6.70	7.31	7.28	8.10	9.61	9.95	8.67
22	9.35	10.13	11.17	10.81	9.91	8.04	7.36	8.15	7.99	9.03	10.82	10.48	9.44
23	9.00	10.32	11.75	11.27	10.25	8.56	7.97	9.00	8.72	9.83	11 45	10.50	9.96
Period of 24 hours	8.56	8.87	9.86	8.50	7.37	5.91	5.44	6.24	5.96	6.81	9.15	9.75	7.70

TABLE LV.

MEAN VELOCITY OF THE WIND, FOR EACH OF THE SIXTEEN POINTS OF THE WIND'S DIRECTION, WITH THE NUMBER OF OBSERVATIONS FROM WHICH THE MEANS ARE DERIVED, FOR THE YEARS 1853-59 INCLUSIVE.

Years.	N.		N.N.E.		N.E.		E.N.E.		E.		E.S.E.		S.E.		S.S.E.	
	No.	Velocity.	No.	Velocity.	No.	Velocity.	No.	Velocity.	No.	Velocity.	No.	Velocity.	No.	Velocity.	No.	Velocity.
		Miles.		Miles.		Miles.		Miles.		Miles.		Miles.		Miles.		Miles.
1853	142	6.00	148	4.66	108	5.72	93	6.09	90	5.23	46	4.77	64	4.65	64	4.91
1854	113	6.44	77	5.96	87	5.20	87	6.00	145	7.40	103	6.48	48	4.31	56	5.01
1855	168	7.53	79	6.45	69	7.39	74	7.94	136	9.61	95	6.38	42	5.71	54	6.35
1856	127	9.22	61	7.43	65	6.71	68	9.47	123	10.34	69	6.21	42	6.00	39	6.87
1857	102	7.22	39	5.86	60	6.92	126	9.18	108	7.62	57	5.34	48	6.22	54	5.50
1858	120	6.72	57	6.03	76	7.15	175	11.26	156	9.16	49	6.75	45	5.08	60	5.90
1859	104	7.34	68	7.44	75	7.96	160	8.86	179	8.35	65	6.76	35	4.90	47	6.06
1853-59	876	7.31	529	6.03	540	6.92	783	8.77	937	8.40	484	6.05	322	5.22	374	5.73

Years.	S.		S.S.W.		S.W.		W.S.W.		W.		W.N.W.		N.W.		N.N.W.	
	No.	Velocity.	No.	Velocity.	No.	Velocity.	No.	Velocity.	No.	Velocity.	No.	Velocity.	No.	Velocity.	No.	Velocity.
		Miles.		Miles.		Miles.		Miles.		Miles.		Miles.		Miles.		Miles.
1853	123	5.84	129	5.67	68	6.02	95	5.71	102	6.90	76	9.02	115	7.63	156	8.08
1854	70	5.20	112	6.18	111	8.06	109	7.83	103	9.08	125	9.30	112	11.34	163	9.29
1855	74	7.75	118	7.22	124	8.16	137	10.29	168	11.23	132	10.88	134	11.13	146	11.16
1856	69	6.67	122	8.12	131	8.93	191	11.80	174	10.94	170	11.06	121	10.03	144	11.05
1857	71	7.45	139	8.38	154	8.37	160	10.23	136	10.84	129	10.78	149	11.06	165	10.73
1858	83	6.85	93	8.50	64	8.08	111	9.86	132	11.47	144	10.42	147	11.40	150	10.61
1859	75	6.49	144	8.14	104	7.67	123	10.81	156	12.10	137	12.82	130	12.02	145	8.56
1853-59	574	6.53	857	7.46	756	8.06	926	9.85	971	10.72	913	10.89	908	10.90	1069	9.63

TABLE LVI.

RATIOS SHEWING THE COMPARATIVE DURATION OF DIFFERENT WINDS IN EACH IN THE MONTH EXPRESSED IN TERMS OF THE

	N.	N.N.E.	N.E.	E.N.E.	E.	E.S.E.	S.E.	S.S.E.	S.
January	1.15	0.74	0.96	0.72	0.75	0.44	0.23	0.21	0.25
February	1.24	0.85	0.73	0.68	0.06	0.37	0.20	0.28	0.37
March	0.68	0.33	0.34	1.10	1.01	0.44	0.46	0.24	0.47
April	1.29	0.96	0.84	1.40	1.71	0.89	0.48	0.52	0.75
May	1.31	0.50	0.71	1.00	2.08	1.03	0.56	0.87	1.08
June	0.91	0.44	0.66	1.34	1.85	0.84	0.51	0.50	1.40
July	1.06	0.70	0.59	1.10	1.40	0.90	0.72	1.18	1.39
August	1.20	0.85	0.65	0.77	1.10	0.66	0.75	0.67	1.15
September	1.20	0.84	0.78	1.04	1.14	0.64	0.69	0.72	0.96
October	0.99	0.66	0.85	1.02	1.12	0.47	0.22	0.45	0.91
November	0.75	0.65	0.68	1.21	1.47	0.49	0.43	0.43	0.42
December	1.29	1.10	1.02	0.86	0.72	0.42	0.22	0.19	0.18
	1.09	0.72	0.73	1.09	1.28	0.64	0.46	0.50	0.78

TABLE LVII.

RATIOS SHEWING THE COMPARATIVE DURATION OF EACH SEPARATE WIND IN TERMS OF THE ANNUAL MEANS

	N.	N.N.E.	N.E.	E.N.E.	E.	E.S.E.	S.E.	S.S.E.	S.
January	1.06	1.03	1.31	0.66	0.59	0.69	0.50	0.42	0.32
February	1.14	1.18	1.00	0.62	0.75	0.58	0.44	0.56	0.48
March	0.62	0.46	0.46	1.00	0.79	0.69	1.00	0.48	0.60
April	1.18	1.34	1.14	1.28	1.34	1.39	1.05	1.03	0.97
May	1.20	0.70	0.97	1.74	1.63	1.61	1.24	1.13	1.38
June	0.84	0.61	0.90	1.22	1.45	1.31	1.12	1.17	1.82
July	0.97	0.98	0.80	1.00	1.09	1.55	1.58	2.34	1.78
August	1.10	1.18	0.88	0.70	0.86	1.03	1.65	1.33	1.49
September	1.10	1.17	1.06	0.95	0.89	1.00	1.51	1.43	1.23
October	0.91	0.92	1.16	0.93	0.88	0.73	0.48	0.89	1.18
November	0.69	0.90	0.93	1.11	1.15	0.77	0.94	0.85	0.54
December	1.18	1.53	1.39	0.79	0.56	0.66	0.48	0.38	0.23

TABLE LVI.

SEPARATE MONTH, BEING THE ABSOLUTE DURATIONS OF THE DIFFERENT WINDS MONTHLY MEAN DURATION FOR ALL WINDS.

S.S.W.	S.W.	W.S.W.	W.	W.N.W.	N.W.	N.N.W.	Calms.	
0.78	1.58	2.61	1.78	1.00	1.18	1.38	1.23	January.
1.00	1.18	2.01	2.08	1.47	1.19	1.58	0.83	February.
0.90	1.30	1.27	1.81	2.27	2.05	1.44	0.80	March.
1.03	0.73	0.71	0.93	1.13	1.12	1.51	1.00	April.
1.30	0.70	0.36	0.49	0.79	0.97	1.69	0.96	May.
1.63	1.35	0.60	0.90	0.84	1.20	1.18	0.76	June.
1.61	0.72	0.46	0.53	0.86	1.00	1.48	1.22	July.
1.27	0.83	0.51	0.92	1.38	1.49	1.69	1.11	August.
1.50	0.98	0.65	0.78	1.05	1.12	1.35	1.56	September.
1.05	1.01	0.90	1.35	1.67	1.37	1.29	1.67	October.
0.86	1.50	2.08	1.78	1.34	1.01	1.03	0.89	November.
0.49	1.42	2.61	1.98	1.11	1.08	1.29	1.02	December.
1.12	1.12	1.23	1.28	1.24	1.23	1.41	1.09	

TABLE LVII.

THE DIFFERENT MONTHS, BEING THE NUMBERS IN TABLE LVI. EXPRESSED IN GIVEN AT THE FOOT OF EACH COLUMN.

S.S.W.	S.W.	W.S.W.	W.	W.N.W.	N.W.	N.N.W.	Calms.	
0.70	1.42	2.12	1.39	0.81	0.96	0.98	1.13	January.
0.89	1.06	1.63	1.63	1.19	0.97	1.12	0.76	February.
0.80	1.25	1.03	1.41	1.83	1.67	1.02	0.73	March.
0.92	0.65	0.58	0.73	0.91	0.91	1.07	0.92	April.
1.16	0.63	0.29	0.38	0.64	0.79	1.20	0.88	May.
1.46	1.21	0.49	0.70	0.68	0.97	0.84	0.70	June.
1.44	0.64	0.37	0.41	0.69	0.81	1.05	1.20	July.
1.13	0.74	0.41	0.72	1.11	1.21	1.20	1.02	August.
1.34	0.88	0.53	0.61	0.85	0.91	0.96	1.43	September.
0.94	0.91	0.73	1.06	1.31	1.11	0.91	1.53	October.
0.77	1.34	1.69	1.39	1.08	0.82	0.73	0.82	November.
0.44	1.27	2.12	1.55	0.90	0.88	0.92	0.94	December.

TABLE LVIII.

RATIOS SHEWING THE COMPARATIVE DURATION OF DIFFERENT WINDS FOR EACH
IN TERMS OF THE MEAN DURATION

Toronto Astronomical time.	N.	N.N.E.	N.E.	E.N.E.	E.	E.S.E.	S.E.	S.S.E.	S.
0	0.61	0.33	0.43	0.86	1.61	1 02	0.78	0.96	1.65
1	0 55	0.28	0.44	0.93	1.54	1.04	0.80	0.90	1.65
2	0.50	0.29	0.43	0.86	1.78	1.05	0.70	0.94	1.62
3	0.54	0.28	0.30	0.96	1.76	1.12	0.69	0.96	1.31
4	0.61	0.31	0.45	1.01	1.84	1.00	0.71	0.81	1.16
5	0.74	0.34	0.53	1.14	1.72	0.86	0.54	0.75	1.00
6	0.70	0.40	0.59	1.30	1.58	0.67	0.46	0.66	0.97
7	0.83	0.44	0.68	1.32	1.38	0.71	0.38	0.51	0.71
8	0.94	0.53	0.66	1.24	1.30	0.51	0.46	0.39	0.54
9	1.08	0.68	0.73	1.22	1.18	0.46	0.33	0.41	0.44
10	1.27	0.80	0.77	1.22	1.04	0.43	0.37	0.35	0.40
11	1.46	0.88	0.85	1.00	1.05	0.41	0.38	0.31	0.39
12	1.59	0.97	0.86	1.08	0.88	0.41	0.31	0.25	0.37
13	1.54	1.14	0.98	1.01	0.79	0.35	0.31	0.25	0 39
14	1.62	1.26	1.02	0.98	0.84	0.35	0.27	0.23	0.37
15	1.72	1.24	0.97	1.01	0.82	0.34	0.27	0.21	0.42
16	1.66	1.18	0.98	1.12	0.76	0.33	0.21	0.27	0.35
17	1.62	1.18	1.03	1.16	0.77	0.34	0.19	0.33	0.37
18	1.54	1.17	1.07	1.13	0.86	0.33	0.24	0.29	0.39
19	1.46	1.07	1.02	1.18	1.07	0.35	0.27	0.24	0.41
20	1.19	0.86	0.92	1.34	1 36	0.54	0.35	0.27	0.44
21	0.96	0.64	0.84	1.18	1.55	0.75	0.46	0.37	0.66
22	0.79	0.53	0.53	1.04	1.57	0.93	0.70	0.62	1.12
23	0.62	0.43	0.44	0.96	1.52	1.06	0.80	0.78	1.52

TORONTO METEOROLOGICAL OBSERVATIONS. 127

TABLE LVIII.

SEPARATE HOUR, BEING THE ABSOLUTE DURATIONS FOR THE HOUR EXPRESSED OF ALL WINDS FOR THE SAME HOUR.

S.S.W.	S.W.	W.S.W.	W.	W.N.W.	N.W.	N.N.W.	Calms.	Toronto Astronomical time.
1.82	1.16	1.05	1.23	1.14	1.10	1.00	0.25	0
1.87	1.16	1 12	1.19	1.12	1.14	0.96	0.22	1
1.91	1.04	1.16	1.23	1.08	1.04	1.08	0.27	2
1.83	1.11	1.12	1.23	1.08	1.05	1.22	0.36	3
1.57	1.21	1.09	1.22	1.06	1.12	1.27	0.55	4
1.48	1.30	1.11	1.13	1.20	1.04	1.28	0.86	5
1.24	1.34	1.20	1 13	1.13	1.29	1.35	0.99	6
1.11	1.37	1.28	1.10	1.31	1.21	1.55	1.11	7
0.70	1.36	1.34	1.29	1.25	1.22	1.66	1.46	8
0.77	1.06	1.35	1.29	1.31	1.31	1.69	1.68	9
0.68	1.00	1.34	1.46	1.28	1.24	1.67	1.67	10
0.74	0.94	1.38	1.40	1.22	1.30	1.66	1.63	11
0.68	0.95	1.34	1.34	1.26	1.29	1.59	1.82	12
0.65	0.90	1.40	1.30	1.22	1.35	1.61	1.80	13
0.74	0.90	1.38	1.24	1.35	1.44	1.52	1.49	14
0.68	0.95	1.26	1.23	1.36	1.35	1.62	1.52	15
0.67	0.99	1.22	1.28	1.48	1.28	1.65	1.56	16
0.65	0.92	1.22	1.33	1.38	1.33	1.70	1.47	17
0.69	1.05	1.14	1.22	1.38	1.31	1.60	1.60	18
0.75	1.08	1.22	1.34	1.32	1.25	1.48	1.49	19
0.96	1 25	1.26	1.42	1.24	1.25	1.40	0.96	20
1.28	1.29	1.26	1.40	1.28	1.31	1.12	0.64	21
1.55	1.22	1.21	1.29	1.20	1.24	1.06	0.41	22
1.69	1.17	1.05	1.26	1.12	1.14	1 06	0.39	23

TABLE LIX.

RATIOS SHEWING THE COMPARATIVE DURATION OF EACH SEPARATE WIND EXPRESSED IN TERMS OF THE MEAN DURA-

Toronto Astronomical time.	N.	N.N.E.	N.E.	E.N.E.	E.	E.S.E.	S.E.	S.S.E.	S.
0	0.56	0.46	0.59	0.79	1.26	1.59	1.71	1.90	2.12
1	0.51	0.39	0.61	0.85	1.21	1.62	1.75	1.96	2.12
2	0.46	0.40	0.59	0.79	1.40	1.64	1.53	1.86	2.08
3	0.50	0.39	0.53	0.88	1.38	1.75	1.51	1.90	1.70
4	0.56	0.43	0.61	0.92	1.44	1.56	1.55	1.60	1.49
5	0.68	0.47	0.72	1.04	1.34	1.34	1.18	1.48	1.29
6	0.64	0.56	0.80	1.19	1.24	1.05	1.01	1.30	1.25
7	0.76	0.61	0.93	1.21	1.08	1.11	0.83	1.01	0.91
8	0.86	0.74	0.90	1.13	1.02	0.80	1.01	0.77	0.69
9	0.99	0.94	0.99	1.12	0.96	0.72	0.72	0.81	0.57
10	1.17	1.11	1.05	1.12	0.82	0.67	0.80	0.69	0.51
11	1.34	1.23	1.16	0.91	0.82	0.64	0.83	0.61	0.50
12	1.46	1.35	1.17	0.99	0.69	0.64	0.67	0.49	0.48
13	1.41	1.59	1.34	0.92	0.62	0.55	0.67	0.49	0.50
14	1.49	1.75	1.39	0.90	0.66	0.55	0.59	0.45	0.48
15	1.58	1.73	1.32	0.92	0.60	0.53	0.59	0.41	0.54
16	1.52	1.64	1.34	1.02	0.60	0.52	0.46	0.58	0.46
17	1.49	1.64	1.40	1.06	0.60	0.53	0.41	0.65	0.47
18	1.41	1.63	1.46	1.03	0.68	0.51	0.52	0.57	0.50
19	1.34	1.49	1.39	1.06	0.84	0.55	0.59	0.47	0.53
20	1.09	1.20	1.25	1.23	1.07	0.84	0.77	0.53	0.57
21	0.88	0.89	1.14	1.06	1.22	1.17	1.01	0.73	0.85
22	0.73	0.74	0.72	0.95	1.23	1.45	1.53	1.23	1.44
23	0.57	0.60	0.61	0.88	1.19	1.66	1.75	1.54	1.96

TABLE LIX.

IN THE DIFFERENT HOURS, BEING THE ABSOLUTE DURATIONS AT THE HOUR
TION OF THE SAME WIND FOR ALL HOURS.

S.S.W.	S.W.	W.S.W.	W.	W.N.W.	N.W.	N.N.W.	Ca'ms.	Toronto Astronomical time.
1.62	1.04	0.85	0.97	0.92	0.89	0.71	0.23	0
1.67	1.04	0.91	0.94	0.90	0.93	0.68	0.20	1
1.70	0.93	0.95	0.97	0.87	0.85	0.77	0.25	2
1.63	1.00	0.91	0.97	0.87	0.85	0.87	0.33	3
1.40	1.09	0.89	0.96	0.85	0.91	0.90	0.50	4
1.32	1.17	0.90	0.89	0.97	0.85	0.91	0.79	5
1.11	1.20	0.98	0.89	0.91	1.04	0.96	0.90	6
0.99	1.23	1.04	0.87	1.06	0.96	1.10	1.02	7
0.78	1.22	1.09	1.02	1.01	0.99	1.18	1.34	8
0.69	0.95	1.10	1.02	1.05	1.06	1.20	1.54	9
0.61	0.90	1.00	1.18	1.03	1.01	1.19	1.53	10
0.66	0.84	1.12	1.06	0.98	1.06	1.18	1.49	11
0.61	0.85	1.09	1.03	1.01	1.04	1.13	1.67	12
0.66	0.81	1.14	0.98	0.98	1.00	1.14	1.65	13
0.06	0.81	1.12	0.97	1.00	1.17	1.08	1.36	14
0.61	0.85	1.03	0.97	1.11	1.09	1.15	1.39	15
0.60	0.89	0.99	1.01	1.19	1.04	1.17	1.43	16
0.58	0.83	0.99	1.05	1.11	1.08	1.20	1.35	17
0.62	0.94	0.93	0.96	1.11	1.06	1.13	1.47	18
0.67	0.97	0.99	1.06	1.07	1.01	1.05	1.37	19
0.86	1.12	1.03	1.12	1.00	1.01	0.90	0.88	20
1.14	1.16	1.03	1.10	1.03	1.00	0.80	0.59	21
1.38	1.10	0.96	1.02	0.97	1.01	0.75	0.38	22
1.51	1.05	0.85	1.00	0.90	0.93	0.75	0.36	23

TABLE LX.

THE NUMBER OF DAYS IN WHICH RAIN FELL, ITS APPROXIMATE DURATION IN HOURS, AND DEPTH IN INCHES, FOR EACH MONTH OF THE YEARS 1854—1859 INCLUSIVE.

NUMBER OF DAYS.

	January.	February.	March.	April.	May.	June.	July.	August.	September.	October.	November.	December.	Year.
1854	7	5	9	12	11	9	9	5	14	15	13	5	114
1855	5	2	5	8	6	17	13	7	12	14	8	6	103
1856	0	0	0	13	14	13	8	12	13	10	10	6	99
1857	3	11	4	10	15	21	15	13	11	10	14	7	134
1858	6	1	10	13	17	12	13	11	8	17	12	11	131
1859	6	6	15	9	11	10	12	11	15	11	12	3	127
Mean of the Six Years.	4	4	7	11	12	15	12	10	12	13	12	6	118
Mean of Fifteen Years.	5	4	6	9	12	12	10	10	9	12	11	6	106

APPROXIMATE DURATION IN HOURS.

1854	39	25	63	42	40	26	29	5	50	45	34	19	417
1855	10	20	20	23	31	75	37	8	44	47	57	29	401
1856	0	0	0	63	89	28	10	24	55	28	42	26	365
1857	6	73	11	40	95	66	43	67	32	42	74	64	613
1858	33	1	31	81	104	47	31	56	22	49	85	44	584
1859	39	17	76	37	51	29	40	41	36	26	94	28	514
Mean of the Six Years.	21	23	33	48	68	45	32	34	40	39	64	35	482

DEPTH IN INCHES.

1854	1.270	1.460	2.425	2.685	4.630	1.460	4.805	0.455	5.375	1.495	1.115	0.590	27.765
1855	0.525	1.770	1.485	2.030	2.565	4.070	3.245	1.455	5.585	2.485	4.590	1.845	31.650
1856	0.000	0.000	0.000	2.780	4.580	3.200	1.120	1.680	4.105	0.875	1.375	1.790	21.505
1857	*	3.050	0.335	1.755	4.145	5.000	3.475	5.265	2.640	1.040	3.235	3.205	33.205
1858	1.152	*	0.917	1.642	6.367	2.943	3.072	3.890	0.735	1.707	3.870	1.657	28.051
1859	1.449	0.455	4.054	2.527	3.410	4.065	2.611	3.990	3.525	0.940	5.193	1.035	33.274
Mean of the Six Years.	0.733	1.123	1.536	2.235	4.283	3.470	3.055	2.789	3.661	1.439	3.231	1.687	29.242
Mean of Fifteen Years.	1.293	0.953	1.405	2.434	3.537	2.969	3.222	2.820	4.050	2.562	3.266	1.556	29.867

In Tables LX to LXII, the sign * denotes that the amount of Rain or Snow was too small for measurement, and the sign † that its duration was less than half an hour.

TABLE LXI.

THE NUMBER OF DAYS IN WHICH SNOW FELL, ITS APPROXIMATE DURATION IN HOURS, AND DEPTH IN INCHES, FOR EACH MONTH OF THE YEARS 1854 TO 1859 INCLUSIVE.

NUMBER OF DAYS.

	January.	February.	March.	April.	May.	June.	July.	August.	September	October.	November.	December.	Year.
1854	11	15	3	4	...	...	...	...	...	3	4	12	52
1855	13	14	11	3	2	...	...	...	...	5	6	10	64
1856	14	8	12	3	1	...	...	...	...	2	9	20	69
1857	16	11	15	11	1	...	...	...	...	2	9	14	79
1858	11	16	6	2	...	...	...	...	...	1	13	18	67
1859	19	14	8	8	...	2	...	...	...	4	9	23	87
Mean of the six years.	14	13	9	5	1	...	...	...	...	3	8	16	69
Mean of fifteen years.	11	12	9	3	1	...	...	...	...	2	6	13	57

APPROXIMATE DURATION IN HOURS.

	January.	February.	March.	April.	May.	June.	July.	August.	September	October.	November.	December.	Year.
1854	42	61	10	9	...	...	...	...	...	†	17	63	202
1855	70	96	44	8	7	...	...	...	...	10	11	55	303
1856	88	51	75	3	†	...	...	...	...	2	30	62	311
1857	88	34	49	42	1	...	...	...	...	11	46	52	323
1858	45	96	11	3	...	...	...	...	...	†	48	74	277
1859	96	87	13	21	...	2	...	...	...	4	13	163	379
Mean of the six years.	71	68	34	14	1	...	...	...	...	5	28	78	299

DEPTH IN INCHES.

	January.	February.	March.	April.	May.	June.	July.	August.	September	October.	November.	December.	Year.
1854	7.5	18.0	2.8	2.7	...	...	...	...	...	*	1.3	17.2	49.5
1855	23.3	21.8	18.1	1.6	0.9	...	...	...	...	0.8	3.0	29.5	99.0
1856	13.6	9.7	16.2	0.1	*	...	...	...	...	0.1	9.5	16.3	65.5
1857	22.5	11.7	11.3	12.9	*	...	...	...	...	0.2	6.9	9.0	73.8
1858	4.0	26.7	0.2	0.1	...	...	...	...	...	*	4.0	10.4	45.4
1859	16.4	8.3	1.0	1.2	...	*	...	...	...	*	0.6	37.4	64.9
Mean of the six years.	14.4	16.0	8.3	3.1	0.1	...	...	...	...	0.2	4.2	20.0	66.3
Mean of fifteen years.	12.1	17.7	9.4	2.6	0.1	...	...	...	...	0.3	2.7	16.6	61.5

TABLE LXII.

NUMBER OF DAYS IN WHICH EITHER RAIN OR SNOW FELL, THEIR APPROXIMATE DURATION IN HOURS, AND DEPTH IN INCHES, FOR EACH MONTH OF THE YEARS 1854 TO 1859 INCLUSIVE; ONE INCH OF SNOW BEING RECKONED AS EQUIVALENT TO ONE-TENTH OF AN INCH OF RAIN.

NUMBER OF DAYS.

	January.	February.	March.	April.	May.	June.	July.	August.	September.	October.	November.	December.	Year.
1854	18	20	12	16	11	9	9	5	14	18	17	17	166
1855	18	16	16	11	8	17	13	7	12	19	14	16	167
1856	14	8	12	16	15	13	8	12	13	12	19	26	168
1857	19	22	19	21	16	21	15	13	11	12	23	21	213
1858	17	17	16	15	17	12	13	11	8	18	25	29	198
1859	25	20	23	17	11	18	12	11	15	15	21	26	214
Mean of the six years.	18	17	16	16	13	15	12	10	12	16	20	22	187
Mean of fifteen years.	16	16	15	12	13	12	10	10	9	14	17	19	163

APPROXIMATE DURATION IN HOURS.

	January.	February.	March.	April.	May.	June.	July.	August.	September.	October.	November.	December.	Year.
1854	81	86	73	51	40	26	29	5	50	45	51	82	619
1855	80	118	64	31	38	75	37	8	44	57	68	84	704
1856	88	51	75	66	89	98	10	74	65	30	72	88	676
1857	94	107	60	82	96	66	43	67	32	55	120	116	938
1858	78	97	42	84	104	47	31	56	22	49	133	118	861
1859	135	84	89	58	51	31	40	41	36	30	107	101	803
Mean of the six years.	93	90	67	62	70	45	32	34	40	44	92	113	782

DEPTH IN INCHES.

	January.	February.	March.	April.	May.	June.	July.	August.	September.	October.	November.	December.	Year.
1854	2.020	3.260	2.705	2.955	4.630	1.460	4.805	0.455	5.375	1.495	1.245	2.310	32.715
1855	2.855	3.050	3.295	2.190	2.655	4.070	3.245	1.455	5.585	2.565	4.890	4.795	41.550
1856	1.300	0.970	1.620	2.790	4.580	3.200	1.120	1.080	4.105	0.885	2.325	3.420	28.055
1857	2.180	4.220	1.465	3.045	4.145	5.060	3.475	5.205	2.640	1.060	3.925	4.105	40.585
1858	1.552	2.670	0.937	1.652	6.367	2.943	3.072	3.890	0.735	1.797	4.279	2.597	32.561
1859	3.080	1.285	4.154	2.647	3.410	4.065	2.611	3.990	3.525	0.940	5.253	4.775	39.764
Mean of the six years.	2.176	2.726	2.363	2.546	4.298	3.470	3.055	2.789	3.661	1.457	3.653	3.664	35.877
Mean of fifteen years.	2.503	2.723	2.345	2.694	3.367	2.969	3.222	2.820	4.050	2.592	3.536	3.196	36.017

TABLE LXIII.

COMPARATIVE DURATION OF THE SEVERAL WINDS DURING THE DAYS IN ANY PART OF WHICH RAIN OR SNOW FELL, FROM OBSERVATIONS IN THE YEARS 1853 TO 1859 INCLUSIVE.

	Absolute duration of the several winds in hours.				Relative duration of each wind on days of precipitation, as compared with its duration on all days.			Ratios of the numbers in (5) (6) and (7) to their respective means for all winds.		
	During days of Rain.	During days of Snow.	During days of Rain or Snow.	During days with and without Rain or Snow.	Rain. Ratio of (1) to (4).	Snow. Ratio of (2) to (4).	Rain or Snow. Ratio of (3) to (4).	RAIN.	SNOW.	RAIN OR SNOW.
	(1)	(2)	(3)	(4)	(5)	(6)	(7)	(8)	(9)	(10)
N.	969	909	1758	3908	0.248	0.233	0.450	0.72	1.21	0.90
N.N.E.	687	705	1286	2579	.266	.273	.499	0.77	1.41	1.00
N.E.	961	766	1566	2635	.365	.291	.594	1.06	1.51	1.19
E.N.E.	2142	533	2501	3929	.545	.136	.637	1.58	0.70	1.27
E.	2375	526	2656	4572	.519	.115	.581	1.50	0.60	1.16
E.S.E.	977	330	1190	2298	.425	.144	.518	1.23	0.75	1.04
S.E.	606	212	743	1647	.368	.129	.451	1.07	0.67	0.90
S.S.E.	681	165	781	1818	.375	.091	.430	1.09	0.47	0.86
S.	965	239	1105	2795	.345	.086	.412	1.00	0.45	0.82
S.S.W.	1538	350	1838	4021	.382	.087	.457	1.11	0.45	0.91
S.W.	1421	800	2120	4000	.355	.200	.530	1.03	1.04	1.06
W.S.W.	1297	1372	2430	4415	.294	.311	.550	0.85	1.61	1.10
W.	1249	1509	2578	4571	.273	.330	.564	0.79	1.71	1.13
W.N.W.	1157	1161	2150	4455	.260	.261	.483	0.76	1.35	0.97
N.W.	1160	1000	2005	4426	.262	.226	.453	0.76	1.17	0.91
N.N.W.	1256	1223	2317	5061	.249	.241	.458	0.72	1.25	0.92
Calms.	1283	504	1703	3921	.327	.129	.434	0.95	0.67	0.87

TABLE LXIV.

COMPARATIVE DURATION OF THE SEVERAL WINDS DURING THE HOURS IN ANY PART OF WHICH RAIN OR SNOW FELL, FROM OBSERVATIONS IN THE YEARS 1857 TO 1859, INCLUSIVE.

	Absolute duration of the several winds expressed in hours.				Relative duration of each wind during the hours in which rain or snow fell, as compared with its duration on all days.			Ratios of the numbers in (5) (6) and (7) to their respective means for all winds.			Ratios from Table LXIII corresponding to those in columns (8) (9) and (10) of Table LXIV.		
	During Rain. (1)	During Snow. (2)	During Rain or Snow. (3)	With and without Rain or Snow. (4)	Rain. Ratio of (1) to (4) (5)	Snow. Ratio of (2) to (4) (6)	Rain or Snow. Ratio of (3) to (4) (7)	Rain. (8)	Snow. (9)	Rain or Snow. (10)	Rain.	Snow.	Rain or Snow.
N.	92	105	195	1489	0.062	0.071	0.131	0.68	1.24	0.81	0.72	1.21	0.90
N.N.E.	118	100	217	770	.153	.130	.282	1.68	2.27	1.01	0.77	1.41	1.00
N.E.	102	143	245	1022	.100	.140	240	1.10	2.45	1.63	1 06	1.51	1.19
E.N.E.	471	139	604	2140	.219	.065	.281	2 41	1.14	1.91	1.58	0.70	1.27
E.	288	82	364	2192	.131	.037	.166	1.44	0.65	1.13	1.50	0.60	1.16
E.S.E.	116	28	144	876	.132	.032	.164	1.45	0.56	1.11	1.23	0.75	1.04
S.E.	68	31	97	661	.103	.047	.146	1.12	0.82	0.99	1.07	0.67	0.90
S.S.E.	75	36	110	781	.096	.046	.141	1.05	0.80	0.96	1.09	0.47	0.86
S.	94	21	115	1166	.081	.018	.099	0.89	0.32	0.67	1.00	0.45	0.82
S.S.W.	172	49	221	1799	.096	.027	.123	1.05	0.47	0.86	1.11	0.45	0.91
S.W.	129	85	212	1760	.073	.048	.120	0.80	0.84	0.84	1.03	1.04	1.06
W.S.W.	103	113	215	1945	.053	.058	.110	0.58	1.01	0.75	0.85	1.61	1.10
W.	107	110	216	1975	.054	.056	.109	0.59	0.96	0.74	0.79	1.71	1.13
W.N.W.	92	125	217	2044	.045	.061	.106	0.49	1.07	0.72	0.76	1.35	0.97
N.W.	80	91	170	2027	.039	.045	.084	0.43	0.79	0.57	0.76	1.17	0.91
N.N.W.	115	125	230	2213	.052	.056	.108	0.57	0.98	0.73	0.72	1.25	0.92
Calms.	85	48	133	1388	.061	.035	.096	0.67	0.61	0.65	0.95	0.67	0.87

TORONTO METEOROLOGICAL OBSERVATIONS.

TABLE LXV.

COMPARATIVE DURATION OF THE SEVERAL WINDS DURING THE DAYS IN ANY PART OF WHICH SNOW FELL, FROM OBSERVATIONS IN THE YEARS 1853 TO 1859 INCLUSIVE; THE SNOW STORMS BEING ARRANGED IN FOUR CLASSES ACCORDING TO THE AMOUNT OF SNOW, AND EACH CLASS BEING TAKEN TO INCLUDE ALL THE HIGHER CLASSES.

	Absolute duration of the several winds in hours.					Relative duration of each wind on days of snow as compared with its duration on all days.				Ratios of the numbers in (6), (7), (8) and (9) to the respective means for all winds.			
	Snow generally	Snow 1 inch and upwards.	Snow 3 inches and upwards.	Snow 6 inches and upwards.	During days with and without snow	Ratio of (1) to (5)	Ratio of (2) to (5)	Ratio of (3) to (5)	Ratio of (4) to (5)	Snow generally.	1 inch and upwards.	3 inches and upwards.	6 inches and upwards.
	(1)	(2)	(3)	(4)	(5)	(6)	(7)	(8)	(9)	(10)	(11)	(12)	(13)
N.	909	236	97	11	3908	0.233	0.060	0.025	0.003	1.21	1.15	1.18	0.83
N.N.E.	705	294	119	10	2579	.273	..114	.046	.007	1.41	2.19	2.17	1.94
N.E.	766	403	190	38	2635	.291	.153	.072	.014	1.51	2.94	3.40	3.89
E.N.E.	533	269	171	34	3929	.136	.068	.044	.009	0.70	1.31	2.08	2.50
E.	526	236	128	27	4572	.115	.052	.028	.006	0.60	1.00	1.32	1.67
E.S.E.	330	125	74	22	2298	.144	.054	.032	.010	0.75	1.04	1.51	2.78
S.E.	212	75	27	4	1647	.129	.046	.017	.002	0.67	0.88	0.80	0.56
S.S.E.	165	43	12	1	1818	.091	.024	.007	.001	0.47	0.46	0.33	0.28
S.	239	62	15	0	2795	.086	.022	.005	.000	0.45	0.42	0.24	0.09
S.S.W.	350	102	14	4	4021	.087	.025	.003	.001	0.45	0.48	0.14	0.28
S.W.	800	147	27	7	4000	.200	.037	.007	.002	1.04	0.71	0.33	0.56
W.S.W.	1372	161	50	10	4415	.311	.036	.011	.002	1.61	0.69	0.52	0.56
W.	1509	212	56	3	4571	.330	.046	.012	.001	1.71	0.85	0.57	0.28
W.N.W.	1161	165	45	3	4455	.261	.037	.010	.001	1.35	0.71	0.47	0.28
N.W.	1000	176	64	5	4426	.226	.040	.014	.001	1.17	0.77	0.66	0.28
N.N.W.	1223	261	107	2	5061	.241	.052	.021	.000	1.25	1.00	0.99	0.00
Calms.	504	81	28	2	3921	.129	.021	.007	.001	0.67	0.40	0.33	0.28

TABLE LXVI.

COMPARATIVE DURATION OF THE SEVERAL WINDS DURING THE HOURS IN ANY PART OF WHICH SNOW FELL, FROM OBSERVATIONS IN THE YEARS 1857 TO 1859 INCLUSIVE; THE SNOW STORMS BEING ARRANGED IN FOUR CLASSES ACCORDING TO THE AMOUNT OF SNOW, AND EACH CLASS BEING TAKEN TO INCLUDE ALL THE HIGHER CLASSES.

	Absolute duration of the several winds expressed in hours.					Relative duration of each wind during the hours in which snow fell, as compared with the duration on all days.				Ratios of the numbers in (6), (7), (8) and (9), to their respective means for all winds.			
	Snow generally.	Snow 1 inch and upwards.	Snow 3 inches and upwards.	Snow 6 inches and upwards.	During days with and without Snow.	Ratio of (1) to (5).	Ratio of (2) to (5).	Ratio of (3) to (5).	Ratio of (4) to (5).	Snow generally.	1 inch and upwards.	3 inches and upwards.	6 inches and upwards.
	(1)	(2)	(3)	(4)	(5)	(6)	(7)	(8)	(9)	(10)	(11)	(12)	(13)
N.	105	43	9	0	1489	0.071	0.029	0.006	0.000	1.24	1.07	0.59	0.00
N.N.E.	100	72	10	2	770	.130	.094	.013	.003	2.27	3.48	1.29	2.04
N.E.	143	117	60	11	1022	.140	.114	.059	.011	2.45	4.22	5.84	7.48
E.N.E.	130	80	64	14	2140	.065	.041	.030	.007	1.14	1.52	2.97	4.76
E.	82	58	34	8	2192	.037	.026	.016	.003	0.65	0.96	1.58	2.04
E.S.E.	28	15	11	0	876	.032	.017	.013	.000	0.56	0.63	1.29	.00
S.E.	31	14	2	0	661	.047	.021	.003	.000	0.82	0.78	0.20	.00
S.S.E.	36	9	4	0	781	.046	.012	.005	.000	0.80	0.44	0.49	.00
S.	21	7	3	0	1166	.018	.006	.003	.000	0.32	0.22	0.29	.00
S.S.W.	49	20	7	0	1790	.027	.011	.004	.000	0.47	0.41	0.39	.00
S.W.	85	26	5	0	1760	.048	.015	.003	.000	0.84	0.56	0.29	.00
W.S.W.	113	19	6	0	1945	.058	.010	.003	.000	1.01	0.37	0.29	.00
W.	110	16	5	0	1975	.056	.008	.003	.000	0.98	0.30	0.29	.00
W.N.W.	125	21	2	0	2044	.061	.010	.001	.000	1.07	0.37	0.10	.00
N.W.	91	25	2	0	2027	.045	.012	.001	.000	0.79	0.44	0.10	.00
N.N.W.	125	47	10	0	2213	.056	.021	.005	.000	0.98	0.78	0.49	.00
Calms.	48	13	6	1	1388	.035	.010	.004	.001	0.61	0.37	0.39	0.68

www.ingramcontent.com/pod-product-compliance
Lightning Source LLC
Chambersburg PA
CBHW030242170426
43202CB00009B/597